EVIDENCE-BASED PARENTING EDUCATION

This is the first book to provide a multidisciplinary, critical, and global overview of *evidence-based* parenting education (PEd) programs. Readers are introduced to the best practices for designing, implementing, and evaluating effective PEd programs in order to teach clients how to be effective parents. Noted contributors from various disciplines examine *evidence-based* programs from the USA, Canada, Europe, Asia, Australia, as well as web-based alternatives. The best practices used in a number of venues are explored, often by the developers themselves. Examples and discussion questions encourage application of the material. Critical guidance for those who wish to design, implement, and evaluate PEd programs in various settings is provided.

All chapters feature learning goals, an introduction, conclusion, key points, discussion questions, and additional resources. In addition to these elements, chapters in Part III follow a consistent structure so readers can easily compare programs—theoretical foundations and history, needs assessment and target audience, program goals and objectives, curriculum issues, cultural implications, evidence-based research and evaluation, and professional preparation and training issues. The editor has taught parenting and family life education courses for years. This book reviews the key information that his students needed to become competent professionals.

Highlights of the book's coverage include:

- Comprehensive summary of *evidence-based* PEd training programs in one volume.
- Preparing readers for professional practice as a Certified Family Life Educator (CFLE) by highlighting the fundamentals of developing and evaluating PEd programs.
- Exposing readers to models of parenting education from around the world.

Ideal for advanced undergraduate or graduate courses in parent education, parent–child relations, parenting, early childhood or family life education, family therapy, and home, school, and community services taught in human development and family studies, psychology, social work, sociology, education, nursing, and more, the book also serves as a resource for practitioners, counselors, clergy members, and policy makers interested in evidence-based PEd programs or those seeking to become CFLEs or parent educators.

James J. Ponzetti, Jr. is an Emeritus Faculty member at the University of British Columbia, Canada.

Textbooks in Family Studies Series

The *Textbooks in Family Studies Series* is an interdisciplinary series that offers cutting-edge textbooks in family studies and family psychology. Volumes can be complete textbooks and/or supplementary texts for the undergraduate and/or graduate markets. Both authored and edited volumes are welcome. Please contact the series editor, Robert Milardo at rhd360@maine.edu, for details in preparing a proposal that should include the goal of the book, table of contents, an overview of competing texts, the intended market including course name(s) and level, and suggested reviewers.

These are the books currently in the series:

Father–Daughter Relationships: Contemporary Research and Issues
written by *Linda Nielsen* (2012)

Stepfamilies: A Global Perspective on Research, Policy and Practice
written by *Jan Pryor* (2014)

Serving Military Families: Theories, Research, and Application, Second Edition
written by *Karen Rose Blaisure, Tara Saathoff-Wells, Angela Pereira, Shelley MacDermid Wadsworth, and Amy Laura Dombro* (2016)

Evidence-based Approaches to Relationship and Marriage Education
edited by *James J. Ponzetti, Jr.* (2016)

Evidence-based Parenting Education: A Global Perspective
edited by *James J. Ponzetti, Jr.* (2016)

Evidence-based Approaches to Sexuality Education: A Global Perspective
edited by *James J. Ponzetti, Jr.* (2016)

EVIDENCE-BASED PARENTING EDUCATION

A Global Perspective

Edited by James J. Ponzetti, Jr.

NEW YORK AND LONDON

First published 2016
by Routledge
711 Third Avenue, New York, NY 10017

and by Routledge
27 Church Road, Hove, East Sussex BN3 2FA

Routledge is an imprint of the Taylor & Francis Group, an informa business

Library of Congress Cataloging in Publication Data
Evidence-based parenting education: a global perspective/edited by James J. Ponzetti, Jr.
pages cm.—(Textbooks in family studies)
Includes bibliographical references and index.
1. Parenting—Study and teaching. I. Ponzetti, James J.
HQ755.7.E955 2016
649′.1071—dc23
2015007723

ISBN: 978-1-84872-589-8 (hbk)
ISBN: 978-1-84872-590-4 (pbk)
ISBN: 978-1-31576-667-6 (ebk)

Typeset in Bembo and Stone Sans
by Florence Production Ltd, Stoodleigh, Devon, UK

Printed and bound in the United States of America by
Edwards Brothers Malloy on sustainably sourced paper

CONTENTS

ABOUT THE EDITOR

James J. Ponzetti, Jr., Ph.D., D.Min., CFLE, CCFE is an Associate Professor of Family Studies at the University of British Columbia. He has served on the faculty at the University of New Mexico, Central Washington University and Western Illinois University. He founded the Oregon Family Nurturing Center, Inc. before coming to Canada. As a Certified Family Life Educator in both Canada and the USA (CCFE, Family Services Canada, and CFLE, National Council on Family Relations), he is committed to the promotion of family life education. He has been an editor for several reference publications such as *International Encyclopedia of Marriage and Family* (2003), *Encyclopedia of Human Emotions* (1999), and *Encyclopedia of Marriage and the Family* (1995). He currently serves on the editorial board for *Personal Relationships*, *Journal of Intergenerational Relationships*, *Journal of Family and Community Ministries*, and *Family Science Review*.

ABOUT THE CONTRIBUTORS

Ana Almeida, Ph. D., is Associate Professor at the Department of Psychology of Education and Special Education of the University of Minho, Portugal. She has conducted studies and integrated international and Luso-Brazilian research networks on children's bullying and school-based prevention programs and on parenting and family intervention programs. She is founding director of the Master's course on Psychosocial Intervention with Children, Youth and Families with scientific responsibility for courses on models and methods for psychosocial intervention in contexts related to family and school contexts. She has published and co-authored in national and international works targeted at academic and professional audiences.

Rozumah Binti Baharudin, Ph.D., is a Malay Malaysian and a professor in family ecology specializing in parenting at the Department of Human Development and Family Studies, Faculty of Human Ecology, Universiti Putra Malaysia. She has served the university since 1982, and in recognition received awards for her excellent contributions in teaching, research, and publications. She actively presents papers at national and international conferences. For several years she served on an expert panel for the Ministry of Education, Malaysia Fundamental Research Grant. In 2011 she was a visiting professor at the Australian National University, Canberra and in 2013 at Macquarie University, Sydney.

Leslie A. Barker, B.Sc.N., R.N., is a registered nurse and parenting educator in Calgary, Alberta. Leslie's career has encompassed a wide scope of experiences from acute care to community health. Her passion is helping families provide the kind of care children need to grow, learn, and thrive. She has coordinated the production of several professional and parenting resources and led a number of community initiatives across the Prairie Provinces in Canada. Her research interests are parents as adult learners and evaluation of prevention-focused parenting approaches.

Ana A. Baumann, Ph.D., is a research associate at the Brown School, Washington University in St. Louis, MO. Dr. Baumann also coordinates the Dissemination and Implementation Research Core (DIRC) for Washington University's Institute of Clinical and Translational Sciences (ICTS). Her research involves reducing racial and ethnic disparities in access to and utilization of services in the treatment and quality of care by adapting, implementing, and disseminating evidence-based interventions for ethnic minority populations. She is also interested in international implementation and dissemination of evidence-based interventions. Dr. Baumann's work in this book is supported by the following grants: R25 MH080916–01A2, UL 1 TR 000448, and NCI U54CA155496.

Stephen J. Bavolek, Ph.D., received his doctorate at Utah State University in 1978 and completed a postdoctoral internship at the Kempe Center for the Prevention and Treatment of Child Abuse and Neglect in Denver, Colorado. He has held university faculty positions at the University of Wisconsin Eau Claire, and the University of Utah. He is a recognized leader in the fields of child abuse and neglect treatment and prevention, and parenting education. Dr. Bavolek has received numerous awards for his work, including induction in 1989 into the Royal Guild of the International Social Work Round Table in Vienna, Austria. Since 1983 he has conducted numerous workshops, has appeared on multiple radio and television talk show programs, and has published numerous books, articles, programs, and newsletters. He is the principal author of the Nurturing Parenting Programs®, programs designed to prevent and treat child abuse and neglect, and the Adult-Adolescent Parenting Inventory (AAPI), an inventory designed to assess high-risk parenting attitudes. Dr. Bavolek is President of Family Development Resources, Inc. and Executive Director of Family Nurturing Centers International.

Karen M. Benzies, B.Sc.N., MN, Ph.D., R.N., is a Professor of Nursing and Adjunct Research Professor with the Department of Pediatrics at the University of Calgary. She received a Ph.D. from the University of Alberta and completed postdoctoral fellowships at Stockholm University and the University of Ottawa. Dr. Benzies leads a program of research in early brain and biological development with a focus on evaluating interventions for children at risk for poor outcomes. She has published over sixty peer-reviewed publications and over forty technical reports, and given hundreds of presentations to conference and community audiences. In 2010, she received the Nursing Excellence in Research Award, the highest honor for nurse scientists in Alberta. In 2013, she received the Westbury Legacy Award in recognition of her commitment to research mentorship. Her most satisfying accomplishments come from creating linkages among researchers, clinicians, and policy makers to improve the health of young children and their families.

Gail Chislett works as a health promoter in Child Health at the Peterborough County-City Health Unit, Peterborough, Ontario. For the past 15 years she has been involved at the community and program level in resource development and parenting education, mainly with the Nobody's Perfect Parenting Program.

Carolyn Pape Cowan, Ph.D., Professor Emerita in Psychology at the University of California at Berkeley, has co-directed and published three longitudinal studies examining the effectiveness of a couples group intervention for working-class, middle-class, and low-income parents, and focusing on the effects of these interventions on the parents and children. The previous 10 years of work with parents have been collaborations with Philip Cowan, Marsha Kline Pruett, and Kyle Pruett in the California-based Supporting Father Involvement project.

Philip A. Cowan, Ph.D., Professor Emeritus in Psychology at the University of California at Berkeley, has co-directed, and broadly published the results of, two longitudinal studies of couples group interventions for parents of young children with Carolyn Pape Cowan, and a third study of these interventions for low-income children, in collaboration with Carolyn Pape Cowan, Marsha Kline Pruett, and Kyle Pruett in the award-winning Supporting Father Involvement project in California. He has written in the areas of family systems, adult attachment, couple relationships, parenting styles, and children's development.

Karen DeBord, Ph.D., has over 37 years of experience with higher education serving three universities (Virginia Tech, University of Missouri, and North Carolina State University) as a professor, cooperative extension specialist, researcher, and Director of Graduate Programs. Among her contributions is the leadership she gave to co-authoring the National Extension Parenting Educators' Framework, which was instrumental nationally in shaping the field of professional development and preparation for family life and parenting education.

Maja Deković earned her Ph.D. in developmental psychology. She is a full professor at Utrecht University, chair of the Department Clinical Child and Family Studies, and director of the research program Development and Treatment of Psychosocial Problems. Her research interests include development of problem behavior, parent–child relationships, family interaction, and the effects of family-based interventions.

Jodi Dworkin, Ph.D., is an associate professor in the Department of Family Social Science with Minnesota Extension at the University of Minnesota. Her research and outreach focus on healthy exploration among adolescents and college students, exploring adolescents' developmental processes in youth activities, promoting positive family development, and parenting adolescents and college students. A critical part of her work is developing research-based outreach to promote positive family development.

Marion S. Forgatch, Ph.D., is Senior Scientist Emerita at Oregon Social Learning Center (OSLC), where she developed interventions that are part of the package of evidence-based programs known as Parent Management Training, the Oregon Model (PMTO®). In 2001 she founded Implementation Sciences International Inc. (ISII), a nonprofit affiliate of OSLC that implements PMTO programs in the USA and internationally. She serves as Executive Director and Director of Research for ISII. She has co-authored two books and numerous articles, book chapters, and parenting materials.

Donald A. Gordon, Ph.D., has a Ph.D. in clinical child psychology. He is currently president of Family Works Inc. and is Director of the Center for Divorce Education. He is an Emeritus Professor of Psychology of Ohio University, where he was employed for 23 years training doctoral students in family interventions and conducting research evaluating family and parenting interventions that he refined or developed. The programs Dr. Gordon refined were Functional Family Therapy, and he developed the Children in Between (formerly Children in the Middle) program and the Parenting Wisely interactive CD-ROM parent training program.

Jeanie Ahearn Greene, Ph.D., is founder and Executive Director of Ahearn Greene Associates, an independent health and human services consulting firm. She received her Ph.D. from Syracuse University, Maxwell School of Citizenship and Public Administration in Social Science and her MSW from Syracuse University. She is a researcher, program evaluator, and technical assistant with expertise in workforce development, cross-cultural studies, and advancing effective evidence-based practices through research and program evaluation. She is particularly interested in social policy and programs that improve the lives of women, children, and underserved populations. Her recent publications include the book, *Blue Collar Women at Work with Men: Negotiating the Hostile Environment.* She has provided training, technical assistance, fidelity assurance, and program evaluation for the Strengthening Families Program since 1998.

Arminta I. Jacobson, Ph.D., is the Elaine Millikan Mathes Professor at the College of Education at the University of North Texas, and is a Fellow of the National Council on Family Relations. She is the founding director of the Center for Parent Education and for 19 years has directed the International Annual Conference on Parent Education. She also founded the Texas Association of Parent

Educators. Jacobson has served as principal investigator and director of state evaluation for the Texas HIPPY Corps Project, a parent education home visitation program for parents of preschoolers.

Nolrajsuwat Kannikar, Ed.D., is an assistant professor in the Faculty of Psychology, Chulalongkorn University, Thailand, specializing in counselor education and supervision and family counseling. In 2013, she was a co-author of the American Counseling Association's "Counseling in Thailand" in *Counseling around the World: An International Handbook*. She has written many Thai articles in applied psychology and has conducted several workshops on applying psychology in life and work, counseling and helping skills, and interpersonal communication for private and government organizations. Currently, she is a committee member of the Psychological Association of Thailand.

Deborah J. Kennett, Ph.D., is the Associate Chair & Director of Graduate Studies, Professor, Department of Psychology, and Director of the Centre for Health Studies at Trent University in Peterborough, Ontario, Canada. She is interested in health promotion with special emphasis on program development and on the personal and social factors influencing lifestyle practices.

Patricia L. Kohl, Ph.D., is an associate professor in the Brown School, Washington University in St. Louis, Missouri. She was awarded her Ph.D. at the University of North Carolina at Chapel Hill. Through her research, which is informed by several years of clinical practice with children and families, she seeks to close the gap between research and community-based practice. Dr. Kohl is currently carrying out a randomized control trial to determine whether Pathways Triple P results in better behavioral and safety outcomes than current treatment for children in the child welfare system, and to evaluate the cost-effectiveness of Pathways Triple P. Support for this chapter was provided Dr. Kohl by the National Institute for Child Health and Human Development (1R01HD061454–04A1). Dr. Kohl is a past fellow with the Implementation Research Institute (IRI) at the George Warren Brown School of Social Work, Washington University in St. Louis, through an award from the National Institute of Mental Health (R25 MH080916–01A2) and the Department of Veterans Affairs, Health Services Research & Development Service, Quality Enhancement Research Initiative (QUERI).

Karol L. Kumpfer, Ph.D., is an American Indian (Pawnee) psychologist and University of Utah Professor of Health Promotion specializing in cross-cultural research and EBP family strengthening interventions, including her Strengthening Families Program. SFP is culturally adapted in 36 countries to prevent substance abuse/delinquency and child maltreatment. Until 2000 she was the Director of the SAMHSA Center for Substance Abuse Prevention in Washington, DC.

In 2008, she was awarded the prestigious Society for Prevention Research Community and Cultural Research Award, and in 2010 the University of Utah Career Diversity Award. She has over 450 publications and presents widely and internationally.

Nicholas Long, Ph.D., is Professor of Pediatrics and Director of Pediatric Psychology at the University of Arkansas for Medical Sciences and Arkansas Children's Hospital. He also serves as Director of the Center for Effective Parenting and Director of the Arkansas Home Visiting Network Training Institute. His primary areas of educational, clinical, and research interest are in the areas of parenting, parenting education, and family influences on child behavior and adjustment. Dr. Long is the author of over eighty publications and has co-authored/edited three books on parenting.

Cátia Magalhães, Ph.D., is a psychologist and professor at the Polytechnic Institute of Viseu, Portugal. Her areas of research include prevention, cross-cultural research, and evidence-based parenting interventions. Her Ph.D. dissertation evaluated the effectiveness of a culturally adapted Strengthening Families Program for Portuguese families in the USA and Portugal. She has also conducted a gender analysis of the total SFP database of 4,000 families as well as examining the relationship of father involvement and qualities of good implementers to SFP outcomes. She has prepared a UNODC gender effectiveness guideline with Dr. Kumpfer and others publications in the areas mentioned above.

Lynn McDonald, Ph.D., was awarded her Ph.D. in psychology from the University of California-Irvine. Before that she obtained a Master's in social work from the University of Maryland-Baltimore campus. Dr. McDonald joined Middlesex University in 2008 as the Professor of Social Work. She currently serves on the NHS National Council for Equity and Diversity in London. Since 2010, Dr. McDonald has consulted for the United Nations (UNODC) for delivering evidence-based family skills programs in developing countries (Kazakhstan, Tajikistan, Kyrgyzstan, Turkmenistan, Uzbekistan, Brazil, and Iran). She also consults with Tavistock Institute (TIHR) and gives lectures at the Institute of Psychiatry, King's College. She volunteered with the British Psychological Society to produce a report on child mental health and social inclusion of low-income parents through adapting evidence-based parenting programs. She previously worked for a family counseling agency and is a certified family therapist who had a private practice in family therapy and taught family therapy for 10 years. In 1988, Dr. McDonald applied sociological and psychological theory to develop an after-school multi-family group program to increase child well-being and reduce inequalities, called Families and Schools Together (FAST). Her husband is British. She is the mother of two, and grandmother of four.

Kim S. Miller, Ph.D. is the Senior Advisor for Youth Prevention at the Centers for Disease Control and Prevention (CDC), Division of Global HIV/AIDS Prevention. She joined CDC 25 years ago after completing her doctoral studies at Emory University in Atlanta, Georgia. Her current international research and prevention activities focus on pre-risk prevention approaches to sexual risk reduction, understanding and reducing sexual risk among youth, youth development approaches to sexual risk prevention, and the role of the family in the promotion of sexual risk reduction and protection of children.

Judith A. Myers-Walls, Ph.D., is Professor Emerita at Purdue University's Department of Human Development and Family Studies. She worked with Cooperative Extension on the topics of child development and parenting for 31 years, focusing especially on adolescent pregnancy and parenthood, methods of parenting education, and talking with children about difficult topics such as war and peace and helping them deal with disasters. She also taught in the classroom. In retirement she is continuing writing, research, and reviewing activities.

Methinin Pinyuchon, Ph.D., was an associate professor at Srinakharinwirot University in Bangkok and later at Thaksin University in Songkhla, Thailand. Her specialty is in the areas of counselor education and supervision, school counseling, cross-cultural understanding, and family counseling. She specializes particularly in parenting skills and social skills training. In 2007, she was invited by the Office of the Narcotics Control Board (ONCB) of Thailand to select evidence-based family skills training programs for implementation in Thailand. The Strengthening Families Program was implemented successfully with Thai families in several regions. The evaluation found outcomes improved if fathers also attended.

Byron J. Powell, Ph.D., is a Fellow at the Leonard Davis Institute of Health Economics and Postdoctoral Researcher in the Department of Psychiatry, Perelman School of Medicine, University of Pennsylvania, Philadelphia, PA.

Enola K. Proctor, Ph.D., is the Shanti K. Khinduka Distinguished Professor and Associate Dean for Faculty in the George Warren Brown School, Washington University in St. Louis. Missouri. Dr. Proctor is also Director, Center for Mental Health Services Research at Washington University. Her teaching and research are motivated by the question, *how do we ensure that people receive the very best possible care?* She currently serves on an Institute of Medicine Committee on Developing Evidence-based Standards for Psychosocial Interventions for Mental Disorder. She has published several books, most recently *Dissemination and Implementation Research in Health: Translating Science to Practice*, with colleagues Ross Brownson and Graham Colditz. Dr. Proctor has been recognized in numerous awards including the Lifetime Achievement Award from the Society for Social Work and Research (2002), the Presidential Award for Excellence in Research (1994), and the Knee-Wittman Award for Lifetime Achievement in Health and Mental Health Practice (2011) from the National Association of Social Workers. Dr. Proctor is supported by the following grants: R25 MH080916–01A2, UL 1 TR 000448, and NCI U54CA155496.

Kyle D. Pruett, MD, is Clinical Professor of Psychiatry at Yale Child Study Center, Yale School of Medicine, where he recently received the Lifetime Achievement and Distinguished Teaching Awards. He served as President of Zero to Three: National Center for Infants, Toddlers, and their Families, and on the Board of Directors of Sesame Workshop while in private practice of child psychiatry. He conducted the only longitudinal study of infants and toddlers being raised primarily by their fathers, publishing his findings in the award-winning *Nurturing Father*, and collaborates with his wife Marsha Kline Pruett, Ph.D. and Phil and Carolyn Cowan in the Supporting Father Involvement longitudinal study.

Marsha Kline Pruett, Ph.D., ABPP is the Maconda Brown Professor at Smith College. She publishes broadly in family research, psychology, and family law and has authored books and articles in these fields nationally and internationally. She develops, implements, and evaluates preventive interventions in courts and family-focused community agencies. Her writings address healthy adjustment to family transitions, shared parenting, father involvement, and work and family. The Supporting Father Involvement project is a 10-year collaboration with Phil and Carolyn Cowan and Kyle Pruett.

Robert E. Pushak, MTS, is the Director of Training for Parenting Wisely. Bob participated in the development of both the Parenting Wisely and Children in the Middle programs, which have been designated as best practice programs in the USA, Canada, and Great Britain. Bob received the 2006–2007 Premiers' Innovation and Special Achievement Award for achieving a fundamental shift in service practice that produces substantial benefits for civil servants and society.

Laura A. Rains, M.S.W., is the Director of Implementation and Training at Implementation Sciences International, Inc. (ISII). She plans and designs ISII's training programs and co-authors educational materials, coding schemes, and infrastructure protocol. She conducts practice as a licensed clinical social worker.

Barbara Reichle, Ph.D., is full Professor of Developmental Psychology and head of the Department of Psychology of Ludwigsburg University of Education, Germany. She has conducted studies on family development after the transition to parenthood, and developed evidence-based prevention programs for new parents and for elementary school children. She has published scientific articles, books, and training manuals targeted at national and international audiences. In 2009, she received the Ludwigsburg University of Education Distinguished Award for the Promotion of Women in Science.

María José Rodrigo, Ph.D., is a professor in psychology at the University of Salamanca, Spain, and Director of the Master's program on Family Intervention and Mediation at the University of La Laguna, Spain. Her research topic is evidence-based parenting programs to promote positive parenting in families under at-risk circumstances and to prevent child maltreatment, on which she has published many international papers. Prof. Rodrigo and her team have designed, implemented, and evaluated group parenting programs targeted at families referred by the local social services, which are widespread in Spain and are currently starting in Portugal and Brazil. Prof. Rodrigo was President of the European Association of Developmental Psychology from 2008 to 2011. Fellow since 2010 of the Association for Psychological Science (APS) for sustained and outstanding distinguished contributions to psychological science, she has been the organizer of several posgraduate courses on Evidence-based Parent Education Programs and Best Practices to Promote Positive Parenting sponsored by the Council of Europe and the Jacobs Foundation. She is currently commissioned by the Spanish Ministry of Health, Social Policy and Equality to promote good practices among professionals in the use of evidence-based and preventive approaches for family work.

Matthew R. Sanders, Ph.D. is Professor of Clinical Psychology and Director of the Parenting and Family Support Centre at The University of Queensland. As the founder of the Triple P—Positive Parenting Program—Professor Sanders is considered a global leader in the field of evidence-based parenting intervention and research, and is one of The University of Queensland's Innovation Champions. The Triple P system is currently in use across 25 countries, with over 60,000 practitioners and having delivered to over 7 million families worldwide.

Margrét Sigmarsdóttir, Ph.D. is a clinical child psychologist. She is an implementation leader at the Government Agency for Child Protection in Iceland and leads a nationwide PMTO project in that country. She is Director of Fidelity and a senior mentor at Implementation Sciences International, Inc. (ISII). She has authored articles, book chapters, and educational materials.

Sabine Stoltz, Ph.D., developmental psychologist, works as an assistant professor at the Behavioral Science Institute of the Radboud University. Her research interests include childhood externalizing behavior, social cognitive functioning in children, personality, temperament, and interventions for externalizing behavior.

Karen M.T. Turner, Ph.D. is Deputy Director of the Parenting and Family Support Centre at The University of Queensland. She is a clinical psychologist and research academic and has had a major role in the development of Triple P resources for practitioners and parents. She has co-authored a range of professional manuals and teaching aids, parent workbooks and tip sheet series, DVDs, and award-winning interactive online programs. A primary focus is reducing barriers to accessing evidence-based parenting and family support.

Carolyn Webster-Stratton, Ph.D. Professor Emeritus at the University of Washington School of Nursing and founding director of the University of Washington Parenting Clinic, has spent more than twenty-five years researching ways to help prevent and treat aggressive behavior in young children. Professor Webster-Stratton, a licensed clinical psychologist and nurse practitioner, has developed evidence-based prevention and treatment programs that have been translated into eight languages and are now used by teachers and mental health specialists in 20 countries around the world. She has published numerous scientific articles, books, and training videotapes. In 1997, Professor Webster-Stratton received the National Mental Health Lela Rowland Prevention Award from the National Mental Health Association for her interventions with families. She also has received the prestigious National Mental Health Research Scientist Award from the National Institute of Mental Health. Recently she received the University of Washington Annual Faculty Award (2006–2007) and the University of Washington Education Department Outstanding Alumnae (2006).

Jing Xie, Ph.D., a national of China, holds a doctoral degree in Health Promotion and Education from the University of Utah. She has worked on program evaluation in the Strengthening Families Program since graduation. Her research interests include program cultural adaptation and evaluation, evidence-based family intervention, and immigrant youth behavioral and mental health. She has contributed to several publications in this direction, and presented the study findings at various national and international conferences, one of which concerns a pilot study of implementing the Strengthening Families Program among immigrant Chinese families in San Francisco. She worked on translation of the program curriculum and evaluation questionnaires, as well as cultural consultation for program evaluation and implementation.

FOREWORD

Few issues are more important to families than raising healthy and successful children who develop interests and occupations that contribute to their communities and lead to rewarding relationships throughout life; few activities are more challenging. Parents routinely report their children are among the most important areas of their lives, among the most satisfying, and among the most difficult. There is little disagreement among professionals in family studies and human development that raising healthy, well-socialized children is important and complex. Not surprisingly, parenting, parent–child relationships, and the broad area of children's cognitive and social development are among the most active areas of research in the family sciences. Researchers are keenly interested in the features of parenting that best support optimum child and adolescent development as well as the influence of siblings, extended family like grandparents, uncles and aunts, and other important influences like schools and relationships with peers. Parallel to the work of social scientists is the work on developing parenting education programs and delivering such programs to parents and caregivers. The best circumstance is when these two areas mutually influence one another. When the outcomes of social science research inform the design and delivery of parenting education programs, and conversely when the experiences of practitioners inform the conduct of research.

In his second book in the series,[1] author and editor James Ponzetti aims to engage the design, delivery, and optimization of parenting education programs in their many forms. *Evidence-based Parenting Education: A Global Perspective* consists of 21 chapters that critically examine parenting education programs offered in health facilities, schools, community centers, public assistance offices, places of worship, universities, and a host of similar settings. These programs share an interest in teaching parents and child caregivers of any age how to become skillful at understanding the needs of a child and fully informed of the course of a child's development through adolescence and well into early adulthood. Evidence-based parenting education programs draw on current research and systematically design programs to teach caregivers essential skills, basic knowledge of child and adolescent development, and otherwise promote optimal child development and healthy parent/caregiver relationships with children. The book intends to inform readers about the design and delivery of specific programs while also addressing the question of how we go about critically evaluating programs given their content and intended purpose and audiences. The book is comprehensive, unique in its purpose, and benefits from the contributions of leading experts in the field throughout North America, Europe, and Asia.

Robert M. Milardo, Ph.D.
Professor of Family Relations
University of Maine
Series Editor

Note

1 The companion volume is: J. J. Ponzetti (Ed.). (2015). *Evidence-based approaches to relationship and marriage education*. New York: Routledge.

PREFACE

Parent–child relationships are a source of well-being for many people. Parenting education (hereafter PEd) is designed to provide caregivers with the information and proficiencies necessary to develop the essential skills, knowledge, and abilities to foster children's healthy development. The primary goal of PEd is to make available to caregivers the necessary knowledge and tools that contribute to children's overall development and socialization. PEd aims at preventing adverse experiences with childrearing through instruction, which involves gaining knowledge, exploring attitudes and values, and/or developing skills to build positive parent–child relationships and facilitate optimal circumstances for guidance and nurturance.

PEd has spread in popularity over the past five decades. The growth of PEd has generated a concurrent proliferation of descriptors from parent education to parent support, parent involvement, and parenting education. PEd best practices focus on the advantages of designing programs based on content and pedagogical practices that have documented effectiveness. Parenting programs have been found to be effective in changing parenting practices, leading to improvements in children's behavior. Yet, evidence of such benefits is dispersed in diverse literature, and is not easily found or readily accessible.

PEd based on substantive evidence offers a more reliable approach. Historically, professional practice has been based on loose, diffuse bodies of knowledge rather than systematic investigation. Much of this knowledge is no more than folklore, custom, or clinical insights, with little, if any, valid scientific evidence on which to justify practice. In response to this circumstance, evidence-based practice (or EBP) was formulated. Evidence-based practice involves complex and conscientious decision making, which details best practices supported in empirical studies to inform the improvement of whatever professional task is at hand. EBP is defined as approaches to prevention or treatment that are based in theory and have undergone scientific evaluation on the U.S. government's National Registry of Evidence-based Programs and Practices online database developed by the Substance Abuse and Mental Health Services Administration (see www.samhsa.gov). EBP stands in contrast to approaches that are based on tradition, convention, belief, or anecdotal evidence. However, this definition must be interpreted broadly so as to not limit EBP only to practices that have supportive random control trials available. EBP, as used in this book, is the integration of preeminent empirical evidence, professional expertise, and client values and preferences in the decision-making process associated with best practice. Thus, EBP is concerned with extant research studies but considers secondary publications, such as systematic reviews, meta-analyses, and clinical guidelines, too. EBP is a philosophical approach initially applied to medicine but expanded since to a disparate collection of professions that includes nursing and allied health professions, family studies, developmental psychology, social work, early intervention, child mental health, and education among others. The time has come for PEd to join these professions in using an evidence-based approach in the design, implementation, and evaluation of PEd practice.

A diverse collection of PEd programs are currently available in a number of venues. These programs are available from government, research, and voluntary organizations. PEd programs are offered in mental hospitals, community centers, public assistance offices, churches, or universities among other places. Programs vary by curricular focus, learning format, and target audience. Curricula usually deal with various childrearing skills or dynamics such as guidance and communication. Providers utilize formats that are preventive and group-oriented. Programs operate with different group sizes and treatment dosage amounts (i.e., length of program). In particular, PEd targets individuals at risk for problems related to parenting. However, programs exist for many groups, including single parents, gay and lesbian parents, grandparents raising grandchildren, in addition to traditional two-parent families.

While the interpretation of outcomes research is complex, parent educators and scholars suggest there is promising evidence that caregivers can learn about developmentally appropriate practices, modify attitudes and beliefs, and hone specific skills to improve parenting in general and their relationships with the children they are responsible for in particular.

Purpose of *Evidence-based Parenting Education: A Global Perspective*

The aim of *Evidence-based Parenting Education: A Global Perspective* is to provide a critical appraisal of evidence-based approaches to parenting education. Accordingly, it offers an accessible and comprehensive overview of best practices when designing and implementing preventive educational programs for parents or primary caregivers. PEd is addressed by numerous professionals representing an array of disciplines (e.g., family studies, psychology, counseling, social work, and other related disciplines). This book aims to bring the diffuse evidence regarding PEd together in one volume readily available to students, scholars, and practitioners alike. It offers the foremost resource for those who plan to design, implement, and evaluate preventive PEd. In addition, future or current practitioners may find the knowledge presented herein of assistance for their professional practice.

Content Overview

The comprehensive coverage of this book is unique and innovative. An introductory chapter presents a concise historical overview of PEd development and expansion. It is followed by 20 chapters written by notable experts who are eminently qualified to present the latest research on a range of pertinent topics to EBP in PEd. The initial six chapters focus on fundamentals of parenting education; namely, program development, implementation, and evaluation as well as the Parent Educator's Framework developed by the U.S. Cooperative Extension Service as a valuable guide to professional practice. Part II, which includes the next three chapters, reviews the status of parenting education in Europe, Asia, and the virtual world created by the Internet. Best practices reviewed in Part III (Chapters 10–19) constitute the core of the book describing 10 stellar evidence-based parenting programs offered around the world. Each chapter in this section presents an overview and history of a particular program as well as the theoretical foundations of the program, discussion of needs assessment and target audience, program goals and objectives, curriculum and other program issues, cultural implications, evidence-based research and evaluation, and additional resources for the reader. Finally, Chapters 20–21 in Part IV review future directions for PEd and conclusions.

Intended Audience

The chapters are organized in a way that is useful to advanced undergraduate and graduate students in family studies, marriage and family therapy, social work, family life education, psychology, mental health and psychiatry programs. The information on parenting education and program development offered here may be utilized in general courses such as parent–child relations or family life education. In addition, advanced classes in family nursing, family psychology, family studies, or early childhood education may find this topic pertinent to professional interests. PEd as a field of professional practice is thriving within several disciplines such as family studies, education, nursing, social work, and mental health counseling.

Acknowledgments

It would be a serious omission not to acknowledge the expertise and willingness of chapter contributors to share their remarkable insight on an array of topics pertinent to readers interested in evidence-based PEd. They have made editing this book a privilege and certainly a pleasure. Robert Milardo, editor for the *Textbooks in Family Studies Series*, has been very supportive. Similarly, Debra Riegert and Angela Halliday at Routledge/Taylor & Francis have been helpful in numerous ways. I also want to thank the reviewers who provided very helpful feedback on the manuscript: Karen S. Myers-Bowman, Kansas State University; Rhonda A. Richardson, Kent State University; Jeffrey J. Angera, Central Michigan University; and Wallace E. Dixon, Jr., East Tennessee State University. However, the most important people have been my family, especially my mother, Jo Ann, and my father, James Sr., who have believed in me and encouraged endeavors such as conceiving and editing this book.

James J. Ponzetti, Jr.

PART I

Fundamentals of Parenting Education Programs

1

OVERVIEW AND HISTORY OF PARENTING EDUCATION

James J. Ponzetti, Jr.

Introduction

Parenting is a difficult and challenging responsibility. Although childbearing may appear instinctive, childrearing is not. It is immensely time consuming and requires much effort. Parenting is an incredible journey, but the **parent–child relationship** can be wearisome and often bewildering. Of the many different relationships people form over the course of the lifespan, the relationship between parent and child is among the most important. The quality of the parent–child relationship is affected by both parent attributes (e.g., age, experience, self-confidence, and marital stability) and child attributes (e.g., age, sex, physical appearance, and temperament). Modern parenthood is too demanding and complex to undertake merely because one was a child once. Changing roles and values may create ambiguity and uncertainty for contemporary parents. Numerous myths and misconceptions persist about parenthood complicated by the lack of sufficient and reliable guidelines for effective parenting. In addition, economic and social conditions increase stress on contemporary families (Hicks & Williams, 1981).

Parenting is one of the most ambitious tasks one can undertake. If done well, however, it can be incredibly rewarding. Contemporary parenting offers both wonders and worries to parents and their children. Zepeda, Varela, and Morales (2004) pointed out that parenting is a learned skill adults can learn or improve through education and experience. Because many believe that parenting comes naturally, they don't always recognize the need for formal parenting education. Whether education occurs on an individual basis, in a group, or even from reading popular magazines and books, the goal is to acquire the knowledge and tools necessary to contribute to a child's overall development and socialization. Nevertheless, the vast majority of caregivers who are expected to nurture and guide children receive little, if any, formal preparation. Learning how to raise children to be healthy, well-adjusted adults is not something a wise society leaves to chance. The importance of parenthood and parenting demands earnest recognition and attention (Fine, 1980, 1989).

What is Parenting Education?

Parenting education is not a new phenomenon. As the field of parenting education has evolved, its definition has changed as well. Although the purpose of parenting programs may be clear, the terminology used to define them can be confusing. Just what is the difference between parent education, parent support, parent involvement, and parenting education? The term "parent education" is often used to refer to instruction on fulfilling the parental role. Brim (1959) described parent education as the use of educational techniques in order to effect change in the role parents enact in raising children. Such a definition is somewhat limited in scope as it focuses only on parental role performance. Parent support, on the other hand, typically described the provision of services to assist parents or primary caregivers to develop and utilize available psychological and material resources to promote family self-sufficiency, and peer support. Parent support approaches often focus on the social context of parenthood, and on techniques to enhance a family's social network, social support, and community linkages as buffers against stress and isolation (Powell, 1988a; Weissbourd, 1994). Parent involvement described parents' interactions with schools and with their children to parents' participation in school efforts to help promote their child's success at school (Kroth, 1989; Editorial Projects in Education Research Center, 2004). Schlossman (1978a) combined parent involvement with early childhood education programs in his definition of parent education.

While role support, activities that build on family strengths instead of centering on deficits, and participation in children's lives are essential resources, parenting education is more inclusive. Anyone who has committed to nurture a child through infancy and beyond can participate and acquire evidence-based methods of child management and childrearing abilities. Note the use of the word "parenting" rather than "parent" before education. This choice is deliberate to include individuals who are not biological or legal parents but who nonetheless carry the primary responsibility of raising a child. Parenting is the act of behaving in a manner conducive to optimal childrearing and positive socialization (Carter, 1996). Accordingly, instruction attends to expanding knowledge of growth and development, and teaching specific behaviors and interpersonal skills. The primary focus of formal parenting education programs is to help caregivers develop the skills, knowledge, and abilities they need to contribute to children's healthy physical, emotional, social, and cognitive development. Grandparents, foster and adoptive parents, or a variety of other significant adults can be instructed in the means to address the needs of a child without ignoring personal needs (Galinksy, 1987).

Historical Overview

Parenting information and skills were traditionally passed down from generation to generation. Further, popular literature augmented childrearing advice garnered through other means (Stendler, 1950; Bigner, 1972; Bigner & Yang, 1996). These informal processes may no longer suffice with the advent of modernization and increased globalization; richer worldviews incorporating the salience of effective parenting in the development of emotionally healthy children are required.

Educational programs for parents have existed in some form since the early 1800s (Sunley, 1955), but these efforts eventually foundered later (Florin & Dokecki, 1983). However, mothers met regularly before this time in study groups called "maternal associations" to talk about concerns related to child-rearing (Croake & Glover, 1977; Lewis-Rowley, Brasher, Moss, Duncan, & Stiles, 1993). Later, these study groups came together to create the National Congress of Mothers which, in turn, became the Parent Teacher Association or PTA. Though separate, both the PTA and the child study movement did much to further parent education; both saw knowledge as the key to improving the lives of children (Schlossman, 1978a).

Early research on children focused on delinquency and pathology. Relatively little was known about normal children and normal development. *Child study* developed with the application of scientific methods to normal child development. The child study movement arose in the last decade of the nineteenth century in several Western countries and was inspired by a number of social reform movements that aimed to improve the health and welfare of children. G. Stanley Hall, a charismatic psychologist who addressed the PTA often, introduced the child study movement in the USA in the 1880s. The decisive impulse to endorse child study as an area of scientific inquiry came in 1923 when the Laura Spelman Rockefeller Memorial (LSRM) awarded a grant to the Society for the Study of Child Nature, founded in 1888, to stimulate the child study movement. Lawrence K. Frank, who directed parent education efforts funded by the LSRM, thought that child study was essential for understanding parent education and childrearing practices. The following year, an extension of the grant was made and the Society incorporated under the name Child Study Association of America. The Child Study Association of America existed from 1890 to 1972, and constituted the oldest organization in the USA to have a continuous parent education program. The LSRM also started funding interdisciplinary research in 1924 at a number of child development centers in the USA and Canada (Schlossman, 1983).

Government support for parent education in the USA preceded private organizations' efforts to offer parent education on a large scale. The White House Conference on Child Welfare was held in 1909, followed by the creation of the Children's Bureau in 1912, Cooperative Extension Service in the Department of Agriculture placed county agents across the country in 1914, and health-oriented parent programs under the auspices of the Public Health Service in 1918 (Brim, 1959).

The influx of immigrants early in the twentieth century created a host of problems related to child and family issues, and sparked sundry social movements to help parents deal with them (Skrypnek, 2002). The home economics movement began in the late nineteenth century and emphasized the importance of hygiene and proper nutrition in caring for children. It expanded in the early decades of the twentieth century when a number of major universities such as Cornell, Illinois, Oregon State, and the University of California at Berkeley advanced research and training in their child development and family life programs. The public health movement performed a significant role in the scientizing of parenting in North America (Dickinson, 1993).

With the advent of behaviorism in the 1920s and its authority in childrearing literature through the 1930s, child care began to lose the political affect and concern for maternal well-being that marked the Progressive era. John B. Watson, the founder of behaviorism, wrote popular articles on childrearing espousing the salience of children's environment over maternal nurturance. Parent education saw dramatic progress in professionalization. In 1929, the National Society for the Study of Education published its yearbook entitled *Preschool and Parent Education*. The National Council on Parent Education was also incorporated during this time and produced a professional journal. The early 1930s saw much activity in the area of parent education. Arnold Gesell brought new insight to parents through his observations of child development in the 1930s. Although the Works Progress Administration made available teachers and other trained personnel for groups interested in child behavior during the depression, financial support for further professional development in parent education was not available (Croake & Glover, 1977). Thus, interest seems to wane late in the decade.

The childrearing advice doled out by various professionals during the first half of the twentieth century was welcomed by mothers of all backgrounds. For instance, the publication of Benjamin Spock's *Baby and Child Care* in the 1940s had a profound effect on parenting in America (Weiss, 1977). Yet, not until the aftermath of World War II and the emergence of the Great Society programs of the 1960s did parent education increase again, this time in the form of energized commitments to parent involvement and empowerment. Behaviorism made a comeback during the 1950s as B.F. Skinner introduced operant conditioning, and used the reward technique and strict environmental control to shape young children's behavior. Ginott (1957) began promoting parent education and guidance groups in the early 1950s as a means of supplanting the conflict, distress, or simple clumsiness that often abides in the parental role due to the lack of preparation. Alene Auerbach published *State of the Art of Parent Education* in 1960. This report raised important questions about parenting education as a field, many of which have yet to receive adequate attention (Palm, 1999).

Formal parent education programs became not only more prevalent in the latter half of the century, but more diverse in terms of sponsorship, which affirmed their appeal and perceived utility (Goetz, 1991). Rudolph Dreikurs, a follower of Alfred

Adler and one of the pioneers in the parent education movement, promoted neighborhood parent discussion groups in Chicago during this time. He later wrote the popular book *Children: The Challenge* (Dreikurs, 1964). Parent education efforts during the 1970s were deemed by government agencies and organizations as the panacea for an array of social ills (de Lissovoy, 1978; Schlossman, 1978b; Clarke-Stewart, K. (1981). Many commercially produced parent programs including Parent Effectiveness Training (Gordon, 1970), Active Parenting (Popkin, 1983), and Systematic Training for Effective Parenting (Dinkmeyer & McKay, 1976) became available. Missouri implemented the Parents as First Teachers program (Vartuli & Winter, 1989) in 1981 based on White's (1981) seminal work with the Harvard Preschool Project. Fine published the *Handbook of Parent Education* (1980) and *The Second Handbook of Parent Education* (1989).

By the beginning of the twenty-first century, numerous reviews of parent education offered cautious optimism regarding program effectiveness and recommendations for best practices (Carter, 1996; Lloyd, 1999; Brown, 2005; Center for Disease Control and Prevention, 2009; Samuelson, 2010). Parenting programs can be effective in changing parenting practices, leading to improvements in children's behavior (Powell, 1988b). Effective parent education programs have been linked with decreased rates of child abuse and neglect; better physical, cognitive, and emotional development in children; increased parental knowledge of child development and parenting skills; improved parent–child communication; and more effective parental monitoring and discipline. The expansion of parenting programs has taken place in a number of countries over the past decade with the growing involvement of voluntary organizations in their provision.

Parenting education is directed at the education and support of adults who are entrusted to raise children in emotionally healthy ways so that the children can thrive personally, academically, and socially. The goal of parenting education is to provide a mechanism to learn positive parenting techniques and attitudes from sources outside one's own upbringing. The ability to provide parent education programming that has proven to be effective is crucial as funders increasingly require evidence-based programming (Todres & Bunston, 1993). The demand for evidence-based programming began primarily in the 1990s from federal agencies addressing problems of substance use and poor mental health among youth. "Evidence-based" is the most common term used to describe either an entire intervention or individual components of the interventions, but terms such as "research-based", "science-based", "effective", and "efficacious" are sometimes used within the broad purview of prevention science (Kellam & Langevin, 2003).

Evidence-based Parenting Education Format

Evidence-based Parenting Education: A Global Perspective provides a systematic outline for individuals who are looking for a guide to professional practice as parenting educators. There is a need for a resource that identifies best practices. This book presents a current, comprehensive overview of evidence-based programmatic parenting education with insightful chapters written by distinguished scholars worldwide. It examines the existing status and provides a critical appraisal of professional practice. The text serves as the preeminent resource for both professors who teach and those preparing to practice parenting education.

This book is about evidence-based programmatic parenting education that minimizes intrusive and expensive remedial efforts. It offers a broad and in-depth look at instruction concerning how children grow and development at particular life stages, what childrearing skills are important to enhance parent–child interaction, how parenting programs are designed and implemented, and how evaluation is accomplished to affirm an evidence-based program. Parenting education efforts can focus on specific topics such as appropriate and recommended disciplinary practices, or on more general subjects, such as developmental stages or fostering physical and mental health in children. The goals and objectives of parenting education may encompass a variety of parent and child outcomes. Parenting education is also delivered in a variety of places and by a range of professionals and paraprofessionals with differing levels of preparation. Its global perspective is multidisciplinary, exploring the range of psychosocial, economic, family, and individual factors that influence the program development and evaluation. The contributors include scholars and practitioners from different disciplines, including human development and family studies, education, sociology, developmental psychology, psychiatry, pediatrics, and health policy. The impetus for preparing the book was to provide an articulate exposition of the state of evidence-based parenting education that can be used in courses concerning parents and children or family life education. This book provides clear information about what research has shown to work (i.e., best practices) when designing and implementing parenting educational programs. This information is critical for competence of both new and practicing professionals.

One of the challenges in writing a book such as this is to balance the many perspectives that inform parenting education. Parenting education is addressed by numerous professionals representing an array of disciplines (e.g., early childhood education, family studies, psychology, nursing, counseling, social work, philosophy, and other related disciplines). As a result, this book is quite deliberate in maintaining breadth, while at the same time limiting the scope to a manageable extent of detail. Such comprehensive coverage is unique and the focus on application is innovative. A multidisciplinary approach is taken to insure the review of significant evidence-based practice of parenting education. Few books integrate similar breadth.

The book chapters have been organized in a way that corresponds with an upper division or graduate-level course. This introduction is followed by 20 chapters written by notable scholars on specific topics. The advantage of this format is the eminent qualifications of contributors to present the latest research in their areas of expertise.

The present chapter has provided an introduction to the field and a concise history of parenting education. Part I includes chapters focusing on basic principles of evidence-based practice and general frameworks. The main part of the book is Part II, which reviews specific parenting programs. Renowned contributors address the development of a program, training required of providers, delivery systems and implementation, and program evaluation or research evidence supporting best practice. Part III focuses on the best available research supporting parenting education efforts. Finally, Part IV considers future trends and directions, especially via the Internet.

References

Bigner, J. (1972). Parent education in popular literature: 1950–1970. *Family Coordinator, 21*, 313–319.

Bigner, J., & Yang, R. (1996). Parent education in popular literature: 1972–1990. *Family and Consumer Sciences Research Journal, 25*, 3–27.

Brim, O., Jr. (1959). *Education for child rearing.* New York: Free Press.

Brown, M. (2005). *Recommended practices. A review of the literature on parent education and support.* Newark, DE: Cooperative Extension, University of Delaware. See http://extension.udel.edu/fcs/human-development-and-families/parent-education-literature-review/

Carter, N. (1996), *See how we grow: A report on the status of parent education in the US.* Philadelphia, PA: Pew Charitable Trusts. Available at www.pewtrusts.com/ideas/ideas_item.cfm?content_item_id=411&content_type_id=17 or ERIC Number: ED412022

Centers for Disease Control and Prevention (2009). *Parent training programs: Insights for practitioners.* Atlanta, GA: Centers for Disease Control.

Clarke-Stewart, K. (1981). Parent education in the 1970s. *Educational Evaluation and Policy Analysis, 3*, 47–58.

Croake, J., & Glover, K. (1977). A history and evaluation of parent education. *Family Coordinator, 26*, 151–158.

de Lissovoy, V. (1978). Parent education. White elephant in the classroom? *Youth & Society, 9*, 315–338.

Dickinson, H. (1993). Scientific parenthood: The mental hygiene movement and the reform of Canadian families. *Journal of Comparative Family Studies, 24*, 387–403.

Dinkmeyer, D., & McKay, G. (1976). *Systematic training for effective parenting.* Circle Pines, MN: American Guidance Service.

Dreikurs, R. (1964). *Children: The challenge.* New York: Plume/Penguin Books.

Editorial Projects in Education Research Center. (2004, August 4). Issues A–Z: Parent Involvement. *Education Week.* Retrieved from www.edweek.org/ew/issues/parent-involvement/

Fine, M. (Ed.). (1980). *Handbook on parent education.* New York: Academic Press.

Fine, M. (Ed.). (1989). *The second handbook on parent education.* San Diego, CA: Academic Press.

Florin, P., & Dokecki, P. (1983). Changing families through parent and family education. Review and analysis, in I. Sigel & L. Laosa (Eds.), *Changing families* (pp. 23–63). New York: Plenum.

Frank, L. (1962). The beginnings of child development and family life education in the twentieth century. *Merrill-Palmer Quarterly, 8*, 207–227.

Galinsky, E. (1987). *The six stages of parenthood.* Reading, MA: Addison-Wesley.

Ginott, H. (1957). Parent education groups in a child guidance clinic. *Mental Hygiene, 41,* 82–86.

Goetz, K. (1991). *Programs to strengthen families.* Chicago, IL: Family Resource Coalition.

Gordon, T. (1970). *P.E.T. parent effectiveness training.* New York: Wyden Books.

Hicks, M., & Williams, J. (1981). Current challenges in educating for parenthood. *Family Relations, 30,* 579–584.

Kellam, S., & Langevin, D. (2003). A framework for understanding "evidence" in prevention research and programs. *Prevention Science, 4,* 137–153.

Kroth, R. (1989). School-based parent involvement programs, in M. Fine (Ed.), *The second handbook on parent education* (pp. 119–143). San Diego, CA: Academic Press.

Lewis-Rowley, M., Brasher, R., Moss, J., Duncan, S., & Stiles, R. (1993). The evolution of education for family life, in M. Arcus, J. Schvaneveldt, & J. Moss (Eds.), *Handbook of family life education: Vol. 1. Foundations of family life education* (pp. 26–50). Newbury Park, CA: Sage.

Lloyd, E. (1999). *Parenting matters: What works in parenting education.* Essex, UK: Barnardo's Publications. See ERIC documents ED456893.

Medway F. (1989). Measuring the effectiveness of parent education, in M. Fine (Ed.) *The second handbook of parent education: Contemporary perspective* (pp. 237–255). San Diego, CA: Academic Press.

Palm, G. (1999, March). 100 Years of Parenting Education. National Council on Family Relations Report, pp. 3–14.

Popkin, M. (1983). *Active parenting handbook.* Atlanta, GA: Active Parenting.

Powell, D. (1988a). Emerging directions in parent-child early intervention, in D. Powell (Ed.) *Parent education as early childhood intervention: Emerging directions in theory, research and practice* (pp. 1–22). Norwood, NJ: Ablex.

Powell D. (1988b). Challenges in the design and evaluation of parent-child intervention programs, in D. Powell (Ed.) *Parent education as early childhood intervention: Emerging directions in theory, research and practice* (pp. 229–237). Norwood, NJ: Ablex.

Samuelson, A. (2010, August). Best practices for parent education and support programs. *What Works, Wisconsin—Research to practice series, issue 10,* Madison, WI: University of Wisconsin Extension.

Schlossman, S. (1978a). Before Home Start: Notes toward a history of parent education in America, 1897–1929. *Harvard Educational Review, 46,* 436–467.

Schlossman, S. (1978b). The parent education game: The politics of child psychology in the 1970s. *Teachers College Record, 79,* 788–808.

Schlossman, S. (1983). The formative era in American parent education: Overview and interpretation, in R. Haskins & D. Adams (Eds.) *Parent education and public policy* (pp. 7–39). Norwood, NJ: Ablex.

Skrypnek, B. (2002). Parent education in Canada: Yesterday, today, and tomorrow. *Canadian Home Economics Journal, 51,* 5–9.

Stendler, C. (1950). Sixty years of child training practices. *Journal of Pediatrics, 36,* 122–134.

Sunley, R. (1955). Early nineteenth-century American literature on child rearing, in M. Mead & M. Wolfenstein (Eds.) *Childhood in contemporary cultures.* Chicago, IL: University of Chicago Press.

Todres, R., & Bunston, T. (1993). Parent education program evaluation: A review of the literature. *Canadian Journal of Community Mental Health, 12,* 225–257.

Vartuli, S., & Winter, M. (1989). Parents as first teachers, in M. Fine (Ed.) *The second handbook on parent education* (pp. 99–117). San Diego, CA: Academic Press.

Weiss, N. (1977). Mother, the invention of necessity: Dr. Benjamin Spock's *Baby and Child Care, American Quarterly, 29,* 519–546.

Weissbourd, B. (1994). The evolution of the family resource movement, in S. Kagan & B. Weissbourd (Eds.) *Putting families first: America's family support movement and the challenge of change* (pp. 28–47). San Francisco, CA: Jossey-Bass.

White, B. (1981). Education for parenthood 1981. *Journal of Education, 163,* 205–218.

Zepeda, M., Varela, F., & Morales, A. (2004). Promoting positive parenting practices through parenting education, in N. Halfon, T. Rice, & M. Inkelas (Eds.) *Building State Early Childhood Comprehensive Systems Series, No. 13.* National Center for Infant and Early Childhood Health Policy.

2

PROGRAM DESIGN

Arminta L. Jacobson

Learning Goals

1. To identify the characteristics of efficacy-based design.
2. To design effective parenting education through a systematic process.
3. To identify the theoretical and knowledge basis of parenting education content across the lifespan.
4. To explain how learning outcomes, learning activities, and evaluation of parenting education are related.

Introduction

The goal of program design in parenting education is to create a learning experience that will help strengthen families through more effective parenting. The goal of a particular parenting education program is based on assessed or perceived needs of a particular target audience, a community, or the society at large. When designing a program, consider differences in the target audience, the setting, stage(s) of parent development (Hill, 1986), interests, and learning needs. Specific objectives will vary for program and target audience. Concomitant learning may also take place through supportive relationships or changes in attitudes toward different aspects of parenting.

Parenting education is designed and taught across the lifespan (NCFR, 2011). Concepts of parenting may be introduced in childhood, for example, through programs such as *Parents under Construction* through ChildBuilders (see http://childbuilders.org/). Parenting education meets different needs of different life stages including adolescence, early and middle adulthood, and older adulthood, when grandparenting is the main interest.

Efficacy-based Design

Efficacy-based parenting education programs have been reviewed and recognized for research and evaluation evidence that they achieve their learning goals and objectives. In other words, they work. Efficacy-based parenting education provides evidence of statistically significant and positive effects on children/youth development, behavior, or academic achievement as well as positive changes in parent (or pre-parent), or other caregiver's knowledge, behaviors, and attitudes. These programs, or curriculum, are reviewed by a number of organizations and government entities and posted as directories of evidence-based programs and practices on accessible websites. Directories focus on programs and practices in a particular professional field or support interventions to address particular issues, such as child abuse.

Programs apply to be listed and provide supporting research evidence for meeting the criteria of the registry. This evidence includes the number and demographic descriptions of participants, how research/evaluation was conducted, and the outcomes. Evidence often includes evidence of success with replication and with significant numbers of participants. There is often research evidence of short- and long-term significant change. Criteria require valid and reliable assessment measures and research/evaluation methodology that follow best practices and align with program goals and objectives.

Why is the establishment and use of efficacy-based programs important? On the University of Wisconsin Cooperative Extension website and *Directory of Evidence-based Programs*, the argument is made for the economic advantages of using evidence-based programs. Since evidence-based parenting programs have a high likelihood of positive impact on target issues, the adoption and implementation of evidence-based programs can help organizations obtain and sustain funding. The use of resources can be more effective, especially when staff training and technical assistance are included. For existing programs, using the principles of evidence-based programs can enhance quality and impact of parenting education through evidence-informed program improvement (Small, Cooney, & O'Connor, 2009).

Existing curriculum and programs can be found on national searchable registries of evidence-based programs and practices that review research/evaluation evidence and post those that meet its criteria or categorize programs. Registries are both broad and focused on outcomes in programs within particular areas of interest. Criteria are based on research and stand up to the rigors of research design. Through the CYFERNet (Children, Youth, and Families Education and Research Network) website, one can access lists and links to registries and guidelines for selecting an evidence-based program. One of the registries is The National Registry of Evidence-based Programs and Practices (NREPP), a database focused on mental health and substance abuse that includes parenting education programs. Another example is *What Works, Wisconsin* (see http://

whatworks.uwex.edu/), a project of the School of Human Ecology and the Cooperative Extension Family Living Program at the University of Wisconsin-Madison, initiated in 2004. The *What Works* project focuses on gleaning the latest research in a directory of evidence-based programs; the parenting program must have met accepted empirical standards for an evidence-based program and been listed on one or more national registries of evidence-based programs.

The Department of Health and Human Services launched Home Visiting Evidence of Effectiveness (HomVEE) through Mathematica Policy Research, which conducted a thorough search of the research literature on home visiting outcomes for pregnant women or families with children, aged 0–5 years, assessed the quality of research studies, and evaluated the strength of evidence for specific home visiting program models. This website describes evidence for each home visiting parent education model that received a high or moderate rating and measured outcomes in at least one of the eligible outcome domains.

Steps in Design

Strategic and thoughtful design and implementation are foundational for effective parenting education. A number of factors may influence how well a parenting education program works. Each step of the design process should be informed by research, or evidence-informed. These steps include clear and specific goals and learning outcomes that inform evaluation of outcome and planning of learning activities for target audiences.

Vision

The initial step in designing parenting education is a vision of how parenting education will contribute to the well-being of families and communities. A vision is based on an educational model that strengthens parenting and family relationships. Stakeholders, including individuals who will plan and implement the program, parents, and relevant community members should develop a consensus about the vision. A vision employs insight, imagination, and foresight leading to anticipation of the process and outcome of the parenting education program. This vision is based on assumptions about the target audience, their parenting knowledge, practice, culture, and values, as well as what they need to learn. It may be a vision for a prevention model designed for parents to apply knowledge of human development and effective parenting characteristics and strategies while overcoming challenges and risks and preventing problems. Or an intervention model may be envisioned when target parents and other caregivers need knowledge and support for overcoming problems such as child abuse or mental illness. Design and implementation should align carefully with this vision.

Target Audience and Needs Assessment

Parenting education can only be efficacious if it meets the needs of the **target audiences** and issues they face. The second step in program design is to conduct a **needs assessment** of representative individuals. A needs assessment may be conducted through (a) observation, (b) research of issues and demographic characteristics, (c) knowledge of field, (d) informed experts, (e) surveys, (f) focus groups of stakeholders, (g) surveys, and (h) community forums. Assessment strategies need to align with your organization or school's vision and overall program goals and be feasible with your availability of resources. For more information about conducting needs assessments, read the information on the CYFERNet website.

In addition to needs assessment, planning will be informed by a review of research literature about the characteristics of parents targeted, including their (a) culture, resources, challenges and strengths; (b) interests, needs, and norms for different age groups and across the lifespan; (c) education, learning styles, and needs for different age groups and across the lifespan; (d) issues in the community or society; and (e) research knowledge of proposed content.

Content

At this point in program design, a general framework or outline of concepts and topics that fit the vision and understanding of the proposed program recipients can be developed. The review of research literature helps validate what is included. This third step involves developing or identifying an existing conceptual framework in which core knowledge, competencies, and/or dispositions for parenting are identified. Not only does this provide a pattern upon which to develop specific outcomes and activities, but if communicated to parents can meet their interest in clearer structure and framework for content (Petersson, Petersson, & Håkannsson, 2004).

Building a conceptual framework begins with a body of knowledge needed for effective parenting education and guidance. This body of knowledge includes knowledge of parenting processes, parenting roles, parent–child relationships, effective guidance, human development, dynamics of family development and relationships, knowledge of diverse cultures and special needs of families, and learning processes across the lifespan (Jacobson & Hirschy, 2000).

Ten family life education content areas for which Certified Family Life Educators (CFLEs) are prepared suggest the depth and breadth of knowledge and understanding, which can be considered as content in designing programs. The content areas include (a) families and individuals in societal context; (b) internal dynamics of families; (c) human growth and development across the lifespan; (d) human sexuality; (e) interpersonal relationships; (f) family resource management; (g) parent education and guidance; (h) family law and public policy; (i) professional ethics and practice; and (j) family life education methodology.

The NCFR Framework for Life-Span Family Life Education (Bredehoft, 2001) conceptualizes family life education as a lifelong process from childhood to later adulthood. Key concepts in the Curriculum Guidelines (NCFR, 1984) for parenting education and guidance include an understanding of how parents teach, guide, and influence children and adolescents based on knowledge of (a) parenting as a process; (b) parental rights and responsibilities; (c) parental roles over the life cycle: and (d) variations in parenting practices. Learning to parent is a lifelong process.

Some topics identified in the Curriculum Guidelines (NCFR, 1984) are listed across ages. For example, parent–child communications, conflict resolution, meeting developmental needs of children, and childrearing practices are identified for both adolescents and adults. Parenting education content in emotional communication has been showed to make a significant difference in participants as well (Kaminski et al., 2008).

Adults with, or about to have, children have a wide range of knowledge and understanding of their roles and responsibilities related to the care and nurturance of child and adolescent development. Parenting situations, environmental influences on parenting, education level, and learning preferences are other examples of differences leading to different content decisions of parenting education. Needs assessments that identify parent development, parenting goals, needs for information and resources, and family strengths provide insights for content that will motivate parents to participate and learn. Another way of conceptualizing content is to design parenting education around ages and stages of children, acknowledging that children and parents move concurrently through predictable stages of development (Galinsky, 1987) and that family systems change as a result of that development. Appropriate care and guidance can be applied to different stages of child and adolescent development.

The National Extension Parent Education Model (NEPEM) (Smith et al., 2004, chapter 6), which includes content organized around priority practices for parents, provides an example of a conceptual framework for organizing parenting education. Identified content includes (a) self-care, with emphasis on strengthening the parenting unit; (b) understand, described in terms of parents understanding children; (c) guide, or guidance of children; (d) nurture, including support of emotional and social development; (e) motivate, the parental role in encouraging learning; and (f) advocate, in speaking for children and identifying needed resources. If adopted, the NEPEM priority practice areas would be emphasized which best met the vision and needs of parents for whom the program is being designed.

Theory

Part of what family life educators bring to the design of parenting education is an understanding or theoretical underpinning about teaching and change for improved parenting. In this program design step, identify a theory or theories, which align with the program vision, the needs of the audience, and research evidence for effective motivation and learning. A theory helps explain knowledge. As an example, consider the priority topics in the NEPEM conceptual framework. As the corresponding body of knowledge is reviewed, family life educators may find that different theories help explain different topics or concerns of parents. If a program is planned for immigrant parents, for example, bio-ecological theory (Bronfenbrenner & Morris, 2006) would help understand and explain knowledge related to *Self-care* for parenting in a complex, bicultural environment. Systems theory (White & Klein, 2008), as applied to the family, provides the basis for parents to understand how their own development and well-being interact with that of other members of the family and affect parenting.

Developmental theories help parent educators conceptualize and teach parents to *Understand* and apply knowledge of child and adolescent development to parenting. Developmental theories developed by Vygotsky (1962) and Piaget (1969) and the knowledge built on them are an excellent basis for teaching parents to *Guide* appropriately for the developmental stage and competencies of their children and youth. This could include guidance in supporting moral development as well as learning. Adlerian theory (Adler, 1956), widely used in published curriculum, can support the guidance needs of parents in considering causes and consequences of behavior and developing appropriate strategies.

The support of emotional and social development and well-being (*Nurture*) is aligned with attachment theory (Bowlby, 1969). Cognitive developmental theories fit a program emphasis on encouraging learning and achievement in children (*Motivate*). Teaching parents to identify opportunities and strategies for *Advocacy* for children and youth can be framed through a bio-ecological theoretical framework (Bronfenbrenner & Morris, 2006). Teaching parents to identify community connections for parenting and ways of improving the lives of their family can have lasting and positive effects.

Outcomes

Before planning specific learning content and activities for parenting education, take the step of writing goals and learning outcomes that meet the priority needs and interests of participants. An example of a goal that is more general might be "Learn how to communicate with teenagers". **Specific learning outcomes** (SLOs) describe what you want parents to know or be able to do at the end of the program. These should include a verb and be measureable, reasonable and fair, and doable (Carriveau, 2010). The learning outcomes you develop become the baseline for parent satisfaction and evaluating the success of your program. SLOs include process, knowledge, skills, and other outcomes. An example of a specific outcome related to process is "To identify situations in which communications are ineffective". A knowledge-based outcome could be "To discuss how the need to develop a personal identity in adolescence is related to arguing with their parents". A specific learning outcome for a skill would be "Demonstrate active listening techniques appropriately". In writing SLOs give consideration to the expected participants' (a) stage(s) of parenting; (b) educational background; and (c) regional and cultural uniqueness as well as requirements for teacher/facilitator knowledge and skills or training, and availability of funding, and whether the program is primarily for prevention or intervention.

The next step in program design is planning how to assess whether planned SLOs are successfully met. Write questions for each SLO that can be answered through learning activities, observation, surveys, or interviews with parents. Specific evaluation strategies can later be developed that answer these questions. Decisions about indicators and measurement for assessment will be based on available resources such as expertise, time, staff or volunteers, technology, and participants' literacy level. Benchmarks for success can be established based on pre-assessment of knowledge or research evidence. The evaluation process may also include other considerations such as content, quality of teaching plans, and appropriateness of instructional processes (Duncan & Goddard, 2011, chapters 4 and 5).

One of the techniques of evaluation for determining efficacy is replication of the significant positive effects through replication of the program with different groups of parents. This is known as implementation fidelity. This requires that parent educators adhere to the **core components** of the program and be flexible in processes and strategies only in ways that still enable the accomplishment of strategic learning outcomes (Fixsen et al., 2005). Implementation supports, such as training and financial support for preparation, help increase implementation fidelity (Fixsen et al., 2005).

Learning Activities

Strengthening parenting and families is the focus of a variety of programs and models, with group and individual approaches, across a wide range of settings. The next step a program designer would take would be deciding on the model or delivery system that best fits their program vision, target parents, and expertise of parent educators. There are a variety of models to meet the diverse needs of parents and resources and skills of parent educators.

Traditionally, parenting education has followed a lecture or discussion group model. Small group discussion, facilitated by a leader, can be structured or unstructured and may be based on content in a curriculum, book, or videos. Small groups are an effective venue for parents to develop knowledge and skills as well as support from the group facilitator and other parents. One-on-one parenting education with a professional or trained peer home visitor includes home visiting and parent coaching.

Programming can vary from direct instruction to modeling of parent–child interactions. Designing parenting education for delivery by or assisted by technology follows design principles and makes parenting education more accessible for busy, working parents with computer skills and access. Design of online instruction provides information but generally is not designed to facilitate discussion of ideas or application to personal issues. The lack of a support group with a parent educator and other parents may discourage some parents from participating. In designing a delivery model, the number and length of sessions and format of parenting education depends on the needs of the target audience as well as practical consideration of the sponsoring organization.

The next step is to identify and plan step-by-step instructions for learning activities that will help participants in the program achieve SLOs. Learning activities should be designed that provide meaningful learning. Program participants, through interaction with course materials, the parent educator, and other parents, can build knowledge and cognitive skills that help them problem solve and achieve parenting goals independently. Learning activities that help parents apply knowledge in a meaningful way are those in which learners co-construct their own knowledge (Mayer, 2002).

Skilled parent educators can devise strategies that facilitate interaction with content as well as other group members. This includes interest approaches, which arouse curiosity and focus learners on the content. Interest approaches range from case studies to film clips to thought-provoking questions. Facilitated discussion then follows with an emphasis on core knowledge related to the topic. Questions or activities that check for understanding and the ability to apply knowledge can be planned into the group experience.

Case studies or video clips can be paired with problem-solving techniques that can be generalized to future parenting dilemmas. Higher-level thinking skills are required that support parents in co-constructing knowledge and hopefully lead to a practice of metacognitive practice in relation to their parenting.

The opportunity to practice new skills and apply new knowledge with their children or teens will reinforce and deepen learning. One of the findings of the meta-analysis of 128 parent training studies by Kaminski et al. (2008) was the positive effect on both parenting behavior outcomes and child externalizing behaviors when content included training in creating positive interactions with a child and required parents to practice new skills with their child during sessions. Creating opportunities for practicing skills can be designed as an integral part of the program, either through structured family activity nights or homework activities that fit naturally into the day-to-day lives of families.

Logic Models

Logic models are widely used in program design, implementation, and evaluation. A logic model serves as a visual map for how the program runs and why it offers services. As a tool, a logic model presents a visual of the relationship between different parts of the program and its outcome and usefulness in evaluation. One of the most helpful resources for program design, information, and a template are on the University of Wisconsin Cooperative Extension website at www.uwex.edu/ces/.

The five core components included in a basic logic model are:

1. Inputs: resources, contributions, investments that go into the program;
2. Outputs: activities, services, events, and products that reach people who participate or who are targeted;
3. Outcomes: results or changes for individuals, groups, communities, organizations, communities, or systems;
4. Assumptions: the beliefs we have about the program, the people involved, and the context and the way we think the program will work;
5. External factors: the environment in which the program exists includes a variety of external factors that interact with and influence the program action.

Conclusion

The steps in parenting education program design include developing a vision, assessing the needs of individuals to be served, identifying a conceptual framework, determining goals and specific learning outcomes, planning assessment of effectiveness, and designing learning activities. The design of parenting education involves assessment of the audience, issues, and research-based content. Knowledge of its effectiveness requires fidelity of content and delivery, training of facilitators, and evaluation to assess effectiveness and need for improvement. For sustainability, marketability, and funding the efficacy of a program needs to be investigated and monitored over time. The goal of efficacy-based parenting education is to demonstrate the capacity to facilitate positive changes in the lives of individuals and families.

Key Points

1. The goal of program design for parenting education is strengthening families through a learning experience.
2. Steps in parenting education program design include visioning, assessing needs, conceptualizing a framework, writing goals and learning outcomes, planning evaluation, and designing learning activities.
3. Efficacy-based parenting education is supported by evidence of positive changes in parenting and child/youth development and achievement.
4. Content and learning activities are based on a body of knowledge based on theoretical underpinnings.

Discussion Questions

1. If you were on the board of directors of a community family resource center, what argument would you make for adopting efficacy-based parenting curriculum?
2. What might be some of the barriers for implementing an efficacy-based parenting education program?
3. If you were the team leader to develop a new parenting education program design, what information and training could be helpful for you and the team to have success?

Additional Resources

Suggested Reading

Campbell, D., & Palm, G. (2004). *Group parent education: Promoting parent learning and support.* Thousand Oaks, CA: Sage.

Darling, C., & Cassidy, D. (2014). *Family life education: Working with families across the life span* (3rd ed.). Long Grove, IL: Waveland.

Duncan, S., & Goddard, H. (2011) *Family life education: Principles and practices for effective outreach* (2nd ed.). Thousand Oaks, CA: Sage.

Keim, R., & Jacobson, A. (Eds.) (2011). *Wisdom for parents: Key ideas from parent educators.* Whitby, ON, Canada: de Sitter.

Websites

Children, Youth, and Families Education and Research Network (CYFERNet): https://cyfernetsearch.org/ilm_1_9

Directory of Evidence-based Programs—University of Wisconsin Extension: http://whatworks.uwex.edu/Pages/2parentsinprogrameb.html

Home Visiting Evidence of Effectiveness (HomVEE): http://homvee.acf.hhs.gov/

Maternal, Infant, Early Childhood Home Visiting program (MIECHV): http://mchb.hrsa.gov/programs/homevisiting/

National Parenting Education Network: www.npen.org

National Registry of Evidence-based Programs and Practices (NREPP): http://nrepp.samhsa.gov/

Parents under Construction: www.childbuilders.org

The University of Wisconsin—Extension evaluation website: www.uwex.edu/ces/pdande/evaluation/evallogicmodel.html

References

Adler, A. (1956). *The individual psychology of Alfred Adler: A systematic presentation in selections from his writings.* New York: Basic Books.

Bowlby, J. (1969). *Attachment and loss.* New York: Basic Books.

Bredehoft, D. (2001). The framework for life span family life education revised and revisited. *The Family Journal, 9*, 134–139.

Bredehoft, D., & Walcheski, M. (Eds.). (2011). *The family life education framework and powerpoint*. Minneapolis, MN: National Council on Family Relations.

Bronfenbrenner, U., & Morris, P. (2006). The bioecological model of human development, in W. Damon & R. Lerner (Eds.) *Handbook of child psychology, Vol. 1: Theoretical models of human development* (6th ed., pp. 793–828). New York: John Wiley.

Campbell, D., & Palm, G. (2004). *Group parent education: Promoting parent learning and support*. Thousand Oaks, CA: Sage.

Carrivou, R. (2010). *Connecting the dots: Developing student learning outcomes and outcome based assessments*. Denton, TX: Fancy Fox Publications.

Darling, C., & Cassidy, D. (2014). *Family life education: Working with families across the life span* (3rd ed.). Long Grove, IL: Waveland.

Duncan, S., & Goddard, H. (2011) *Family life education: Principles and practices for effective outreach* (2nd ed.). Thousand Oaks, CA: Sage.

First, J., & Way, W. (1995). Parent education outcomes: Insights into transformative learning. *Family Relations, 44*, 104–109.

Fixsen, D., Naoom, S., Blase, K., Friedman, R., & Wallace, F. (2005). *Implementation research: A synthesis of the literature*. Tampa, FL: University of South Florida.

Hill, R. (1986). Life cycle stages for types of single parent families: of family development theory. *Family Relations, 35*, 19–29.

Jacobson, A., & Hirschy, S. (2000). *Core knowledge for parent educators and professionals who work with families* [brochure]. Denton, TX: University of North Texas, Center for Parent Education. Retrieved from http://parenteducation.unt.edu/core-knowledge-attitudes-and-skills

Kaminski, J., Valle, L., Filene, J., & Boyle, C. (2008). A meta-analytic review of components associated with parent training program effectiveness. *Journal of Abnormal Child Psychology, 36*, 567–589.

Knapp, P., & Deluty, R. (1989). Relative effectiveness of two behavioral parent training programs. *Journal of Clinical Child Psychology, 18*, 314–322.

Lengua, J., Roosa, M., Schupak-Neuberg, E., Michaels, M., Berg, C., & Weschler, L. (1992). Using focus groups to guide the development of a parenting program for difficult-to-reach, high-risk families. *Family Relations, 41*, 163–168.

Mayer, R. (2002). Rote versus meaningful learning. *Theory into Practice, 41*, 226–232.

National Council on Family Relations (NCFR) (2011). *Family Life Education Content Guidelines*. Minneapolis: Author. Retrieved at www.ncfr.org/sites/default/files/downloads/news/FLE_Content_Areas_2011.pdf

Petersson, K., Petersson, C., & Håkannsson, A. (2004). What is good parental education? Interviews with parents who have attended parental education sessions. *Scandinavian Journal of Caring Sciences, 18*, 82–89.

Piaget, J., & Inhelder, B. (1969). *The psychology of the child*. New York: Basic Books.

Radey, M., & Randolph, K. (2009). Parenting sources: How do parents differ in their efforts to learn about parenting? *Family Relations, 58*, 536–548.

Rossie, P. Lipsey, M., & Freeman, H. (2004). *Evaluation: A systematic approach* (7th ed.). Thousand Oaks, CA: Sage.

Small, S., Cooney, S., & O'Connor, C. (2009). Evidence-informed program improvement: Using principles of effectiveness to enhance the quality and impact of family-based prevention programs. *Family Relations, 58*, 1–13.

Smith, C., Cudaback, D., Goddard, H., & Myers-Walls, J. (1994). *National extension parent education model.* Manhattan, KS: Kansas Cooperative Extension Service. Retrieved from www.k-state.edu/wwparent/nepem/

Vygotskiĭ, L. (1962). *Thought and language.* Cambridge, MA: MIT Press.

Webster-Stratton, C. (1992). Individually administered videotape parent training: "Who benefits?" *Cognitive Therapy & Research, 16*, 31–52.

White, J., & Klein, D. (2008). *Family theories* (3rd ed.). Thousand Oaks, CA: Sage.

3

PROGRAM IMPLEMENTATION

Ana A. Baumann, Patricia L. Kohl, Enola K. Proctor, & Byron J. Powell

Learning Goals

1. To increase awareness of implementation strategies as a means to increase adoption and sustainability of evidence-based parenting interventions.
2. To enhance knowledge about provider training and supervision as implementation strategies.
3. To understand the importance of agency context in the selection of implementation strategies.
4. To learn the reasons for, and the importance of, maintaining fidelity when delivering parenting interventions.

Introduction

A robust literature about parent education spans over five decades. With the assumption that parents' behaviors mediate children's behavior, parent education and training programs have been created to prevent and/or intervene on child disruptive behavior (Beauchaine, Webster-Stratton, & Reid, 2005; Hagen, Ogden, & Bjørnebekk, 2011; Forehand, Jones, & Parent, 2013; Honeycutt et al., 2013). The parent education field is fortunate to have a set of effective programs that could benefit families were they to be implemented well in community settings (Substance Abuse and Mental Health Services Administration, 2012; California Evidence-based Clearinghouse for Child Welfare, 2012); however, dissemination and implementation initiatives and the evaluation of the current practices are still in relative infancy (Becker, Nakamura, Young, & Chorpita, 2009; Kohl, Schurer, & Bellamy, 2009). For example, an evaluation of parent training programs in one midsized Midwestern city revealed that only about 11 percent of agencies had adopted evidence-based programs (Kohl et al., 2009).

The low rates at which evidence-based parenting interventions are delivered suggests that simply publishing reports on their availability and effectiveness, while necessary, is not sufficient given the myriad of barriers at the client, clinician, team, organizational, policy, and funding levels (e.g., Shapiro, Prinz, & Sanders, 2012; Flottorp et al., 2013; Powell, Hausmann-Stabile, & McMillen, 2013). More thought should be put into the process of implementation, and several models can provide guidance as to how to implement parent interventions in usual care (Tabak, Khoong, Chambers, & Brownson, 2012). This chapter is focused on two aspects that can facilitate the uptake of parent interventions: implementation strategies and implementation outcomes.

Strategies for Implementing Parenting Education

Implementation refers to the process of integrating an intervention within a setting (Rabin & Brownson, 2012). It extends efficacy and effectiveness research that focuses on discovering *what* works to understanding *how* the implementation works *in specific contexts* (Damschroder, Peikes, & Peterson, 2013). **Implementation strategy** is defined as a "systematic intervention process to adopt and integrate evidence-based health innovations into usual care" (Powell et al., 2012, p. 124). Implementation strategies offer a way to answer the question set forth by Asgary-Eden and Lee (2011): "So now we've picked an evidence-based program, what's next?" (p. 169). While the literature reflects a wide range of different implementation strategies (Powell et al., 2012), the evidence to support the use of specific implementation strategies in mental health and social services is still scarce (Powell, Proctor, & Glass, 2013). The recent prioritization of implementation research by the Institute of Medicine (2009) and the National Institutes of Health (2013) will, however, undoubtedly increase the number of empirical studies testing innovative approaches to implementation. This chapter addresses one implementation strategy, namely, provider training, as it is the most frequently used in parent intervention. The importance of effectively using and measuring implementation strategies will then be briefly discussed.

Provider Training in Evidence-based Practices

For many evidence-based programs and interventions, training of frontline providers is a critical component of implementation (Beidas & Kendall, 2010; Becker & Stirman, 2011; Lyon et al., 2011). How should providers be trained to deliver parenting education programs? To understand training from an implementation perspective, consideration of the effects of training on provider behavior, the contextual factors such as organizational variables, the mode and quality of training, and client variables is necessary (Sanders & Turner, 2005; Turner & Sanders, 2006; Beidas & Kendall, 2010). Training does not happen in a vacuum and contextual factors affect the success of implementation efforts (Beidas &

Kendall, 2010). Usually, training of practitioners to deliver parent interventions is provided via workshops and supervision (Sholomskas, Syracuse-Siewert, Rounsaville, Ball, & Nuro, 2005; Beidas & Kendall, 2010). However, much still needs to be learned about which training components, doses, and modalities are the most effective for specific contexts and target populations. Below we briefly describe the literature on workshops and clinical supervision.

Training with Workshops

Training workshops are effective in increasing providers' knowledge and provider confidence in delivering the intervention (Walters, Matson, Baer, & Ziedonis, 2005; Lyon, Stirman, Kerns, & Burns, 2011), and are relatively cheap as several providers can be trained simultaneously at a one-time event. Workshops are particularly effective if they involve active learning. This is because evidence suggests that the use of training skills that will be employed in the clinical context can improve trainee fidelity (Beidas & Kendall, 2010; Cross, Seaburn, Gibbs, Schmeelk-Cone, White, & Caine, 2011). However, workshops alone do not promote consistent or sustained behavior change (Lyon et al., 2011). Training workshops may be more effective if they are bundled with ongoing coaching (Lyon et al., 2011; Herschell, Reed, Mecca, & Kolko, 2014), but the costs of providing ongoing training and consultation remain a considerable barrier to implementing evidence-based treatments in the community (Powell et al., 2013). One promising means of reducing training costs is to provide online training and support (e.g., Beidas et al., 2012).

Supervision

Supervision offers another familiar approach to provider training and can be provided by the clinical supervisor in the agency and/or by the treatment developer and team. Supervision accounts for a significant proportion of variance in client outcomes (Callahan, Almstrom, Swift, Borja, & Heath, 2009). One of the challenges inherent to supervision is tailoring it to the individual needs of given providers. For example, students in practice were more satisfied with their practice when supervisors provided feedback and titrated their supervisory approach according to the developmental needs of the supervisees (Everett et al., 2011; Bennett & Deal, 2012; Deal & Clements, 2016). Moreover, several studies indicate that provider characteristics, such as age, professional degree, theoretical orientations and attitudes towards evidence-based treatments, and language in addition to years of experience, mediate the provider's willingness to attend supervision and implement the intervention as desired (Beidas & Kendall, 2010; Schwartz, Domenech-Rodríguez, Santiago-Rivera, Arredondo, & Field, 2010; Bennett & Deal 2012; Bearman et al., 2013;). These variables make it difficult to provide consistent and effective supervision, and more research is needed to understand how to provide supervision to a variety of providers in an efficient manner.

Effective Use of Implementation Strategies

Regardless of the approach chosen for implementing efficacious parenting training programs, the chosen implementation strategy must be carefully selected and evaluated for its effectiveness. Theory may help guide the selection of a strategy. Theories, conceptual models, and/or frameworks can ensure that essential contextual and process elements related to implementation are not overlooked (Proctor, Powell, Baumann, Hamilton, & Santens, 2012; Tabak et al., 2012). Moreover, frameworks provide a systematic way of evaluating the interventions and facilitating replication of the implementation process in different settings. While there are numerous implementation frameworks and models (Tabak et al., 2012), evidence from healthcare suggests that theory is underutilized in implementation studies (Davies, Walker, & Grimshaw, 2010; Colquhoun et al., 2013).

Considering how a given strategy fits with the contextual elements of the practice settings for parent training programs is also important, as the success of any implementation effort depends on provider perspectives and on team, organizational, and political factors (Aarons, Wells, Zagursky, Fettes, & Palinkas, 2009; Asgary-Eden & Lee, 2011). Once a strategy is chosen—be it workshop, supervision, or learning collaborative—its deployment should be documented and, if possible, measured. Proctor et al. (2013) have urged greater precision in defining and operationalizing implementation strategies in terms of seven dimensions: actor, the action, action targets, temporality, dose, implementation outcomes addressed, and theoretical justification. The success of an implementation strategy should be evaluated in relation to the implementation outcome targeted, as explained below. Certain strategies may be more effective in increasing the acceptability of a parent training program to providers, while other strategies may be needed to ensure sustained use with fidelity over time.

Implementation Outcomes

It is critical that implementation studies evaluate **implementation outcomes**. Proctor and colleagues (2011; 2012) have suggested a taxonomy of implementation outcomes, including acceptability, adoption, appropriateness, cost, feasibility, fidelity, penetration, and sustainability. Evaluation of implementation outcomes can help investigators disentangle implementation effectiveness from treatment effectiveness and to know, for example, if an intervention failed because it was ineffective or it was implemented incorrectly (Proctor et al., 2011). Furthermore, assessing implementation outcomes may improve our understanding of which implementation strategies work best with given interventions, settings, and conditions. We focus here on fidelity of implementation, as it is one of the most complex but highly important outcomes when implementing parent intervention.

Fidelity

Evidence-based interventions are often manualized as a means to train and support practitioners delivering an intervention. However, the use of a manual in and of itself is not a guarantee that the intervention was delivered as intended by the treatment developers (Forgatch, Patterson, & DeGarmo, 2005). Being faithful to the treatment model is of importance because of the association between accurate implementation of an intervention and outcomes (Proctor et al., 2011). If outcomes in usual care settings are not as favorable as they were found to be in clinical trials, it could be because the intervention was poorly implemented and not that it is an ineffective intervention when delivered in usual care settings (Dobson & Cook, 1980).

Gearing and colleagues (Gearing, El-Bassel, Ghesquiere, Baldwin, Gillies, & Ngeow, 2011) identify four components of **fidelity**: (a) intervention design and protocols; (b) intervention training; (c) monitoring of intervention delivery; and (d) monitoring of intervention receipt. Fidelity of protocol entails the framework, standards, and essential components guiding the assessment and measurement of the intervention. The intervention training refers to the manual review as well as training of providers. As an example of implementation of Parent Management Training, the Oregon Model (PMTO) in Mexico City, the intervention delivery was monitored via supervision of the training by the treatment developer and her team, as well as by observation of the providers' sessions with their clients (Baumann, Domenech Rodriguez, Amador, Forgatch, & Parra Cardona, 2014). Fidelity monitoring involves provider adherence and competence (Waltz et al., 1993), as well as component differentiation (Proctor et al., 2011). Adherence refers to whether or not the intervention is delivered as intended (Carroll et al., 2007) and competency refers to the way in which the intervention was delivered (Carroll et al., 2007; Proctor et al., 2011). Component differentiation focuses on the exclusion of other practices that are not specifically delineated as part of the practitioner training in the intervention. It is crucial, however, to balance fidelity with adaptation during the implementation process when delivering the intervention to a new population and/or in a new setting (Cabassa & Baumann, 2013). To summarize, the successful implementation of evidence-based interventions into usual care service settings requires assurance that treatment models with proven effectiveness in clinical trials are provided by practitioners as they were intended by the treatment developers. If the intervention is poorly implemented it likely will not reach its full potential impact.

Conclusion

While there are several evidence-based parent interventions available, they are either not adopted, not implemented, not sustained, or are implemented poorly in usual care. There is urgency for implementers to carefully monitor the implementation process so as to increase the uptake of parent interventions. Training practitioners as the sole implementation strategy is, however, not enough to change practitioner behavior and achieve sustained implementation in community-based practice settings. Without attention to implementation strategies and outcomes, these interventions will likely not reach their full potential impact. An implementation framework, and evaluation process along the way, will facilitate the process and hopefully increase the number of evidence-based parent interventions successfully implemented in usual care.

Key Points

1. Despite the availability of evidence-based parenting interventions, they are often not delivered in usual care settings.
2. Little is known about the most efficient and effective means to implement evidence-based parenting interventions into usual care settings, and more research on implementation strategies is needed.
3. Provider training and supervision are common strategies used to implement parenting interventions.
4. To ensure the best possible outcomes for children and families, it is important that treatment models are delivered with fidelity.

Discussion Questions

1. Workshops have been widely used to train providers in parent training interventions. Discuss why training alone is not an effective way to support the implementation of evidence-based parent intervention.
2. What strategy could you use to support the implementation of an evidence-based parent intervention in an agency?
3. What are the effective ways of using implementation strategies?

Additional Resources

Website

http://nirn.fpg.unc.edu/learn-implementation

References

Aarons, G., Wells, R., Zagursky, K., Fettes, D., & Palinkas, L. (2009). Implementing evidence-based practice in community mental health agencies: A multiple stakeholder analysis. *American Journal of Public Health, 99*, 2087–2095.

Asgary-Eden, V. & Lee, C. (2011). So now we've picked an evidence-based program, what's next? Perspectives of service providers and administrators. *Professional Psychology: Research and Practice, 42*, 169–175.

Baumann, A., Domenech Rodríguez, M., Amador, N., Forgatch, M., & Parra Cardona, J. (2014). Parent Management Training–Oregon model (PMTO™) in Mexico City: Integrating cultural adaptation activities in an implementation model. *Clinical Psychology: Science and Practice, 21*, 32–47.

Bearman, S., Weisz, J., Chorpita, B., Hoagwood, K., Ward, A., Ugueto, A., & Bernstein, A. (2013). More practice, less preach? The role of supervision processes and therapist characteristics in EBP implementation. *Administration and Policy in Mental Health and Mental Health Services Research, 40*, 518–529.

Beauchaine, T., Webster-Stratton, C., & Reid, M. (2005). Mediators, moderators, and predictors of 1-year outcomes among children treated for early-onset conduct problems: a latent growth curve analysis. *Journal of Consulting and Clinical Psychology, 73*, 371–388.

Becker, K., Nakamura, B., Young, J., & Chorpita, B. (2009). What better place than here, what better time than now? Advancing the dissemination and implementation of evidence-based practices. *Behavior Therapists, 32*, 89–96.

Becker, K. & Stirman, S. (2011). The science of training in evidence-based treatments in the context of implementation programs: Current status and prospects for the future. *Administration and Policy in Mental Health, 38*, 217–222.

Beidas, R. & Kendall, P. (Eds.). (2014). *Dissemination and implementation of evidence-based practices in child and adolescent mental health*. New York: Oxford University Press.

Bennett, S., & Deal, K. (2012). Supervision training: What we know and what we need to know. *Smith College Studies in Social Work, 82(2–3)*, 195–215.

Brownson, R., Colditz, G., & Proctor, E. (Eds.). (2012). *Dissemination and implementation research in health: Translating science to practice*. New York: Oxford University Press.

Cabassa, L., & Baumann, A. (2013). A two-way street: Bridging implementation science and cultural adaptations of mental health treatments. *Implement Science, 8*, 90. Available at www.implementationscience.com/content/8/1/90

California Evidence-based Clearinghouse for Child Welfare. (2014). Retrieved January 10, 2014, from www.cebc4cw.org/

Callahan, J., Almstrom, C., Swift, J., Borja, S., & Heath, C. (2009). Exploring the contribution of supervisors to intervention outcomes. *Training and Education in Professional Psychology, 3*, 72–77.

Carroll, C., Patterson, M., Wood, S., Booth, A., Rick, J., & Balain, S. (2007). A conceptual framework for implementation fidelity. *Implementation Science, 2*, 40.

Colquhoun, H., Brehaut, J., Sales, A., Ivers, N., Grimshaw, J., Michie, S., Carroll, K., Chalifoux, M., & Eva, K. (2013). A systematic review of the use of theory in randomized controlled trials of audit and feedback. *Implementation Science, 8*, 66.

Cross, W., Seaburn, D., Gibbs, D., Schmeelk-Cone, K., White, A., & Caine, E. (2011). Does practice make perfect? A randomized control trial of behavioral rehearsal on suicide prevention gatekeeper skills. *Journal of Primary Prevention, 32*, 195–211.

Damschroder, L., Peikes, D., & Peterson, D. (2013). *Using implementation research to guide adaptation, implementation, and dissemination of patient-centered medical home models.* Rockville, MD: Agency for Healthcare Research and Quality. Retrieved from http://pcmh.ahrq.gov/portal/server.pt/community/pcmh__home/1483/Implementation_Research

Davies, P., Walker, A., & Grimshaw, J. (2010). A systematic review of the use of theory in the design of guideline dissemination and implementation strategies and interpretation of the results of rigorous evaluations. *Implementation Science, 5*, 14.

Deal, K. & Clements, J. (2006). Supervising students developmentally: Evaluating a seminar for new field instructors. *Journal of Social Work Education, 42*, 291–306.

Dobson, D. & Cook, T. (1980). Avoiding type III error in program evaluation: Results from a field experiment. *Evaluation and Program Planning, 3*, 269–276.

Everett, J., Miehls, D., DuBois, C., & Garran, A. (2011). The developmental model of supervision as reflected in the experiences of field supervisors and graduate students. *Journal of Teaching in Social Work, 31*, 250–264.

Flottorp, S., Oxman, A., Krause, J., Musila, N., Wensing, M., Godycki-Cwirko, M., Baker, R., & Eccles, M. (2013). A checklist for identifying determinants of practice: A systematic review and synthesis of frameworks and taxonomies of factors that prevent or enable improvements in healthcare professional practice. *Implementation Science, 8*, 35.

Forehand, R., Jones, D., & Parent, J. (2013). Behavioral parenting interventions for child disruptive behaviors and anxiety: What's different and what's the same. *Clinical Psychology Review, 33*, 133–145.

Forgatch, M., Patterson, G., & DeGarmo, D. (2006). Evaluating fidelity: Predictive validity for a measure of competent adherence to the Oregon model of parent management training. *Behavior Therapy, 36*, 3–13.

Grol, R., Wensing, M., Eccles, M., & Davis, D. (Eds.). (2013). *Improving patient care: The implementation of change in health care* (2nd ed.). Chichester: John Wiley.

Hagen, K., Ogden, T., & Bjørnebekk, G. (2011). Treatment outcomes and mediators of parent management training: A one-year follow-up of children with conduct problems. *Journal of Clinical Child & Adolescent Psychology, 40*, 165–178.

Herschell, A., Reed, A., Mecca, L., & Kolko, D. (2014). Community-based clinicians' preferences for training in evidence-based practices: A mixed-method study. *Professional Psychology: Research and Practice, 45*, 188–199.

Honeycutt, A., Khavjou, O., Jones, D., Cuellar, J., & Forehand, R. (2013). Helping the noncompliant child: An assessment of program costs and cost-effectiveness. *Journal of Child and Family Studies*, retrieved at http://link.springer.com/article/10.1007/s10826-013-9862-7

Kohl, P., Schurer, J., & Bellamy, J. (2009). The state of parent training: Program offerings and empirical support. *Families in Society, 90*, 247–254.

Landsverk, J., Brown, C., Rolls Reutz, J., Palinkas, L., & Horwitz, S. (2011). Design elements in implementation research: A structured review of child welfare and child mental health studies. *Administration and Policy in Mental Health and Mental Health Services Research, 38*, 54–63.

Lyon, A., Stirman, S., Kerns, S., & Bruns, E. (2011). Developing the mental health workforce: Review and application of training approaches from multiple disciplines. *Administration and Policy in Mental Health and Mental Health Services Research, 38*, 238–253.

McHugh, R. & Barlow, D. (2012). Training in evidence-based psychological interventions, in R. McHugh & D. Barlow (Eds.) *Dissemination and implementation of evidence-based psychological interventions* (pp. 43–58). New York: Oxford University Press.

Palinkas, L., & Soydan, H. (2012). *Translation and implementation of evidence-based practice*. New York: Oxford University Press.

Powell, B., Hausmann-Stabile, C., & McMillen, J. (2013). Mental health clinicians' experiences of implementing evidence-based treatments. *Journal of Evidence-based Social Work, 10*, 396–409.

Powell, B., McMillen, J., Proctor, E., Carpenter, C., Griffey, R., Bunger, A., Glass, J., & York, J. (2012). A compilation of strategies for implementing clinical innovations in health and mental health. *Medical Care Research and Review, 69*, 123–157.

Powell, B., Proctor, E., & Glass, J. (2013). A systematic review of strategies for implementing empirically supported mental health interventions. *Research on Social Work Practice, 24*, 192–212.

Proctor, E., & Brownson, R. (2012). Measurement issues in dissemination and implementation research, in R. Brownson, G. Colditz, & E. Proctor (Eds.), *Dissemination and implementation research in health: Translating science to practice* (pp. 261–280). New York, NY: Oxford University Press.

Proctor, E., Powell, B., Baumann, A., Hamilton, A., & Santens, R. (2012). Writing implementation research grant proposals: Ten key ingredients. *Implementation Science, 7*, 96.

Proctor, E., Silmere, H., Raghavan, R., Hovmand, P., Aarons, G., Bunger, A., Griffey, R., & Hensley, M. (2011). Outcomes for implementation research: Conceptual distinctions, measurement challenges, and research agenda. *Administration and Policy in Mental Health and Mental Health Services Research, 38*, 65–76.

Rabin, B., & Brownson, R. (2012). Developing terminology for dissemination and implementation research, in R. Brownson, G. Colditz, & E. Proctor (Eds.) *Dissemination and implementation research in health: Translating science to practice* (pp. 23–51). New York: Oxford University Press.

Sanders, M., & Turner, K. (2005). Reflections on the challenges of effective dissemination of behavioural family intervention: Our experience with the Triple P–Positive Parenting Program. *Child and Adolescent Mental Health, 10*, 158–169.

Schwartz, A., Rodríguez, M., Santiago-Rivera, A., Arredondo, P., & Field, L. (2010). Cultural and linguistic competence: Welcome challenges from successful diversification. *Professional Psychology: Research and Practice, 41*, 210–220.

Shapiro, C., Prinz, R., & Sanders, M. (2012). Facilitators and barriers to implementation of an evidence-based parenting intervention to prevent child maltreatment: The Triple P-positive parenting program. *Child Maltreatment, 17*, 86–95.

Sholomskas, D., Syracuse-Siewert, G., Rounsaville, B., Ball, S., Nuro, K., & Carroll, K. (2005). We don't train in vain: A dissemination trial of three strategies of training clinicians in cognitive-behavioral therapy. *Journal of Consulting and Clinical Psychology, 73*, 106–115.

Straus, S., Tetroe, J., & Graham, I. (Eds.). (2013). *Knowledge translation in health care: Moving from evidence to practice* (2nd ed.). Chichester: John Wiley.

Substance Abuse and Mental Health Services Administration. (2012). *NREPP: SAMHSA's national registry of evidence-based programs and practices*. Retrieved April 18, 2012 from www.nrepp.samhsa.gov/

Tabak, R., Khoong, E., Chambers, D., & Brownson, R. (2012). Bridging research and practice: Models for dissemination and implementation research. *American Journal of Preventive Medicine, 43*, 337–350.

Turner, K., & Sanders, M. (2006). Dissemination of evidence-based parenting and family support strategies: Learning from the Triple P—Positive Parenting Program system approach. *Aggression and Violent Behavior, 11*, 176–193.

Waltz, J., Addis, M., Koerner, K., & Jacobson, N. (1993).Testing the integrity of a psychotherapy protocol: Assessment of adherence and competence. *Journal of Consulting and Clinical Psychology, 61*, 620–630.

Wilson, C. (2012). Special issue of *Child Maltreatment* on implementation: Some key developments in evidence-based models for the treatment of child maltreatment. *Child Maltreatment, 17*, 102–106.

4

PROGRAM EVALUATION

What Works in Parenting Education?

Karen M. Benzies & Leslie A. Barker

Learning Goals

1. Delineate the rationale to conduct evaluation for community-based parenting education programs.
2. Describe the steps in planning for program evaluation.
3. Discuss basic elements that an evaluator should consider when planning a program evaluation.
4. Compare and contrast the advantages and challenges associated with basic program evaluation designs.
5. Describe critical elements of effective parenting education program evaluation outcome measures.

Introduction

The Convention on the Rights of the Child states that all children have the right to protection (Article 3) and nurturing care (Article 27) (United Nations General Assembly, 1989). Parents (i.e., mothers, fathers, or anyone who has assumed the responsibility for the care of a child) are the most significant influence in the development of their children (Bruner, 2010; Canadian Association of Family Resource Programs, 2011) and most parents can benefit from information, guidance, and support for this role (Heath, 2006). Yet, there is a substantial gap in what parents *believe* they know and what they *need* to know to support their child's development (Rikhy, Tough, Trute, Benzies, Kehler, & Johnston, 2010). Prevention-focused parenting programs (PFPPs) are generally accepted as effective strategies to improve parental capacity and prevent problems before they occur (Lundahl, Risser, & Lovejoy, 2006; Bell, 2007; Kaminski, Valle, Filene, & Boyle,

2008). Yet, there is insufficient evidence of the effectiveness of PFPP without program evaluation. The need for evidence is critically important because preventive, community-based programs have been shown to be six times more cost-effective than clinical interventions for children with problems (Cunningham, Bremmer, & Boyle, 1995). The aim of this chapter is to provide an overview of evaluation for **prevention-focused parenting programs (or PFPPs)** and describe a new, reliable, and valid measure designed specifically for this purpose.

Why Evaluate Parenting Education Programs?

Rather than "parent education" (Fine, 1980, p. 5) that suggests training of individuals who are parents, the term "parenting education" is used because it suggests education for the role of parenthood. While considered a type of parenting education, "parent training" (see below) generally refers to interventions delivered by licensed professionals (e.g., clinical psychologist, social worker, or psychiatrist) for parents of children with a clinical diagnosis of developmental delay or disability, and families experiencing serious dysfunction (Medway, 1989). Historically and in the present day, evidence of the effectiveness of parenting education programs has been inadequate (Fine, 1980; McLennan & Lavis, 2006; Deković, Asscher, & Manders, 2012). The majority of evidence focuses on secondary and tertiary prevention (or treatment) programs that target parents of children with high social (e.g., Karoly et al., 2001; Temple & Reynolds, 2007) or medical (e.g., Benzies, Magill-Evans, Hayden, & Ballantyne, 2013) risk for problems, and families or children with diagnosed problems (Cunningham et al., 1995; Sanders, Markie-Dadds, & Turner, 2003; Webster-Stratton & Reid, 2003). While the effectiveness of clinical treatment programs has been well documented (Webster-Stratton & Reid, 2003; Wilson et al., 2012), these results cannot necessarily be applied to prevention programming, because the mechanisms (treatment/intervention versus education/prevention) are quite different (Posavac & Carey, 2007).

The demand for accountability has driven a trend toward more rigorous program evaluation with a focus on outcomes (Carman, 2010). Neither government nor philanthropic funders are satisfied with documentation of program outputs, such as number of participants served. While parental satisfaction with the program remains important, it is no longer sufficient. The focus today has shifted to answering the question, "Did the program make a difference to *outcomes* for parents and their children?" Progressive program leaders recognize that evaluation is a mechanism for continuous quality improvement (Caffarella, 2002).

While community agencies recognize the need for and benefits of program evaluation, frequently they are hampered by a lack of expertise, time, and resources. The collective impact movement (Turner, Merchant, Kania, & Martin, 2012) has spawned efforts to build a collaborative culture of evaluation within and across family-serving agencies. Given the demands of frontline program delivery and increasingly sophisticated approaches to evaluation, program leaders are engaging in communities of learning and practice whereby they can collaborate with other agencies and university researchers to design and conduct rigorous program evaluation (Benzies, 2013).

Planning for Program Evaluation

A well-defined plan is critical to the success of program evaluation. Evaluations impact, and are impacted by, all other aspects of program planning, therefore planning for a program's evaluation must be an integral part of early, overall planning for any new programming, and more than a quick add-on to existing activities (Caffarella, 2002). There are multiple elements to consider in planning a program's evaluation.

Identifying Context

The evaluator must identify the theoretical underpinnings of the prevention-focused parenting programs (i.e., PFPP) in order to understand how to evaluate it. Given the complexity of parenting programs, it may be useful to consider a number of mid-range theories overlaid on a systems theory (Bronfenbrenner, 2005). For example, attachment (Bretherton, 1992), parent–child interaction theories (Trivette, Dunst, & Hamby, 2010), and neurobiological development (Shonkoff, 2010; Boivin & Hertzman, 2012) may be useful to explain child development and behavior, and strategies to strengthen the parent–child relationship within the family.

Parenting education programs have embedded social values by virtue of their intent to influence parenting beliefs, enhance parenting knowledge and skills, and ultimately, to impact the developmental health of the next generation of citizens (Fine, 1980). These values inform decisions about program goals, components, and outcome measurement. Thus, the value that society places on parenting and child outcomes indirectly influences program evaluation.

The more immediate context within which a program occurs can also impact its evaluation. Consultations with program stakeholders (Posavac & Carey, 2007) can inform and strengthen the development of an evaluation plan. The funders' priorities, the mandate and support of the agency, the facilitators' skills, and parental experiences within the program are factors that can impact outcomes and thus should be considered, not only in program planning, but also in planning the evaluation (Caffarella, 2002; Posavac & Carey, 2007). Defined responsibilities for planning, implementation, analysis, reporting, and quality improvement; secured agency and funder support; and identified timelines, budget, and necessary resources are key contextual factors to consider during planning to prevent problems in the evaluation's implementation.

Characteristics of PFPPs

Typically, PFPPs are offered by health or social service agencies and are one component of community-based supports for parenting (Bell, 2007; Berlin, Brooks-Gunn, & Aber, 2001). PFPPs offer parents a chance to (a) learn how typical children grow and learn; (b) normalize day-to-day parenting challenges; (c) develop effective parenting strategies; (d) build parental sense of competence; and (e) create vital social support networks and a strong sense of community (Benzies, Clarke, Barker, & Mychasiuk, 2013). When parents are more knowledgeable about child development, know when to be concerned, and have effective ways to interact with their child, they are more likely to parent effectively (Trivette et al., 2010). Typically, PFPPs are facilitated by licensed professionals or program certified leaders with a defined number of group sessions. PFPPs may target parents alone or provide multiple components, including interaction time for parents and children together. PFPPs target families with low to moderate risk of poor outcomes in an effort to foster family resiliency (Benzies & Mychasiuk, 2009) for coping and thriving through the inevitable ups and downs of life (Benzies & Mychasiuk, 2009). Generally, PFPPs are not the appropriate starting point for parents with serious family issues such as substance abuse, child abuse, or parents or children with a clinical diagnosis as these issues require more intensive, therapeutic interventions. Recognizing the difference between these approaches is essential for effective evaluation planning.

Purpose of the Evaluation

Typically, the purpose of a PFPP evaluation is to inform immediate policy and program application. Program leaders are a key audience; they depend on evaluations to provide information for continuous quality improvement (Hertzman, 2013). A beneficial side effect of the evaluation planning process is that it may uncover opportunities to refine the program content and processes prior to program implementation, thus increasing the likelihood that the program will be able to achieve the desired outcomes. For example, if informal social support is identified as a desired outcome, program activities need to be designed to enable participants to connect informally both inside and outside of designated program time.

Scope of the Evaluation

The evaluation questions frame the scope of the evaluation and generally address utility, feasibility, propriety, accuracy, and accountability (Yarbrough, Shulha, Hopson, & Caruthers, 2011; Joint Committee on Standards for Educational Evaluation, 2012). A program evaluation should include both formative (process) and summative (outcomes) components. Formative evaluation determines whether all the necessary processes are in place to achieve success, including whether the program's activities are aligned with the evaluation design, measurements, and intended outcomes using tools such as a program logic model (Helitzer, Hollis, de Hernandez, Sanders, Roybal, & Van Deusen, 2010). Formative evaluation determines fidelity to program design and can provide immediate feedback to enable real-time refinement of a program. In addition, formative evaluation can help identify synergistic and unanticipated outcomes or spin-off effects (Edwards, Mill, & Kothari, 2004). Synergistic effects result from the way specific components of a parenting program work together to create additive or multiplicative effects on outcomes. Spin-off effects are intended or unintended indirect consequences of parenting programs, such as the emergence of similar programs in other agencies. Formative evaluation measures should include open-ended responses to capture both positive and negative effects. Summative evaluation identifies whether the larger and more generalizable outcomes of the program have been achieved. Outcome evaluation informs both recommendations for internal decision making and considerations for external application to other populations and settings.

Participants

Program evaluation is conducted in real-life conditions with all eligible participants. Mistakenly, many program facilitators and evaluators believe that groups of parents are fundamentally homogeneous. However, family situations, parenting knowledge, beliefs, attitudes, and skills vary. Thus, it is important to include detailed information about access to the program and detailed descriptions of participants in order to understand to whom program evaluation findings may be generalizable.

Decisions about the participants become more complex as the critical nature of the proximal environment on child development becomes apparent and greater emphasis is placed on the combined contributions of adults (mothers and fathers) to create an optimal proximal environment for child development (Bronfenbrenner, 2005). Typically, parenting program evaluation targets an individual parent (mother or father) as the unit of analysis. In the case of two-generation programs (i.e., the parent and child attend together), the mother– or father–child dyad, mother–father–child triad, or the family may be the unit of analysis. There are challenges inherent in selecting each unit of analysis and the selected unit needs to reflect the program target and outcome variables. For example, selecting mothers only as the unit of analysis may facilitate data collection and analyses. However, providing only the mother's perspective on outcomes may misrepresent actual outcomes in a complex family system. Selecting triads as the unit of analysis is more challenging because true triadic measurement is rare, except in the case of family observations. In addition, selecting dyads or triads requires greater sophistication in terms of underlying theory and data analyses.

Choosing an Evaluation Design

There are many issues to consider when choosing an evaluation design. Randomized controlled trials (RCT) are the "gold standard" in terms of level of evidence (Centre for Evidence-based Medicine, 2009) and typically compare two groups: one group that receives the program and one group that receives standard care (comparison) or no program at all (control). However, RCT designs present ethical implications for PFPPs. Randomization to a standard care group or a wait-list control group may be particularly problematic for populations that require age-appropriate interventions for parents of children experiencing rapid change (i.e., during infancy). Comparison of early start and late start groups may be a useful strategy in some evaluation designs. For example, the evaluator could compare programs that provide information about parent–child relationships starting prenatally versus programs that start in toddlerhood when negative patterns of interaction may have become well established. Non-inferiority designs comparing outcomes for a new PFPP versus an existing PFPP may be useful, particularly for new programs with a limited evidence base. Alternatively, the new PFPP could be considered an additive component and comparison made between a standard of care group (existing PFPP) versus standard of care plus new PFPP. "Dose" optimization studies that identify the optimal number of sessions required to achieve an outcome may be particularly useful. In this design, the PFPP would be conducted over various lengths of time (e.g., four, six, or eight sessions) and outcomes compared. Finally, program evaluations may be designed to compare its effects on different subpopulations. For example, some PFPPs may benefit some cultural groups more than others, which is important information in determining a target population. A mixed methods approach to program evaluation with integration of the results of quantitative and qualitative data can provide a more holistic understanding of the PFPP impact (Creswell & Plano Clark, 2011). A longitudinal approach to evaluation is required if a PFPP is expected to have delayed effects or long-term consequences. However, follow-up studies take time and are expensive.

Choosing Outcome Measures

Although both program evaluators and program providers agree that outcomes must be accurately assessed to provide meaningful information upon which to implement quality improvements, they may have different needs and expectations for program evaluation. Program evaluators may insist on "gold standard" research measures that have been developed in the context of treatment-focused programs, and tend to be lengthy with a high reading level (Benzies et al., 2008). Typically, program evaluators search for measures that (a) are related to the program's theoretical framework and program logic model, (b) capture the outcomes of interest, (c) have satisfactory psychometric properties, (d) have been used in a population similar to the one being evaluated, and (e) are acceptable to the population being evaluated. A measure with a published history of use in other evaluations will enable comparison of results across programs. On the other hand, program providers typically want to know (a) what knowledge and skills were learned; (b) the program's impact on participants' experiences as parents, and (c) whether participants were satisfied with the program. Providers want evaluation tools that are (a) as unobtrusive as possible, (b) take up minimal program time, and (c) do not alienate respondents. If program evaluation is burdensome, it can actually interfere with desired program outcomes by annoying participants or by absorbing important program time (Benzies et al., 2008). Finally, program providers require evaluation tools that are inexpensive, easy to interpret and report, and give useful information for quality improvement. The ideal tool for community-based programs would be brief and parent-friendly, while maintaining strong psychometric properties.

Planning for evaluation includes identifying the type of measures needed (e.g., observational tools for parent–child interactions; parental self-rated tools for knowledge, self-efficacy, or mental health outcome measures). Choosing and using an outcome measure can be fraught with challenges. First, evaluators unfamiliar with a particular area of program evaluation may have limited knowledge of existing instruments. Although, there are multiple online repositories of information about measures, it is challenging to find sites with dependable assessment of reliability and validity of measurement tools. A few sites (e.g., Early Childhood Measurement and Evaluation Resource Centre) provide detailed reports of screening, assessment, and program evaluation tools.

Another challenge may be a lack of measures to capture outcomes for an innovative parenting program. While it is always advisable to use existing measures with published reliability and validity information, in some cases an evaluator may have to design a new measure. After data have been collected, at a minimum, evaluators should provide principal components analysis and Cronbach's alphas for any new measures. Although not ideal, an existing measure may need to be adapted to suit the needs of the population or program. Evaluators need to be aware that adapting measures invalidates the original psychometric properties. Contacting the developer for permission and advice about adaptations may save valuable time.

Bias

Bias is ever-present in all forms of measurement. Self-report measures and observations of behavior are subject to social desirability response bias. While parent self-report measures are the most practical method of assessment, they have been shown to have little relationship to observed behaviors (Offord et al., 1996). Behavioral reactions to unnatural observational measures (e.g., video recordings) can be mitigated somewhat with observations conducted in the home versus the agency. The addition of a measure of social desirability or defensive responding may be useful to control for this type of bias. Interviews with parents are subject to recall bias, ability to verbally articulate responses, and interviewer skills. Weiss and colleagues (2005) suggest triangulation of multiple measures to capture one concept with both observational and self-rated data. However, inter-rater reliability (parent–parent, parent–child, parent–teacher/observer) can be an issue with multiple measures of the same construct. Being aware of inherent biases is critical when considering the design of a program's evaluation, and evaluators must take mitigating steps as much as possible.

Control for Confounding Variables

Program evaluation is less concerned with controls for confounding variables than consideration of real-life context. Thus, program evaluation has certain advantages over RCTs. Mobilization of knowledge from program evaluation has shorter timelines than RCTs, and evaluation results delivered directly to program leaders have the potential to implement immediate change and quickly increase program effectiveness.

Fidelity to the Program Design

In the case of manualized programs, fidelity to the program as designed is critical to achieve similar outcomes (Dane & Schneider, 1998; Boivin & Hertzman, 2012). Implementation science approaches and process evaluation may be particularly effective to monitor program fidelity (Durlak & DuPre, 2008). Other individual components to consider are the program facilitator's knowledge and beliefs about the program, individual stage of change, personal identification with the organization, and other personal attributes such as training, intellectual ability, ability to tolerate ambiguity and change, motivation, values, and learning style (Damschroder et al., 2009; Weiner, 2009).

Data Collection, Analysis, and Utilization

Planning for an evaluation includes identifying all sources of data to be collected; from whom, where and how they will be gathered; and how they will be stored, analysed, and reported. Be aware of additional, emergent opportunities that may arise over the course of the program evaluation period. Documenting the ethical considerations that have been taken into account ensures all participants are working from the same frame of reference. Identifying these components in the planning stage can save time, money and frustration later on (Hertzman, 2013).

Designing Databases

Program evaluations should provide continuous and accurate reporting of program philosophy and goals, processes, participants, measurement tools, and outcomes, as well as successes and failures (Fine, 1980). Program evaluations every two to five years are no longer sufficient for agencies to be responsive to the competing demands of multiple funders with different reporting requirements. Agencies that truly espouse a culture of evaluation are integrating the collection of administrative and research data as a standard of practice for ongoing evaluation and quality improvement. By customizing existing software platforms, agencies are designing databases for simultaneous data analysis and administrative reporting. Typically, the design of these databases requires a comprehensive, multi-level program logic model with clearly defined program inputs, activities, outputs, and outcomes. Given that the database is owned and operated by the agency, outcomes may be both short and long term when there is the possibility of follow-up. Integrated databases enable the ongoing collection of outcome data to generate administrative reports at specific intervals (e.g., quarterly reports to funders). With embedded outcomes, monitoring and evaluation for quality improvement is much easier.

In summary, rigorous planning for program evaluation will contribute to the evidence that is needed to bolster our current knowledge about the effectiveness of PFPPs. In the next section we describe a new, reliable, and valid measure designed specifically to evaluate PFPPs.

Development and Evaluation of the UpStart Parent Survey–Early Years Version

Background

The UpStart Parent Survey was developed in 2010 through a partnership of community agencies, researchers, and policy makers convened by UpStart of United Way of Calgary and Area: Champions for Children and Youth. The development of the UpStart Parent Survey was influenced by decades of research (Kaminski et al., 2008) and a consensus conference on common outcomes that could be expected of evidence-based parenting programs (Alberta Centre for Child Family & Community Research, 2007). However, typical research measures of these common outcomes created substantial respondent burden and limited the number of outcomes that could be captured (Benzies et al., 2008). Consultations with Wisconsin Children's Trust Fund (Wisconsin Children's Trust Fund, 2014) and British Columbia Parenting Vision Working Group (Munro, 2009) elicited other ideas that informed the content and design of the UpStart Parent Survey. Through a collaborative process that involved multiple meetings with community partners, these ideas were refined to create the initial version of the UpStart Parent Survey.

Description

The UpStart Parent Survey includes three separate scales: (a) Parenting Knowledge/Skills, (b) Parenting Experience, and (c) Program Satisfaction. There are four open-ended questions that ask what parents have learned and applied as a result of participation in PFPPs, what they need more information about, and what suggestions they have for program improvement. The final section of the survey collects basic demographic information about the participants and their families.

Parenting Knowledge/Skills Scale

The 10-item Parenting Knowledge/Skills scale captures concepts such as growth and development, parental responses to everyday challenges, discipline strategies, child health and safety, and parent–child interactions. A seven-point Likert scale ranging from 1 (*Strongly Disagree*) to 7 (*Strongly Agree*) is used. Scores on individual items are summed to create a total scale score. The theoretical range of scores is 10 to 70, with higher scores indicating greater parenting knowledge and skills. Each item offers a *Not Covered* response option for concepts that were not addressed. With permission, the knowledge items on the survey can be adapted to reflect the individual program curriculum (e.g., strategies for sleep and self-calming for programs for toddlers versus the impacts of separation and divorce on children for a program designed for that purpose). Aligning knowledge items with the curriculum content is critical to ensuring effective evaluation.

Parenting Experiences Scale

The Parenting Experiences scale includes 11 items that capture common outcomes of parenting programs using a seven-point Likert scale from 1 (*Strongly Disagree*) to 7 (*Strongly Agree*). These common outcomes are indicative of the participant's experience in their role as a parent, and include self-efficacy, morale, social support, stress, emotional health, advocacy, and family functioning. Scores on individual items are summed to create a Parenting Experiences total score. The theoretical range of scores is 11 to 77, with higher scores indicating a more positive parenting experience.

Program Satisfaction Scale

The Program Satisfaction scale is a posttest only. It contains seven items that capture engagement in, and satisfaction with, the program on a five-point Likert scale ranging from 1 (*Strongly Disagree*) to 5 (*Strongly Agree*). Scores on individual items are summed to create a Program Satisfaction total scale score. The theoretical range of scores is 7 to 35, with higher scores indicating greater satisfaction with the parenting program.

3–2–1 Questions

The survey includes a section that asks participants to share: "Three things I learned from the program", "Two things I have done differently because of this program", and "One thing I still have a question about". This format allows participants to reflect on what they have learned, and on how they have applied that knowledge in daily life. Asking participants what they still have a question about provides additional feedback to the program by identifying content areas that might need expansion. At the end of this section, there is a short space for participants to make suggestions and to comment on any area of the program.

Design

The Parenting Knowledge/Skills and Parenting Experiences scales were designed as posttest/retrospective pretests. That is, the survey was designed to be administered once at the conclusion of the program. The parent reports a "today" (posttest) score then a "before this program" (retrospective pretest) score for each item. The design was chosen for the following reasons. First, administering program evaluation tools takes time. With a posttest/retrospective pretest design, use of program and staff time is reduced. It is more convenient and efficient to conduct evaluation as a single survey during the last session of the program than to administer traditional pretest and posttest surveys. Second, a common concern expressed by program providers was reluctance to administer a traditional pretest survey prior to building rapport and trust with the parents. In addition, the traditional pretest may establish an uncomfortable feeling that parenting is being "tested" rather than supported through learning. Third, a retrospective pretest/posttest design is useful when an evaluation goal includes an assessment of individual perception of change through a guided reflection on personal growth related to the program (Howard et al., 1979), a concept in keeping with adult education best practices (Jarvis, 2006; Marienau & Segal, 2006). Finally, a traditional pretest requires that participants answer questions about concepts for which they may have an unrealistic frame of reference. In essence, parents may think they know about some aspect of parenting, yet realize after taking the course they did not know as much as they thought they knew. This is called response shift bias (Howard & Dailey, 1979), which can be avoided by the use of a posttest/retrospective test design.

Evaluation

The UpStart Parent Survey was evaluated between June 2010 and September 2012 with 536 diverse participants in 10 PFPPs offered by six agencies. The majority of the programs targeted parents of children less than age 6 years, and were offered for a defined length of time that varied from 4 to 11 weeks; weekly classes lasted between 2 and 3 hours.

The psychometric evaluation assessed (a) internal consistency reliability, (b) temporal stability (test–retest) reliability, and (c) concurrent validity of individual items on the UpStart Parent Survey Parenting Experiences scale with established measurements previously deemed psychometrically valid and reliable.

The 536 participants who completed the UpStart Parent Survey represented a broad range of household income, education, ethnicity, language, number of children, and previous participation in other parenting programs. The majority (97.6 percent) rated the survey as "average" or "easy" to complete; 2.4 percent rated the survey as "hard" to complete. Ease of completion was not affected by participants' age, level of education, or first language, suggesting that the survey is easily completed by a wide range of participants. The UpStart Parent Survey readability is rated at a 4.6 grade level on the Flesch–Kincaid Grade Level scale, 4 to 5 on the Canadian Language Benchmark score, and 80.5 on the Flesch Reading Ease test, which means it is generally readable by 12- to 15-year-olds. The UpStart Parent Survey–Early Years version is free; the Survey and User's Manual can be obtained by contacting the first author. The UpStart Parent Survey–Prenatal version is also available from the authors.

Conclusion

Program evaluation is essential to demonstrate the effectiveness of community-based, prevention-focused, parenting education programs. With thorough planning and appropriate design, program evaluations can capture useful information for both ongoing quality improvement and furthering our broader understanding of the role these programs can play in promoting the health and well-being of children and their families.

Key Points

1. Increasing demand for fiscal accountability has driven a trend toward more rigorous evaluation of parenting education programs with a focus on outcomes.
2. A well-defined plan is critical to the success of program evaluation and includes identifying the context and characteristics of the program and participants; defining the purpose and scope of the evaluation; and selecting an evaluation design and outcome measures.
3. The evaluation plan needs to address bias in measurement and control for confounding variables.
4. Determining fidelity to the program design is a critical component of evaluation, along with identifying procedures for data collection and analysis, and database designs.
5. There is limited evidence of the effectiveness of prevention-focused parenting education programs, which is due, in part, to lack of reliable and valid evaluation tools.
6. Typical research measures create substantial respondent burden and limit the number of outcomes that can be captured in a program evaluation.

7. The UpStart Parent Survey–Early Years version was developed as a brief, user-friendly tool to evaluate prevention-focused parenting programs.
8. Psychometric evaluation of the UpStart Parent Survey–Early Years version suggests that it holds promise as a reliable and valid measure to evaluate prevention-focused parenting education programs.
9. Program evaluation can capture useful information for both ongoing quality improvement and furthering our understanding of the role of prevention-focused parenting programs in promoting the health and well-being of children and their families.

Discussion Questions

1. Why is it important to conduct evaluation of prevention-focused parenting programs?
2. What are the critical elements that an evaluator should consider when planning an evaluation of a prevention-focused parenting program?
3. What are the advantages and challenges associated with various program evaluation designs?
4. What are the most important considerations when identifying outcome measures for program evaluation?
5. When evaluating prevention-focused parenting programs that are manualized, what are the challenges inherent in capturing fidelity to the program design?
6. How can an evaluator support the design of data collection systems to guide organizational improvement?
7. In what ways does program evaluation benefit parents and children?

Additional Resources

Websites

Alberta Family Wellness Initiative: www.albertafamilywellness.org/
Harvard Center on the Developing Child: http://developingchild.harvard.edu/

References

Alberta Centre for Child Family & Community Research. (2007). *Common Outcomes Initiative: Roundtable final report.* Edmonton, AB: ACCFCR.

Bell, M. (2007). Community-based parenting programmes: An exploration of the interplay between environmental and organizational factors in a Webster Stratton project. *British Journal of Social Work, 37*, 55–72.

Benzies, K. (2013). *Backgrounder for the Alberta Early Childhood Development Priority Initiative Research and Innovation Strategy.* Calgary, AB: University of Calgary.

Benzies, K., Clarke, D., Barker, L., & Mychasiuk, R. (2013). UpStart Parent Survey: A new psychometrically valid tool for the evaluation of prevention-focused parenting programs. *Maternal and Child Health Journal, 17*, 1452–1458.

Benzies, K., Ghali, L., Clyne, G., Barker, L., Friesen, L., Dennis, D., & Otis, B. (2008). *Community Parenting Program Evaluation Project (CPPEP) Aggregate Report.* Calgary, AB: University of Calgary.

Benzies, K., Magill-Evans, J., Hayden, A., & Ballantyne, M. (2013). Key components of early intervention programs for preterm infants and their parents: A systematic review and meta-analysis. *BMC Pregnancy and Childbirth, 13(Suppl. 1)*, S10.

Benzies, K., & Mychasiuk, R. (2009). Fostering family resiliency: A review of the key protective factors. *Child and Family Social Work, 14*, 103–114.

Berlin, L., Brooks-Gunn, J., & Aber, J. (2001). Promoting early childhood development through comprehensive community initiatives. *Children's Services: Social Policy, Research & Practice, 4(1)*, 1–24.

Boivin, M., & Hertzman, C. (2012). Early childhood development: Adverse experiences and developmental health. Ottawa, ON: Royal Society of Canada.

Bretherton, I. (1992). The origins of attachment theory: John Bowlby and Mary Ainsworth. *Developmental Psychology, 28*, 759–775.

Bronfenbrenner, U. (2005). *Making human beings human: Bioecological perspectives on human development*: Thousand Oaks, CA:Sage.

Bruner, C. (2010). What young children and their families need for school readiness and success, in R. Tremblay, R. Barr, R. Peters & M. Boivin (Eds.), *Encyclopedia on early childhood development* (pp. 1–7). Montreal, QC: Centre of Excellence for Early Childhood Development.

Caffarella, R. (2002). *Planning programs for adult learners: A practical guide for educators, trainers, and staff developers.* San Francisco, CA: Jossey-Bass.

Canadian Association of Family Resource Programs. (2011). *Family is the foundation: Why family support and early childhood education must be a collaborative effort.* Ottawa, ON: Canadian Association of Family Resource Programs.

Carman, J.G. (2010). The accountability movement: What's wrong with this theory of change? *Nonprofit and Voluntary Sector Quarterly, 39*, 256–274.

Centre for Evidence-based Medicine. (2009, March). Oxford Center for Evidence-based Medicine (OCEBM)—Levels of Evidence. Retrieved from www.cebm.net/oxford-centre-evidence-based-medicine-levels-evidence-march-2009/

Creswell, J., & Plano Clark, V. (2011). *Designing and conducting mixed methods research* (2nd ed.). Thousand Oaks, CA: Sage.

Cunningham, C., Bremmer, R., & Boyle, M. (1995). Large group community-based parenting programs for families of preschoolers at risk for disruptive behavior disorders: Utilization, cost effectiveness, and outcomes. *Journal of Child Psychology and Psychiatry and Allied Disciplines, 36(7)*, 1141–1159.

Damschroder, L., Aron, D., Keith, R., Kirsh, S., Alexander, J., & Lowery, J. (2009). Fostering implementation of health services research findings into practice: A consolidated framework for advancing implementation science. *Implementation Science, 4*, 50.

Dane, A., & Schneider, B. (1998). Program integrity in primary and early secondary prevention: Are implementation effects out of control? *Clinical Psychology Review, 18*, 23–45.

Deković, M., Asscher, J., & Manders, W. (2012). Changing parenting: Lessons (to be) learned from evaluations of parenting programs. *International Society for the Study of Behavioural Development Bulletin, 62*, 19–22.

Durlak, J., & DuPre, E. (2008). Implementation matters: A review of research on the influence of implementation on program outcomes and the factors affecting implementation. *American Journal of Community Psychology, 41*, 327–350.

ECMERC. The Early Childhood Measurement and Evaluation Resource Centre. Retrieved from www.cup.ualberta.ca/projects-initiatives/ecme/past-projects/the-early-childhood-measurement-and-evaluation-resource-centre-ecmerc

Edwards, N., Mill, J., & Kothari, A. (2004). Multiple intervention research programs in community health. *Canadian Journal of Nursing Research, 36*, 40–54.

Fine, M. (1980). *Handbook on parent education*. Orlando, FL: Academic Press.

Heath, H. (2006). Parenting: A relationship-oriented and competency-based process. *Child Welfare, 85*, 750–766.

Helitzer, D., Hollis, C., de Hernandez, B., Sanders, M., Roybal, S., & Van Deusen, I. (2010). Evaluation for community-based programs: The integration of logic models and factor analysis. *Evaluation and Program Planning, 33*, 223–233.

Hertzman, C. (2013). The significance of early childhood adversity: Commentary. *Pediatric Child Health, 18*, 127–128.

Howard, G., & Dailey, P. (1979). Response-shift bias: A source of contamination in self-report measures. *Journal of Applied Psychology, 64*, 144–150.

Howard, G., Ralph, K., Gulanick, N., Maxwell, S., Nance, D., & Gerber, S. (1979). Internal validity in pretest-postest, self-report evaluations and a re-evaluation of retrospective pretests. *Applied Psychological Measurement, 3*, 1–23.

Jarvis, P. (2006). *Towards a comprehensive theory of human learning*. New York: Routledge.

Joint Committee on Standards for Educational Evaluation (2012). *Program evaluation standards*. Retrieved from www.evaluationcanada.ca/site.cgi?s=6&ss=10&_lang=en

Kaminski, J., Valle, L., Filene, J., & Boyle, C. (2008). A meta-analytic review of components associated with parent training program effectiveness. *Journal of Abnormal Child Psychology, 36*, 567–589.

Karoly, L., Kilburn, M., Bigelow, J., Caulkins, J., Cannon, J., & Chiesa, J. (2001). *Assessing costs and benefits of early childhood intervention programs: Overview and application to the Starting Early Starting Smart Program*. Santa Monica, CA: Rand Corporation.

Lundahl, B., Risser, H. J., & Lovejoy, M. C. (2006). A meta-analysis of parent training: Moderators and follow-up effects. *Clinical Psychology Review, 26*, 86–104.

McLennan, J., & Lavis, J. (2006). What is the evidence for parenting interventions offered in a Canadian community? *Canadian Journal of Public Health, 97*, 454–458.

Marienau, C. & Segal, J. (2006). Parents as developing adult learners. *Child Welfare, 85*, 767–784.

Medway, F. (1989). Measuring the effectiveness of parent education, in M. Fine (Ed.) *The second handbook on parent education: Contemporary perspectives* (pp. 237–255). San Diego, CA: Academic Press.

Munro, C. (2009). *Planning for parenting education and support in British Columbia*. Retrieved from www.playvictoria.org/assets/news/pdfs/Planning%20for%20Parent%20Education.pdf

Offord, D., Boyle, M., Racine, Y., Szatmari, P., Fleming, J., Sanford, M., & Lipman, E. (1996). Integrating assessment data from multiple informants. *Journal of the American Academy of Child and Adolescent Psychiatry, 35*, 1078–1085.

Posavac, E., & Carey, R. (2007). *Program evaluation: Methods and case studies* (7th ed.). Upper Saddle River, NJ: Pearson Prentice Hall.

Rikhy, S., Tough, S., Trute, B., Benzies, K., Kehler, H., & Johnston, D. (2010). Gauging knowledge of developmental milestones among Albertan adults: A cross-sectional survey. *BMC Public Health, 10*, 183.

Sanders, M., Markie-Dadds, C., & Turner, K. (2003). *Theoretical, scientific and clinical foundations of the Triple P-Positive Parenting Program: A population approach to the promotion of parenting competence.* Retrieved from www.cimharchive.trilogyir.com/downloads/handouts/Theoret%20Scientific%20Clinical%20Foundation%20for%20Triple%20P.pdf

Shonkoff, J. (2010). Building a new biodevelopmental framework to guide the future of early childhood policy. *Child Development, 81*, 357–367.

Temple, J. & Reynolds, A. (2007). Benefits and costs of investments in preschool education: Evidence from the Child-Parent Centers and related programs. *Economics of Education Review, 26*, 126–144.

Trivette, C., Dunst, C., & Hamby, D. (2010). Influences of family-systems intervention practices on parent-child interactions and child development. *Topics in Early Childhood Special Education, 30*, 3–19.

Turner, S., Merchant, K., Kania, J., & Martin, E. (2012). Understanding the value of backbone organizations in collective impact. *Stanford Social Innovation Review.* Retrieved from www.ssireview.org/blog/entry/understanding_the_value_of_backbone_organizations_in_collective_impact_1

United Nations General Assembly (1989). *Convention on the Rights of the Child. Treaty Series*, vol. 1577, p. 3. Retrieved from www.refworld.org/docid/3ae6b38f0.html

Webster-Stratton, C. & Reid, M. (2003). Treating conduct problems and strengthening social and emotional competence in young children: The Dina Dinosaur treatment program. *Journal of Emotional & Behavioral Disorders, 11*, 130–143.

Weiner, B. (2009). A theory of organizational readiness for change. *Implementation Science, 4*, 67.

Weiss, H., Kreider, H., Mayer, E., Hencke, R., & Vaughan, M. (2005). Working it out: The chronicle of a mixed-methods analysis, in T. S. Weisner (Ed.), *Discovering successful pathways in children's development: Mixed methods in the study of childhood and family life* (pp. 47–64). Chicago, IL: The University of Chicago Press.

Wilson, P., Rush, R., Hussey, S., Puckering, C., Sim, F., Allely, C., Doku, P., McConnachie, A., & Gillberg, C. (2012). How evidence-based is an 'evidence-based parenting program'? A PRISMA systematic review and meta-analysis of Triple P. *BMC Medicine, 10*, 130.

Wisconsin Children's Trust Fund. (2014). Children's Trust Fund. Retrieved from http://wichildrenstrustfund.org/index.php

Yarbrough, D., Shulha, L., Hopson, R., & Caruthers, F. (2011). *The program evaluation standards: A guide for evaluators and evaluation users* (3rd ed.). Thousand Oaks, CA: Sage.

5

MODERATORS AND MEDIATORS OF PARENTING PROGRAM EFFECTIVENESS

Sabine Stoltz & Maja Deković

Learning Goals

After reading this chapter, the reader will increase their awareness of the following:

1. The importance of high-quality evaluation of effects of parenting programs and about criteria for high-quality research on program effectiveness.
2. Differential effectiveness of parenting programs for subgroups of parents and children and about the need for more research on moderators of program effects.
3. Other factors that might influence program effects, such as dosage of a program, quality of implementation and integrity, and about the need for more knowledge of the influence of program characteristics on the effects of parent programs.
4. The need for more research on underlying processes, or working mechanisms, by which parenting programs have their effects.
5. The importance of a strong theoretical base and a clear objective of parenting programs, to be able to test mediation effects.
6. How research on mediators of program effects can enhance clinical practice by refining current programs and focus on active ingredients of a program.

Introduction

Research over the last half century has proven the important role parenting plays in development of children (Grusec, 2011). Parents are children's most important and influential socializing agents. It is then not surprising that many different prevention and intervention programs that focus on parenting exist and are frequently used in clinical practice. These programs are based on the assumption that improvements in parenting behavior will lead to improvements in the child's functioning and may thus prevent or decrease child problem behavior.

Parenting interventions, when used as intended, can indeed be effective in improving child outcomes, and can be even more effective than interventions that focus solely on the child (Chorpita, Daleiden, Ebesutani, Young, Becker, & Starace, 2011). Although "evidence-based practice" (i.e., practitioners focus on working with proven effective, well-researched interventions) is increasing, and there are several parenting programs that have been properly evaluated (see Part III), still many parenting programs in use to date are not empirically tested for their effectiveness (Scott, 2006). As a result, it is often unclear which programs are successful in improving parenting and/or child behavior, which programs are benign, and which programs actually have negative effects. For example, from evaluation of cognitive behavioral intervention for antisocial youth it is known that group treatment, which is widely implemented to reduce antisocial behavior, actually increases conduct problems via processes of "deviancy training" among peers (Dishion, McCord, & Poulin, 1999; MacGowan & Wagner, 2005). Although there is less evidence for such general negative effects of parenting programs, it is quite possible that parenting programs, at least for some parents, do produce undesirable effects. For example, Asscher, Deković, Prinzie and Hermanns (2008) found that Home-Start in general had a positive effect on parenting, but still, 15 percent of mothers who followed Home-Start programs showed an increase, rather than a decrease, in harsh parenting. Moreover, one can even argue that programs which are not effective (i.e., do not lead to improvements in parenting and/or child outcome) actually do more harm than good. Parents, especially those who most need it, might be difficult to motivate for a parenting program (Whittaker & Cowley, 2012). If they do engage in a program, but the expected positive outcomes are not realized, it might lead to demoralization and helplessness. Finally, programs that do not work are a waste of human resourses, time, and money. Therefore, the evaluation and documentation of effectiveness of parenting programs remain very important: only the most effective prevention and intervention practices should be implemented.

In the present chapter, conceptual and methodological issues related to the evaluation of parenting programs are reviewed. This discussion is organized according to three questions that are often posed in evaluation research: (a) Does it work (effectiveness)? (b) For whom and under which conditions does a program lead to positive outcomes (moderators of program effects)? And (c) how does it work (mediators of program effects)?

Does it Work? Quality of Examining Effectiveness

The central and most traditional questions asked in parenting program evaluation research are: Does the intervention work? Does participation in the intervention result in expected effects? Because of the increased attention for evidence-based practice in the last few years, an increasing number of studies are being conducted to evaluate the effects of parent programs (La Greca, Silverman, & Lochman, 2009). Although progress has been made in research on parenting programs, it is important to realize that the quality of the conducted research on parenting programs is not always adequate.

The confidence of results of an evaluation study increases with the quality of the study. The randomized controlled trial (RCT) has been the standard of proof in behavioral intervention studies in the last half century (Consolidated Standards of Reporting Trials, 2010). Although some of the programs have been evaluated in a scientifically rigorous manner, this is not the case for many. Moreover, many evaluations are "university based", so-called efficacy trails, conducted under optimal circumstances (well-trained practitioners, carefully selected participants, high program integrity), rather than effectiveness trials conducted in applied settings, with "real-world" clinicians and participants (Kazdin, 2008; Michelson, Davenport, Dretzke, Barlow, & Day, 2013). It has been suggested that effectiveness studies are better comparable to clinical practice. Indeed, these studies can be informative to determine whether parent programs can be rolled out into regular practices (i.e., testing implementation; Gardner et al., 2010). However, results of these trials can only be meaningful when they meet the quality criteria for evaluation research (Deković et al., 2012).

Implementing an RCT design in clinical practice is very challenging. Many studies have problems with including a no-treatment control group, because it is difficult to motivate participants for a study when they do not receive an intervention. As a result, many evaluation studies do not include a control group or only include a selective population that is willing to participate in a study and therefore not representative for the targeted population (Asscher, Deković, van der Laan, Prins, & van Arum, 2007). Second, in intervention trials, researchers must cooperate with care-providing agencies. It is not always easy to convince them to evaluate a program under strict research conditions, with validated measures, long-term measures, multiple informants, and so on (see for more extensive review on this topic: Deković, Stoltz, Schuiringa, Manders, & Asscher, 2012). As a consequence, concessions have been made in evaluation studies and as a result research designs are not as perfect as intended. Studies suffer from important limitations such as small sample size, reliance on self-reports only, poor quality of measurement instruments, no long-term follow-up measurements, or failure to evaluate program integrity (Weisz, Jensen, Doss, & Hawley, 2006). These concessions to the design make it difficult to draw reliable conclusions about the effectiveness of a program (see also Asmussen & Weizel, 2010).

To sum up: in recent years progress has been made, there is more awareness of the importance of evidence-based practice, there is an increase in efficacy and effectiveness studies of parenting programs, however, great care should be taken to ensure the high quality of evaluation studies. Next, efforts should be made to bring knowledge from these studies to the field, so that practitioners know where to find good-quality programs underpinned by a solid evidence base.

Five key research directions in evaluation of parenting programs were identified. First, evaluation studies should follow their samples for a longer period of time to examine long-term effects of parent programs. Despite the belief that preventive interventions can produce long-term beneficial effects, very few studies actually tested the long-term effects of parent programs (Deković, Slagt, Asscher, Boendermaker, Eichelsheim, & Prinzie, 2011).

Second, very little systematic research has been conducted on the effects of different program intensities on outcome. Therefore, evaluation studies should include a measure of intensity, or dosage, of an intervention. Especially in parent programs, attendance can be highly variable. Some parents never attend any of the intervention sessions, or are only minimally engaged, while some parents attend all sessions. Several studies show that dosage can be related to program outcome (e.g., Reid, Webster-Stratton, & Baydar, 2004). Parent attendance may have a substantial impact on evaluation findings for prevention and intervention programs (Lochman, Boxmeyer, Powell, Rothe, & Windle, 2006).

Third, careful attention should be paid to the selection of the outcome measures. Obviously, a program should be evaluated based on its aims. In the case of parenting programs, the target, and thus the main outcome, is the parenting behavior. However, in evaluation studies, often broad categories, such as positive parenting, are used to assess the main outcome, rather than more specific parenting behaviors that are targeted within the program, such as praising appropriate child behavior, ignoring, or using time out. In future research, a tighter link between what is actually targeted in the program and what is assessed in the evaluation studies is desirable. Moreover, parenting programs are designed not only to enhance parenting skills, but also to increase knowledge, to improve self-beliefs in their own capacities in raising the child, to alter negative attributions, etc. These cognitive outcomes are not often assessed, although they might be important for explaining why parents do or do not change their behavior due to the parenting programs (Deković, Asscher, & Manders, 2012). Moreover, in many evaluations of parenting programs only parents' outcomes are measured, while it is also important to see whether child behavior improves as a result of parenting programs. For example, some studies on parenting programs revealed positive results on parent outcomes, but did not result in changes in child outcomes (e.g., McCord, 1992). In addition to measuring child outcomes, a child's perspectives on changes in parenting behavior should be also assessed. It is likely that changes in child behavior would only occur if children perceive changes in parenting or if children change in their interpretations of parental behavior. Inclusion of measures on a child's perspective on parenting can reveal important information for interpretation of both positive and negative effects of parenting programs (Deković & Stoltz, 2015).

Regarding sources of information, many evaluation studies, especially those for parents with older children, rely on questionnaires. However, especially for parent programs, the use of a more objective, observational, measure of parenting change would improve confidence in findings regarding effectiveness. Parents might be biased in reporting positive effects of parenting programs given the fact that they invest a lot to participate in a parent program (Deković & Stoltz, 2015).

Finally, evaluation studies should include indices that reflect clinically relevant changes. Especially for intervention programs, it is informative to know whether it is possible with a certain intervention to move children into a normative range on important outcomes after participation (Kazdin, 2008).

For Whom? Moderators of Effectiveness

Parenting programs can be effective in improving various child and parent outcomes, such as reducing disruptive child behavior (Lundahl, Risser, & Lovejoy, 2006), and improving parental warmth and parental self-efficacy and reducing parental stress (Thomas & Zimmer-Gembeck, 2007). However, these programs do not have the same effects on all participants: a program that works for one family may not work for another. Instead, it is much more likely to expect that some participants will benefit more than others from a specific program. Questions about who benefits most from an intervention and under what circumstances are investigated through moderator analyses.

Even the most effective interventions are only effective for two-thirds of children (Dumas, Moreland, Gitter, Pearl, & Nordstrom, 2008). Especially in parent programs, drop-out rates (i.e., parents who were offered a parent program but did not participate) are often high (28–50 percent; Reyno & McGrath, 2006), often as a result of a non-suitable intervention (Kraemer et al., 2002; Beauchaine, Webster-Stratton, & Reid, 2005). Moreover, effect sizes of parent education programs are still small to moderate (Dumas et al., 2008). Moderator analyses in evaluation studies can reveal important information about the differential effectiveness of a program. It is very well possible that programs for which no, or only small, overall effects emerge are still effective for specific subgroups of children and families (Kraemer et al., 2002). Knowledge about characteristics of these children and families that might influence intervention effects can lead to better selection of participants for a specific intervention, and in turn result in lower drop-out rates. For example, a specific intervention may be particularly suitable for boys, so for girls extra (or other) efforts may be necessary. In this way, moderator analyses are important for directly informing clinical practice. However, they also contribute to scientific knowledge by elucidating whether developmental processes can be changed under certain conditions (Kellam & Rebok, 1992). When analyzing factors that might be related to program effects, it is essential to distinguish moderators from predictors. A moderator is a variable that is measured before random assignment to the intervention condition and is differentially associated with the outcome of a program compared to control groups

(Hinshaw, 2007). This is in contrast to predictors of outcome, which may be associated with outcome equally across intervention and control groups (Beauchaine et al., 2005).

Program effects might differ as a function of demographic characteristics, such as age, gender, or ethnicity, or as a function of more substantive characteristics, such as personality of child or parents or parental mental health. Moderator analyses indicating these characteristics that influence program effects are often based on routinely obtained information, such as age or gender (Kazdin, 2007). This is because of practical issues (this information is included in the study anyway), but also because there is a lack of theoretical models explicitly covering moderator effects in parenting interventions (Gardner, Burton, & Klimes, 2010). Therefore we only have limited knowledge of what works for whom.

For example, it is found that parenting programs are less effective for children of low-income parents, lower-educated parents, and single parents (Lundahl et al., 2006; Reyno & McGrath, 2006; Leijten et al., 2013). It has been suggested that children from these socially or economically "disadvantaged" parents have more psychological, financial, or social stressors and are, as a result, less sensitive for positive change (Deković & Stoltz, 2015). Some evaluation studies include child gender as a potential factor that might influence intervention outcomes (e.g., CPPRG, 2002; Beauchaine, Webster-Stratton, & Reid, 2005; McGilloway et al., 2012), however, proposed effects, based on evidence from longitudinal studies, are often not found and there is still insufficient evidence regarding the question of whether programs work equally well for boys and girls (Hipwell & Loeber, 2006). Based on the few evaluation studies that actually test moderation, it can be concluded that demographical factors do not have very large or straightforward influences on intervention effects.

These inconsistent findings suggest that research on moderators should be theoretically based: what factors can we expect to influence program effects based on theory and empirical findings? From an ecological perspective (Bronfenbrenner, 1979; Sameroff, 2010), behavior is a result of interactions between factors at both the individual level (child and parent characteristics) and environmental level. Risk factors for specific behaviors as demonstrated in empirical studies, at an individual or environmental level, can be expected to influence treatment outcome as well. An example of a theoretically based moderator at an individual level is adolescent psychopathy. In an intervention study for antisocial adolescents (Manders, Deković, Asscher, van der Laan, & Prins, 2013) adolescent psychopathy, characterized by callous/unemotional traits, narcissism, and impulsiveness, was assessed as moderator, based on longitudinal studies demonstrating that psychopathic traits in adolescents place them at risk for severe forms of antisocial behavior. In agreement with the expectations, the intervention was not effective for adolescents with higher levels of psychopathic traits, suggesting that the intervention should be tailored for these adolescents to achieve the same intervention gains as for adolescents with low levels of psychopathic traits.

Other factors that might be considered when studying moderator effects are characteristics of the program (e.g., integrity, quality of implementation) being evaluated. Even well-structured and well-worked-out programs have variations in delivery of the program. For example, programs might differ in dosage (i.e., how much of the program). Very little systematic research has been conducted on the effects of different treatment intensities. In general it is expected that more frequent and more intensive interventions with a longer duration and broader scope may be more effective, however, more recently it is argued that brief approaches may result in larger effects (Bakermans-Kranenburg, van IJzendoorn, & Juffer, 2003). Further program-related factors, such as program integrity (i.e., is the program conducted as intended?) or level of experience of persons who deliver the program, might also influence program effects (Kaminski, Vallew, Filene, & Boyle, 2008). To date, very little is known about the influence of program characteristics on the effects of parent programs.

To conclude, testing moderation effects in parent evaluation studies is very important because it can show effectiveness for certain subgroups of participants when there are no overall effects, and it can lead to program adaptation for those groups that are not responsive to a specific program (personalized programs). To date, there is a lack of studies that include moderator analyses (Weersing & Weisz, 2002), partially due to the fact that larger samples are needed to have enough power for these analyses (Hinshaw, 2007). Studies that do include moderators include mainly demographic information or test prediction rather than moderation.

How? Mediators of Effectiveness

A final, but perhaps most important, question that can be answered through evaluation studies is *how* does the intervention work? Through which mechanisms does the intervention exert its effects? What are the active ingredients of an intervention? Mediation analyses can signify the working mechanisms of an intervention. Knowledge about how an intervention exerts its effects and which components of an intervention are associated with larger effects can enhance clinical practice. It can result in more tailored interventions in which effective components are added and less effective components are changed or omitted (Weisz et al., 2006; Kaminski et al., 2008;). Moreover, results from mediation analyses can increase knowledge on developmental theories of specific behavior, since these give insight into how and through what processes behavior can be changed. For example, evidence exists that cognitive behavior therapy is effective for reducing anxiety, which establishes cognitive distortions as an important process in the development and maintenance of anxiety (Kraemer et al., 2002). Although there is a growing body of studies that tries to identify mediators, in a recent review of 46 parenting intervention trials it was concluded that the knowledge of underlying processes by which these interventions have effects is very limited (Sandler, Schoenfelder, Wolchik, & MacKinnon, 2011).

To increase knowledge on mediators of parenting programs, it is essential to know first what is actually targeted in these programs. In other words, developers of parenting programs have to make clear, before the intervention and evaluation of the intervention start, what aspects of parenting and child behavior need to be changed with the intervention. A clear objective and the content of the program, underpinned by a strong theoretical base, make it possible to identify tentative mediators (Deković et al., 2012). This is the first step necessary to test for mediator effects in intervention trials.

For example: parent interventions are based on the assumption that changes in parenting behavior would result in changes in child behavior. A study on the effectiveness of a specific parent intervention (multi-systemic therapy; Deković et al., 2012) hypothesized that changes in parental cognitions (i.e., their confidence in their ability to manage parenting tasks) are the working mechanism through which the intervention induces changes in parenting behavior, which in turn results in changes in child behavior. This assumption was based on the rationale of the intervention and on substantial evidence in the literature for the relationship between high sense of competence and positive parenting. Through mediation analyses it was found that indeed changes in parental sense of competence resulted in change in parenting (and adolescent) behavior. These findings thus give support for parental sense of competence as an active ingredient of the parent intervention and for a sense of competence as an important process in development of adaptive parenting behavior (Deković et al., 2012).

However, to date only a few studies have actually tested theoretical models on which parenting interventions are based, and many parent programs actually lack a clear theoretical rationale on which the program is based (Hinshaw, 2002; Sandler et al., 2011).

The few studies that have examined mediation often suffer from design problems. For example, to know which changes in parenting behavior lead to improvements in child outcome behavior, it is necessary to include several time points to be able to make causal interpretations (Maric, Wiers, & Prins, 2012). Ideally, trials should include measures *during* and *after* the intervention to see what changes when. Otherwise, it is not possible to prove that the proposed mediator actually is a *process* that is causally responsible for bringing about improvements in outcome, rather than just an alternate outcome measure (Kazdin & Nock, 2003). This is in contrast to a moderator, which is a variable assessed at baseline (e.g., SES) and which is assumed to influence intervention effects. To be a mediator, a change (e.g., change in SES as results of improvement in a family's social standing) in a variable during the period of the intervention should mediate outcomes (Hinshaw, 2002). The few studies that attempt to test mediation are often not able to include multiple time points and have therefore not the optimal study design to support causal mechanisms (e.g., Gardner et al., 2010).

Offering only minimal intervention parent training methods is especially important in the light of findings showing that it is difficult to motivate parents to attend and participate in a meaningful way in parent education programs (Scogin, Bynum, Stephens, & Calhoon, 1990; Dumas et al., 2008). The commonly held assumption "the more, the better" does not hold in parent interventions (Bakermans-Kranenburg, van IJzendoorn, & Juffer, 2003), and adding more components to an intervention might actually impede parental ability of focus on learning parenting skills and thus can lead to less positive outcomes (Lundahl et al., 2006; Kaminski et al., 2008). Parenting education programs should be brief and focused to decrease the burden on both parents and practitioners, containing only those components that do actually work.

To summarize, knowledge about mediating mechanisms, or active ingredients, of parent education programs can result in more focused, tailored, interventions in which only the most effective components are included. These focused interventions will be more effective and less time consuming and can enhance clinical practice. Importantly, it can lead to suggestions of variables to be experimentally manipulated in subsequent clinical trials, to establish more conclusively their causal relation to core outcomes (Hinshaw, 2007).

Conclusion

The efforts on examining if parenting programs work should be continued, however, more studies are necessary to examine moderators and mediators to answer the questions how, for whom, and under what circumstances parenting education programs produce their effects. Effectiveness of parenting programs can be enhanced by information from these studies by better identification of children and parents who are likely to respond and by selecting other programs for children and parents who are not helped by a specific program. Moreover, current programs could be refined by focusing on active ingredients of a program and leaving out those components that do not work (Deković & Stoltz, 2015). This is important for dissemination: complexity of programs is a key problem when adopting evidence-based programs in clinical practice (Comer & Barlow, 2014).

A next step in evaluation research is to take a closer look at what actually happens during the program. When and how do changes in parental behavior occur? Is the impact of a program the largest at the beginning of a program, or at the end? From previous studies on multi-systemic therapy (MST) we can conclude that intervention effects on parenting emerge only after improvement in parental cognitions (Deković et al., 2012). To increase knowledge about processes of change during the course of a program, multiple measurements during the program should be included, rather than focusing on pre and post assessment.

Moreover, more attention should be paid to the inclusion of fathers. In parenting programs, mothers are most often the main attendees. More effort should be given to engagement of fathers in such programs (Stahlschmidt, Threlfall, Seay, Lewis, & Kohl, 2013). Not only have fathers an important role as socializing agents, the involvement of only mothers in parental programs might lead to diverging parenting in the families. If mother takes home new ideas acquired in parenting programs which are in conflict with existing ideas of fathers, it might be very difficult for her to change her behavior and it might lead to discord between the parents.

A parenting program can be well designed and proven effective when delivered properly (i.e., with a high level of program integrity), but it might still fail if it is not conducted as it should. The process of taking evidence-based parenting programs from research laboratories to the community is full of challenges. We still do not know which factors ensure a successful implementation of parenting program in everyday practice (Sanders & Kirby, 2015).

Key Points

1. The evaluation and documentation of effectiveness of parenting programs are important: only the most effective prevention and intervention practices should be implemented.
2. Evaluation studies should meet quality criteria for evaluation research to provide meaningful results.
3. Despite the belief that preventive interventions can produce long-term beneficial effects, very few studies actually tested the long-term effects of parent programs.
4. Careful attention should be paid to the selection of the outcome measures; both child and parenting outcomes should be measured.
5. Evaluation studies should include indices that reflect clinically relevant changes.
6. Moderator analyses in evaluation studies can reveal important information about the differential effectiveness of a program.
7. Program effects might differ as a function of demographic characteristics, such as age, gender, or ethnicity, or as a function of more substantive characteristics, such as personality of child or parents or parental mental health.
8. To date, very little is known about the influence of program characteristics on the effects of parent programs.
9. Mediation analyses can signify the working mechanisms of an intervention.
10. A clear objective and the content of the program, underpinned by a strong theoretical base, make it possible to identify tentative mediators.
11. Knowledge about mediating mechanisms of parent education programs can result in more focused, tailored, interventions in which only the most effective components are included.

Discussion Questions

1. What might be some of the barriers for conducting scientific studies to the effectiveness of parenting education programs?
2. How would you determine whether effects of a parenting program are clinically relevant?
3. What would you decide when, from moderator analyses, it could be concluded that a program does not have the same effects for all participants?
4. What does it mean for implementation of a program?
5. What might be the best way to identify and test the working mechanisms of a parenting education program?

Additional Resources

Websites

For information about different parenting programs, see:

www.education.gov.uk/commissioning-toolkit
www.parentinguk.org/your-work/programmes/
www.actionforchildren.org.uk/our-services/family-support/parenting-support/parenting-programmes
http://whatworks.uwex.edu/attachment/Directoryofeb.pdf
http://whatworks.uwex.edu/Pages/2parentsinprogrameb.html

References

Asmussen, K., & Weizel, K. (2010). *Evaluating the evidence: What all practitioners need to know to deliver evidence-based parenting support.* London: King's College, National Academy for Parenting Research.

Asscher, J., Deković, M., van Laan, P., Prins, P., & van Arum, S. (2007). Implementing randomized experiments in criminal justice settings: An evaluation of multi-systemic therapy in the Netherlands. *Journal of Experimental Criminology, 3*, 113–129.

Asscher, J., Deković, M., & Prinzie, P., & Hermanns, J. (2008). Assessing change in families following the Home-Start parenting support program: Clinical significance and predictors of change. *Family Relations, 57*, 351–364.

Bakermans-Kranenburg, M., Van IJzendoorn, M. & Juffer, F. (2003). Less is more: Meta-analysis of sensitivity and attachment interventions in early childhood. *Psychological Bulletin, 129*, 195–215.

Beauchaine, T., Webster-Stratton, C., & Reid. M. (2005). Mediators, moderators, and predictors of 1-year outcomes among children treated for early-onset conduct problems: A latent growth curve analysis. *Journal of Consulting and Clinical Psychology, 73*, 371–388.

Bronfenbrenner, U. (1979). Contexts of child rearing. *American Psychologist, 34*, 844–858.

Chorpita, B., Daleiden, E., Ebesutani, C., Young, J., Becker, K., & Starce, N. (2011). Evidence-based treatments for children and adolescents: An updated review of indicators of efficacy and effectiveness. *Clinical Psychology: Science and Practice, 18*, 154–172.

Comer, J., & Barlow, D. (2014). The occasional case against broad dissemination and implementation. *American Psychologist, 69*, 1–18.

CPPRG. (2002). Predictor variables associated with positive fast track outcomes at the end of third grade. *Journal of Abnormal Child Psychology, 30*, 37–52.

Deković, M., Asscher, J., & Manders, W. (2012). Changing parenting: Lessons (to be) learned from evaluations of parenting programs. *ISSBD Bulletin, 62*, 19–22.

Deković, M., Asscher, J., Manders, W., Prins, P., & van der Laan, P. (2012). Within-intervention change: Mediators of intervention effects during multisystemic therapy. *Journal of Consulting and Clinical Psychology, 80*, 574–587.

Dekovic, M., Slagt, M. I., Asscher, J. J., Boendermaker, L., Eichelsheim, V. I. &, Prinzie, P. (2011). Effects of early prevention programs on adult criminal offending: A meta-analysis. *Clinical Psychological Reviews 31*, 532–544.

Dekovic, M., & Stoltz, S. (2015). Treatment of youth who show externalizing problem behavior, in M. Maric, P. Prins, & T. Ollendick (Eds.), *Mediators and moderators of youth treatment outcomes* (pp. 97–122). New York: Oxford University Press.

Deković, M., Stoltz, S., Schuiringa, H., Manders, W., & Asscher, J. (2012). Testing theories through evaluation research: Conceptual and methodological issues embedded in evaluations of parenting programmes. *European Journal of Developmental Psychology, 9*, 61–74.

Dishion, T. J., McCord, J., & Poulin, F. (1999). When interventions harm: Peer groups and problem behavior. *American Psychologist, 54*, 755–764.

Dumas, J., Moreland, A., Gitter, A., Pearl., A., & Nordstrom, A. (2008). Engaging parents in preventative parenting groups: Do ethnic, socio-economic, and belief match between parents and group leaders matter? *Health Education & Behaviour, 35*, 619–633.

Flay, B., Biglan, A., Boruch, R., González Castro, F., Gottfredson, D., Kellam, S., et al. (2005). Standards of evidence: Criteria for efficacy, effectiveness and dissemination. *Prevention Science, 6*, 151–175.

Gardner, F., Burton, J., & Klimes, I. (2006). Randomized controlled trial of a parenting intervention in the voluntary sector for reducing child conduct problems: Outcomes and mechanisms of change. *Journal of Child Psychology and Psychiatry, 47*, 1123–1132.

Gardner, F., Hutchings, J., Bywater, T, & Whitaker, C. (2010). Who benefits and how does it work? Moderators and mediators of outcome in an effectiveness trial of a parenting intervention. *Clinical Child and Adolescent Psychology, 39*, 568–580.

Grusec, J. (2011). Socialization processes in the family: Social and emotional development. *Annual Review of Psychology, 62*, 243–269.

Hinshaw, S. (2002). Intervention research, theoretical mechanisms, and causal processes related to externalizing behavior patterns. *Development and Psychopathology, 14*, 789–818.

Hinshaw, S. (2007). Moderators and mediators of treatment outcome for youth with ADHD: Understanding for whom and how interventions work. *Journal of Pediatric Psychology, 32*, 664–675.

Hipwell, A. E., & Loeber, R. (2006). Do we know which interventions are effective for disruptive and delinquent girls? *Clinical Child and Family Psychology Review, 9*, 221–255.

Kaminski, J., Vallew, L., Filene, J., & Boyle, C. (2008). A meta-analytic review of components associated with parent training program effectiveness. *Journal of Abnormal Child Psychology, 36*, 567–589.

Kazdin, A. (2007). Mediators and mechanisms of change in psychotherapy research. *Annual Review of Clinical Psychology, 3*, 1–27.

Kazdin, A. (2008). Evidence-based treatment and practice: New opportunities to bridge clinical research and practice, enhance the knowledge base, and improve patient care. *American Psychologist, 63*, 146–159.

Kazdin, A., & Nock, M. (2003). Delineating mechanisms of change in child and adolescent therapy: Methodological issues and research recommendations. *Journal of Child Psychology and Psychiatry, 44*, 1116–1130.

Kellam, S. & Rebok, G. (1992). Building developmental and etiological theory through epidemiologically based preventive intervention trials, in J. McCord & R. Tremblay (Eds.) *Preventing antisocial behavior: Intervention from birth through adolescence* (pp. 162–195). New York: Guilford.

Kraemer, H., Wilson, T., Fairburn, C., & Agras, W. (2002). Mediators and moderators of treatment effects in randomized clinical trials. *Archives of General Psychiatry, 59*, 877–883.

La Greca, A., Silverman, W., & Lochman, J. (2009). Moving beyond efficacy and effectiveness in child and adolescent intervention research. *Journal of Consulting and Clinical Psychology, 77*, 373–382.

Leijten, P., Raaijmakers, M., De Castro, B., & Matthys, W. (2013). Does socioeconomic status matter? A meta-analysis on parent training effectiveness for disruptive child behavior. *Journal of Clinical Child & Adolescent Psychology, 42*, 384–392.

Lundahl, B., Risser, H. J., & Lovejoy, M. C. (2006) A meta-analysis of parent training: Moderators and follow-up effects. *Clinical Psychology Review, 26*, 86–104.

McCord, J. (1992). The Cambridge-Somerville study: A pioneering longitudinal experimental study of delinquency prevention, in J. McCord & R. E.Trembley (Eds.) *Preventing antisocial behaviour: Interventions from birth through adolescence.* New York: Guilford.

McGilloway, S., Ni Mhaille, G., Bywater, T., Furlong, M., Leckey, Y., Kelly, P., et al. (2012). A parenting intervention for childhood behavioral problems: A randomized controlled trial in disadvantaged community-based settings. *Journal of Consulting and Clinical Psychology, 80*, 116–127.

MacGowan, M., & Wagner, E. (2005). Iatrogenic effects of group treatment on adolescents with conduct and substance use problems: A review of the literature and a presentation model. *Journal of Evidence-based Social Work, 2*, 79–90.

Manders, W., Deković, M., Asscher, J., Van der Laan, P., & Prins, P. (2013). Psychopathy as predictor and moderator of multisystemic therapy outcomes among adolescents treated for antisocial behavior. *Journal of Abnormal Child Psychology, 41*, 1121–1132.

Maric, M., Wiers, R., & Prins, P. (2012). Ten ways to improve the use of statistical mediation analysis in the practice of child and adolescent treatment research. *Clinical Child and Family Psychological Review, 15*, 177–191.

Michelson, D., Davenport, C., Dretzke, J., Barlow, J., & Day, C. (2013). Do evidence-based interventions work when tested in the "real world?" A systematic review and meta-analysis of parent management training for the treatment of child disruptive behavior. *Clinical Child and Family Psychology Review, 16*, 18–34.

Reid, M. J., Webster-Stratton, C., Baydar, N. (2004). Halting the development of externalizing behaviors in Head Start children: The effects of parenting training. *Journal of Clinical Child and Adolescent Psychology*, 33, 279–291.

Reyno, S. & McGrath, P. (2006). Predictors of parent training efficacy for child externalizing behavior problems—a meta-analytic review. *Journal of Child Psychology and Psychiatry, 47*, 99–111.

Sameroff, A. (2010). A unified theory of development: A dialectic integration of nature and nurture. *Child Development*, *81*, 6–22.

Sanders, M., & Kirby, J. (2015). Surviving or thriving: Quality assurance mechanisms to promote innovation in the development of evidence-based parenting interventions. *Prevention Science*, *16*, 421–431.

Sandler, I., Schoenfelder, E., Wolchik, S., & MacKinnon, D. (2011). Long-term impact of prevention programs to promote effective parenting: Lasting effects, but uncertain processes. *Annual Review of Psychology*, *62*, 299–329.

Scogin, F., Bynum, J., Stephens, G., & Calhoon, S. (1990). Efficacy of self-administered treatment programs: meta-analytic review. *Professional Psychological Research Practices*, *21*, 42–47.

Scott, S. (2006). Improving children's lives, preventing criminality: Where next? *The Psychologist*, *19*, 484–487.

Stahlschmidt, M., Threlfall, J., Seay, K., Lewis, E., & Kohl, P. (2013). Recruiting fathers to parenting programs: Advice from dads and fatherhood program providers. *Children and Youth Services Review*, *35*, 1734–1741.

Thomas, R., & Zimmer-Gembeck, M. (2007). Behavioral outcomes of parent-child interaction therapy and Triple P—Positive Parenting Program: A review and meta-analysis. *Journal of Abnormal Child Psychology*, *35*, 475–495.

Weersing, R., & Weisz, J. (2002). Mechanisms of action in youth psychotherapy. *Journal of Child Psychology and Psychiatry*, *43*, 3–29.

Weisz, J., Jensen Doss, A., & Hawley, K. (2006). Evidence-based youth psychotherapies versus usual clinical care: A meta-analysis of direct comparisons. *American Psychologist*, *61*, 671–689.

Whittaker, K., & Cowley, S. (2012). An effective programme is not enough: A review of factors associated with poor attendance and engagement with parenting support programmes. *Children & Society*, *26*, 138–149.

Zhou, Q., Sandler, I., Millsap, R., Wolchik, S., & Dawson-McClure, S. (2008). Mother-child relationship quality and effective discipline as mediators of the 6-year effects of the New Beginnings Program for children of divorced families. *Journal of Consulting and Clinical Psychology*, *76*, 579–594.

6

U.S. COOPERATIVE EXTENSION PARENT EDUCATOR'S FRAMEWORK

Karen DeBord

Learning Goals

1. Understand the distinction between content and process in the National Extension Parenting Educators' Framework.
2. Self-critique their strengths and gaps as a family life educator according to the 12 practice areas of the NEPEF model.
3. Apply the NEPEF model to structuring a professional development conference.

Introduction

Parents, whether parenting as single, dual, grandparents, teen parents, stepparents, or first-time parents, share similar apprehensions relative to how to prepare children for school and life, how to keep them healthy, and how to nurture a sense of independence. Obviously, becoming a parent differs from "being" a parent. As Galinsky (1987) notes, once parents are aware that they will be having a child, they begin envisioning what it will be like and how the child will change their lives. However, once the child is part of the family, the reality of the parenting experience becomes evident and they begin to question their judgment and decisions, and pave the way for what kind of parents they will become. It's not an easy journey and one that few are prepared to take. Who will support them in this journey? While parents of all ages, genders, and ethnicities need to build their parenting skills, where do they turn for information and what qualifies those educators to deliver such programs?

Parents differ in where they receive information about parenting. For many, the first source of information and advice is generally friends and family. For others, medical practitioners are often a first source of information (DeBord, 1996). Besides the immediate and extended family network and the medical profession, there is a growing army of professionals who are qualified, interested, and willing to support parents in their journey to raise their children.

Parenting professionals are busier than ever supporting parents from all sectors of society. Caregivers, nonprofit agencies, and other consulting organizations spanning the fields of education, health and social work, community service, and cooperative extension are engaged with families who are seeking to maintain custody of their children, seeking to improve their family relationships, and seeking to help their children do well in school. The field of parenting education is a young field and one that has been built with many jagged edges. Since there is such diversity in professionals contributing to supporting families, determining how to approach parents with a foundation of knowledge, skills, and information to raise children had not been defined until in more recent years. And, with the diversity among outreach professionals, how to educate parents about parenting practices continues to be debated.

For well over 100 years, the **Cooperative Extension Service** (hereafter CES) has supported families in raising their quality of life. As early as 1910, agents were teaching heads of households how to raise crops, cook and store food safely, rear children, and build a sense of community. Local educators in over 3,500 counties nationwide, called extension agents, have been supportive of children's learning and civic engagement through 4-H programs, supportive of family nutrition and finance, and supportive of farmers in efficiently reaping their harvests. But in more recent years, this outreach has become even more strategically important as economic social issues intervene in the lives of families and parents who find difficulty managing the stress of their jobs in addition to tracking the activities of their children while still maintaining a healthy household. Life, it seems, has gotten more and more complicated.

The CES is housed nationally in the National Institute of Food and Agriculture (NIFA), an agency within the U.S. Department of Agriculture (USDA). Meeting public needs at the local level, extension educators in over 100 Land Grant universities and over 3,000 counties partner with other agencies to address a wide range of human, plant, and animal needs through research, teaching, and outreach.

The CES has led the way in many of the developments in parenting education, engaging in multi-state collaborations while disseminating parenting information, and evaluating educational programs. One of the most significant contributions has been the development of the **National Extension Parenting Education Model** (NEPEM).

NEPEM provides a definition of parenting as well as offering 29 critical parenting skills divided into six categories of parenting practices to be learned by parents and taught by parenting educators. Smith, Cudaback, Goddard, and Myers-Walls (1994) created the NEPEM model. It represents a consolidation of the empirical literature to provide a foundation for all parent educators, and presents a sound framework focusing on the content that parenting educators teach parents.

Detailing the National Extension Parenting Education Model

As it was conceptualized, NEPEM served as a framework to review, design, and evaluate parenting education programs and as a guide to the key **content areas** of parenting education. Once the model was released, educators were hard-pressed to find any new topic that would not fit within these six areas. This information was initially shared by Charles Smith, professor at Kansas State University, with the other authors; then later imparted broadly through a National Extension Network called CYFERnet (CYFERnet, 2014). His co-authors all were extension faculty representing different land grant universities. NEPEM's six critical practices are prioritized as what seems to be most important for parents with caring for one's self as the number one priority. The six content areas include **Care for Self**, **Understand**, **Guide**, **Nurture**, **Motivate**, and **Advocate**.

The first category of parenting skills is called **Care for Self** and refers to knowing and understanding oneself, managing life's demands, and establishing clear direction. When parents care for themselves, they can influence the lives of everyone in the family. For example, a parent who is motivated in her or his own life will be more capable of motivating a child. A parent who feels interpersonally connected and supported will find it natural to nurture a child. To care for self means to be able to:

1. Manage personal stress.
2. Manage family resources.
3. Offer support to other parents.
4. Ask for and accept support from others when needed.
5. Recognize one's own personal and parenting strengths.
6. Have a sense of purpose in setting childrearing goals.
7. Cooperate with one's childrearing partners.

The second parenting skill category, **Understand** captures the notion that it is critical for parents to *understand* children as well as understand themselves as parents. Understanding children's development and understanding that each child's needs are different can help enhance parent effectiveness. Understanding children and their developmental needs can result in less conflict in relationships with them. Understanding is also an important part of helping children become secure and healthy as they grow. When parents are able to know their child and what to expect as they grow and develop, they become more confident as well as competent in their parenting journey. Parents who actively observe their children, watch them, and pick up on their cues, understand them better.

Guide focuses on the development of self-control and strength in children and the effective expression of authority by parents. Parents are faced with a difficult balancing act in establishing authority using their power to identify, introduce, and enforce reasonable limits while gradually giving freedom to children by encouraging them to be appropriately responsible for themselves. Parents have the responsibility to set limits that protect their children and show concern for the welfare of others. Children, on the other hand, seek freedom from such constraint even as they need guidance and structure. Their growth as individuals depends on making choices and facing the consequences of their own decisions.

For parents to understand how *to guide* their children means they must:

1. Model appropriate desired behavior.
2. Establish and maintain reasonable limits.
3. Provide children with developmentally appropriate opportunities to learn responsibility.
4. Convey fundamental values underlying basic human decency.
5. Teach problem-solving skills.
6. Monitor children's activities and facilitate their contact with others.

The next parenting skills category is **Nurture**, which means parents attend to the needs of children. When parents exhibit caring behaviors within the context of the family, children learn to be nurturing as well. To build positive, loving relationships between parents, children, and all extended family, consistent messages of love and support must be sent. Being nurturing is difficult when a family's emotional resources are overextended or when a child has difficulty accepting nurturing in the way parents deliver it. Children also have different needs and different preferences for nurturing behavior. To be effective, parents should:

1. Express affection and compassion.
2. Foster children's self-respect and hope.
3. Listen and attend to children's feelings and ideas.
4. Teach kindness.
5. Provide for the nutrition, shelter, clothing, health, and safety needs of one's children.

Motivate is the next category of parenting skills. Motivate involves parents promoting intellectual development and school success. Parents who help children develop a sense of curiosity and desire to learn, develop confident children who become skilled learners. Parents motivate their children by teaching children about themselves and the world around them, stimulating imagination and a search for knowledge, creating beneficial learning conditions, and helping children process and manage information.

Lastly, **Advocate** is the outward support parents have of their children. Parents who connect with community resources increase the probability that their children's and family's needs are met. Parents may seek out programs, institutions, and professionals that provide services important to their children and/or family, or they may represent their children's needs to those organizations or individuals to facilitate a linkage between that community service and the child. When policies

Icon	*Category*	*Priority Practice*
	**Care for Self**	■ Manage personal stress. ■ Manage family resources. ■ Offer support to other parents. ■ Ask for and accept support from others when needed. ■ Recognize one's own personal and parenting strengths. ■ Have a sense of purpose in setting child-rearing goals. ■ Cooperate with one's child-rearing partners.
	**Understand**	■ Observe and understand one's children and their development. ■ Recognize how children influence and respond to what happens around them.
	**Guide**	■ Model appropriate desired behavior. ■ Establish and maintain reasonable limits. ■ Provide children with developmentally appropriate opportunities to learn responsibility. ■ Convey fundamental values underlying basic human decency. ■ Teach problem-solving skills. ■ Monitor children's activities and facilitate their contact with peers and adults.
	**Nurture**	■ Express affection and compassion. ■ Foster children's self-respect and hope. ■ Listen and attend to children's feelings and ideas. ■ Teach kindness. ■ Provide for the nutrition, shelter, clothing, health, and safety needs of one's children. ■ Celebrate life with one's children. ■ Help children feel connected to family history and cultural heritage.
	**Motivate**	■ Teach children about themselves, others, and the world around them. ■ Stimulate curiosity, imagination, and the search for knowledge. ■ Create beneficial learning conditions. ■ Help children process and manage information.
	**Advocate**	■ Find, use, and create community resources when needed to benefit one's children and the community of children. ■ Stimulate social change to create supportive environments for children and families. ■ Build relationships with family, neighborhood, and community groups.

FIGURE 6.1 The National Extension Parent Education Model

Source: Smith et al. (1994). Reprinted with permission.

and procedures in the community impede children's growth or make it difficult for families to function, advocate parents speak up and take action to change those policies. Children whose parents *advocate* for them are less likely than other children to get lost between the cracks or to be offered services that simply do not fit. Parents practice being an advocate by finding and using community resources, creating supportive environments for children and families, and building relationships with family, neighborhood, and community groups. Figure 6.1 represents the only graphic representation of the six categories of parenting skills.

NEPEM Next Steps

NEPEM offers a significant contribution by suggesting a framework as opposed to a new curriculum. It proved useful to parenting educators by providing a model for understanding the critical content to be learned by parents and taught by parenting educators. Curriculum could now be planned according to these six parenting skill areas, programs now could be evaluated with the critical areas as guiding factors, and educational programs could be planned by these themes. NEPEM was broadly accepted within cooperative extension and by others in the field of family support and science.

However, there remained a gap between what parents need to know and what parenting educators need to know to teach and support parents. Those outside of the field have commented that "anyone can be a parent" or that "parenting is innate". However, court judges, social workers, emergency room staff, and others can show time and time again that poor parenting leads to bad results for children. There are many skills and attitudes about how adults interact with children that simply must be taught. Parents who have been reported for neglect or abusive interactions with their children find themselves before a judge being ordered to attend parenting education classes. Parents who become frustrated with their children seek out information to solve immediate problems, and parents of adolescents and teens finally start paying attention to their children's emerging personalities once they reach a level of independence that they display irresponsible behavior or do poorly in school. By then, parenting education becomes more of a family intervention as opposed to a preventive educational measure.

If parents are indeed ordered to seek parenting education, or frustrated parents are looking for advice, where do they turn? Who is qualified to provide reliable information, teach parenting strategies, and help parents guide their child safely through to adulthood?

Challenging others in the profession of educating parents to consider important questions to shape the field was the next step. A round table discussion was convened at the National Conference conducted by the National Council on Family Relations in 1997. The questions were posed regarding what is needed for parenting educators to be qualified to teach parents. Should one be a parent? Should one have a degree in a particular field? Are there particular and specific qualifications needed to qualify as a parent educator to be effective? Karen DeBord led a team of discussants to address these questions. Along with DeBord, Charles Smith, the first author of NEPEM and others came forth to help convene and show support for addressing these critical questions. Subsequently, she led a second team of extension scholars to examine the practices and critical areas of knowledge and expertise of parenting educators.

Through email discussions, ideas emerged that other professionals felt were critical to organizing the field of professional development. A content analysis was used to summarize the ideas into themes. Then a systematic exploration of the issues, concerns, and potential components to be included followed.

By 2001, the NEPEM model that included skills to be taught to parents was expanded. This expansion served as an important next step for moving the field of parenting education forward. The expanded framework addressed skills needed for parenting educators as opposed to addressing the education of parents. It described the competencies and skills necessary for parenting educators to be effective. The framework referred to as the **National Extension Parent Educators' Framework** (NEPEF) included categories of parent educator practice identified as critical for parenting educators. Within those categories, 42 specific practices were identified that are associated with implementing high-quality parenting programs. NEPEF was distributed and content validity was gathered through a process of expert review. Experts representing the areas of practice and research in child development, family studies, diversity education, and human development made comments and suggestions that were incorporated.

For the draft document, eight extension faculty experts conducted a thorough literature search then critiqued each section. An additional 50 experts from multiple states were queried for their feedback during two national conferences: Children, Youth and Families at Risk (CYFAR) and the National Council on Family Relations. The 42 items that comprise the list of critical parenting educator practices were drawn from the literature addressing educational leadership, adult education, family life education, and parenting education. Finally, six overarching areas were identified in the literature:

1. *Grow*ing personally as a professional in the field of parenting education.
2. Understanding theoretical *Frame*works that undergird practices and recommendations for families.
3. The ability to *Develop* educational programs that are effective.
4. Understanding how to teach and effectively *Educate.*
5. Understanding the importance of *Embrac*ing diversity.
6. Continuing to *Build* the field of parenting education.

The six new areas (**Grow**, **Frame**, **Develop**, **Educate**, **Embrace, and Build**) are **process skills**. These are skills that parenting educators must possess in order to teach parenting content. For example, a parent educator must know how to plan an educational program using objectives and effective instructional delivery (captured under Develop and Educate). Or, parent educators must continue to learn about the family and child development field including available parenting curriculum and best practices about what works and doesn't work for parents to learn to change their interactions with their children. These skills are encompassed in the process area of Grow.

Thus, the team referred to these six new areas as *process* skills and the six categories of parenting skills already offered within NEPEM as *content*. The content is the subject matter that is taught while the process skills involved how one teaches, markets, or evaluates programs. For example, content-wise, consider that a parent educator must teach parents how to guide their children's behavior by teaching listening skills or effective ways to make and incorporate rules. These fall into the NEPEM content skill area of Guide. Another example is that parents must learn to take care of themselves in order to take care of their children. Thus, stress reduction techniques, adapting healthy lifestyles, or networking for support within the community may become the focus of educational outreach. The processes go beyond the skills taught to parents. In order to support parents, parenting educators need to understand both the skill (or content) areas as well as the processes such as how to teach a variety of learners, how to embrace differences in families and ethnicities, and how to design and evaluate programs.

Summarily, the total new framework includes 12 total areas. Six were lifted from the NEPEM model to become the *content* areas and six additional areas were added to become the *process* areas. Together the six original areas of the NEPEM folded into a new model to become the National Extension Parenting Educators' Framework (NEPEF).

Examining the Six Process Areas

The first process that parent educators must understand is that it is important to stay current in research and development for their own profession. This is referred to as *Grow*. Grow reflects the process by which parenting educators become professionals and associate themselves with colleagues through professional development activities. In order to be effective educators, it is important for parenting educators to develop a philosophical basis for teaching about families and thoroughly reflect the origin of their personal beliefs (Myers-Walls & Myers-Bowman, 1999; Powell & Cassidy, 2001).

The term *Grow* is used to suggest that the development of these skills begins with the earliest educational and experiential preparations for becoming a parenting educator and continues as an ongoing developmental process. Affiliation, mentoring, supervision, and professional development are all critical to personal growth (Katz, 1977; Schor, 1988; Fenichel, 1992; Rothenberg, 1992; Carter & Kahn, 1996; Powell & Cassidy, 2001).

The second process category, *Frame* refers to skills related to a parenting educator's knowledge of theoretical frameworks that describe human growth and development. Frameworks guide a parent educator's practice in the field of parenting education. Frame includes the ability to effectively conceptualize and apply the philosophies, perspectives, theories, frameworks, paradigms, schools of thought, worldviews, and models that guide educational parenting programs and recommendations for children, parents, and families. Skilled parenting educators draw on appropriate frameworks and assumptions when they develop or choose parenting materials, when they discuss with parents how to deal with difficulties in their relationships with children, and when they make referrals for and recommendations to families (Thomas, 1992; Brock, Oertwein, & Coufal, 1993; Myers-Walls & Myers-Bowman, 1999; Campbell & Palm, 2004).

For example, to guide a parent in understanding how to prepare their child for public school, an overview of Erikson's stages of development including independence and taking initiative may be helpful to teach parents of preschoolers. Thus, the parent educator must know theories in order to determine which would be most helpful to explain to parents.

The *Develop* category includes the skills used in creating parenting education programs. Although there are many packaged curricula available, few of those curricula provide all of the information, materials, and methods needed to effectively meet the needs of a specific audience without the facilitator adapting or changing the curriculum (Brown, 1998). The program development process, especially as it pertains to community-based adult education, has been thoroughly conceived and tested (Boone, 1985; Jacobs, 1988; Rockwell & Bennett, 2000). This body of literature emphasizes the necessary sequence and interconnectedness of needs assessments, targeted outcomes, program design and implementation, progress tracking, and evaluation designed to measure specific outcomes.

Effective parenting education programs are those that (a) include flexible structures and sensitive staff members; (b) respond to participant needs; and (c) use a coherent, research-based training design (Cataldo, 1987). Many scholars recommend a comprehensive program-development process that includes specifying target-audience needs and assets, considering facilitator resources, conducting interventions, considering delivery formats, and designing appropriate evaluation and reporting methods (Brown, 1998; DeBord, 1998; Matthews & Hudson, 2001). Medway (1989) and others reinforce the fact that the design of program evaluation is integral to the entire planning process, not a step added at the conclusion. It is also clear that skill in the Develop category of practices is significantly enhanced by building skills in the other areas of NEPEF simultaneously. For example, parent educators need to evaluate their effectiveness. In order to evaluate their effectiveness, they must have a marker against which to measure. Writing learning objectives prior to teaching is a process skill needed in order to truly develop an educational program that is organized in a way that intentionally is planned with the learner in mind and with the end result planned from the beginning. Educators then evaluate against the learning objectives.

Educate is a category that is also not likely to be overlooked by parenting educators. It comprises the skills of being an effective teacher, knowing how to use various delivery methods, helping parents learn, and challenging them to higher parenting goals. Educate includes the process of building relationships with participants to help them more effectively solve problems, resolve conflicts, set goals, and gain knowledge and skills to guide and nurture their child(ren). Educate involves being effective by knowing and using a variety of effective teaching strategies, skills, techniques, and methods. It includes adapting these teaching tools to meet specific learners' needs.

The dimension of Educate recognizes that individual participants within each audience bring different knowledge, skills, expectations, and goals to the program. Participants do not exist in a vacuum; they bring with them a variety of psychosocial experiences and learning styles that influence their perception of learning as well as their ability to understand and utilize the content and skills taught (Hilgard, 1967; Galbraith, 1991). As an example, parent educators may be faced with a group of disinterested, court-mandated parents who are unwilling to listen to what an educator has to say. A skilled educator builds rapport through sensitive listening, engagement, and even humor to open the minds of the learners to gain new knowledge and learn skills through the educational program.

The category of *Embrace* posits that all parenting educators need to be knowledgeable about, and sensitive to, the specific populations with which they are working. Several researchers and authors (Cross, 1996; Weissbourd & Kagan, 1989; Myers-Walls, 2000) have outlined the importance of such sensitivity. Some skills are related to an understanding of specific cultural groups while recognizing that parents have differing parenting styles and values depending on their degree of acculturation or biculturalism (DeAnda, 1984; Wasserman, Rauh, Brunelli, Garcia-Castro, & Necos, 1990), their socioeconomic status, and their individual history and background.

Other approaches focus on understanding cultural characteristics that may vary in different ways across subcultures and over time (Myers-Walls, Myers-Bowman, & Dunn, 2003). Teaching should be customized to the learner for greatest effectiveness (Weissbourd & Kagan, 1989; Arcus, 1992, 1995; Cross, 1996; Myers-Walls, 2000). By the very nature of their work, parenting educators interact with diverse groups of parents and caregivers who differ in preferred communication and learning approaches, levels of literacy, sexual orientation, family composition, English language proficiency, access to basic resources, and many other dimensions (Doherty, 2000).

Involving parents in the design, governance, and delivery of parenting education programs has been found to improve program effectiveness, participant responsiveness, and cultural sensitivity of program materials and activities, resulting in greater family trust and empowerment, greater family enrollment and retention, and positive outcomes for children and families (Ahsan, 1999; Foster, 1999). In programs in which families are seen as partners with program staff in an atmosphere of mutual respect, the expertise of families is brought into the educational process, and program effectiveness is increased (Weissbourd & Kagan, 1989; Doherty, 2000). For example, if assigned to teach a group of Spanish-speaking families, educators are wise to engage a translator who can communicate family needs and then tailor the program to meet the needs of the parent learners.

The final category, *Build*, refers to the parenting education practice of being actively involved in building professional networks, being a community advocate and an advocate for parents and families, and connecting with organizations to expand the field of parenting education. Scholars have suggested that the professional success of the field will depend upon knowledgeable stakeholders coming together to share resources, to work collectively to overcome obstacles, and to meet the challenge of building a public agenda that strengthens parents and families (Schorr, 1987; Weiss, 1990).

While many networks are informal in nature, some studies have found that membership in professional associations or organizations provides critical linkages with others in the field working toward similar goals (Brown & Rhodes, 1991; Arcus & Thomas, 1993). Small and Eastman (1991) suggest that, when parenting educators understand how political, educational, legal, and medical systems operate, they can be more effective in selecting information to present to policy makers and others. Building networks and partnerships that support children, parents, and families at local and state levels and sometimes at a regional, national, or international level will ultimately build the field of parenting education.

The Total Framework

NEPEM, the companion piece that originally inspired subsequent expansion, offered the content piece contributing the areas of Care for Self, Understand, Guide, Nurture, Motivate, and Advocate. When used in tandem, the six *content* categories and the six *process* categories (Grow, Frame, Develop, Educate, Embrace, and Build) form a competency framework to provide guidance and structure for the preparation, training, and assessment of parenting educators.

NEPEF provides a way to organize, plan, and evaluate. This framework may be used to design and deliver professional development opportunities, to assist with self-assessment of professional progress, to guide curriculum development, and to build and refine certification programs. Figure 6.2 provides a visual representation of the framework and Table 6.1 provides an example of an application of the framework.

NEPEF has been used as a framework to plan graduate curriculum to prepare parenting educators. Some states have used NEPEF as a reference to frame their professional parent educator credentialing programs or professional development programs.

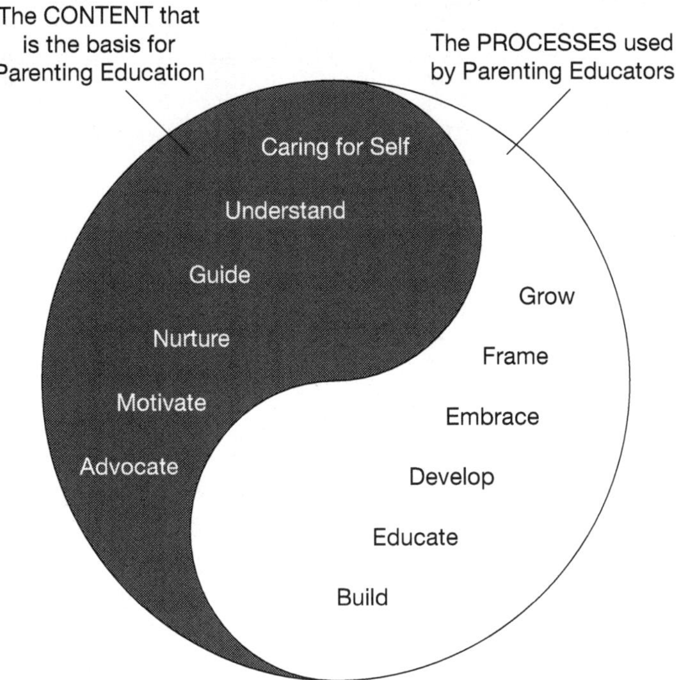

FIGURE 6.2 The National Extension Parenting Educators' Framework

Source: DeBord et al. (2006). Reprinted with permission of the Cooperative Extension System, U.S. Department of Agriculture.

Using the Framework

Imagine being given the task of planning a conference for parenting educators and others who support families. What content should be offered? Should it be whoever and whatever is readily available or should a more intentional approach be taken to plan as well as educate about the field of parenting education? One way to approach this would be to use NEPEF to frame the conference planning. Table 6.1 shows example topics associated with each dimension of the National Extension Parenting Educators' Framework.

Going further with the application seen in Table 6.1, leaders might give conference attendees certificates of completion based on the number of hours completed in the various competency areas. Further, professional portfolios are often based on completion of professional development. Using a framework like NEPEF that can summarize professional growth can bring an element of organization and professionalism to the field.

After NEPEF was introduced, the discussion continued to build among leaders in the field of parenting education. The field continues to modify and adapt the

TABLE 6.1 Application of National Extension Parenting Educators' Framework to Planning Professional Development

	Care for self	*Understand*	*Guide*	*Nurture*	*Motivate*	*Advocate*
Conference sessions offered (Content)	Managing personal stress	What to expect of teens	Teaching children to self-monitor	Reading together is more than literacy	Children and chores	Making referrals for families in need
	Grow	*Frame*	*Embrace*	*Develop*	*Educate*	*Build*
Conference sessions offered (Process)	Developing your personal portfolio	How Vygotsky explains children's thinking	Working with migrant families	Evaluation tips for those who hate evaluation	Teaching using Skype	Round table discussion: Designing a parenting educator credential

skills and competencies needed to be a parent educator. The National Council on Family Relations (NCFR) continues to monitor the field and support professional development; and the National Parenting Education Network (NPEN) continues to give leadership in the professional development arena, particularly with regard to parent educator credentials. Several states have developed professional associations to recognize personal and professional growth.

In 1997, the word "emerging" was used to describe the field of parenting education (DeBord et al., 1997). "Emerging" is descriptive yet today, as a common set of credentials, a common set of principles, and a common set of standards has yet to be agreed upon to guide the field. Most likely this is due to the diversity of professionals who comprise the field, each with their own lingo and values.

Since NEPEF

Being a parent educator and exhibiting good skills as outlined in NEPEF is critical. In recent years, the field of parenting education has moved in new directions making the qualifications of those who work with parents even more worthy of attention. There is a growing emphasis on accountability as publicly appropriated dollars have been used to support parenting education. To meet this accountability swell, new terms have been evolved including *best practices, promising practices, and evidence-based* programs. Many designers of parent education curriculum have diligently collected data about the effectiveness of their programs by conducting controlled studies on a quest to have their program marketed as "evidence-based". Once a program is labeled "evidence-based" there is a good chance that funders would include this on lists of approved programs for funded grants or contracts. A concern, however is that many times, evidence-based programs are not delivered in the way they were designed. If they are not implemented as recommended by the program designer, fidelity is not upheld and programs cannot claim the same results as when they were implemented in a controlled setting. Parenting educators must be prepared to follow trends, critically review and select curriculum, and make good decisions about how and what to teach.

Program evaluation is another area that is a concern for parent educators. Funders want to know that parenting education works and what form of parenting education reveals the best results. Several studies have guided how we evaluate parent education effectiveness. Parenting education is best evaluated by using a combination of quantitative and qualitative techniques (DeBord et al., 2002). Seeking to understand what aspects of educational programs change behaviors in parents, Kaminski, Valle, Filene, and Boyle (2008) conducted a meta-analysis of parenting programs. They found that changes in knowledge do not guarantee changes in behavior and that parents who are able to practice newly learned skills directly with their children improve in that skill. Others have reviewed the length of educational interventions and find that the intensity of the intervention matters. The more intense the interactions and the more often the parent educators are in contact with parents (3–4 times per week), the greater chance that parenting skills will improve. The length of the connection with parents is critical (referred to as duration), however intensity is said to be more important by some (Howing, Wodarski, Gaudin, & Kurtz.1989; Whipple & Wilson, 1996; Zepeda, Morales, & Varela, 2004). Again, understanding the process elements of Develop and Educate is critical to applying ever-evolving research to educational settings with parents.

More recent trends are to embrace a philosophy of partnering with parents whereby educators share power with families. This work falls under the process element of Build. Finding suitable ways to involve families and community members in planning, establishing policy, and making decisions is often a challenge (Henderson & Mapp, 2002; Hepburn, 2004), as is designing professional development ladders to recognize non-professionals' contributions in the larger scheme of family support.

Recent work by the National Parenting Education Network (Jones, Stranik, Hart, Wolf, & McClintic, 2013) proposes recognition of the value of peer educators and paraprofessionals through a credentialing model. As the field continues to grow and emerge, parenting education will become a highly sought commodity and the work of parenting educators will continue to be recognized as critical to raising children and supporting all families. The specific qualifications of those who work with parents and teach them skills to raise children to build relationships with them are worthy of continued discussion.

Conclusion

As the field continues to grow and emerge, parenting education will become a highly sought commodity and the work of parenting educators will continue to be recognized as critical to raising children and supporting families. The specific qualifications of those who work with parents and teach them skills to raise and build relationships with children are worthy of continued discussion. The Cooperative Extension Parent Framework advances a lucid and functional guide to professional practice in parenting education.

Key Points

1. The National Extension Parenting Education Model (NEPEM) is a framework to understand the critical content to be learned by parents and taught by parenting educators.
2. The National Extension Parenting Educator's Framework (NEPEF) includes the NEPEM content areas in addition to six process areas for parenting educators.
3. Qualifications to serve as a parenting educator are becoming more prevalent, but states vary how they approach credentialing processes.
4. NEPEF provides a way to organize, plan, and evaluate professional development activities for parenting educators.

Discussion Questions

1. What qualifies one to be a parenting educator?
2. Parenting education is embedded in many fields of practice and study. Which fields can you think of where parenting education is used? How could all of these fields agree on a common definition of quality parenting education programs?
3. How do you think that involving parents in the design of parenting education program would affect the program?
4. How does a framework (like NEPEF) guide the work of a professional educator or researcher?
5. Parent educators need to understand the content they are teaching as well as understand processes that help them design educational programs. Give three examples of content. Give three examples of processes.
6. What are the pros and cons of using evidence-based curriculum?
7. What is the best way to evaluate parenting education programs?
8. How much parenting education is enough? One hour as in a workshop? A series of classes over 12 weeks? More or less?

Additional Resources

Websites

National Extension Parent Education Model (NEPEM): www.ksu.edu/wwparent/nepem/
National Extension Parenting Educator's Framework (NEPEF): https://cyfernetsearch.org/sites/default/files/cyfar_research_docs/National%20Extension%20Parenting%20educators%20framework.pdf

References

Ahsan, N. (1999). Forging equal partnerships. Special focus: Parents are leaders. *America's Family Support Magazine, 18(1)*, 19–20.

Arcus, M. E. (1992). Family life education: Toward the 21st century. *Family Relations, 41*, 390–393.

Arcus, M., & Thomas, J. (1993). The nature and practice of family life education, in M. E. Arcus, J. Schvaneveldt, & J. Moss (Eds.) *Handbook of family life education: The practice of family life education* (Vol. 2, pp. 1–32). Newbury Park, CA: Sage.

Azar, S. T. (1989). Training parents of abused children, in C. E. Schaefer & J. M. Briesmeister (Eds.) *Handbook of parent training* (pp. 414–441). New York: Wiley.

Boone, E. (1985). *Developing programs in adult education.* Englewood, Cliffs, NJ: Prentice-Hall.

Brock, G., Oertwein, M., & Coufal, J. (1993). Parent education: Theory, research, and practice, in M. E. Arcus, J. Schvaneveldt, & J. Moss (Eds.), *Handbook of family life education: The practice of family life education* (Vol. 2, pp. 87–114). Newbury Park, CA: Sage.

Brown, M. (1998). *Recommended practices: Parent education and support.* Newark, DE: University of Delaware Extension.

Brown, W. & Rhodes, W. (1991). Factors that promote invulnerability and resiliency in at risk children, in W. Rhodes & W. Brown (Eds.) *Why some children succeed despite the odds* (pp. 171–177). New York: Praeger.

Campbell, D, & Palm, G. (2004). *Group parent education: Promoting parent learning and support.* Thousand Oaks, CA: Sage.

Carter, N., & Kahn, L. (1996). *See how we grow: A report on the status of parenting education in the U.S.* Philadelphia, PA: Pew Charitable Trusts.

Cataldo, C. (1987). *Parent education for early childhood: Child-rearing concepts and program content for the student and practicing professional.* New York: Teachers College Press.

Cross, T. (1996). Developing a knowledge base to support cultural competence. *Prevention Reports, 1*, 2–5.

CYFERnet (2014). National Extension Parenting Educators' Framework. https://cyfernetsearch.org/sites/default/files/cyfar_research_docs/National%20Extension%20Parenting%20educators%20framework.pdf

De Anda, D. (1984). Bicultural socialization: Factors affecting the minority experience. *Social Work, 29*, 101–107.

DeBord, K. (1996). A study of Euro-American, Hispanic, Native American, Asian and African American parents. *Forum for Family & Consumer Issues, 1(2)*. Retrieved from http://ncsu.edu/ffci/publications/1996/v1-n2–1996-spring/parent.php

DeBord, K. (1998). Planning, conducting, and evaluating parenting education programs. Retrieved from www.ces.ncsu.edu/depts/fcs/temp/parent_ed/pdfs/planning%20family%20programs.pdf

DeBord, K., Bower, D, Goddard, H., Kirby, J., Kobbe, A., Myers-Walls, J., Mulroy, M., & Ozretich, R., (2002). *The National Extension Parenting Educators' Framework*. Retrieved from www.ces.ncsu.edu/depts/fcs/NEPEF/NEPEF.pdf

DeBord, K., Bower, D., Goddard, H., Wilkins, J., Kobbe, A. Myers-Walls, J., Mulroy, M., & Ozretich, R. (2006). A professional guide for parenting educators: The National Extension Parenting Educators' Framework. *Journal of Extension, 44(3)*, Article No. 3FEA8. Retrieved from www.joe.org/joe/2006june/a8p.shtml

DeBord, K., Smith, C., Mulroy, M., Tanner, P., & Silliman, B. (1997, November). The emergence of the parenting profession, National Council for Family Relations annual conference, Arlington, VA.

Doherty, W. (2000). Family science and family citizenship: Toward a model of community partnership with families. *Family Relations, 49*, 319–325.

Fenichel, E. (Ed.) (1992). *Learning through supervision and mentorship to support the development of infants, toddlers, and their families: A sourcebook*. Arlington, VA: Zero to Three/National Center for Clinical Infant Programs.

Foster, R. (1999). Who best represents the voice of parents? Special focus: Parents are leaders. *America's Family Support Magazine, 18(1)*, 19–20.

Galbraith, M. (1991). Adult learning methods and techniques, in M. Galbraith (Ed.) *Facilitating adult learning: A transactional process* (pp. 103–134). Malabar, FL: Krieger.

Galinsky, E. (1987). *The six stages of parenthood*. Reading, MA: Addison-Wesley.

Grotberg, E. (1977). *200 years of children*. DHEW Publication No. (OHD) 77–30103. Washington, DC: U.S. Department of Health, Education, and Welfare.

Hamner, T., & Turner, P. (2001). *Parenting in contemporary society* (4th ed.). Boston, MA: Allyn and Bacon.

Henderson, A., & Mapp, K. (2002). *A new wave of evidence: The impact of school, family, and community connections on student achievement*. Austin, TX: Southwest Educational Development Laboratory.

Hepburn, K. S. (2004). *Families as primary partners in their child's development & school readiness*. The Annie E. Casey Foundation. Retrieved from www.aecf.org

Hilgard, E. (1967). *A basic reference shelf on learning theory*. Stanford, CA: Clearinghouse on Educational Media and Technology.

Howing, P., Wodarski, J., Gaudin, J., & Kurtz, P. (1989). Effective interventions to ameliorate the incidence of child maltreatment: The empirical base. *Social Work, 34*, 330–338.

Jacobs, F. (1988). A five-tiered approach to evaluation: Context and implementation, in H. Weiss & F. Jacobs (Eds.) *Evaluating family programs* (pp. 37–68). New York: Aldine de Gruyter.

Jones, S., Stranik, M., Hart, M. Wolf, J., & McClintic, S. (2013). National Parenting Education Network. Retrieved from http://npen.org/wp-content/uploads/2012/03/diverse-roles-in-PE-white-paper_-12_17_13.pdf

Kaminski, J., Valle, A., Filene, J., & Boyle, C. (2008). A meta-analytic review of components associated with parent training program effectiveness, *Journal of Abnormal Child Psychology, 36*, 567–589.

Katz, L. (1977). The nature of professions: Where is early childhood education? *Montessori Life, 5(2)*, 31–35.

Kumpfer, K., & Alvarado, R. (1998). *Effective family strengthening interventions*. Washington, DC: US Department of Justice (Office of Juvenile Justice and Delinquency Prevention), Bulletin # NCJ171121.

Matthews, J., & Hudson, A. (2001). Guidelines for evaluating parent training programs. *Family Relations, 50*, 77–86.

Medway, F. (1989). Measuring the effectiveness of parent education, in M. Fine (Ed.) *The second handbook on parent education: Contemporary perspectives* (pp. 237–255). New York: Academic Press.

Myers-Walls, J. (2000). Family diversity and family life education, in D. H. Demo, K. R. Allen, & M. A. Fine (Eds.) *Handbook of family diversity* (pp. 359–379). Oxford, UK: Oxford University Press.

Myers-Walls, J., & Myers-Bowman, K. (1999). Sorting through parenting education materials: A values approach and the example of socially conscious parenting. *Family Science Review, 12*, 69–86.

Myers-Walls, J., Myers-Bowman, K., & Dunn, J. (2003). Cultural characteristics questionnaire: What does your target population look like?, in D. Bredehoft & M. Walcheski (Eds.). *Family life education: Integrating theory and practice.* Minneapolis, MN: National Council on Family Relations.

Powell, L., & Cassidy, D. (2001). *Family life education: An introduction.* Mountain View, CA: Mayfield.

Rockwell, K. & Bennett, C. (2000). *Targeting Outcomes of Programs (TOP)*. Retrieved from http://citnews.unl.edu/TOP/english/

Rothenberg, B. (1992). *Parentmaking educators training programs: A comprehensive skills development course to train early childhood parent educators.* Menlo Park, CA: Banster.

Schorr, L. (1987). Early interventions to reduce intergenerational disadvantage: The new policy context. *Teachers College Record, 90(3)*, 362–374.

Schorr, L. (1989). Early interventions to reduce intergenerational disadvantage: The new policy context. *Teachers College Record*, 362–374.

Small, S., & Eastman, G. (1991). Rearing adolescents in contemporary society: A conceptual framework for understanding the responsibilities and needs of parents. *Family Relations, 40*, 455–462.

Smith, C., Cudaback, D., Goddard, H., & Myers-Walls, J. (1994). *National Extension Parent Education Model of Critical Parenting Practices.* Manhattan, KS: Kansas Cooperative Extension Service. Retrieved from www.ksu.edu/wwparent/nepem/

Thomas, R. (1992). *Comparing theories of child development.* Belmont, CA: Wadsworth.

Wasserman, G., Rauh, V., Brunelli, S., Garcia-Castro, M., & Necos, B. (1990). Psychosocial attributes and life experiences of disadvantaged minority mothers: Age and ethnic variations. *Child Development, 61*, 566–580.

Weiss, H. (1990). Beyond parens patriae: Building policies and programs to care for our own and others' children. *Children and Youth Services Review, 12*, 269–284.

Weissbourd, B., & Kagan, S. L. (1989). Family support programs: Catalysts for change. *American Journal of Orthopsychiatry, 59*, 20–31.

Whipple, E. E., & Wilson, S. R. (1996). Evaluation of a parent education program for families at risk for child abuse. *Families in Society, 77(4)*, 227–239.

Zepeda, M., Morales, F., & Verela, A. (2004). *Promoting positive parenting practices through parenting education.* National Center for Infant and Early Childhood Health Policy. Retrieved from www.healthychild.ucla.edu/NationalCenter/bb.brief.no13.pdf

PART II

Parenting Education

A Global Perspective

7

EVIDENCE-BASED PARENT EDUCATION PROGRAMS

A European Perspective

María José Rodrigo, Ana Almeida, & Barbara Reichle

Learning Goals

1. Learn more about European family and parenting policies and their impact on family lives.
2. Reflect on the modern view of parenting in our societies.
3. Know more about the best ways to parent children and their impact on child development.
4. Discover different forms of parental support in Europe.
5. Know what is meant by evidence-based parent education programs.
6. Identify parent education programs currently implemented in Europe.
7. Recognize the benefits of incorporating parent education programs to the family services.
8. Reflect on the changing role of professionals and their training needs.

Introduction

On January 1, 2013, the population of the European Union (EU), involving 28 countries, was estimated at 505.7 million. There is a rich cultural diversity (e.g., 24 official languages), increased by the presence of immigrants from many other regions (e.g., North Africa, eastern Europe, and Latin America). Although historically the most important objective of the EU was the establishment of a common market (e.g., Treaty of Maastricht, 1993), subsequent treaties (e.g., Treaty of Lisbon, 2009) have broadened the scope, including the promotion of peace and the well-being of the Union's citizens and the endorsement of important values such as the respect for human dignity, liberty, and democracy. However, despite these common goals and values, diversity is still the rule when it comes to the particular lives of ordinary citizens. The reason is that there are significant cross-national differences between EU members in their legal systems, welfare structures, education institutions, health and social services systems, and economic and financial systems. European family forms and functions as well as family policy trends are also quite diverse, and so are the living conditions of the families.

The main objective of this chapter is to present a contemporary view of parenting in Europe, including policies, support initiatives, and parent education programs that may have an impact on the well-being of the child and the family. This broader view is necessary to properly understand the political, social, and practical context in which evidence-based parent education programs are delivered. More specifically, contents focus on two related topics: how parenting is collectively envisioned, and the way parenting support is conceived and put into practice. These topics are related because the modern conceptualization of parenting has brought about recent developments in parenting support in Europe, with the use of evidence-based parent education programs being the flagship of these initiatives.

The chapter commences with an overview of European family and parenting policies. Although they are still far from following a unitary schema, there is an increasing interconnectedness of European states at a governmental and legislative level through the adoption of common rules and recommendations. Underlying these efforts is the increasing recognition that parents play a central role in promoting healthy child development, because they are a key source of early diagnosis and primary care for young children and the most important protective factor against high-risk behaviors in adolescents, such as substance use, early or unhealthy sexual involvement, and delinquent behavior (e.g., Kumpfer & Alvarado, 2003; O'Connor & Scott, 2006). As a consequence, there is broad consensus that parenting should be included under the umbrella of public policies.

The chapter continues by addressing how parenting is collectively conceived in Europe within the framework of positive parenting policy. Traditionally, competent parenting was taken for granted except in problem cases in which parents failed to behave properly. By contrast, in the modern view, parenting is a task that requires a set of aptitudes and skills that can be learned (Reder, Duncan, & Lucey, 2003; Budd, 2005). It is also recognized that the quality of parenting depends not only on the psychological qualities of the parents, but also on the ecological conditions (e.g., informal and formal support and community resources) that surround the family.

Parental capacities and resources involved in responsible parenting are promoted through public support in Europe. Parenting support is different from other types of family policies (e.g., work–family reconciliation measures, income support, and social welfare measures) and other family/child services (e.g., child care services and mainstream child health services). There are three core features: (a) parents and their parenting role is the first-line target; (b) the support provided is a service in kind; and (c) the focus is on parents' resources and childrearing competencies define parenting support services (Daly, 2014). The chapter illustrates the different ways in which European countries provide and deliver services to the families.

The provision of evidence-based parent education programs singularizes a principal type of parental support in Europe. Parenting education consists of structured programs aimed at strengthening parents' abilities and skills to promote an adequate climate of family relationships that enhance well-being. It is acknowledged that services are needed to demonstrate the effectiveness of parenting education; therefore some evidence-based programs are briefly illustrated. Finally, an overview of the achievements and limitations of European policies and parenting support and parent education programs in Europe is presented.

It is important to note that the chapter is limited in its ability to provide a complete overview of the parent support services and education programs available in the European countries. The little cross-national research that has been done does not allow for a sound comparison, and even less for a systematic account of effective programs. With this limitation in mind, an inclusive approach based on the reviews of the available scientific literature and reports delivered by European institutions and stakeholders (e.g., European Commission, Council of Europe, Eurochild, Eurofound) is offered. The aim is to promote the readers' learning about initiatives of parenting support services, and parenting programs relevant for illustrating the progress that is being achieved in Europe.

Family and Parenting Support Policies in Europe

Traditionally, family policies in the EU were a part of wider policies including employment, social protection, housing, education, and health policies. The role of a welfare state in relation to families was mostly to protect the social position of particular "at-risk" groups in a reactive and remedial way. Since the 1990s, many family-related issues have been on the European agenda, although family policy is not an explicit area of competence of the EU but is relegated to Member States. The list of issues includes gender equality, immigration, and the free movement of populations, social protection, reconciliation of work and family life, intergenerational solidarity, lifelong learning, and the expansion of day-care systems for children. In addition, the "Europe 2020" strategy called for a reduction in early school-leaving to increase students' opportunities for a productive life, the decline of social inequalities, and decreasing poverty and social exclusion in the EU.

Nevertheless, it took time for the European governments and international organizations to set the stage for a parenting support policy. Several factors may explain this shift from family policy being part of a wider set of employment-related polices to a parenting support policy in Europe (Hermanns, 2014). First, the recognition that children's rights, articulated in the United Nations Convention on the Rights of the Child signed in 1989, are better preserved and enhanced in appropriate family contexts has put the need for parenting support at the forefront of the policies directed to promote children's well-being. Second, there has been a change in the objectives of welfare states in Europe from a passive and compensating state to an active and empowered state with an acknowledgment of citizens' capabilities and the need for them to rely upon their own resources. Third, the emphasis on family policy has shifted from corrective measures toward more preventive initiatives. Early intervention and prevention are essential for developing more effective and efficient policies, as the public expenses needed to address the consequences of child poverty and social exclusion tend to be greater than what is needed to intervene at an early age. Finally, the modernization of parenthood itself was an impetus for developments in parenting support. We are living in a time in which Europe has a great diversity of family models and cultural backgrounds; therefore, the traditional ways of parenting are no longer valid models to be followed as a matter of custom. Those deciding to have children want to do it well and may seek support. This change in the motivation of parents is one of the important factors driving the development of parenting support policies in Europe.

The national and local policies of parenting support are very much influenced by the general policies marked at the cross-national European level; therefore, it is worthwhile to pay attention to them. The recent EU European Commission recommendation (European Commission, 2013) addresses child poverty and social exclusion as a key issue within the Europe 2020 Strategy. This is an important development especially given the severe negative impact of the current economic crisis on children and their families, and the budget cuts that have put the preventive and support services under threat. There are two issues in the recommendation that are especially relevant for a parenting support policy. The first issue enhances the importance of family support and the quality of alternative care settings by strengthening child protection and social services in the field of prevention. It also mentions the need to help families develop parenting skills and the promotion of family preservation services to prevent the unnecessary displacement of children from their homes. The second issue strengthens the use of evidence-based approaches by promoting evidence-based policy development and social policy innovation. This includes the following measures among others: (a) making full use of existing statistics and administrative data to monitor the impact of policies on children and their families; (b) encouraging the evidence-based evaluation of program outcomes targeted toward parents and children and the sharing of results; and (c) promoting the exchange of good practice and knowledge, the testing of intervention models, and taking measures to foster solidarity in the wider community and to empower local communities to work together.

The Positive Parenting Initiative in Europe

The Council of Europe's recommendations for providing guidance on how governments can support positive parenting are also an important policy development for parenting support in Europe. As a major intergovernmental organization that currently includes 47 Member States, the Council of Europe has a long record on family matters. It has been focusing on parenting since the 1970s and on the quality of family life since the 1980s. The Council of Europe launched its recommendation on the *Policy to Support Positive Parenting* (Council of Europe, 2006), which is of major importance for family and social policy. Positive parenting is defined as: "parental behavior based on the best interest of the child that is nurturing, empowering, nonviolent and provides recognition and guidance which involves setting of boundaries to enable the full development of the child". The concept involves a view of children as active subjects of their own lives who contribute to shaping their own development (Daly, 2007). The role of parents is to facilitate the child to exercise his or her rights, by providing direction and guidance appropriate to the child's developmental needs and evolving capacities. There must be a perfect match between the key aspects of parenting and the fulfillment of the child's needs in order to obtain positive child outcomes (see Table 7.1).

Within this view, more research is needed to identify the parental capacities required to establish the scenario of parent–child collaboration during the socialization process beyond those required to control the child's behavior (Reder, Duncan, & Lucey, 2003; Budd, 2005; Rodrigo, 2010). These capacities might include: observing the child's characteristics and the situational constraints on actions; paying attention to and recognition of the child's new achievements and points of view; designing appropriate leisure activities with children and family members; promoting mid- to long-term educational goals (e.g., pro-social and collaborative behavior, self-direction, and autonomy) instead of short-term goals based on immediate child compliance; and promoting parental reflections on the consequences of their educational practices on child and family outcomes. In sum, the enjoyment of the parental role is associated with parents' sense of competence and personal fulfillment, which are experienced as a result of a positive atmosphere of parent–child relationships and a healthy and successful development of their children.

The emergence of parenting support policies in Europe has been accompanied by the recognition that all parents need informal and formal support to perform the task of parenting (Daly, 2007; Rodrigo, 2010). Support networks can be informal, such as family members, friends, a group of parents on a playground, or neighbors. They can also be more formal, such as school and community associations, networks through one's job, and relationships with professionals (e.g., teachers, healthcare providers, and community workers). Member states are encouraged to support parents in their upbringing tasks through adequate family

TABLE 7.1 Key Aspects of Positive Parenting, the Child's Needs, and Child Outcomes (Rodrigo, Byrne, & Rodríguez, 2014)

Positive parenting	*Child's needs*	*Child outcomes*
Nurturing: Showing positive feelings of love, acceptance, and joy to the child	Healthy and protective parent–child bonds	Security, confidence, and sense of belonging
Structuring: Creating an environment with well-established routines and habits	Clear and flexible limits and supervision	Internalization of norms and values and a capacity to negotiate
Stimulation: Providing guided support to the children's informal and formal learning	Opportunities to participate with adults in learning activities	Promotion of cognitive, emotional, and social competences
Recognition: Showing interest in their world and taking into account their ideas for decision making in the family	Be acknowledged and have his or her personal experience responded to and confirmed by parents	Self-concept, self-esteem, and sense of mutual respect in the family
Empowerment: Displaying the parental capacity to grow in a relationship as children develop	Enhance their strengths and sense of capacity as active agents who can change the world around them	Self-regulation, autonomy, and a capacity to cooperate with others
Free from violence: excluding any form of verbal and physical violence against children	Preserve their rights and dignity as human beings	A respect for themselves and self-protection against violent relationships with others

Source: Rodrigo, M. et al. (2014). Parenting styles and child well-being (ch. 86, fig. 86.3), with kind permission from Springer Science and Business Media.

policy measures that provide the necessary material conditions for families and the services needed to support parents, especially those parents and children facing adverse circumstances (Rodrigo, Byrne, & Álvarez, 2012).

Concerning services, the Council of Europe's recommendation specifically proposes that psycho-educational resources such as parenting programs should be made available to all parents. Communities should also be empowered because families are heavily dependent on the quality of their neighborhoods and the existence of cohesive and well-resourced environments to satisfy their many needs.

Finally, the recommendation also emphasizes the best ways to deliver parental support in a nonstigmatizing and respectful way, especially for the most vulnerable families.

Scope of Parenting Support in Europe

Under the impetus provided by the new policies on positive parenting, the services and resources specifically addressing parents' needs in bringing up children have undergone a rapid expansion and impressive changes across and within the European countries. The variety of definitions and formulations of parenting support that can be found is summarized in Daly's definition (2014): "Parenting support refers to a range of information, support, education, training, counseling and other measures or services that focus on influencing how parents understand and carry out their parenting role" (p. 17). Complementarily, another definition refers to the promotion of child outcomes (Moran, Ghate, & van der Merve, 2004): "Parenting support includes any intervention for parents and caregivers aimed at reducing risks and/or promoting protective factors for their children, in relation to their social, physical and emotional well-being" (p. 21).

The extent and prominence of support for parents across European countries mirror "the model and history of social policy, the prevailing philosophy and approach to child welfare and family well-being, the traditions of service organizations, the amount of funding available, where the demand comes from (family networks or parent associations, NGOs' commissioners and practitioners, government and other public authority) and the degree of importance attributed to interventionist as against preventive policies" (Daly, 2014, p. 19). Each of these influential factors accounts for the commonalities as well as for the distinctive aspects of parenting support across the European countries that shape the resources made available for supporting parents and parenting. In Table 7.2, some of the common and distinctive aspects of support are grouped to provide a more comprehensive view of the underlying dimensions involved.

TABLE 7.2 Trends in Parenting Support Initiatives in Europe

Common features	*Distinctive features*
Variety of sources of support	Drivers for parenting support
Multi-level responsibility of support delivery	Universal services
Multi-agency coordination and integrative working	Targeted services to vulnerable families
Focus on prevention and strengthening	Professional development

The variety of sources of support used as one of the commonalities found across European countries is highlighted. The provision of parenting support encompasses a wide range of services and resources that can be grouped into three main forms: (a) general information made available to parents through written material, telephone helplines, e-parenting, and face-to-face contact such as a seminar series on positive parenting; (b) one-on-one advisory or coaching sessions, especially in relation to health and/or behavior management; and (c) workshops in the form of training or education programs that are highly structured and delivered mainly through group psychosocial interventions (ChildONEurope Secretariat, 2007; Daly, 2014).

A common schema was also identified in the way the parenting support is delivered through many levels of responsibility in Europe (Molinuevo, 2013). The development of parental support policies is generally the responsibility of the national/federal government. The central authorities (e.g., ministries dealing with child protection, families, or social inclusion issues) are responsible for the legislative framework and regulations, the drafting of national action plans, and financial support. In turn, the implementation of the programs through the provision of parenting support activities is, in most cases, a responsibility of the public regional and local/municipal agencies and private and volunteer sector organizations, with different degrees of coordination and funding.

Another common feature is that multi-agency coordination and multi-disciplinary integrative working is recognized as an important feature of service provision across countries. It is still a far-reaching goal for some countries with less tradition in family and parenting policies. However, European countries are devoting increased attention to the introduction of a family support dimension to the provision of health, education, and social services. The universality and gratuity of health services and social services is a clear asset in many countries. The services are usually provided by a variety of professionals including, not only social educators, psychologists, social workers, lawyers, and family mediators, but also health professionals such as maternity and public health nurses and doctors.

Finally, there is a shared concern about providing services with a preventive focus that is based on empowering parents and families in the context of family–services partnerships. In this regard support is intended to be provided in nonjudgmental, nonstigmatizing, participatory, inclusive, needs-led ways that require that parents be placed at the very center of the services (Fukkink, Vink, & Bosscher, 2014).

Concerning some distinctive features of the provision of support across Europe, we will now highlight some remarkable differences in the way support is delivered, providing some prototypical examples of countries (for reviews, see Moran et al., 2004; Boddy et al., 2009; Crepaldi et al., 2011; Rodrigo, Almeida, Spiel, & Koops, 2012; Molinuevo, 2013). First, the drivers for parental support differ across the European countries. For instance, in France, the organization of parenting support comes from the ground or bottom-up (mainly from the parents themselves) because provision has strong roots in activism on the part of parents and NGOs. One of the most significant initiatives is a national infrastructure of networks of parents "REAAPs" (Parental Consultation, Care, and Social Support Networks), which are regional organizations that focus on general support to parents and also on parents' difficulties in protecting the child. Other countries that represent a top-down provision system (in the sense of being led by the central government) are England, Ireland, the Netherlands, Belgium, and Germany. These countries have a high standardization of services, programs, and professional practices (e.g., English Children's Centres, Flemish Parenting Shops, the Netherland Centers for Youth and Family, the German Home Visiting program for young infants, the Northern Ireland Family Support Hubs). A halfway approach is found in Estonia, with local authorities assuming responsibility for the delivery of services through NGOs. At this level, funding has been a critical issue both for the regularity and quality of service provision, especially for NGOs that work on a project basis that faces many uncertainties.

A second distinctive feature is the universalization of parenting support services and resources, typical of the Nordic European countries and England. For example, Denmark has an extensive net of resources for parenting support embedded in universal services such as early child care and education, schools, and health services with professionalized workforces (European Alliance for Families, 2013). Sweden's 2009 National Strategy for Parental Support has the main objective of reducing mental health problems among children, and it includes measures for improving cooperation between parents and institutions, increasing health promotion activities, providing more meeting places, and training its staff to deal with parents. In England the provision system is also intended to tackle a multiplicity of issues, with an impact on parenting such as the promotion of health, early intervention through education, the improvement of parent–child relations, and the intensification of intervention projects for families involved in antisocial behavior, and for families of children at risk or likely to become so (Molinuevo, 2013; Daly, 2014). The provision of parenting support involves an extensive range of services and resources, combining counseling and individual interventions, home visits, and group work with parents into a framework of "progressive universalism", defined as support for all, with more support for those who need it most (Boddy et al., 2009).

As a third distinctive feature, in other countries support for parents has been developed mainly with the aim of preventing child maltreatment in vulnerable families by providing assistance for improving living conditions and enhancing parents' skills (e.g., Italy, Portugal, Spain, Poland, Bulgaria, Hungary, Lithuania, Latvia). Progressively, the services' exclusive focus on child protection/child safety issues has changed to include general concerns about parenting issues and family well-being. Thus, there is a trend to create family guidance centers located in public health services to provide education and support services to enhance parent–child relations (Molinuevo, 2013). Support is also provided in family preservation services located in basic and specialized municipal social services to avoid unnecessarily displacing at-risk children to institutionalized care. Targeting and accessibility issues continue to be objects of concern for those countries in which statutory services in charge of at-risk family referrals still stress a deficit-focused approach to parenting support. To deal with this problem, Spain is especially committed to providing support to vulnerable families in the context of community-based interventions involving at-risk and not-at-risk parents, and with more of a focus on prevention and strengthening. To this aim, a partnership schema was created with the Spanish Ministry of Health, Social Services and Equality, the Spanish Federation of Provinces and Municipalities, several NGOs, and a consortium of Spanish universities to design a new model of professional training and family intervention based on the use of evidence-based parent education programs, according to the European policy of positive parenting (Rodrigo et al., 2012).

Finally, some countries have successfully developed professional training in parenting support, but this is not a general trend (Crepaldi et al., 2011). The prevention and strengthening approach requires new job qualifications basically informed by the set of competencies that are necessary for the professional work with families. As an exception, in Austria, parent support practitioners are required to undergo an extensive training program that is focused on parenting education. Likewise, in England, the National Academy for Parenting Practitioners (NAPP) was created to design, commission, and offer a rolling program of training and support for parenting practitioners. One important emphasis is the need for sound evaluations of services and programs because this is an essential element for reflecting and qualifying the role of family practitioners (Asmussen, 2011). In this regard, Portugal has undertaken a nationwide study aimed at identifying a variety of ongoing family interventions targeting at-risk families and evaluating them using the same protocol to assess their impact on several parental and outcome measures. The results of this study, which involved a network of universities and practitioners who were running the programs, are necessary for policy makers in the regulation of parent education programs as the best practices to support child protection in that country (Almeida et al., 2012).

Evidence-based Parenting Programs in Europe

Asmussen (2011) referred to evidence-based methods as those that "have been proven, beyond anecdote or chance, to make a positive difference in the lives of parents and children" (pp. xvi–xvii). This evidence includes the results from rigorously conducted studies that verify the extent to which parenting interventions are beneficial and provide value for money, thus allowing well-informed decisions to be made about policies and programs. To further clarify what is meant by "evidence", international standards of evidence that have been widely adopted by the scientific community have been proposed to establish quality levels for the evaluation of a program, placing the use of randomized controlled trials (RCTs) at the highest level (e.g., American Psychological Association, Presidential Task Force on Evidence-based Practice, 2006; Society for Prevention Research, Flay et al., 2005; see Chapters 4 and 5, this volume). Other researchers and practitioners propose that there should be a broader definition of the term "strong evidence base", which is not exclusively the domain of RCTs (Boddy, Smith, & Statham, 2011; Eurochild, 2013). There should be a consideration of other standards of evidence that can embrace a holistic multi-agency delivery of practice in community settings, including prevention and strength-based approaches. For instance, equally important achievements that deserve attention consist of the level of effectiveness of the program in getting communities and practitioners to want the program; modifying the program to make it acceptable to a wide range of socioeconomic groups in order to achieve higher retention rates in poor communities; ensuring that the program is implemented with fidelity by agencies and staff; and assuring its sustainability by integrating the program into the network of community resources (McCall, 2009; Davis, McDonald, & Axford, 2012; Rodrigo et al., 2012).

The European policy places a strong emphasis on the "evidence base" as an underlying principle for the investment and transferability of good practice, which is particularly relevant for services providing family and parenting support. The need to establish a unified European system of evidence-based practices, or at least to share outcomes of the evaluation of different databases and systems, has been stressed to facilitate the exchange of the best practices across the European countries (Eurochild, 2013). Table 7.3 presents a summary of some initiatives of evidence-based systems operating in Europe managed by different organizations with more or less coverage and proposing quality levels and/or dimensions to evaluate programs (for more details, see the web-page links at the end of this chapter).

Parent education programs are generally meant to help parents develop and enhance their parenting skills by trying alternate approaches to childrearing, improving the family learning environment, fostering their sense of personal competence, and strengthening their capability to draw upon available resources for their own well-being and the well-being of their young and adolescent children. In the following, in the absence of previous systematic reviews of scientific journals articles, we will report the results of a search carried out *ad hoc* by the authors and aimed at identifying evidence-based parenting programs implemented in the European countries. We focused on structured evidence-based parenting programs with the prevention- and strength-based approach whose evaluations were reported in journals in the PsycInfo database from 1980 to 2014. The results showed that there is a general trend in Europe to adopt international programs (USA, Canada, and Australia) that have been successfully evaluated according to evidence-based standards: *FAST—Families and Schools Together* (McDonald & Sayger, 1998; McDonald et al., 2012); *Incredible Years* (Webster-Stratton, 1999;

TABLE 7.3 Initiatives of Evidence-based Systems in Europe

Source	*Organization/coverage*	*Levels/dimensions*
European Platform for Investing in Children (EPIC)	European Commission DG Employment, Social Affairs, and Equal Opportunities (EU), and operated by Rand Europe/EU	– Emergent practice – Promising practice – Best practice
Blueprints in Europe	Social Research Unit at Dartington in the UK and University of Colorado, USA/EU	– Evaluation quality – Intervention impact – Intervention specificity – System readiness
Parenting Programme Evaluation Tool (PPET)	National Academy for Parenting Practitioners (NAPP), Department for Education, UK/UK	– Specificity of the target population – Contents – Implementation systems – Evaluation evidence
System for Assessment, Accreditation, and Publication of Youth Interventions	Netherlands Youth Institute/Netherlands	– Potential intervention – Plausible intervention – Functional intervention – Efficacious intervention

Jones, Daley, Hutchings, Bywater, & Eames, 2008); *Pathways to Competence* (Landy, 2002; Skreitule-Pikse, Sebre, & Lubenko, 2010); *Strengthening Families Program* (Kumpfer, Molgaard, & Spoth, 1996; Kumpfer, Magalhães, & Xi, 2012); and *Triple P* (Sanders, 1999; Nowak & Heinrichs, 2008).

The results of the search helped identify national programs of European origin that have undergone rigorous evaluations: (a) *Personal and Family Support* (Apoyo Personal y Familiar, Spain) develops inductive parenting, maternal self-efficacy, internal control, and reduces maternal role problems, nurturist and nativist beliefs, and neglect-permissive and coercive practices in at-risk parents to prevent child maltreatment (Rodrigo, Máiquez, Correa, Martín, & Rodríguez, 2006; Salmela-Aro, Read, & Rodrigo, 2013); (b) *Parent Start–Beginnings Matter (Elternstart–Auf den Anfang kommt es an*, Germany), a second version of a universal primary prevention program for expecting and new parents during the first year of their newborn child's life, develops parents' knowledge about early child development, parental emotion control in stressful situations, security in interactions with the child, and prevents the usual postpartum decrease in marital satisfaction (Reichle, Backes, & Dette-Hagenmeyer, 2012); (c) *Empowering Parents, Empowering Communities* (EPEC, United Kingdom) is a community-based program, training local parents to run parenting groups to develop positive parenting and prevent social behavior problems in children on a secondary prevention level (Day, Michelson, Thomson, Penney, & Draper, 2012); (d) *International Child Development Programme* (ICP, Norway) develops positive attitudes toward child management, child management, and parental strategies, and decreases child difficulties in preschool children on a primary or secondary prevention level (Sherr, Skar, Clucas, von Tetzchner, & Hundeide, 2014); *Keiner faellt durchs Netz* (KFDN; Nobody slips through the net, Germany) develops positive interactions between mothers and newborn children during the child's first year of life, prevents an increase in depression in mothers of newborns, and prevents mothers' perception of their child as difficult on a secondary level of prevention (Sidor, Kunz, Eickhorst, & Cierpka, 2013); (f) *Preparedness for Childbirth and Positive Motherhood in Fear of Childbirth for Women* (LINNEA, Finland) develops positive parenting via preparedness for childbirth in nulliparous pregnant women with an intense fear of childbirth in psycho-educational group sessions during pregnancy and after childbirth (Salmela-Aro, 2012; Salmela-Aro et al., 2012); (g) *Supporting Parents on Kids' Education* (SPOKES, United Kingdom) combines behavioral (Incredible Years group parenting program) and literacy training to train parents to support their children's reading at home, develops children's word reading and writing skills and parents' use of reading strategies with their children (Sylva, Scott, Totsika, Ereky-Stevens, & Crook, 2008); (h) *Video-feedback Intervention to Promote Positive Parenting and Sensitive Discipline* (VIPP-SD, the Netherlands), develops sensitivity and attachment to parents of young children who were identified as being at risk for developing externalizing behavior problems, making the parents more responsive to the needs of the child and more consistent in their parenting (Bakermans-Kranenburg, van IJzendoorn, & Juffer, 2003; Juffer, Bakermans-Kranenburg, & van IJzendoorn, 2008). More systematic scientific research is needed to fully identify evidence-based parenting programs implemented in the European countries and to examine their relative impact on a variety of outcomes, also relying on non-English sources.

Conclusion

The goal of this chapter was to bring attention to the development of European family and parenting policies and how they shape the well-being of the child and family. The motivation for taking such a broad scope was that European family policies offer an interesting viewpoint from which to envision the task of parenting as it is collectively conceived nowadays. After many years of neglecting their importance, parents are considered to play a key role in society, and it is recognized that the task of parenting needs public support, according to the Council of Europe's (2006) initiative on positive parenting. The European family policy is also an interesting resource by which to identify a variety of programs and interventions on parenting support currently carried out by the European countries at national, regional, and local levels. The array of initiatives and approaches that support parents is impressive and demonstrates a huge potential to develop innovative practice in prevention and intervention and to improve outcomes for children and families, especially for the most vulnerable.

A closer view of the initiatives for parental support across the European countries reveals the great diversity of political, cultural, and social traditions. There is an intrinsic richness in the diversity of families and socioeconomic and cultural differences. But there is also a potential danger underlying this plurality as it may hide economic and social inequalities between countries. Such inequalities may hinder the supportive network that families offer for parenting children and may limit the life chances of family members. A lesson to be drawn is that European policies clearly make a difference, but their success depends on how they are put into practice in the different countries. In this chapter, we have seen many instances of how public support is conceived and delivered to the families. In the dialectic tension between universal and targeted services, we have noticed that the former are more likely to be found in countries with greater resources and/or with a large tradition in family services because universality is costly. By contrast, an exclusive reliance on targeted services is more frequently found in countries with more economic restrictions and/or less of a tradition of family support, because scarce resources tend to be used more intensively to remedy problems. There is a need to study appropriate solutions for enhancing the involvement of vulnerable groups while at the same time avoiding the risks of stigmatization and the lack of social integration of at-risk families. Accordingly, "progressive universalism"—support for all, with more support for those who need it most—seems to be the most suitable way of intervening. A further way to "normalize" the use of parental support for all families is to open up the group parenting programs not only to the target population but also to a broader group of families in the neighborhood, helping to build informal networks and to promote social inclusion and community partnerships.

Concerning evidence-based policy, there is a potential transfer of "know-how" knowledge across the European countries that could be facilitated by promoting more comparative research to identify programs that work in different countries. In this regard, the dissemination of results to the researchers, practitioners, policy makers, stakeholders, and the general public is absolutely crucial, as shown by the initiatives to develop European evidence-based systems. This information could be very useful for informing social actions and social policies. As the evidence-based movement advances in the family domain across countries, broader quality standards and design criteria for implementation, sustainability, and cost factors should be included.

The incorporation of evidence-based parent education programs into local family services, especially those involving groups of parents, has several advantages. First, it contributes to changing the focus of intervention from the therapeutic–clinical sphere, characterized by an exclusive individual approach to support families, to the psychosocial–educational sphere, with an emphasis on prevention and on strengthening the capacities of families and developing communities. Second, the implementation of these programs improves the skills of professionals, as they should learn how to integrate the program into their casework with families as well as how to run group interventions. Finally, the quality of the services themselves is improved because programs are evaluated according to standards of quality assurance, achieving a better coordination of the services and resources in the community.

In spite of the benefits, international and national evidence-based parenting programs are implemented in Europe with different levels of intensity and quality depending on the political, economic, and social conditions of the countries. Some countries embrace and promote the development of evidence-based programs, whereas others have little knowledge or resources that can be used to make them a reality. Thus, in some countries, it is remarkable that there is a lack of consolidation of these initiatives and that they have limited availability in terms of geographical and socioeconomic distribution due to a lack of clear policies, budget shortcuts, and difficulties in networking between the different help providers. The implementation of parent education programs should be integrated into a clear policy framework in which the different levels of governance (national, regional, and local) play a specific role in ensuring the congruence of interventions as well as the continuity of funding for parenting support. In this regard, the delivery of evidence-based parenting programs should be part of a broader strategy for supporting families. Moreover, even the large-scale implementation of a single parenting program may posit organizational, structural, and systemic challenges that need to be addressed to ensure the program's sustainability.

Concerning professional work with parents, a consensus has yet to be reached on the qualification level needed for the professionals involved in prevention work in the EU: this holds even at a national level. And yet, to work effectively with parents, professionals have to be prepared, skilled, and have a clear idea of the boundaries of their role within this (relatively new) prevention- and strength-based approach. This is especially needed when they are involved in building a sense of "partnership" with families. They need to value the establishment of good relationships with families, building their resilience and empowering them to be autonomous instead of promoting their dependence on the service. To summarize this new approach, "Think parents", "Think partnership", and "Think communities" are the lemmas proposed by European organizational networks (e.g., Eurochild) as indicating good practices in their work with families. In conclusion, there is a growing consensus in Europe that the task of parenting should be framed in terms of a "community" of key parties: parents, children, local and national service providers, and the communities themselves.

Key Points

1. It is important to take into account the development of family and parenting policies as these are shaping the well-being of the child and family.
2. The positive parenting framework has channeled the way the task of parenting is collectively perceived and supported in Europe.
3. Advanced scientific knowledge about the importance and consequences of parenting has brought about a new focus on prevention and has strengthened parental capacities as the main way to protect children, preserve their rights, and promote their development.
4. The provision of parental support is a public responsibility that takes multiple forms and is displayed in a variety of services aimed at universal and targeted interventions.
5. Evidence-based policies are a growing concern in Europe but are not assumed to the same extent across countries.
6. International and national evidence-based parenting programs are implemented in Europe with different levels of intensity and quality depending on the political, economic, and social conditions of the countries.
7. Quality assurance, collaborative schema with parents, and professional training are important to improve parental support services.

Discussion Questions

1. To what extent do family policies shape the lives of children and their families?
2. What has the modernization of the parenting task brought about to family intervention?
3. In which ways do evidence-based parenting programs benefit families and services?
4. Can you think of advantages of universally preventive programs (i.e., programs which target all parents, even the ones with no obvious risks)?
5. How can we identify target variables for the selection of parents with a special need or risk factors for parenting interventions (secondary prevention)?
6. Which are the child outcome variables that positive parenting programs try to influence?
7. Why does a good implementation of a program in real-life conditions matter?
8. Describe the role of professionals in the promotion of positive parenting.
9. To what extent do professionals need specific training to work with families in prevention programs?
10. Can you think of the resentments of practitioners towards the manualization of programs and resentments towards evaluations of program effects? Can you think of means to prevent such resentments?

Additional Resources

Websites

Blueprints in Europe: http://dartington.org.uk/projects/blueprints-for-success

ChildONEurope work on family and parenting support: www.eurochild.org/en/policy-action/family-and-parenting-support/index.html

Council of Europe Family Policy Database: www.coe.int/t/dg3/familypolicy/database/default_en.asp

EU Peer Review "Building a coordinated strategy on parenting support". Peer review on social protection and social inclusion organized by the European Commission took place in Paris in October, 2011. More information at: http://ec.europa.eu/social/main.jsp?catId=1024&langId=en&newsId=1391&furtherNews=yes

European Platform for Investing in Children (EPIC): http://europa.eu/epic/practices-that-work/index_en.htm

Parenting Programme Evaluation Tool (PPET): www.education.gov.uk/commissioning-toolkit

System for Assessment, Accreditation and Publication of Youth Interventions: www.youthpolicy.nl/yp/Youth-Policy/Youth-Policy-subjects/Netherlands-Youth-Institute-Effective-youth-interventions

References

Almeida, A., Abreu-Lima, I., Cruz, O., Gaspar, M., Brandão, T., Alarcão, M., Ribeiro Santos, M., & Cunha Machado, J. (2012). Parent education interventions: Results from a national study in Portugal. *European Journal of Developmental Psychology, 9*, 135–149.

American Psychological Association, Presidential Task Force on Evidence-based Practice (2006). Evidence-based practice in psychology. *American Psychologist, 61*, 271–285.

Asmussen, K. (2011). *The evidence-based parenting practitioner's handbook*. Abingdon, UK: Routledge.

Bakermans-Kranenburg, M., van IJzendoorn, M., & Juffer, F. (2003). Less is more: Meta-analyses of sensitivity and attachment interventions in early childhood. *Psychological Bulletin, 129*, 195–215.

Boddy, J., Smith, M., & Statham, J. (2011). Understandings of efficacy: Cross-national perspectives on "what works" in supporting parents and families. *Ethics and Education, 6*, 181–196.

Boddy, J., Statham, J., Smith, M., Ghate, D., Valerie Wigfall, V. & Hauari, H. (2009). *International perspectives on parenting support: Non-English language sources*. DCSF Research Report No DCSF-RR 114. London: Institute of Education, University of London. Retrieved from www.expoo.be/sites/default/files/kennisdocument/UK_international_perspective_on_parenting_support1.pdf

Budd, K. (2005). Assessing parenting capacity in a child welfare context. *Children and Youth Services Review, 27*, 429–444.

Byrne, S., Salmela-Aro, K., Read, S., & Rodrigo, M. (2013). Individual and group effects in a community-based implementation of a positive parenting program. *Research on Social Work Practice, 23*, 46–56.

ChildONEurope Secretariat (2007). *Survey on the role of parents and the support from the governments in the EU*. Florence, Italy: ChildONEurope Secretariat. Retrieved from www.childoneurope.org/issues/support_family/reportSurveyRoleParents.pdf

Council of Europe (2006). *Recommendation of the Committee of Ministers to Member States on Policy to Support Positive Parenting*. Retrieved from https://wcd.coe.int/ViewDoc.jsp?id=1073507

Crepaldi, C. et al. (2011). *Parenting support in Europe: A comparative study of policies and practices, final report*, Dublin, Ireland: European Foundation for the Improvement of Living and Working Conditions.

Daly, M. (2007). *Parenting in contemporary Europe: A positive approach*. Strasbourg, France: Council of Europe.

Daly, M. (2014). *Parenting support policies in Europe: Main developments and trends*, in R. Ruggiero (Coord.) *Public Policies Supporting Positive Parenthood: New policy perspectives*. The proceedings of the ChildONEurope Seminar on positive parenthood (pp. 17–24). Florence, Italy: Instituto degli Innocenti di Firenze. Retrieved from www.childoneurope.org/issues/publications/COEseries8-Positiveparenthood.pdf

Davis, F., McDonald, L., & Axford, N. (2012). *Technique is not enough: A framework for ensuring that evidence-based parenting programmes are socially inclusive*. Discussion Paper. Leicester: British Psychological Society. Retrieved from www.bps.org.uk/system/files/images/tine.pdf

Day, C., Michelson, D., Thomson, S., Penney, C., & Draper, L. (2012). Evaluation of a peer led parenting intervention for disruptive behaviour problems in children: Community based randomised controlled trial. *British Medical Journal, 344*, 1–10.

Eurochild (2013). *Family and Parenting Support in Challenging Times: Round table report* 7. Brussels, Belgium: Eurochild. Retrieved from www.eurochild.org/fileadmin/Events/2013/05_FPS_roundtable/Eurochild_FPS_round_table_7_May_2013_Report.pdf

European Alliance for Families (2013). *Parenting Support Policy Brief*. Retrieved from http://europa.eu/epic/studies-reports/docs/eaf_policy_brief_-_parenting_support_final_version.pdf

European Commission (2013). *Investing in Children: Breaking the cycle of disadvantage* (20.3.2013). Recommendation. Retrieved from http://ec.europa.eu/social/BlobServlet?docId=9762&langId=en

Flay, B., Biglan, A., Boruch, R.., Castro, F., Gottfredson, D., Kellam, S., Mościcki, E., Schinke, S., Valentine J., & Ji, P. (2005). Standards of evidence: Criteria for efficacy, effectiveness and dissemination. *Prevention Science, 6*, 151–175.

Fukkink, R., Vink, C., & Bosscher, N. (2014). *Think parents! Putting parents at the heart of parenting support*. Amsterdam: SWP.

Hermanns, J. (2014). Parenting support in Europe. What it brings and what it can take away, in R. Fukkink, C. Vink, & N. Bosscher, (Eds.). *Think parents! Putting parents at the heart of parenting support* (pp.11–25). Amsterdam: SWP.

Jones, K., Daley, D., Hutchings, J., Bywater, T., & Eames, C. (2008). Efficacy of the Incredible Years Basic parent training programme as an early intervention for children with conduct problems and ADHD: Long-term follow-up. *Child: Care, Health and Development, 34*, 380–390.

Juffer, F., Bakermans-Kranenburg, M. J., & van IJzendoorn, M. (Eds.) (2008). *Promoting positive parenting. An attachment-based intervention*. New York: Lawrence Erlbaum.

Kumpfer, K., & Alvarado, R. (2003). Family strengthening approaches for the prevention of youth problem behaviors. *American Psychologist, 58*, 457–465.

Kumpfer, K., Magalhães, C., & Xie, J. (2012). Cultural adaptations of evidence-based family interventions to strengthen families and improve children's developmental outcomes. *European Journal of Developmental Psychology, 9*, 104–116.

Kumpfer, K., Molgaard, V., & Spoth, R. (1996). The Strengthening Families Program for the prevention of delinquency and drug use, in R. Peters & R. McMahon (Eds.) *Preventing childhood disorders, substance abuse, and delinquency* (pp.241–267). Thousand Oaks, CA: Sage.

Landy, S. (2002). *Pathways to competence. Encouraging healthy social and emotional development in young children*. Baltimore, MD: Paul H. Brookes.

McCall, R. (2009). Evidence-based programming in the context of practice and policy. *SRCD Social Policy Report, 23*, 3–18.

McDonald, L., FitzRoy, S., Fuchs, I., Fooken, I., & Klasen, H. (2012). Strategies for high retention rates of low-income families in FAST (Families and Schools Together): An evidence-based parenting programme in the USA, UK, Holland and Germany. *European Journal of Developmental Psychology, 9*, 75–88.

McDonald, L., & Sayger, T. (1998). Impact of a family and school based prevention program on protective factors for high risk youth. *Drugs and Society, 12*, 61–85.

Molinuevo, D. (2013). Parenting support in Europe (Eurofound report ef1270). Retrieved from www.eurofound.europa.eu/publications/htmlfiles/ef1270.htm

Moran, P., Ghate, D., & van der Merwe, A. (2004). *What works in parenting support? A review of the international evidence*. London: Department for Education and Skills. Retrieved from www.prb.org.uk/wwiparenting/RR574.pdf

Nowak, C. & Heinrichs, N. (2008). A comprehensive meta-analysis of Triple P–Positive Parenting Program using hierarchical linear modeling: Effectiveness and moderating variables. *Clinical Child and Family Psychology Review, 11*, 114–144.

O'Connor, T., & Scott, S. (2006). *Parenting and outcomes for children*. York, UK: Joseph Rowntree Foundation.

Reder, P., Duncan, S., & Lucey, C. (2003). *Studies in the assessment of parenting*. London: Routledge.

Reichle, B., Backes, S., & Dette-Hagenmeyer, D. (2012). Positive parenting the preventive way: Transforming research into practice with an intervention for new parents. *European Journal of Developmental Psychology, 9*, 33–46.

Rodrigo, M. (2010). Promoting positive parenting in Europe: New challenges for the European Society of Developmental Psychology. *European Journal of Developmental Psychology*, 7, 281–294.

Rodrigo, M., Almeida, A., Spiel, C., & Koops, W. (2012). Introduction: Evidence-based parent education programmes to promote positive parenting. *European Journal of Developmental Psychology, 9*, 2–10.

Rodrigo, M., Byrne, S., & Álvarez, M. (2012). Preventing child maltreatment through parenting programmes implemented at the local social services level. *European Journal of Developmental Psychology, 9*, 89–103.

Rodrigo, M., Byrne, S., & Rodríguez, B. (2014). Parenting styles and child well-being, in A. Ben-Arieh, F. Casas, I. Frønes, & J. E. Korbin (Eds.) *Handbook of child well-being* (Vol. 4, pp. 2173—2196). New York: Springer.

Rodrigo, M., Máiquez, M., Correa, A., Martín, J., & Rodríguez, G. (2006). Outcome evaluation of a community center-based program for mothers at high psychosocial risk. *Child Abuse & Neglect, 30*, 1049–1064.

Salmela-Aro, K. (2012). Transition to parenthood and positive parenting: Longitudinal and intervention approaches. *European Journal of Developmental Psychology, 9*, 21–32.

Salmela-Aro, K., Read, S., Rouhe, H., Halmesmaki, E., Toivanen, R., Tokola, M., & Saisto, T. (2012). Promoting positive motherhood among nulliparous pregnant women with an intense fear of childbirth: RCT intervention. *Journal of Health Psychology, 17*, 520–534.

Sanders, M. (1999). Triple P–Positive Parenting Program: Towards an empirically validated multilevel parenting and family support strategy for the prevention of behavior and emotional problems in children. *Clinical Child and Family Psychology Review, 2*, 71–90.

Sherr, L., Skar, A, Clucas, C., von Tetzchner, S., & Hundeide, K. (2014). Evaluation of the International Child Development Programme (ICDP) as a community-wide parenting programme. *European Journal of Developmental Psychology, 11*, 1–17.

Sidor, A., Kunz, E., Eickhorst, A., & Cierpka, M. (2013). Effects of the early prevention program "Keiner faellt durchs Netz" ("Nobody slips through the net") on child, mother, and their relationship: A controlled study. *Infant Mental Health Journal, 34*, 11–24.

Skreitule-Pikse, I., Sebre, S., & Lubenko, J. (2010). Child behavior and mother-child emotional availability in response to parent training program: moderators of outcome. *Procedia—Social and Behavioral Sciences, 5*, 1418–1424.

Sylva, K., Scott, S., Totsika, V., Ereky-Stevens, K., & Crook, C. (2008). Training parents to help their children read: A randomized control trial. *British Journal of Educational Psychology, 78*, 435–455.

Webster-Stratton, C. (1999). *How to promote children's social and emotional competence.* London: Paul Chapman.

8

PARENTING EDUCATION IN THE ASIAN PACIFIC REGION

Karol L. Kumpfer, Methinin Pinyuchon, Rozumah Binti Baharudin, Nolrajsuwat Kannikar, & Jing Xie

Learning Goals

1. Increase awareness of the incidence and prevalence of child maltreatment, delinquency, substance abuse and other child developmental issues in Asia, and potential causal factors unique to the Asian culture and parenting style.
2. Understand the importance of selecting, culturally adapting, and implementing evidence-based family interventions to improve child and adolescent outcomes in Asia.
3. Increase knowledge of the history, structure, content and prior research outcomes of evidence–based parenting programs (EBPs) and non-EBP parenting education being implemented in Asia.
4. Understand the need for the use digital technology to reduce costs and rapidly disseminate EBP parenting programs to reduce the increasing trends in child misbehaviors in Asian families.

Introduction: Child Maltreatment in Asia and the Pacific Region

The World Health Organization (WHO: www.who.int/topics/child_abuse/en/) defines child maltreatment as five types of child abuse and neglect including all forms of physical abuse, sexual abuse, neglect and negligent treatment, emotional abuse, and exploitation. Consequently, these impact on actual or potential harm to the child's health, development, or dignity. Child maltreatment in Asian countries is prevalent. UNICEF (2012) has systematically reviewed studies covering the magnitude of child maltreatment in East Asia and the Pacific Region. By country, the findings show that in Thailand, lifetime prevalence of child abuse in different studies ranged from 11.7 to 66.1 percent (Chaopricha & Jirapramukpitak, 2010). In Vietnam, Nguyen, Dunne, and Le (2009) reported 19.7 percent lifetime prevalence of sexual abuse, 29.3 percent lifetime prevalence of neglect, and 39.5 percent lifetime prevalence of emotional abuse from a sample of 2,591 secondary school students. A child trafficking study in Thailand, Laos, and Myanmar found that 23 of the 103 minors interviewed had been sold as a commodity and 43.2 percent of them had been sold in their villages and transported to Thailand (ILO, 2002).

In Malaysia, the Department of Social Welfare (DSW) statistics suggest that neglect and physical and sexual abuse occur primarily in 7–12-year-olds, followed by infants aged 0 to 3 years. Choo, Dunne, Marret, Fleming, and Wong (2011) found that 22 percent of older children were exposed to more than one type of maltreatment (i.e., physical, emotional, sexual, and neglect). Parents made up 40 percent of child abusers in Malaysia, with mothers more likely to be abusers than fathers. However, many child abuse cases in Malaysia and the rest of Asia are not reported to the authorities due to the social stigma, despite efforts by various agencies to create awareness and combat the child maltreatment problem at the community level.

Child Delinquency in Asia and the Pacific Region

In all of Asia, delinquency is a growing concern with more children committing crimes. For example, the Malaysian government statistics showed a large (47 percent) one-year increase in juvenile index crimes from 3,700 cases in 2012 to 7,816 in 2013. Juveniles, including those who are still in school, are found to be involved in crimes including gangs, motorcycle thefts, burglary, vandalism, extortion, injuring others, pornography, rape, truancy and loafing (Baharudin, Muhamed, Juhari, Abu Samah, Noor, & Abu Talib, 2003; Chiam & Chan, 2011). Recently crimes such as illegal motorcycle racing—popularly known as "hell bikers" (Ismail, Abdul Karim, & Mustapha, 2010) and abandoning newborn babies or "baby dumping" (Mohd Fazly, 2012) have become a significant concern for Malaysians.

In Thailand, a UNICEF (2012) study found children as young as 10 years of age committing crimes; overcrowded conditions; lack of adequate facilities, services, and rehabilitation; limited alternatives to the detention of children; the lack of systematic follow-up and support for children and families after release from detention; and discrimination against ethnic minorities and children in conflict with the law. In Vietnam, Vu Ngoc Binh (1997) reported that juvenile delinquency was a growing problem and the major concern in Vietnamese society. The *Thanhnien News* (2013) reported that Vietnam youth appear to be increasingly crime prone. There was increasing awareness of the family's role in preventing youth crimes, because 80 percent of delinquents had parents who were either divorced, criminals, or gamblers; or were exposed to domestic violence.

The need for Asian authorities and societies to work together is deemed highly important to curb the growth of juvenile delinquency in Asian society.

Substance Abuse in Asian Adolescents

While lower than levels in Western countries, substance abuse is increasing in Asia and Pacific Region countries. Substance use data collected through the Global School-based Student Health Survey on 13- to 15-year-old males and females in schools in various Asian countries reported the rates of alcohol, tobacco, and drug use varied markedly in different Asian countries (WHO, 2014). Thailand had the highest illicit drug use rates in boys, at 15.8 percent, and in girls at 2.8 percent. Similarly the highest alcohol use rates were in Thailand, at 25 percent for boys and 14.8 percent for girls. Pacific Island countries also had high rates of alcohol use but not as high as Thailand. Vietnam had high rates also—7.7 percent in boys and 8.1 percent in girls. These two countries have been the most interested in implementing **evidence-based** parenting interventions to help reduce these high rates of drug and alcohol use in adolescents. China's alcohol use rates of 11.9 percent in boys and 7.8 percent in girls are likely higher today because their school survey was completed over 10 years ago. Tobacco use rates were highest in boys in Indonesia, at 22 percent, and the Philippines, at 18 percent. In Asian countries, the "gender gap" is typically present as in most countries of the world (Kumpfer, 2014; UNODC, in press), with a significantly larger percentage of boys using various substances than girls; but with the exception of drug use in Cambodia and Myanmar, where usage rates were low and similar between girls and boys.

Potential Causes of Family Conflict and Child Maltreatment

This section discusses the potential causes of family dysfunction in Asia, such as massive immigration, family displacement, parents leaving home for work in cities, and differential generational acculturation, that lead to higher parent–child conflict due in part to the permeation of Western values through the media.

Immigration and Family Dysfunction

One major cause of family disruption is the high rates of immigration both within Asia and out of Asia to the more developed Western countries with different cultural values—Australia, Canada, the USA, and the European Union. Malaysian families, especially of Chinese descent, have moved to more developed countries including China, with the percentage of Malaysian Chinese in Malaysia predicted to shrink from 45 in 1957 to 18.6 in 2035. Such immigration has resulted in family and cultural disruption and the need for culturally sensitive social services for these families. Burmese families have been escaping to Thailand and China whenever ethnic purges against the Karen and other hill tribes have broken out. In Vietnam, Chinese families are now being evacuated back to China because of political crises. In Bhutan, families of Nepalese descent who have lived there for generations are being removed from the country and not accepted back into Nepal. Chinese families are migrating from Asian and Southeast Asian countries (e.g., Taiwan, China, Hong Kong, Vietnam, Singapore, Indonesia, and Malaysia) for political, economic, and educational reasons. In Australia, between 1986 and 2001 there was a 778 percent increase in Chinese and Hong Kong immigrants, so that 74 percent of Chinese in Australia are foreign-born (Guo, 2005).

The reliance on low-skilled foreign workers is increasing rapidly in Asian countries that are shifting rapidly to export-oriented industrialization which has consequently created major economic and social issues for families. More women are entering the workforce, creating the need for child care and household support. For example, having a maid is an integral part of most dual-earner families in Malaysia today. By 2008, there were at least 250,000 foreign maids in Malaysian households (Department of Immigration, Malaysia). In 2015, 10 Asian countries formed the Association of South East Asian Nations (ASEAN) and its economically powerful ASEAN Economic Community (AEC) which, by 2020, will consist of 575 million people with trade exceeding US$ 1.4 trillion. Asian families experience benefits and disadvantages requiring them to be more aware of changes in their society and neighboring countries because of increased inflow and outflow of workers.

Within-country Migration for Work

Asia is rapidly changing from an agrarian society to one of large cities focused on manufacturing and tourism. Asian families in less economically prosperous areas are moving to more prosperous areas for jobs in their own or other countries. In China and other Asian countries, millions of parents have left their villages to move to cities for work, unfortunately leaving their children to be raised without parents.

Differential Generational Acculturation

Many Asian youth experience a "dual value system" (Vuttanont et al., 2006) leading to "differential generational acculturation" and family conflict because Eastern cultural values held by older generations (e.g., grandparents and parents) clash with more Westernized children or grandchildren. In other words, young people are becoming more Westernized than their elders because the ubiquitous Western media, movies, music, and fashion have permeated Asia. This "perceived parent–child acculturative gap" or "differential generational acculturation" can significantly damage parent–child relationships and lead to greater **adolescent problem** behaviors (Buki, Ma, Strom, & Strom, 2003). Immigrant parents fear the loss of traditional culture and language in their children (Portes & Rumbaut, 2001). In turn, children may increasingly challenge their parents' authority and disagree with traditional family roles and expectations (Nguyen & Williams, 1989; Rumbaut, 1991). In a study of substance abusers and delinquents in detention centers in four regions of Thailand, Rodnium (2007) found using structural equations modeling (SEM) that the major pathway to delinquency and drug abuse was "differential generational acculturation" leading to increased family conflict. Finding ways to reduce family conflict and improve parent–child attachment is needed to prevent negative adolescent outcomes in Asian and Pacific Region families.

High Expectations for Educational Success

Asian children experience stress because their parents have very high expectations for their school success (Gelles, 1997). Asian and American education systems are culturally different and Asian children study with a purpose because education is the essential path to success (Breitenstein, 2013). Parental demands, fear of failure, competition, and pride together motivate Asian children to study hard.

Eastern versus Western Parenting Styles

Many Asian parents value the family roles dictated by their religious customs and traditions such as Confucian and Islamic teachings: respect for elders, an authoritarian parenting style, and the mother as the primary caregiver (Harun, 2001; Fung & Lau, 2010). These Eastern values conflict with the more democratic Western parenting style which entails more paternal involvement in parenting (Chao & Tseng, 2002). Immigrant Asian children quickly discover the more positive and warm Western parenting style and believe their parents are too strict and "old-fashioned". They also often want their Western peers' additional freedoms and can rebel against their parents' strict discipline and control. **Prevention** programs are particularly well suited for immigrant Asian families because they are reluctant to seek help from mental health services (Sue, Fujino, Hu, Takeuchi, & Zane, 1991). The authors believe that evidence-based family interventions could help to prevent this family acculturation stress and child dysfunction. These studies suggest the need for implementing culturally adapted family strengthening programs for Asian families, especially those who immigrate to non-Asian countries because they face significant acculturation stressors.

Need for Parenting Education in Asian Families

Asians are widely regarded as the "model minority" in Western countries where they immigrate with few visible family problems. Despite the image of "harmonious" and intact families, Asian families experience high levels of stress which, combined with low use of mental health services (Sue, 2005), can lead to high levels of untreated psychological problems. Because Asian families value education, prevention "parenting education or family skills training" classes are more appealing than individual or family therapy, despite being similar in theoretical basis, objectives, content, and intervention techniques. Designers and implementers of family interventions seeking to engage Asian families should understand this cultural preference and the appeal of classes to improve children's outcomes. Because few parents feel a need to improve their parenting skills, despite the stress of East-to-West acculturation on parent–child relationships, enrollment messages stressing children's success in school are the most powerful (Dinh, Sarason, & Sarason, 1994).

Core Elements of Evidence-based Parenting Interventions

Basically, most evidence-based parenting and family interventions are based on cognitive behavioral theory (Bandura, 2001) and family systems theories. They also use similar intervention techniques to engage families and improve parenting behaviors, including personalized recruitment messages, needs assessments, experiential role plays to learn new parent–child attachment enhancement, clear communication and behavioral discipline methods, homework assignments to generalize the new behaviors to the home, and incentives for attendance and graduation. Effective parenting interventions include **cultural adaptation** as part of required fidelity to the model program rather than slavish fidelity. Of course, major program modifications, such as dropping critical core content and moving sessions around, are not considered part of implementation fidelity. Steps to successful cultural adaptation are included in work by Kumpfer and associates (Kumpfer, Pinyuchon, de Melo, & Whiteside, 2008; Kumpfer, Magalhães, & Xie, 2012; Chapter 18, this volume).

Definition of EBPs

Evidence-based programs are programs replicated in multiple randomized control trials (RCTs) by independent research teams with positive results having large effect sizes (Kumpfer et al., 2012). The larger the effect size or amount of improvement, the greater the program's success. The average effect size of family EBPs is nine times larger than youth-only substance abuse prevention programs (Tobler & Kumpfer, 2000). Wider dissemination of culturally adapted family EBPs worldwide can help counter increasing substance abuse and delinquency exacerbated by decreased parental involvement as parents work longer hours in hard economic times (United Nations Office of Drug and Crime, 2009).

The Need for Cultural Adaptation of Family EBPs

EBP parenting programs, based primarily on Western cognitive behavioral reward principles, necessarily conflict with principles of Confucian parenting. Enrolling and engaging Asian parents is difficult unless they are experiencing significant push-back from their children or want to learn more about the Western democratic ways of parenting. Lau and associates (2011) describe the disparity between the *Incredible Years* (IY) prescribed positive parenting skills and traditional, less positive Chinese parenting. Because filial piety is an obligation of children, Chinese parents object to positive reinforcement. Moreover, rewards or even praise for children's achievements are thought to encourage egotism and discourage the drive for improvement. Nevertheless, by establishing partnerships with the Chinese community to develop a sensitive cultural adaptation, 83 percent of the Chinese parents were retained and learned the value of positive play, active listening, problem solving and less punitive discipline that reduced (with large effect sizes) externalizing and internalizing problems among children. Similarly a Chinese cultural adaptation of the *Strengthening Families Program* (SFP 12–16 Years) implemented with immigrant Chinese families in San Francisco achieved significant positive pre- to posttest improvements with relatively large effect sizes in parental involvement, parenting efficacy, positive parenting, family cohesion, family communication, youth overt and covert aggression, and social skills. At pretest, the Chinese families were found to be at higher risk in all parent and family variables except family conflict, but relatively lower in risk for the youth variables as compared with the non-Chinese American comparison groups and SFP 12–16-year norms.

Status of Parenting Programs in Asia

Unfortunately, there has been a slow uptake of these EBPs in Asia and Pacific Region countries because most effective parenting and family interventions were developed primarily in English-speaking countries such as the USA, Australia, and the UK. Further, EBPs have been slow to develop in Asia because geographic distances, the need for language and cultural adaptations, and the lack of funding for efficacy and effectiveness trials have impeded progress. Hence, most of the home grown **parenting education** programs in the Asia and Pacific Region, while probably partially effective, are not considered evidence-based parenting programs.

In Asia often the major parenting education approach is a media campaign because of its reduced cost. In Malaysia, the Thai Ministry of Education conducted a nationwide media campaign on television that stressed parenting techniques to prevent drug abuse and other pressing social issues. The displayed posters, with cartoons of the right and wrong way to address the three major parenting issues —increasing positive appreciations of children's good behaviors, more effective communication, and reducing harsh discipline. The Cambodian government, with the support of UNICEF, promoted home-based parenting education including child development in health and nutrition visits, parent support groups, and early childhood education media broadcasts, such as Sabai Sabai Sesame Street for children.

In Malaysia, the National Population and Family Development Board (NPFDB) under the Ministry of Women, Family and Community Development, is the main government agency dealing with family and parenting education. NPFDB launched its first parenting module in 1993 with the aim of developing happy families through the enhancement of parenting knowledge and skills of parents. In 2008, NPFDB launched KASIH Module, a repackaging of its earlier versions of parenting modules from pre-parenthood to parenting of young children and adolescents, fathering, and parenting at work. To date, no formal evaluation has been done by NPFDB on the effectiveness of all the modules in promoting better parenting among participants who attended their workshops and related short courses. The only attempt for such evaluation was done by Doshi and Baharudin (1999) on the NPFDB's first parenting module. In their quasi-experimental study, parents in the experimental group who attended their three-day training workshops were found to show significant improvement in parenting knowledge, attitude, and practices compared with those in the comparison group. Several other private agencies and NGOs have also been active in offering family and parenting education programs: for example, the Malaysian Paediatric Association (MPA), Islamic and Strategic Studies Institute Berhad (ISSI), Malaysian Parent Collaborative Mimbar (MAPIM), and Organization of Graduates of Educational Institutes of Malaysia (HALUAN). At the more informal level, in Malaysia, Muslim mothers can join groups to volunteer to be "parent educators" to any new mother in their community. They are provided a nurse supervisor/trainer and a room with educational materials and equipment to encourage breastfeeding, healthy weight, nutrition, and effective parenting education. This could represent a lower-cost solution for Asian and non-Asian countries to improving infant outcomes and preventing child maltreatment than the more expensive EBP Nurse Family Partnership home visitation program (Olds et al., 2010). An evaluation is needed, however.

Thailand had been ahead of other Asian countries in adopting EBPs, including the *Strengthening Family Program* (6–12 years) in 2007 and soon after the *Family Matters* program. Several non-EBP family programs have also been evaluated, including parent management training programs, some including both parent and teacher training (Pumpuang, Phuphaibul, Orathai, & Putdivarnichapong, 2012) and others including children's life skills (Kummabutr, Phuphaibul, Suwonnaroop, Villarruel, & Nityasuddhi, 2013). Researchers (Arunothong & Waewsawangwong, 2012) implemented and evaluated a 7-week, 3-hour *Siriraj Parent Management Training* (PMT) clinical program. This PMT program was modified from Dr. James Windell's (1995) **parent training** book *8 Weeks to a Well-Behaved Child: Putting Discipline Skills to Work*. The sessions include case examples, small group role plays, and homework assignments. The study found significant improvements in 41 parents in parenting skills on the Parent Practice Test (PPT) and reductions in troublesome home situations and disruptive child behaviors up to one follow-up. Because Thailand had the second highest rate of mid–late teenage pregnancy in the entire world, Bunpromma (2012) proposed the development of a parenting program for teenage pregnancy in the Thai northeastern region to reduce child maltreatment.

Vietnam has tested the *Incredible Years* (IY) and the *Triple P* intervention. Nam Thanh Tran (2013) reported that Vietnamese parents were fairly willing to try using behavioral parent training (BPT) techniques that could contribute to the successful adoption of parenting EBPs.

Most Popular Evidence-based Parenting Programs in Asia

Many prevention researchers (Biglan & Taylor, 2000; Kumpfer & Alvarado, 2003; UNODC, 2009) have recommended the wide dissemination of evidence-based family skills training programs to improve deteriorating adolescent outcomes worldwide. This chapter focuses on EBPs in the Asia and Pacific Region. Few EBP parenting or family programs have been tested or even implemented in Asia, Pacific Islands except in English-speaking countries like Australia and New Zealand. The EBPs that have been tested or evaluated the most are the *Positive Parenting Program* (Triple P) developed by Matthew Sanders at the University of Queensland in Australia (Chapter 15) because of closer proximity, the *Incredible Years* (IY) by Carolyn Webster-Stratton at the University of Washington (Chapter 10), the *Strengthening Families Program* (SFP) developed by Karol Kumpfer at the University of Utah (Chapter 18), and *Family Matters* by Karl Bauman at the University of Florida (Chapter 17). Research on these four EBP parenting programs in Asia is briefly described below. More in-depth descriptions are found in other chapters in this book.

Triple P—Positive Parenting Program

The *Positive Parenting Program*, "Triple P", is one of the most implemented EBP parenting programs in Asia and, of course, in Australia, most likely because of its close proximity for training, tiered approach, and flexible content to match risk in families, and its excellent results. It is a clinically oriented, behavioral family intervention (Sanders, Markie-Dadds, & Turner, 2003). The therapeutic techniques and content are very similar to all of the other EBP parenting programs stemming from the parent–child therapeutic methods developed by Gerald Patterson and colleagues at the University of Oregon and the Oregon Social Learning Center (Chapter 13). Unlike most EBP parenting programs, Triple P does not rely on written curriculum manuals, but rather uses fact sheets as guides for the different parenting topics. Clinicians work from these materials to individualize the family sessions, making it harder to evaluate dosage and fidelity on outcomes.

Triple P does not specify the degree to which cultural adaptations are included in these versions of the program. It is assumed that, because the program primarily consists of defined goals, cultural adaptations occur naturally because of the training and background of program providers. However, Triple P materials have been translated into several other languages, such as Chinese, Farsi, German, and Japanese.

Evaluations of Triple P in Asian Pacific Region

In Hong Kong, *Triple P* was implemented with a sample 91 Chinese parents of 3- to 7-year-old children with early onset conduct-related problems and recruited from maternal and child health centers and child assessment centers for service (Leung, Sanders, Leung, Mak, & Lau, 2003). Using an experimental wait treatment control design, participants were randomly assigned to the intervention (TP) or a wait-list control group (WL). At baseline program pretest, there was no significant difference in pre-intervention measures between the two groups. However, by post-intervention, parents in the TP group self-reported significantly lower levels of child behavior problems, lower dysfunctional parenting styles, and higher parent sense of competence compared with the WL group. These positive results suggest that Triple P can be effective for families of Chinese descent.

Incredible Years (IY)

Another evidence-based parenting programs being implemented in the Asian region, mostly in Australia and New Zealand, is the *Incredible Years* (IY) program (Webster-Stratton, 1994). IY is a series of interlocking video-based lessons for parents, children, and teachers of 2- to 10-year-olds. IY is implemented in over 20 countries, but most are English-speaking countries; hence, no language translation and little cultural adaptation were needed.

Over 1,500 clinicians have been trained in IY in New Zealand and over 350 in Australia. Their website lists people trained in Korea, Japan, China, Singapore, and Malaysia. The IY programs had been delivered in New Zealand to 12,000 parents and 5,000 teachers by 2014 as part of the NZ Positive Behavior for Learning Action Plan. Dr. Webster-Stratton has made numerous visits to train parent group leaders, and in 2010 she trained Ministry of Education and NGO staff and Resource Teachers: Learning and Behaviour to become group leaders to deliver the classroom management programs to New Zealand teachers. The Ministry of Education has slowly been building its delivery of the IY parent and teacher programs over the past five years. Fergusson and associates (2009), in a pilot study of IY training, found that both Māori and non-Māori parents attending IY reported reductions in problem behavior and increases in child social competence following the program, and high client satisfaction. Also, high retention rates of Māori parents were found in a second qualitative evaluation (Altena & Herewini, 2009).

The most recent pilot evaluation with about 150 families (Sturrock & Gray, 2013) found the greatest improvements for Oppositional Defiant Disorder (d = 0.96) and Self-control (d = 0.96), followed by Social Competence (d = 0.68) and Conduct Disorder (d = 0.62). ADHD (d = 0.55) and Anxiety/Withdrawal (d = 0.51) showed moderate improvement. The changes in parenting behaviors were all statistically significant by the 6-month follow-up but less than those for child behaviors with small to medium effect sizes (d = 0.33–0.68), with poor supervision the least (d = 0.25). The overall median effect size was d = 0.54, excluding the Total Scale. The Total Arnold–O'Leary Parenting Scale maintained a large effect size of d = 0.79 at the fourth interview. The effect sizes on teacher reports of behavior change were much lower than those based on parent reports at d = 0.17. Evaluations of other IY implementations in the Asian Region were not found. A free South Australian networking site provides the opportunity for professionals involved in the Incredible Years programs to share knowledge and experiences.

The Strengthening Families Program

The Strengthening Families Program (SFP), a family skills training program, was selected by the Thai government for cultural adaptation and a randomized control trial in several regions of Thailand. SFP is a 14-session (2.5 hours each) family skills training program attended by the whole family to learn better communication, discipline methods, and ways to increase family attachment (Kumpfer, 2014). It was the first parenting program designed specifically for helping children of drug abusers in treatment. This program is described more in Chapter 18, this volume.

Although SFP has been culturally adapted and found effective in 35 countries including almost all European countries, Russia, the Balkans, Canada, Mexico, Central and South America, and the Middle East (Iran, Palestine), but in only two Asian Pacific Region countries, namely Australia and Thailand (Pinyuchon, 2010), SFP has not been implemented in China despite significant positive outcomes with a Chinese adaptation of SFP in San Francisco's Chinatown (Xie, 2014).

In Australia, the Queensland government hosted Dr. Kumpfer to train practitioners in four communities on the Gold Coast about 10 years ago. Despite enthusiasm for the program, unfortunately no implementation or evaluation funding was provided, so the success and outcomes are uncertain. Recently, a mental health center in Geelong near Melbourne did support an evaluation. The quasi-experimental effect size results were equivalent to the excellent SFP outcomes for parenting, family environment, and youth behavior and mental health improvements found in many sites in the USA and other countries (Kumpfer, Whiteside, Xie, & Cofrin, 2013).

However, in Thailand an extensive implementation funded by the Thai government resulted in a randomized trial with excellent effect size results. Cultural adaptation and implementation in Thailand followed exactly the steps recommended by Kumpfer (Kumpfer, Magalhães, & Xie, 2012). The reported engagement of families and results are excellent (Pinyuchon, 2010). The results of the study indicated statistically significant differences between pretest and posttest scores on outcome variables, such as parenting skills, family strengths, children's behaviors, attitude, and social skills. The parents and children in control groups showed no significant differences on such outcome variables. Participating families reported their high satisfaction with SFP and even two years later many are continuing to meet regularly as a family support group. Of interest is that it was the fathers in these ongoing Thai SFP groups who wanted to continue meeting, since they had found a way to connect to other fathers.

As Kim, Choe, and Webster-Stratton (2010) found in their study of IY with Korean families in the USA, Thai fathers are not particularly involved in childrearing. Thai funders therefore asked why fathers were to attend SFP. So Pinyuchon (2010) randomly assigned the enrolled Thai families to SFP groups for mothers only or both parents. Better outcomes were found for the SFP groups where both parents attended (Pinyuchon, 2010). SFP was effective with families in the Thai cultural context and potentially worth wider dissemination in Asia to reduce the high levels of differential generational acculturation (Rodnium, 2007).

SFP has also been successfully culturally adapted and implemented with Burmese refugees in Mae Sot, Thailand and many other villages by the International Rescue Committee (IRC). These Burmese refugees really like the experiential exercises ("fun and games" to the Burmese) and have almost no family drop-out. The independent outcome evaluation being conducted by the IRC demonstrates the success of this program in improving family relations. The psychiatry department at the University of Shanghai is considering an implementation of the new SFP home use DVD video materials for dissemination on smartphones as a very cost-effective dissemination method.

Thai Family Matters

Family Matters is another evidence-based parenting education program developed by Karl Bauman (Bauman, 2002) for prevention of substance abuse. It was translated, culturally adapted with one lesson on dating and risky sex, and evaluated in a randomized control trial in seven districts in Bangkok, Thailand (Rosati et al., 2012). This is a low-cost, school-based program for 13- to 14-year-olds that involves five parenting booklets being mailed out with follow-up calls by health educators. A completion rate for all five booklets was 85 percent, but the families took an average of 16 weeks to complete the program. The students reported a significant increase in the frequency of general parent–child communication. Parents reported marginal increase in the frequency of parent–child communication about sexual issues with reduced discomfort (Cupp et al., 2013).

Future Recommendations for Parenting Education in the Asian Pacific Region

Because of the rapid changes economically and culturally occurring in the Asian Pacific Region that are leading to increased family and youth dysfunction, it is recommended that parenting and family skills EBPs be culturally adapted, implemented, and evaluated at a more rapid rate. There are major barriers to such widespread dissemination of EBP parenting programs in Asia, including recognition of the growing problem of adolescent and family dysfunction; community readiness for adoption of EBPs; reluctance to implement parenting programs from Western countries with different values; lack of exposure to the notion of EBPs; and certainly lack of sufficient funding to implement more costly but more effective programs.

Funding is a major problem as EBPs cost more money than the most popular currently parenting education programs, namely a media campaign or simple parent education lectures. Although prevention specialists in 13 Asian Pacific Region countries assembled in Ho Chi Minh City by the Bangkok UN Office of Drug Control (UNODC) approved and developed plans for implementation of SFP and one other youth-only EBP with funding supplied by China, the higher government officials later voted to use the money for border controls instead. Hence, political awareness of the importance of EBP parenting programs in supporting **family harmony** and their strong economic development is needed. Also to have a broad public health impact, many more families have to be reached cost-effectively. One major recommendation would be to consider implementing EBPs using digital technology, television, self-help CDs or DVDs, the Internet, YouTube, and smartphone apps. Within-country public and private funding plus external international funding is often needed to culturally adapt and evaluate, in at least quasi-experimental studies, the EBPs discussed in this book as well as the currently popular parent education programs. Another new idea being tried in a few Western countries is attracting private investor funding in the form of Social Impact Bonds. This is the funding mechanism of a new concept called "Pay for Success" for EBPs that can save governments and agencies money and create a return to investors by the government for reduced costs if the EBP produces the expected positive impacts. The first successes were in reducing prison recidivism, which has calculable savings in costs with EBP therapeutic programs.

Television programming of parenting programs has been tried successfully in this region. The impact of a 12-episode television series, "Families" based on Triple P, was evaluated in Australia using a randomized wait-treatment control design with 55 parents of high-risk children aged between 2 and 8 years (Sanders, Montgomery, & Brechman-Toussaint, 2000). At immediate posttest, the parents in the television viewing (TV) condition reported significantly lower levels of disruptive child behavior, which had reduced from 43 to 14 percent of children in clinical range, and higher levels of perceived parenting competence than parents in the control group. A six-month follow-up revealed that all post-intervention effects were maintained. A high level of consumer acceptability was reported by parents in the TV condition.

In China and other Asian countries, specially designed television programs have been shown to improve health behaviors, some even using charismatic hosts, expert speakers, and parents who ask questions. These TV shows could be used more to promote improved parenting. A game show format could be used with a lottery for valuable prizes the following week for correct entries to increase the number of viewers. Still this requires government support and funding as TV programming is not inexpensive. Putting existing video-based EBP parenting programs on TV, the Internet, smartphones, or YouTube would be less expensive over time, but language subtitles or dubbing would be required and probably also reshooting the material with racially and ethnically matched actors who look like average parents and children. Then dissemination mechanisms would be needed, in addition to large national organizations or required homework assignment of students in school, families with children on probation or in youth corrections centers, and women's clubs, as is currently being done with SFP in the USA.

Conclusion

Because of the rapid increase in Westernization, differential generational acculturation, and behavioral health problems among Asian youth, evidence-based family interventions need to be implemented on a larger scale to have a greater public health impact. With such a high population density in Asia and lack of funding for prevention services, the use of lower-cost digital technology (e.g., TV, DVDs, the Internet, and smartphone apps) is recommended. Each country should become creative to figure out the best dissemination methods to engage the largest number of families in parenting and family EBPs. Governments, private companies, and family services agencies should partner to fund and implement family EBPs.

Discussion Questions

1. Why is parenting education of benefit in Asia and the Pacific Region?
2. What parenting programs have been offered in Asia?
3. Why has the development of parenting education in Asian countries and cultures been protracted?
4. What cultural adaptations are important before implementing parenting education programs in Asia?
5. How can parenting education be propagated across Asia and within Asian communities?

Additional Resources

Suggested Reading

Kumpfer, K., Alvarado, R., Smith, P., & Bellamy, N. (2002). Cultural sensitivity and adaptation in family-based prevention interventions. *Prevention Science, 3*, 241–246.

Kumpfer K., & Hansen, W. (2014). Family based prevention programs, in L. Scheier, & W. Hansen, *Parenting and teen drug use* (pp. 166–192). New York: Oxford University Press.

Kumpfer, K., Magalhães, C. & Xie, J. (2012). Cultural adaptations of evidence-based family interventions to strengthen families and improve children's outcomes. *European Journal of Developmental Psychology, 9*, 104–116.

UNODC (2009). *Guide to Implementing Family Skills Training Programmes for Drug Abuse Prevention* (pp. 1–52). Vienna: United Nations Office on Drugs and Crime.

Van Ryzin, M., Kumpfer, K., Falco, G. & Greenberg, M. (Eds.) (2015). *Family-centered prevention programs for children and adolescents: Theory, research, and large-scale dissemination.* New York: Academic Press.

Websites

Center for Substance Abuse Prevention (CSAP): www.prevention.samhsa.gov

National Institute on Drug Abuse: www.nida.nih.gov

OJJDP and CSAP's descriptions of EBP parenting interventions: www.strengthening families.org

Strengthening Families Program: www.strengtheningfamiliesprogram.org

UNODC Compilation of Evidence-based Family Skills Training Programmes: www. unodc.org/documents/prevention/family-compilation.pdf

References

Altena, I., & Herewini, T. (2009). *Incredible Years Marae Based Group*. Auckland: Werry Centre.

Arunothong, W., & Waewsawangwong, S. (2012). An evaluation study of Parent Management Training (PMT) program in Northern Thai. *ASEAN Journal of Psychiatry, 13(1)*, 31–48.

Baharudin, R., Muhamed, A., Juhari. R., Abu Samah, A., Noor, A., & Abu Talib, M. (2003). *Tingkahlaku Pelajar Sekolah Menengah dan Rendah*. Serdang: UPM.

Bandura, A. (2001). Social cognitive theory: An agentic perspective. *Annual Review of Psychology, 52*, 1–26.

Bauman, K. (2002). *Family Matters. A family-directed intervention designed to prevent adolescent alcohol and tobacco use and its evaluation.* Chapel Hill, NC: Department of Health Behavior & Health Education, School of Public Health, University of North Carolina at Chapel Hill. Retrieved from http://familymatters.sph.unc.edu/index.htm

Biglan, A., & Taylor, T. (2000). Increasing the use of science to improve child-rearing. *Journal of Primary Prevention, 21*, 207–226.

Breitenstein, D. (2013, August 4). Asian students carry high expectations for success. *USA Today*. Retrieved from www.usatoday.com/story/news/nation/2013/08/04/asian-students-carry-high-expectations-for-success/2615483

Buki, L., Ma, T., Strom, R., & Strom, S. (2003). Chinese immigrant mothers of adolescents: Self-perceptions of acculturation effects on parenting. *Cultural Diversity and Ethnic Minority Psychology, 9*, 127–140.

Bunpromma, W. (2012). *Development of parenting program for teenage pregnancy Thai Northeastern Region to reduce child maltreatment.* [PDF document]. Retrieved from http://ceu.md.kku.ac.th/site_data/mykku_ceu/130/Final_SC2012/Wallapa_Fina2012l_New.pdf

Chao, R., & Tseng, V. (2002). Parenting in Asians, in M. Bornstein (Ed.) *Handbook of parenting* (Vol. 4): *Social Conditions and Applied Parenting* (pp. 59–93). Mahwah, NJ: Lawrence Erlbaum.

Chaopricha, S., & Jirapramukpitak, T. (2010). Child abuse and risky behaviours among youths. *Journal of the Medical Association of Thailand, 93(S7)*, S160–165.

Chiam, H. & Chan, S. (2011). A profile of delinquents in an approved school. *Akademika, 81(1)*, 101–108.

Choo, W., Dunne, M., Marret, M., Fleming, M., & Wong, Y. (2011). Victimization experiences of adolescents in Malaysia. *Journal of Adolescent Health*, *49*, 627–634.

Cupp, P., Atwood, K., Byrnes, H., Miller, B., Fongkaew, W., Chamratrithirong, A., Rhucharoenpornpanich, O., Rosati, M., & Chookhare, W. (2013). The impact of Thai Family Matters on parent–adolescent sexual risk communication attitudes and behaviors. *Journal of Health Communication, 18(11)*, 1384–1396.

Dinh, K. T., Sarason, B. R., & Sarason, I. G. (1994). Parent–child relationships in Vietnamese immigrant families. *Journal of Family Psychology, 8*, 471–488.

Doshi, A., & Baharudin, R. (1999). Influences on the effectiveness of the National Population and Family Development Board parenting module. *Pertanika Journal of Social Science & Humanities, 7(1)*, 43–57.

Fergusson, D., Stanley, L., & Horwood, L. (2009). Preliminary data on the efficacy of the Incredible Years Basic Parent Programme in New Zealand. *Australian and New Zealand Journal of Psychiatry, 43*, 76–79.

Foxcroft, D., Ireland, D., Lister-Sharp, D., Lowe, G., & Breen, R. (2003). Longer-term primary prevention for alcohol misuse in young people: A systematic review. *Addiction, 98*, 397–411.

Fung, J., & Lau, A. (2010). Factors associated with parent-child (dis)agreement on child behavior and parenting problems in Chinese immigrant families. *Journal of Clinical Child and Adolescent Psychology, 39*, 314–327.

Gelles, R. (1997). *Intimate violence in families* (3rd ed.). Thousand Oaks, CA: Sage.

Guo, X. (2005). *Immigrating to and ageing in Australia: Chinese experiences*. Unpublished PhD thesis. Murdoch University, Perth, Australia.

Harun, D. (2001*). Manusia dan Islam*. Selangor, Malaysia: Dewan Bahasa dan Pustaka.

Ismail, R., Abdul Karim, M. F., & Mustapha, Z. (2010) Golongan muda mat rempit: suatu ekspresi sub budaya. *e-BANGI: Jurnal Sains Sosial dan Kemanusiaan, 5(1)*, 1–10.

Kim, E., Choe, H., & Webster-Stratton, C. (2010). Korean immigrant parents' evaluation of the delivery of a parenting program for cultural and linguistic appropriateness and usefulness. *Family and Community Health, 33*, 262–274.

Kummabutr, J., Phuphaibul, R., Suwonnaroop, N., Villarruel, A., & Nityasuddhi, D. (2013). The effect of a parent training program, in conjunction with a life skills training program for school-age children, on children's life skills, and parents' child-rearing skills and perceptions of support for child life skills development. *Pacific Rim International Journal of Nursing Research, 17(1)*, 3–17.

Kumpfer, K. L. (2014). Family-based interventions for the prevention of substance abuse and other impulse control disorders in girls. *ISRN Addiction*, Article ID 308789. New York: Hindawi Publishing. Retrieved from http://dx.doi.org/10.1155/2014/308789

Kumpfer, K., Alvarado, R., & Whiteside, H. (2003). Family-based interventions for substance abuse prevention. *Substance Use and Misuse, 38(11–13)*, 1759–1789.

Kumpfer, K., Magalhães, C., & Xie, J. (2012). Cultural adaptations of evidence-based family interventions to strengthen families and improve children's outcomes. *European Journal of Developmental Psychology, 9*, 104–116.

Kumpfer, K., Pinyuchon, M., de Melo, A., & Whiteside, H. (2008). Cultural adaptation process for international dissemination of the Strengthening Families Program (SFP). *Evaluation and Health Professions, 33(2)*, 226–239.

Kumpfer, K., Whiteside, H., Xie, J., & Cofrin, K. (2013). *Effectiveness of the Australian Strengthening Families Program*. Evaluation Report. Salt Lake City, UT: LutraGroup.

Lau, A., Fung, J., Ho, L., & Liu, L. (2011). Parent training with high-risk immigrant Chinese families: A pilot group randomized trial yielding practice-based evidence. *Behavior Therapy, 42*, 413–426.

Leung, C., Sanders, M., Leung, S., Mak, R., & Lau, J. (2003). An outcome evaluation of the implementation of the Triple P-Positive Parenting Program in Hong Kong. *Family Process, 42*, 531–544.

Miller, T., & Hendrie, D. (2008). *Substance abuse prevention: Dollars and cents: A cost-benefit analysis*. Center for Substance Abuse Prevention (CSAP), SAMHSA. DHHS Pub. No. 07–4298, Rockville, MD.

Mohd Fazly, M. (2012). *Buang bayi: Bilakah akan berakhir?* Dewan Masyarakat. Retrieved from http://dwnmasyarakat.dbp.my/?p=1568

Nguyen, H., Dunne, M., & Le, A. (2009). Multiple types of child maltreatment and adolescent mental health in Vietnam. *Bulletin of the World Health Organization, 87*, 22–30.

Nguyen, N. & Williams, H. (1989). Transition from East to West: Vietnamese adolescents and their parents. *Journal of the American Academy of Child Adolescent Psychiatry, 28*, 505–515.

Olds, D., Kitzman, H., Cole, R., Hanks, C., Arcoleo, K., Anson, E., Luckey. D., Knudtson, M., Henderson, C. Jr., Bondy, J., & Stevenson, A. (2010). Enduring effects of prenatal and infancy home visiting by nurses on maternal life course and government spending. *Archives of Pediatric and Adolescent Medicine, 164(5)*, 419–424.

Pinyuchon, M. (2010, June 12). Effectiveness of implementing the Strengthening Families Program for families of school children in Songkhla Province, Thailand. Paper presented at NIDA International Forum, Scottsdale, AZ.

Portes, A., & Rumbaut, R. (2001). *The story of the immigrant second generation: Legacies*. Berkeley, CA: University of California Press.

Pumpuang, W., Phuphaibul, R., Orathai, P., & Putdivarnichapong, W. (2012). Effectiveness of a collaborative home-school behavior management program for parents and teachers of children with attention deficit hyperactivity disorder. *Pacific Rim International Journal of Nursing Research, 16(2)*, 138–153.

Rodnium, J. (2007). *Causes of delinquency: The social ecology model for Thai youth*. (Doctoral dissertation). Salt Lake City, UT: Department of Health Promotion and Education, University of Utah.

Rosati, M., Cupp, P., Chookhare, W., Miller, B., Byrnes, H., Fongkaew, W., Vanderhoff, J., Chamratrithirong, A., Rhucharoenpornpanich, O., & Atwood, K. A. (2012). Successful implementation of Thai Family Matters: Strategies and implications. *Health Promotion Practice, 13(3)*, 355–63.

Rumbaut, R. (1991). The agony of exile: A study of the migration and adaptation of Indochinese refugee adults and children, in F. Ahearn & J. Athley (Eds.) *Refugee children: Theory, research and services* (pp. 53–91). Baltimore, MD: Johns Hopkins University Press.

Sanders, M., Markie-Dadds, C., & Turner, K. (2003). Theoretical, scientific and clinical foundations of the Triple P–Positive Parenting Program: A population approach to the promotion of parenting competence. *Parenting Research and Practice Monographs, 1*, 1–21.

Sanders, M., Montgomery, D., & Brechman-Toussaint, M. (2000). The mass media and the prevention of child behavior problems: The evaluation of a television series to promote positive outcomes for parents and their children. *Journal of Child Psychology and Psychiatry, 41*, 939–948.

Sturrock, F., & Gray, D. (2013). *Incredible Years: Pilot Study Evaluation Report*. Centre for Research and Evaluation. Ministry of Social Development, Wellington, New Zealand.

Sue, D. (2005). Racism and the conspiracy of silence. *Counseling Psychologist, 33*, 100–114.

Sue, S., Fujino, D., Hu, L., Takeuchi, D., & Zane, N. (1991). Community mental health services for ethnic minority groups: A test of the cultural responsiveness hypothesis. *Journal of Consulting and Clinical Psychology, 59*, 533–540.

Thanhnien News. (2013, January 14). Vietnam youth increasingly crime prone. Retrieved from www.thanhniennews.com/society/vietnam-youth-increasingly-crime-prone-3763.html

Tobler, N., & Kumpfer, K. (2000). Meta-analyses of family approaches to substance abuse prevention. Report prepared for CSAP, Rockville, MD.

Tran, N. (2013). *Vietnamese parents' attitudes towards Western parenting behaviors and interventions* (Unpublished doctoral dissertation). Nashville, TN: Peabody College of Vanderbilt University.

United Nations Children's Fund [UNICEF] (2012). *Measuring and monitoring child protection systems: Proposed core indicators for the East Asia and Pacific Region, Strengthening Child Protection Series No. 1*. UNICEF EAPRO, Bangkok, Thailand.

United Nations Office of Drug and Crime [UNODC] (2009). *Guide to implementing family skills training programmes for drug abuse prevention* (pp. 1–52). Vienna: United Nations Office on Drugs and Crime.

United Nations Office of Drug and Crime [UNODC] (in press). *Guidelines on drug prevention and treatment for girls and women*. Vienna: UNODC.

Vu, N. (1997). *Children involved with the system of juvenile justice: The case of Vietnam*. UNICEF Vietnam, Hanoi. Retrieved from www.unicef-irc.org/portfolios/documents/490_vietnam.htm

Vuttanont, U., Greenhalgh, T, Griffin, M., & Boynton, P. (2006). "Smart boys" and "sweet girls"—sex education needs in Thai teenagers: a mixed-method study. *The Lancet, 368*, 2068–2080.

Webster-Stratton, C. (1994) Advancing videotape parent training: A comparison study. *Journal of Consulting and Clinical Psychology, 62*, 583–593.

Windell, J. (1995). *8 weeks to a well-behaved child: Putting discipline skills to work*, New York: Wiley.

World Health Organization (2014). *Global School-based Student Health Survey*. Retrieved from www.who.int/chp/gshs/ multicountryfs/en/

Xie, J. (2014). *Effectiveness evaluation of a culturally adapted family skills training program for Chinese American adolescents and their families*. (Doctoral dissertation). Department of Health Promotion and Education, University of Utah, Salt Lake City, UT.

9

PARENTING EDUCATION WITHOUT BORDERS

Web-based Outreach

Judith A. Myers-Walls & Jodi Dworkin

Learning Goals

After reading this chapter, readers will be able to:

1. List several types of online educational resources available to parents (informational sites, blogs, online courses, etc.).
2. Describe several characteristics of parents that may influence whether and how they would use the Internet for parenting education.
3. Describe factors that may facilitate and interfere with effective use of the Internet for parenting education and how those factors apply to a few different groups of parents.
4. Perform an efficient and effective online search for research-based educational materials about and for parenting.
5. Assess the quality of individual web pages, websites, and online courses related to parenting and parenting education.

Introduction

Parenting has always been a challenging task. One of our sets of parents raised children in the 1950s and 1960s and depended on Dr. Spock's *Baby and Child Care* and Hiam Ginott's *Between Parent and Child* along with personal contacts. There was not much more available. The other set of parents raised children in the 1970s and still used Dr. Spock, along with free information pamphlets from the pediatrician. Both of us authors entered our parenthood journeys with academic training that gave us an extensive set of resources, but the one of us who raised children in the 1980s and 1990s also used resources like *Ourselves and Our Children* from the Boston Women's Health Book Collective, and a monthly newsletter called *Growing Child*. By the time the second author began raising her children after the turn of the century, the world of resources had changed. The Internet offered a new way to find parenting information and support. What sources did your parents use? If you are a parent or expect to be one, what do you use or intend to use?

The types of resources available to parents have increased over the years. Now that we are well established in the twenty-first century, trends toward technology innovations and widespread interest in parenting information that began in the previous century (Simpson, 1997) have not only continued, but the pace of change has increased, especially for electronic and virtual information sources. Radey and Randolph (2009) found that 76 percent of parents reported the Internet as a major source of parenting information. In addition, a Google search for the word "parenting" results in 84.8 million options. Even a specific search on "parenting children who bite" brings more than 2 million sources.

As professionals who support parents, we need to learn how parents use the resources available to them, including the Internet. We also need to learn how we can help them become informed consumers of online resources, how to incorporate those materials into our educational efforts, and how to create responsible and useful online parenting materials. As professionals we can support parents in an environment where a single keystroke produces an overwhelming amount of information.

The authors are both experienced parenting educators and have extensive and varied experience with online parenting education. They hold degrees in Child Development or Human and Community Development, and both have served as Cooperative Extension Specialists, helping to extend research-based information to the general public, especially to parents and parenting professionals. The first author has spearheaded the creation of three websites. The second has specialized in technology and family development.

Literature Review

Parents and Access to the Internet: A Snapshot

Although technology use is increasing among all populations (Martin & Robinson, 2007; National Telecommunications and Information Administration [NTIA], 2011; Pew Research Center, n.d.), studies have shown that parents are more connected to and enthusiastic about technology than non-parents. In 2002, 70 percent of parents in the USA reported using the Internet compared with 53 percent of non-parents. More recently, broadband access among U.S. households with children was between 63 and 84 percent compared with 55 percent of households without children (NTIA, 2011). This is true not only for the USA; Internet access among households with children has been found to outpace access among households without children in Canada and England as well (Statistics Canada, 2010; UK Statistics Authority, 2010). This access is not only by computer. In May of 2010, only 3 percent of adults owned a tablet, but this number had increased to 35 percent by September 2013 (Rainie & Smith, 2013). Similarly, in May 2011, 35 percent of adults owned a smartphone, and this number had increased to 56 percent by May 2013 (Smith, 2013). By the time you are reading this chapter, new and different technologies are likely to have displaced those that are considered new and innovative at the time of its writing, continuing to connect parents with quick and abundant virtual information and support.

So data indicate that many parent populations have access to the Internet using a variety of Internet-capable devices (Walker, Dworkin, & Connell, 2011). Greater use of these technologies in households with children may be related to the fact that adults with children at home may be younger than parents without children in the home and therefore more comfortable with new technologies, parents' needs for quick access to information may be greater than non-parents, or children themselves may inspire or demand greater technology resources and connectivity (and often are teaching their parents computer skills!). In fact, researchers have found that parent media use changes with children's use (Wartella, Rideout, Lauriella, & Connell, 2013). So we know some things about the availability of devices among parents, but we know significantly less about how they use new media specifically to support parenting.

Allen and Rainie (2002) found that parents most commonly went online to: send email (92 percent), read news (67 percent), and look for health information (67 percent). More recent studies (Radey & Randolph, 2009) indicated that, while the Internet continues to be a key resource for information, parents still turn to family and friends for parenting advice far more than to online tools. Further, 70 percent of parents of children age 0–8 do not think technology devices make parenting easier (Wartella et al., 2013).

Not all parents look at the Internet in the same way. In a recent study by Doty, Dworkin, and Connell (2012), age and education emerged as significant predictors of the frequency of parents' online social activities, and there was a significant difference in parents' online information-seeking by income, but the effect of these demographic influences was small. However, what was particularly striking was that comfort with technology emerged as the most salient predictor of parents' online activities. Rothbaum and colleagues (2008) found that parents with high incomes were more likely to have refined search skills and were more likely to report success in finding a variety of online information about children and families than low-income parents. These data suggest the need to help parents develop skills that will increase their comfort with seeking parenting information online. (See Dworkin, Connell, & Doty, 2013, for a complete overview of the literature regarding parents' Internet use.)

Activity 9.1

Think about your own family and one or two families with which you work or have contact.

How and when does each family use online resources, if at all? How easily and quickly can they find, view, save, and share online links?

Now think about each family's parenting needs and interests. What are two or three parenting questions each family may have? You could write down actual questions the family has asked or questions you think they may have. *Sample questions: How early can I start teaching my child to use the toilet? Is it normal to sometimes wish I never had kids?*

Parental Use of the Internet

While it is clear many parents "consume" Internet information and resources, studies have shown that parents are often concerned about the credibility of online information and report being very cautious about what to trust (Rothbaum et al., 2008; Plantin & Daneback, 2009). For example, a qualitative study of white, educated mothers in the USA found they consulted blogs, Yahoo! groups, and sites consistent with their philosophies, and reported that "the most important source of information by far . . . was the internet" (Hoffman, 2013, p. 234). But these mothers also reported taking a very critical view of the resources and were reluctant to use recommendations they found there. What is unclear is how they decided what was credible and relevant.

In a similar way, studies have shown that parents who consult the Internet for advice about their children's health were more likely to base their actions on advice from pediatricians or from their mothers (Moseley, Freed, & Goold, 2011). Other studies and our own unpublished research show that many Asian parents also prefer to get parenting advice from family members or experienced friends rather than from experts (Shwalb, Kawai, & Whoji, 1995).

Despite parental skepticism, some authors have identified advantages for parents in using web-based family life education resources and programs when compared with face-to-face methods of delivery. The Internet and other technologies allow information and support to be available at any time and place and in ways that can supplement more traditional parent education (Ebata & Dennis, 2011). For instance, some parents participating in online communities reported satisfaction with the immediacy of support received from other parents (Drentea & Moren-Cross, 2005). Parents can seek answers to questions online anonymously without embarrassment and can pick and choose the sources they consult. Additionally, hyperlinks and multimedia features can help enhance learning by structuring information in relevant ways. The Internet and other new technologies also have also created communication communities such as listservs, chat rooms, blogs, and social networking sites. These technologies allow people to meet, discuss ideas, and share their feelings in new ways (Ebata & Dennis, 2011). These findings suggest it is worthwhile to help parents learn how to find and use online parenting resources.

In addition to finding information and expert advice and participating in online networking, parents are accessing and reporting positive effects from online peer-based prevention and intervention programs (e.g., Metzler et al., 2011). Although there are few published evaluations of online programs, an evaluation of one six-month, computer-mediated social support online community targeting 42 young, single mothers revealed women accessed the online network over 16,000 times, provided social support to each other through online discussion forums, and reported decreased parenting stress (Dunham et al., 1998). Online educational programs aimed at building knowledge and skills also have shown positive impacts. First-time fathers who participated in an online intervention reported significantly higher parenting self-efficacy scores than fathers in a comparison group (Hudson, Campbell–Grossman, Fleck, Elek, & Shipman, 2003). In an experimental study of over 800 Singaporean parents with children under the age of six, parents who accessed an online program providing information about children's development and tips for interacting with children showed a statistically significant increase in knowledge about children's development. Parents who participated in the online program also reported feeling more confident in achieving their parenting goals (Na & Chia, 2008).

There are advantages for parent professionals as well using online resources. The Internet provides them the potential to interact with parents who were previously unreachable with face-to-face delivery methods. Educators can assess needs, use unique educational methods, collect feedback, and/or collect data in addition to providing previously unattainable information and perspectives to large numbers of diverse groups of parents (Madge & O'Connor, 2002; Ebata & Dennis, 2011). Internet resources also can be cost-effective. Web-based information sources are easier to maintain, update, and distribute than print resources.

To get full advantage of these benefits, it is important for family life educators to understand and keep up with the contexts in which learning happens. As technologies shift, the locus of information control moves from the expert or teacher to the consumer or parent. Use of the Internet and other technologies gives parents control in how, where, and when they access information and support—responsibilities that used to rest primarily with the educator. Parents are able to access, create, and share information based on their individual needs and ways of thinking (Ebata & Dennis, 2011). Given these facts and parents' attraction to interactive sites over more passive educational ones, it is important for educators to respond by designing research-based sites with an eye toward

Activity 9.2

Return to the questions you identified in the first activity. Think about the parent who may be asking that question and consider the types of online resources available to that parent. What is the parent's objective or need? How can you match the question and desired outcome with an appropriate type of online resource? You may choose more than one type for each question.

Sample: A parent interested in toilet training may need an informational site on normal child development, an online shopping site for a how-to book or toilet-training equipment, or a blog or chat room to share joys and frustrations with other parents dealing with the same tasks.

participant engagement (Hughes, Bowers, Mitchell, Curtis, & Ebata, 2012). Educators also need to help parents learn to screen those resources to relieve concerns about trustworthiness.

Recognizing the variety of formats available online, educators need to think carefully about what kind of online formats they use or recommend and also attempt to vary those formats. In addition, it is important for educators to consider appropriate outcome objectives for parents when using, recommending, or creating online resources. As Campbell and Palm (2004) point out, it is important to match methods to learning outcomes and to use a variety of methods to increase responsiveness to and the effectiveness of the education.

Developing Internet Skills Related to Parenting Education

Finding Parenting Sources Online

As any Internet user knows, millions of options appear in response to any search. Those options include sources that span the full range of reliability, trustworthiness, and ease of use. The situation can be overwhelming enough to make users want to give up or just accept the first one or two listings they find. Both parents and parenting educators can benefit from learning and using methods for effective searching, screening, and sorting through the jumble.

There are two basic approaches to finding resources on the Internet: browsing or searching. The difference is like going shopping with a list or without. When browsing the web or a specific site, a user just looks around to see what is there and follows whatever links suit his or her fancy at that time—like window-shopping. Searching, on the other hand, begins with a topic or need in mind—

Activity 9.3

Conduct a search with one or two of the questions you identified in the first activity. What additional background do you need to clarify the parent's question? Are you sure you understand what the parent wants to know? Start with a one-word search. Then add clarifying terms. Keep track of what you find with each change. See what happens when you add Boolean search terms. Make notes about ways to teach parents about effective searching based on what you learn from your searching experience.

like shopping with a list. Browsing works best when the user has time and curiosity and does not have a specific need. Searching can be much more effective in meeting a parent's needs, but can also be frustrating. Using effective search skills can help you and your parent clientele find what they need efficiently. Nichols and colleagues (2009) found that over half of parents reported using Google Search to look for information regarding children's learning and development, but in a sample of African American parents with high levels of computer (84 percent) and Internet access (74 percent), the majority expressed the desire to improve their Internet skills (Cohall, Cohall, Dye, Dini, & Vaughan, 2004).

The first step in an effective search is to decide exactly what you want to find. As most users have discovered, it helps to be as exact as you can. Try a few sets of terms. Make sure your terms are clear, and be willing to tweak the search terms during the search process. You could use Boolean search terms to make the search more exact. For example, link terms together by adding "AND" between them so that only sources that include both terms will be found. If you use "OR" between terms, you will find sources with one or the other term. If you want the materials to include a specific word or term, put it in quotes. For more information about Boolean searches, review the relevant link in the resources at the end of this chapter.

Another way to improve the quality of the search is by reviewing multiple sources. Review the first source that appears to be on target. Then look at two or more additional sources to see whether they are consistent with each other. If they all say the same thing or make the same recommendations, you will have a good sense of what is out there. If they disagree, look for credibility levels and value differences. Choose what best fits the situation and the user.

Assessing the Quality of Online Parenting Education Materials

Locating online resources through searching or browsing is just one step in effective use of the Internet in supporting parents. Because it is easy for anyone to post things for others to access, parenting experts are likely to be even more leery of information than parents. It is up to the user to assess the quality of what he or she finds.

A number of authors have examined the factors that contribute to high-quality family life education materials in general and online specifically (Hughes, 1994; Grassian, 2008; Teacher Certification, n.d.; University of Washington, n.d.). Some of the concerns are particular to web-based media and others apply to any family life education efforts. A simple assessment can be done by parents and by professionals who are in a hurry, but a more in-depth assessment may be required at times.

We have summarized key recommendations for a simple assessment in the following four steps:

1. Look at the suffix of the website. It can tell you something about the motivation for creating the site and the credibility of the information. In general, URLs that end in .gov, .edu, and .org are likely to be the most reliable sites for family life education information, but there are exceptions. Suffix interpretation: .com = commercial; .edu = educational; .gov = governmental; .mil = military; .net = network (miscellaneous); .org = nonprofit organization.
2. Does the source answer your questions?
3. Does it apply to you (age of child, ethnicity/national origin, family type, etc.)?
4. Is the technology working on that site? Does it cost anything or require you to enroll or buy something?

These questions provide a basic assessment. But there are many more criteria that should be considered if you will be recommending the site to others, if the topic is sensitive or critical, or if you will use it as an important source of information for programming. Based on the guidelines from many other sources as applied to Family Life Education (FLE), the website Family Life Education Materials Quality Assessment Tool (FLEMatQAT) (www.extension.purdue.edu/purplewagon/FLEMat-QAT/FLEMat-QAT.htm) provides an interactive four-

Activity 9.4

Using the four simple questions above, evaluate at least two of the web resources you found in the previous activity. Make notes about your answers and then reflect on what was easy and what was difficult about this assessment method. Write down your reactions.

step method for professionals to examine written materials, curricula, and online materials using four steps:

1. Choose the type of material to be assessed.
2. Write a description of the material.
3. Determine the quality of the material.
4. Write a recommendation.

Each step is described in detail online and includes links and additional material to clarify each criterion. Although this tool may be used by some highly motivated parents, a professional background is helpful for many of the judgments that need to be made using this process.

The first step is to choose the type of material you are assessing. Regarding online material, it is important to decide whether you are evaluating a single web page that stands by itself, an entire website with a number of pages and links included, or an online curriculum that is set up for a user to complete independently. (See links at the end of the chapter for examples of each of those types.) Each type of online material would be assessed using different criteria. After you determine the type, follow the instructions for opening the Assessment Summary form. Either print or save the form to your computer so that you can use it to record your answers to the assessment items.

The second step is to look carefully at the material to describe it. Often the most difficult task at this step is to determine the philosophy or school of thought, because it is rarely a specified direction. A link provides possible philosophies for parenting materials and gives some clues to help you choose among the options.

The third step is the longest and most involved in FLEMatQAT. Table 9.1 lists the criteria that are used for step 3 and indicates the types of materials to which those criteria were applied. Note the columns that apply to online parenting education: Online Articles, Websites, and Self-study Curricula that are available online. As you rate the material, keep in mind that it would be unusual for materials to be rated at the top level on all criteria. Identify which criteria are most important to the material and audience you are considering, Weigh those items most heavily.

Activity 9.5

Choose one online piece (or more, if desired) to assess using FLEMatQAT. It can be a single page, a website, or an online self-study curriculum. Walk through the online assessment process while reading the next section of this chapter.

TABLE 9.1 Quality Criteria Applicable to Different Parenting Education Materials

Criterion	*Criterion applicable to this type of material*					
	1	*2*	*3*	*4*	*5*	*6*
The author(s) or sponsor(s) of the material has training and/or experience that are clearly related to the topic of the material	x	x	x	x		x
The owner or host of the website is identifiable and appropriate					x	
The material lists the professional references that were consulted when the material was created, and most of the references are current	x	x	x	x	x	x
It is clear how the material is related to the research findings; the material applies the findings effectively	x	x	x	x		
The level of intended impact (awareness, enrichment, prevention, intervention) of this material is clearly evident	x	x	x	x	x	x
The objectives of the material are clear	x	x	x	x	x	x
The values orientation underlying the material is evident	x	x	x	x	x	
The material clearly states why the topics in the program are important for the target audience	x	x	x	x	x	x
There is an appropriate match between the target audience and the content [and methods] of the material	x	x	x	x		x
Materials for parents are attractive, understandable, and useful	x	x	x	x		
The website is attractive and easy to use					x	x
Recommendations in the material suggest other resources that could be used in conjunction with this material	x	x	x	x		
The site includes links to other resources that could be used in conjunction with this website					x	
The self-study curriculum provides connections to additional sources of information and opportunities for learning						x
The material distinguishes among research findings, theories, and opinions	x	x	x	x	x	x
The material recognizes that families live in a world larger than a single family and does not assume that families are solely responsible for everything that happens to them and their children	x	x	x	x	x	x
Instructions for the leader are clear, complete, and easy to follow				x		
Instructions for the user are clear, complete, and easy to follow						x

continued . . .

TABLE 9.1 Continued

Criterion	*Criterion applicable to this type of material*					
	1	*2*	*3*	*4*	*5*	*6*
The curriculum uses a variety of educational techniques that help participants learn in diverse ways				x		x
Evaluation research has demonstrated that the curriculum is effective in reaching its objectives with families				x		
Evaluation strategies and materials are provided for the facilitator to use				x		
The curriculum is complete and includes all materials and information necessary for delivering the program				x		
The site is current and well maintained					x	
The site uses web and electronic media effectively					x	
The flow of the curriculum is appropriately controlled so that users complete the curriculum components in the appropriate order to achieve the objectives of the program						x
Methods are provided for participants to assess their progress and/or for organizers to assess competency for credit						x
The curriculum is complete and includes all materials and information necessary for using the program						x

Key: Types of parenting education materials:

1 Informational pamphlets, newsletters, booklets, online articles
2 Magazines
3 Trade books
4 Curriculum guides/workshop outlines
5 Websites
6 Self-study, online, or on hard copy.

As you use the criteria, read their descriptions carefully and use the links provided. Some were repetitious at first, but there are subtle differences. Several of the criteria are related to credibility and scholarly accountability. Most of these apply to all FLE materials, as do the criteria related to the educational value or structure of the material. There are also items regarding the adequacy of the materials and instructions for the user. The most difficult of these criteria to assess are likely to be the values inherent in the piece, because this is another characteristic that is rarely specified in parenting programming (Myers-Walls & Myers-Bowman, 1999). Finally, some of the criteria in this section are specific to presentation in the online format. As you look at these online-related items, refer to the included FLEMatQAT links and also consider the following list (Doty, Doty, & Dworkin, 2011).

1. Usability
   a. The site and its pages are approachable and easy to look over and digest.
   b. Users always know where they are, how they got there, and how to get back.
   c. The site establishes structural anchors that remain the same from page to page.
   d. There is a clear visual hierarchy on each page with images, structure, or color so the user naturally focuses on important aspects of each page.
   e. Industry conventions are followed regarding the placement of navigation.
   f. Important information can be reached without too many clicks.
2. Attractiveness and accessibility
   a. The first page immediately engages users.
   b. The reading level of the material is appropriate for the target population.
   c. The site uses visuals effectively.
3. Tools and methods
   a. The technology is used effectively and not just for its own sake.
   b. The technical set-up is appropriate for the intended audience and its likely equipment and connectivity.
   c. Meets ADA requirements for users with a variety of abilities.

After you have completed Step 3 in FLEMatQAT, follow the instructions to calculate your final score. Then complete Step 4, the recommendation. Your

Activity 9.6

Look at the results of your assessments of materials using the four simple questions and then using FLEMatQAT. Clearly, the simple questions provide easier and faster feedback, but FLEMatQAT provides a much deeper and more detailed analysis. Reflect on when you might use each of them. Also reflect on what you would need to do to become more proficient with judging the quality of online parenting materials and creating new resources.

recommendation could be shared with anyone who was planning to use the material and wanted your reaction. Maybe it would be part of a program-planning effort at your job or as a search for new resources. Note that the score is for comparative use only; you may want to compare your findings with colleagues or compare scores on one resource to another similar resource. The assessment will be most useful for identifying what you saw as the strongest and weakest areas. Finally, FLEMatQAT could be used when creating your own original materials; refer to the criteria as you build a program that could provide high-quality online parenting programming.

Implications for Parenting Educators

The Internet is an important source of support and information for parents. Educators should help parents use its resources effectively and responsibly. The following recommendations from the literature are reviewed in this chapter.

1. Get to know your audience. A basic guideline in all FLE programming is to tailor education to the audience. That is challenging with the broad and often anonymous reach of Internet-based resources. Review the statistics about parents and connectivity. Survey your target audiences to get specific information. Match each recommended online resource to the specific audience. Specify the target audience for any web-based materials you create.
2. Know what is online for parents and how to find it. Stay informed about new resources and technologies. Refine your browsing and searching skills. Teach those skills to parents.
3. Assess the quality of online materials and provide parents with basic quality guidelines. Use simple assessment techniques when appropriate and more elaborate and in-depth techniques for sensitive topics, materials to be widely disseminated, and major programming topics.

Conclusion

1. Parenting is challenging, and parents have long sought helpful sources of assistance. The Internet is now a major source of advice and support.
2. Parents are more likely than non-parents to use the Internet. Some parents are more confident of their Internet skills and more trusting of web-based information than others.
3. Parents and parenting professionals both need effective skills for browsing and searching for sources of information and support on the Internet.
4. Not all online resources are reliable, trustworthy, and research-based. Parents and parenting professionals need to learn to judge the quality of Internet-based resources.

Key Points

1. Parenting is challenging, and parents have long sought helpful sources of assistance. The Internet is now a major source of advice and support.
2. Parents are more likely than non-parents to use the Internet. Some parents are more confident of their Internet skills and more trusting of web-based information than others.
3. Parents and parenting professionals both need effective skills for browsing and searching for sources of information and support on the Internet.
4. Not all online resources are reliable, trustworthy, and research-based. Parents and parenting professionals need to learn to judge the quality of Internet-based resources.

Discussion Questions

1. Think about your own family and one or two families with which you work or have contact. How and when does each family use online resources, if at all? How easily and quickly can they find, view, save, and share online links?
2. Choose some questions parents may ask. Think about the parent who may be asking that question and consider the types of online resources available to that parent. What is the parent's objective or need? How can you match the question and desired outcome with one or more appropriate type of online resource?
3. What strategies do you use to locate electronic parenting materials? What strategies do you feel are important to teach to parents?
4. How do you assess whether online materials are of sufficient quality? What strategies do or will you teach to parents?

Additional Resources

Information about Searches, Internet Use, and Quality of Web-based Materials

Information about Boolean searches from Joe Barker at the University of California, Berkeley: www.lib.berkeley.edu/TeachingLib/Guides/Internet/Boolean.pdf

Website evaluation guide—Another alternative: www.extension.umn.edu/family/families-with-teens/resources-professionals/research-updates-for-professionals/additional-resources/docs/website-evaluation-criteria.pdf

Parenting-related Sites by the Authors

Provider–parent partnerships—A site for child care providers and the parents in their programs: www.extension.purdue.edu/providerparent/

Teen link—Guide to resources on teen issues: www.extension.umn.edu/family/families-with-teens/resources-professionals/teen-link/

Samples of Web-based Resources to Help Understand Categories in FLEMatQAT

Online self-study curricula

www.familyaffairs.org/
http://kids.lovetoknow.com/wiki/Parenting_Curriculum_Guides.

Websites

www.parentfurther.com/
http://myparenthetical.com/

Individual web pages:

www.webmd.com/parenting/guide/discipline-tactics
http://pubs.ext.vt.edu/350/350–111/350–111.html

References

Allen, K., & Rainie, L. (2002). *Parents online.* Retrieved from Pew Internet and American Life Project website: www.pewinternet.org/Reports/2002/Parents-Online.aspx

Campbell, D., & Palm, G. (2004). *Group parent education: Promoting parent learning and support.* Thousand Oaks, CA: Sage.

Doty, J. L., Doty, M. J., & Dworkin, J. (2011). Web-based family life education: Spotlight on user experience. *Journal of Extension, 49(6).* Retrieved from www.joe.org/joe/2011 december/tt6.php

Doty, J. L., Dworkin, J., & Connell, J. H. (2012). Examining digital differences: Parents' online activities. *Family Science Review, 17*, 18–39.

Drentea, P., & Moren-Cross, J. (2005). Social capital and social support on the web: The case of an Internet mother site. *Sociology of Health and Illness, 27*, 920–943.

Dunham, P., Hurshman, A., Litwin, E., Gusella, J., Ellsworth, C., & Dodd, P. (1998). Computer-mediated social support: Single young mothers as a model system. *American Journal of Community Psychology, 26*, 281–306.

Dworkin, J., Connell, J., & Doty, J. (2013). A literature review of parents' online behavior. *Cyberpsychology: Journal of Psychososcial Research on Cyberspace*, *7(2).* Retrieved from http://cyberpsychology.eu/view.php?cisloclanku=2013052301&article=2

Ebata, A., & Dennis, S. (2011). Family life education on the technological frontier, in S. F. Duncan & H. W. Goddard (Eds.) *Family life education: Principles and practices for effective outreach* (2nd ed.) (pp. 236–262). Thousand Oaks, CA: Sage.

Grassian, E. (2008). *UCLA College Library How-to Guides: Thinking critically about world wide web resources.* Retrieved from www.library.ucla.edu/libraries/college/thinking-critically-about-world-wide-web-resources

Hoffman, D. (2013). Power struggles: The paradoxes of emotion and control among child-centered mothers in privileged America, in C. Faircloth, D. M. Hoffman, & L. L. Layne (Eds.) *Parenting in global perspective* (pp. 229–243). New York: Routledge.

Hudson, D., Campbell–Grossman, C., Fleck, M. O., Elek, S., & Shipman, A. (2003). Effects of the new fathers network on first-time fathers parenting self-efficacy and parenting satisfaction during the transition to parenthood. *Issues in Comprehensive Pediatric Nursing, 26*, 217–229.

Hughes, R., Jr. (1994). A framework for developing family life education programs. *Family Relations, 43*, 74–80.

Hughes, R., Jr., Bowers, J., Mitchell, E., Curtiss, S., & Ebata, A. (2012). Developing online family life prevention and education programs. *Family Relations, 61*, 711–727.

Madge, C., & O'Connor, H. (2002). On-line with e-mums: Exploring the Internet as a medium for research. *Area, 34*, 92–102.

Martin, S., & Robinson, J. (2007). The income digital divide: Trends and predictions for levels of Internet use. *Social Problems, 54*, 1–22.

Metzler, C., Sanders, M., Rusby, J., & Crowley, R. (2011). Using consumer preference information to increase the reach and impact of media-based parenting interventions in a public health approach to parenting support. *Behavior Therapy, 43*, 257–270.

Moseley, K., Freed, G., & Goold, S. (2011). Which sources of child health advice do parents follow? *Clinical Pediatrics, 50*, 50–56.

Myers-Walls, J., & Myers-Bowman, K. (1999). Sorting through parenting education materials: A values approach and the example of socially conscious parenting. *Family Science Review, 12*, 69–86.

Na, J., & Chia, S. (2008). Impact of online resources on informal learners: Parents' perception of their parenting skills. *Computers & Education, 51*, 173–186.

National Telecommunications and Information Administration. (2011). *Digital nation: Expanding Internet usage*. Washington, DC: U.S. Department of Commerce. Retrieved from http://ntia.doc.gov/files/ntia/publications/ntia_internet_use_report_february_2011.pdf

Nichols, S., Nixon, H., Pudney, V., & Jurvansuu, S. (2009). Parents resourcing children's early development and learning. *Early Years, 29*, 147–161.

Pew Research Center. (n.d.) *Pew Research Internet Project*. Retrieved from www.pewinternet.org/

Plantin, L., & Daneback, K. (2009). Parenthood, information, and support on the Internet: A literature review of research on parents and professionals online. *BMC Family Practice, 10*, 34.

Radey, M., & Randolph, K. A. (2009). Parenting sources: How do parents differ in their efforts to learn about parenting? *Family Relations*, 58, 536–548.

Rainie, L., & Smith, A. (2013). *Tablet and e-reader ownership update*. Retrieved from Pew Internet and American Life Project website: www.pewinternet.org/2013/10/18/tablet-and-e-reader-ownership-update/

Rothbaum, F., Martland, N., & Jannsen, J. (2008). Parents' reliance on the web to find information about children and families: Socio-economic differences in use, skills and satisfaction. *Journal of Applied Developmental Psychology, 29*, 118–128.

Shwalb, D., Kawai, H., & Whoji, J. (1995). The place of advice: Japanese parents' sources of information about childrearing and child health. *Journal of Applied Developmental Psychology, 16*, 629–644.

Simpson, A. (1997). *The role of the mass media in parenting education*. Boston, MA: Center for Health Communication, Harvard School of Public Health.

Smith, A. (2013). *Smartphone ownership 2013*. Retrieved from Pew Internet and American Life Project website: www.pewinternet.org/2013/06/05/smartphone-ownership-2013/

Statistics Canada. (2010). *Canadian Internet Use Survey*. Retrieved from www.statcan.gc.ca/daily-quotidien/110525/dq110525b-eng.htm

Teacher Certification. (n.d.). *Evaluation techniques of Internet resources*. Retrieved from www.teachercertification.org/teach/evaluation-techniques-of-Internet-resources.php

UK Statistics Authority. (2010). *Internet access—households and individuals*. Retrieved from www.ons.gov.uk/ons/publications/index.html

University of Washington (n.d.). *Trio training: Assessing website quality*. Retrieved from http://depts.washington.edu/trio/resources/web/proof_assess.php

Walker, S., Dworkin, J., & Connell, J. (2011). Variation in parent use of information and communications technology: Does quantity matter? *Family & Consumer Sciences Research Journal, 40*, 106–119.

Wartella, E., Rideout, V., Lauriella, A & Connell, S. (2013). *Parenting in the age of digital technology: A national survey*. Northwestern University, Center on Media and Human Development. Retrieved from http://web5.soc.northwestern.edu/cmhd/wp-content/uploads/2013/05/Parenting-Report_FINAL.pdf

PART III

Best Practices in Evidence-based Programs

10

THE INCREDIBLE YEARS® PARENT PROGRAMS

Methods and Principles that Support Program Fidelity

Carolyn Webster-Stratton

Learning Goals

1. Learn about Incredible Years parent programs' goals, objectives, and theoretical foundations to promote positive and responsive parenting, build support networks, reduce child disruptive behavior problems, and increase child social and emotional competence.
2. Learn about randomized control group trials related to the IY parent programs.
3. Understand the value of IY Teacher and Child Programs in support of IY parent programs
4. Understand the importance of fidelity implementation of the IY programs using IY training principles and methods and how to balance fidelity delivery with adaptation for the cultural context of every family.
5. Recognize the importance of ongoing consultation and support after initial training.

Introduction

Social, emotional, and behavioral problems in young children are the most common reason parents seek help from mental health professionals. Without intervention, these disruptive behavior problems can lead to poor educational achievement and confer risk for later psychopathology including criminality, substance abuse, and other adverse outcomes (Tremblay, Nagin, & Seguin, 2004). A Cochrane review recently showed that group-based parenting programs improved parenting skills, parental mental health, and children's conduct problems according to parent report and independent observations (Furlong, McGilloway,

Bywater, Hutchings, Smith, & Donnelly, 2012). Interestingly, the severity of conduct issues prior to parents starting the program did not influence program effectiveness. Another recent meta-analysis of 36 controlled trials with preschool children provided robust quantitative support for evidence-based parent interventions being provided as the first-line treatment for early disruptive behavior (Comer, Chow, Chan, Cooper-Vince, & Wilson, 2013). Despite the growing body of evidence to support the effectiveness of group-based parenting programs, the proportion of children and their parents receiving evidence-based programs is decreasing (Comer et al., 2013). Barriers to program availability include financial difficulties, lack of understanding how to deliver such programs with fidelity, and clinician training issues.

This chapter reviews the Incredible Years Parenting Program Series, which is one of the evidence-based, group-based parenting programs for young children included in the reviews and meta-analyses cited above. This chapter will include the theoretical foundation, goals, and core content of these programs as well as the research evidence and the unique methods and principles of delivering the programs with fidelity.

Theoretical Foundations and History

The Incredible Years® Parent Series (IY) was originally developed in 1979 for parents of children ages 4 to 6 years (Webster-Stratton, 1981, 1982). It was designed to reduce the malleable family risk factors that lead to negative outcomes for children, such as ineffective parenting, harsh discipline, neglect and poor attachment, parent isolation and lack of support, and low involvement with day-care providers and teachers. Over subsequent decades the program has continued to be refined and updated based on research and parent feedback with both high-risk prevention populations and treatment populations.

The IY parent training series is grounded in cognitive social learning theories about the development of antisocial behaviors in children (Patterson, Reid, & Dishion, 1992) as well as modeling and self-efficacy theory (Bandura, 1977, 1982), developmental cognitive stages and interactive learning methods (Piaget & Inhelder, 1962), and attachment relationship theories (Ainsworth, 1974; Bowlby, 1980). The parenting program works to break the negative coercive cycle described by Patterson (Patterson et al., 1992) and build positive relationships and attachment between parents and children as well as strengthen parents' support networks with teachers and other parents. The program integrates cognitive, emotional, and behavioral theories, all considered equally important.

Program Goals and Objectives

Currently the BASIC (core) parent training is four different curricula tailored to the developmental stage of the child: Baby Program (4 weeks to 9 months),

Toddler Program (1–2½ years), Preschool Program (3–5 years), and School-Age Program (6–12 years). Each of these programs emphasizes developmentally appropriate parenting skills and includes age-appropriate video examples of culturally diverse families and children with varying temperaments and developmental issues. The specific objectives for each of these programs can be found on the website http://incredibleyears.com/about/incredible-years-series/objectives/. In addition to the BASIC program there are also other adjunct programs such as the ADVANCE curriculum, which are described below.

Short-term program goals for parents are improved parent–child interactions and attachment, lessening of harsh and building nurturing parenting, and increased parental social support and problem solving. These positive parent changes, in turn, lead to child changes including increasing social competence, emotion regulation, positive attributions, problem-solving ability, and academic readiness while preventing or reducing externalizing (aggressive, defiant, oppositional behaviors) and internalizing (anxiety, fears, somatic symptoms) behavior problems. The long-term goals for the program are the prevention of conduct disorders, academic failure, delinquency, and substance abuse.

The IY parent programs were originally developed as a clinic-based treatment program for reducing young children's conduct problems (high rates of aggression, defiance, and oppositional and impulsive behaviors). They were researched in randomized control group trials (RCTs) with parents who had children (ages 3–8) diagnosed (DSM-III and IV) with oppositional defiant disorder (ODD) and attention deficit hyperactivity disorder (ADHD). Many of these children also were comorbid for internalizing problems and developmental delays. Later the program protocols were revised by the developer for use as a selective prevention program in targeted schools addressing socioeconomically disadvantaged children (greater than 70 percent free lunch). These program protocols were also evaluated in RCTs with families enrolled in Head Start and families involved with child protective services. Currently the programs are being offered both as prevention and treatment programs in a variety of settings such as mental health clinics, primary grade schools, Head Start centers, jails, homeless shelters and residential homes, and in businesses as employee benefits.

The Incredible Years® "Core" BASIC Parent Programs

In the IY *Baby and Toddler Programs*, parents are focused on helping their babies and toddlers successfully accomplish three developmental milestones—secure attachment with their parents (or primary caregiver); language and social expression; and beginning development of a sense of self. Program topics for the baby program include: baby-directed play; speaking "parentese" (language that is melodious, high pitched, elongated, sing-song-like, uses repetition and exaggerated facial expressions); providing physical, tactile, and visual stimulation; nurturing parenting; providing a language-rich environment; baby-proofing to assure safety and building a support network. The baby program is a minimum of 9–12 weekly, 2-hour sessions with parents and babies present. Parents use the *Incredible Babies* book (Webster-Stratton, 2011a), which includes journaling and developmental and safety checklists. Program topics for the toddler program include: toddler-directed play; descriptive commenting, social and emotion coaching; language-rich specific praise; understanding toddlers' drive for exploration and need for predictable routines; clear limit setting; toddler-proofing to assure safety; and separation and reunion strategies. The BASIC toddler parent program is completed in a minimum of 12–14 weekly, 2-hour group sessions and has its own *Incredible Toddlers* parent book (Webster-Stratton, 2011b).

In the IY BASIC *Preschool Program*, parents are focused on the developmental milestones of encouraging school readiness skills (pre-writing, pre-reading, discovery learning); emotional regulation; and beginning social and friendships skills. Program topics include continuation of toddler topics as well as academic, persistence, and self-regulation coaching; effective use of praise and encouragement; proactive discipline; and teaching children beginning problem-solving skills. The preschool program is offered in 18–20 weekly sessions for high-risk populations and for parents of children diagnosed with ODD or ADHD. There is also a reduced 14-week protocol of this program for low-risk prevention populations. The text for both the Preschool and the School Age programs is entitled *Incredible Years: A Troubleshooting Guide for Parents of Children Ages 3–8 Years* (Webster-Stratton, 2006).

The *School Age Program* focuses on the developmental milestones of encouraging children's independence; motivation for academic learning; and development of family responsibility and empathy awareness. Program topics continue to build on core relationship skills with special time with parents; incentive systems for difficult behaviors; clear and respectful limit setting; encouragement of family chores; predictable homework routines; adequate monitoring; logical consequences; and working successfully with teachers. The *School Age Program* has protocols for 6–8- and 9–12-year-old children (both are 16+ sessions). The older age protocol includes content on monitoring afterschool activities, and discussions regarding family rules about TV and computer use, as well as drugs and alcohol.

In the *Group-based Delivery of IY Program*, all programs involve group-led discussions of a series of age-appropriate video vignettes of parents interacting with children in family life situations. The vignettes represent Latino, African American, Asian, and Caucasian mothers and fathers with children of varying developmental abilities and temperament. Programs have been translated into more than five languages: Chinese, Danish, Dutch, French, Norwegian, Portuguese, and Russian. Currently efforts are being made to translate the programs into Japanese and Arabic. Trained group facilitators use these video vignettes to facilitate modeling, self-reflection, group discussion, problem solving, and to trigger behavioral and cognitive practices. Group size is 10–14 parents. Group facilitators help parents learn behavior management, self-regulation skills, and developmental principles, which they apply to their goals for themselves and their children.

Home-based delivery. Home-based coach-led versions of all four parenting programs are also available and are recommended as an adjunct to the group model for families referred by child welfare for extra practice with children at home and for makeup sessions when group sessions are missed.

Incredible Years® adjuncts to parent programs

In addition to the core BASIC parenting programs there are also three supplemental or adjunct parenting programs to be used in combination with BASIC for particular populations. First, the ADVANCE parenting program offered after completion of the BASIC preschool or school-age programs was designed for selective high-risk and indicated populations. This program focuses on parents' interpersonal risk factors such as anger, stress and depression management, poor coping skills, lack of support, and ineffective communication skills. The content of this program includes teaching cognitive self-control strategies, problem solving between couples and teachers, communicaton skills, ways to give and get support, how to set up family meetings, and ways to teach children problem-solving skills. This entire program is an additional 9–12-week supplement to the BASIC programs.

A second optional adjunct training to the Preschool Program is the *School Readiness Program* for children ages 3–4 years (4–6 sessions) that is designed to help high-risk and new immigrant parents support their children's preliteracy and interactive reading readiness skills. A third optional adjunct for the Toddler, Preschool and Early School Age programs is the *Attentive Parenting® Program* for children ages 2 to 6 years. This 8–10-session group prevention program is designed to teach parents social, emotional, and persistence coaching, reading skills and how to promote their children's self-regulation skills and problem-solving skills. The Incredible Years Series also includes complementary curricula for teachers, and children, which utilize similar group training methods and processes.

Evidence-based Research and Evaluation

The IY Series programs have been the subject of extensive empirical evaluation over the past three decades. The programs have been widely endorsed by various review groups including the Office for Juvenile Justice and Delinquency Prevention (OJJDP) as 1 of 11 "blueprint" model violence prevention evidence-based programs for treating and preventing disruptive behavior disorders (Webster-Stratton & Mihalic, 2001). Further, the toddler, preschool, and school-age programs have been researched as prevention programs with high-risk populations (Head Start and primary grades addressing low-income families) as well as treatment interventions with children with diagnoses such as ODD, ADHD, and internalizing problems across a variety of settings and cultural contexts with high fidelity (Webster-Stratton & Herman, 2008; Webster-Stratton & Reid, 2010). A recent meta-analytic review examined the IY parent training regarding disruptive and pro-social behavior in 50 control group studies where the IY intervention group was compared to the control group. Results were presented for treatment populations as well as indicated and selective prevention studies. The programs were successful in improving child behavior in a diverse range of families, especially for children with the most severe cases, and the program was considered well established (Menting, Orobio de Castro, & Matthys, 2013).

Treatment and Indicated Populations

The efficacy of the IY BASIC parent treatment program for children (ages 2–8 years) diagnosed with ODD/CD and ADHD was demonstrated in eight published randomized control group trials (RCTs) by the program developer (Webster-Stratton, 1981, 1982, 1984, 1990a, 1992, 1994; Webster-Stratton, Kolpacoff, & Hollinsworth, 1988; Webster-Stratton, Hollinsworth, & Kolpacoff, 1989; Webster-Stratton & Hammond, 1997; Webster-Stratton & Reid, 2003; Webster-Stratton, Reid, & Hammond, 2004; Webster-Stratton, Reid, & Beauchaine, 2011).

The BASIC program has consistently improved parental attitudes and parent–child interactions, and reduced harsh discipline and child conduct problems, compared with wait-list control groups. These results are consistent for toddler, preschool, and school-age versions of the programs (Gross et al., 2003). One study (Webster-Stratton, 1994) indicated the additive benefits of combining the BASIC program with the ADVANCE program on children's pro-social solution generation and parents' marital interactions. Consequently a 20–24-week program that combined BASIC plus ADVANCE became the core treatment for parents of children diagnosed with ODD and/or ADHD and was used for the majority of the treatment studies. Several studies have also shown that IY treatment effects are durable 1–3 years post treatment (Webster-Stratton et al., 1989; Webster-Stratton, 1990b; Webster-Stratton, Reid, & Beauchaine, 2013). Recently two 8- to 12-year follow-up studies of families treated with the IY parent program because of their children's conduct problems (Webster-Stratton, Rinaldi, & Reid, 2010; Scott, Briskman, & O'Connor, 2014) indicated that 75 percent of the teenagers were typically adjusted with minimal behavioral and emotional problems. The later study (Scott et al., 2014) also indicated that in comparison with the control condition who received individualized supportive therapy, the mothers in the IY treatment condition expressed greater emotional warmth, supervised their adolescents more closely, and their children's reading ability was substantially improved on a standardized assessment.

The BASIC programs have been replicated with treatment populations by independent investigators in mental health clinics with families of children diagnosed with conduct problems (Taylor, Schmidt, Pepler, & Hodgins, 1998; Drugli & Larsson, 2006; Gardner, Burton, & Klimes, 2006; Scott, Spender, Doolan, Jacobs, & Aspland, 2001; Drugli, Larsson, Fossum, & Morch, 2010; Scott et al., 2010) and in doctors' offices with toddlers with ADHD symptoms (Lavigne et al., 2008; Perrin, Sheldrick, McMenamy, Henson, & Carter, 2014) Other treatment studies by independent investigators may be found in the recent meta-analytic review described earlier of 50 control group studies evaluating the effectiveness of the IY parent programs (Menting et al., 2013).

Prevention Populations

Additionally, four RCTs have been conducted by the developer with multiethnic, socioeconomically disadvantaged families in schools (Webster-Stratton, 1998; Reid, Webster-Stratton, & Beauchaine, 2001; Webster-Stratton, Reid, & Hammond, 2001). A study on elementary school children evaluated the effects of parent intervention delivered in schools with an indicated, culturally diverse population. Children whose mothers received the intervention showed fewer externalizing problems, better emotion regulation, and stronger parent–child bonding than control children. Mothers in the parent intervention group showed more supportive and less coercive parenting than control mothers (Reid, Webster-Stratton, & Hammond, 2007).

At least six RCTs by independent investigators with high-risk prevention populations have found that the BASIC parenting program increases parents' use of positive attention with their children (praise, coaching, descriptive commenting) and positive discipline strategies, and reduces harsh, critical, and coercive discipline strategies (see review Webster-Stratton & Reid, 2010). These replications were "effectiveness" trials in applied mental health settings, schools, homes post incarceration, and doctor's clinical practices, not a university research clinic, and the IY group leaders were existing staff (nurses, social workers, and psychologists) at the centers or doctors' offices (e.g., Raaijmakers et al., 2008; Posthumus, Raaijmakers, Maassen, Engeland, & Matthys, 2012; Perrin et al., 2014). The program has also been found to be effective with diverse populations including those representing Latino, Asian, African American, and Caucasian background in the USA (Reid et al., 2001), and in other countries such as the UK, Ireland, Norway, Sweden, Holland, New Zealand, Wales, and Russia (Scott et al., 2001; Gardner et al., 2006; Hutchings et al., 2007; Raaijmakers et al., 2008; Larsson et al., 2009; Scott et al., 2010). These findings illustrate the transportability of the IY parenting programs to other cultures and countries.

Fidelity of IY Parent Program Delivery

The fidelity of evidence-based programs (EBP) is an important topic for the delivery of these programs in the field. Fidelity, or intervention integrity, refers to the degree of exactness with which group leaders or clinicians adhere to the original training program model features, with the goal of replicating original research outcomes (Schoenwald & Hoagwood, 2001). Fidelity can be conceptualized in three dimensions: (a) program adherence, or delivery of core program content and intervention dosage (number of sessions) in the recommended sequence; (b) clinician competence, or the IY group leader's skill level in using the training methods, processes, and learning principles employed in the original program model; and (c) program differentiation, or implementation of the program for the population for whom the program was designed. In addition to the three dimensions outlined here, parent responsiveness, or the level of engagement in the program, is an important component of intervention fidelity. In other words, fidelity encompasses both the quality and quantity of EBP training delivery.

Why does fidelity matter? Convincing evidence exists that program delivery fidelity is predictive of significant positive outcomes across a number of different EBPs, notably parent training programs (Henggeler, Schoenwald, Liao, Letourneau, & Edwards, 2002; Wilson & Lipsey, 2007; Eames et al., 2009). Poor program fidelity, including reduced program dosage and poor quality delivery, has been shown to predict little or no change, challenging the view that some exposure to program components is better than no exposure. Numerous studies have shown that dosage (Baydar, Reid, & Webster-Stratton, 2003; Lochman, Boxmeyer, Powell, Roth, & Windle, 2006) and quality of program delivery methods and processes are related to effect size of outcomes (Scott, Carby, & Rendu, 2008; Eames et al., 2009). Adding consultation and supervision for clinicians increases fidelity of program delivery (Henggeler et al., 2002; Raver et al., 2008; Lochman et al., 2009; Webster-Stratton, Reid, & Marsenich, 2014), which in turn leads to better outcomes. Taken together these findings regarding evidence-based parenting programs lend support to the assertion that higher dosages of these programs and quality delivery lead to more robust effects. Despite this compelling research, most mental health agencies are slicing and dicing EBP's dose and content due to budget barriers.

The IY Program Series provides a stellar example of an EBP that embeds fidelity and adaptation within its design. First, the core features of the program are presented along with the methods and processes that make the intervention effective. Second, the dissemination support mechanisms (training, mentoring, consultation, and coaching) necessary to facilitate high fidelity of implementation of IY parent programs are highlighted. The goal is to clarify the underlying principles and layered supports needed to effectively disseminate the IY programs to audiences with diverse cultural backgrounds and with children of varying developmental, academic, and social-emotional needs. Often fidelity and adaptation are thought of as mutually exclusive, but in the IY model they are considered both complementary and necessary. Finally, implications for future research are discussed.

IY Series Training Methods and Delivery Principles

The IY Series is frequently misunderstood as a fixed-dosage, inflexible, curricular-driven EBP. Instead, the IY Series is better understood as a set of principle-driven, dynamic interventions that were developed in applied settings and are flexibly adapted to each cultural context for parents of children with varying developmental abilities based on ongoing dialogue and collaboration between participants and training group leaders (see therapist text Webster-Stratton, 2012). The big ideas or principles, video-based vignettes, and participant books give structure to the programs, but flexible implementation gives voice to the participants and helps ensure the content fits the context of their lives. By using a principle-driven framework and flexible delivery strategies, the IY programs have proven to impact parent, child, and teacher behaviors across a wide range of settings with culturally diverse groups of participants in repeated and rigorous evaluation studies (Webster-Stratton & Reid, 2010).

The IY program utilizes self-reflective and experiential learning, group support and problem solving, and specific training methods that facilitate parents in learning important behavior management skills along with helping parents manage their own self-regulation and stress. Part of using the IY parent program model successfully is for group leaders to understand how to tailor or adapt the program according to the individual needs of each parent. Group leaders can achieve flexible applications of the manual when there is understanding of the program at multiple levels, including the program model, content, training methods, and delivery principles built into the program to promote a culturally and developmentally responsive structure for delivering the program to diverse populations. Evidence of the success of the IY implementation and adaptation processes comes from the high attendance and parent satisfaction ratings by parents in prior IY studies in varied contexts and multiple countries (Menting et al., 2013).

IY Parent Training Methods

The core IY training methods used to support effective parent learning include having trained group leaders or clinicians who (a) facilitate supportive and collaborative parent group processes and problem-solving interactions; (b) utilize video vignettes strategically selected to model effective parent interactions with children representing a variety of developmental abilities and ages; (c) structure role play and practices for parents to self-reflect and have experiential learning utilizing the newly acquired parenting skills; (d) set up small group breakouts for behavior planning and practices; and (e) assign home activities between group sessions. These training methods are utilized in every group session.

Group Process

A key part of the transportability of IY is that it is delivered in groups. Not only is this approach more cost-effective than individual therapy, but it also allows group leaders to capitalize on dimensions of group process that facilitate cooperative learning (Brown & Palincsar, 1989; Eames et al., 2009), motivation, and self-efficacy (Bandura, 1982). IY programs attempt to build social networks among parents and reduce the isolation and stigma that they commonly experience, especially those who are struggling with oppositional children. Another advantage of the group is that it allows the group leader to capitalize on the collective knowledge and wisdom of all the parent participants. They learn from each other as much as they do from the group leader. When resistance emerges, the group leader does not argue against it, but rather draws on the group for other perceptions.

Video Modeling

A core feature of the IY Series is that it utilizes social learning, modeling, and self-efficacy theory (Bandura, 1977), which contends that observation of a model can support the learning of new skills. Video-based modeling involves showing participants actual parents using effective behavior management skills. Video vignettes show parents and children in unrehearsed situations, such as during unstructured play, reading times, mealtimes, bath times, going to bed, getting dressed for school, doing homework, grocery shopping, and doing chores. Scenes depict diverse parents with a variety of parenting styles and skill levels using many different strategies. Children in the scenes represent children of different ages, cultures, developmental abilities, and temperament styles. When delivered in groups, video-based modeling has the added benefit of triggering group discussion, self-reflective learning, and practices to reenact vignettes. The goal is not only to have parents grasp the intended concept, but also to have them become actively involved in problem solving, sharing ideas about the vignette, and practicing. In order to make the training personally relevant and bridge the gap between the specific structure and content of the vignettes and the varied backgrounds, situations, and problems represented by the participating parents, group leaders help parents discuss how the concepts illustrated in the vignettes apply or don't apply to their own unique home situations.

Role Play Practices and Experiential Learning

Role play and performance-based practice of unfamiliar or newly acquired behaviors and cognitions is effective in producing behavioral changes (Twentyman & McFall, 1975). Role play practices help parents anticipate situations more clearly, dramatizing possible sequences of behavior and thoughts that occur every day at home. This allows parents to apply behavioral and cognitive principles to situations that are specific to them and their personal situations. Parents are given ample opportunity to participate in role plays and to give and receive feedback about effective parenting practices. Group leaders direct and scaffold these role play practices and guide discussions through collaborative facilitation strategies and Socratic questioning.

Small Group Breakouts and Buzz Brainstorms

The IY Series uses small group breakouts to stimulate strategies regarding targeting specific "positive opposite" behaviors (that replace negative behaviors) and to engage parents. Thus, the IY Series employs a partnership learning philosophy that uses strategies to give and respect the voices of parents with a reciprocal approach to learning between the parents and the group leaders.

Weekly Home Practice Assignments

The IY group leader assigns home practice activities for every session to help transfer what is learned in the group session to practice at home. Learning about a skill or planning a strategy during the group discussion is one thing, while implementing it with their children at home is another. Parents bring their successes and challenges faced in implementing the strategy at home to the next group session. Thus, the between-weekly sessions practice assignments serve as powerful experiential learning opportunities and stimulus for discussion, review, and refinement of strategies and further role plays in subsequent sessions.

Training and Supporting Clinician/Group Leaders to Deliver the IY Programs

Training for group leaders from experienced IY accredited trainers or mentors is highly recommended because it is more likely to lead to fidelity in program delivery. The 3-day workshops (with a maximum of 25 clinicians) are offered on a regular basis in Seattle, or can be arranged at the agency site through the IY headquarters. The clinician/group leader training process mirrors the methods and processes to be used by group leaders with parents. It includes modeling group leader skills, participant experiential practice mediating vignettes and leading small group discussions, setting up strategic role play practices, collaborative learning, and problem solving (Webster-Stratton, 2006b). However, sending motivated clinicians or group leaders with adequate qualifications to an accredited 3-day training workshop is only the first step in successful program delivery. After initial training, group leaders should be provided with sufficient consultation, support, and video reviews of their group sessions from accredited IY coaches or mentors to ensure quality delivery of the intervention. Research has shown that post workshop coaching, consultation and support leads to high-quality program delivery (Lochman et al., 2009; Webster-Stratton, Reid, & Marsenich, 2014).

In order to ensure fidelity and accreditation/certification it is necessary for group leaders to submit videos of the group sessions they conduct, protocol checklists, parent attendance lists, and parent evaluations. Those who achieve accreditation are then eligible for further training as IY peer coaches or mentors. Peer coaches provide peer supervision and support to newer group leaders within their agencies. Mentors provide support and supervision to new group leaders and are also able to provide accredited workshop training to new group leaders within their agency or geographic areas. Coaches and mentors allow agencies to become more self-sufficient in the ongoing delivery of the IY program (see website for description of the certification/accreditation process http://incredibleyears.com/certification-gl/basic-program/).

Cultural Implications

To enhance parent engagement and maximize outcomes among individuals from diverse backgrounds and experiences, programs must be flexible enough to allow for some tailoring and adaptation. Prevention scientists developing interventions and clinicians implementing evidence-based interventions must be aware of the important balance between adaptation and implementation with high fidelity. The IY parent program utilizes a principle-driven approach that provides a guide to gaining this balance. Given that culture is not static and that relevant cultural dimensions are virtually limitless, it is not realistic to develop and rigorously evaluate a new, culturally adapted intervention for each of these dimensions as they change over time. Consider that race, ethnicity, nationality, socioeconomic status, religion, marital status, family constellation, geography, gender, age/developmental status, and neighborhood (among other cultural factors) all interact to influence responsiveness to interventions. When we appreciate this fact, every intervention truly needs to be tailored to the unique cultural context of every individual's life. The only reasonable way for this to occur is for tailoring to be built explicitly into the design of an intervention. For over thirty years, the IY Series has incorporated a principle-driven collaborative and experiential reflective approach to guide effective tailoring, adaptation, and dissemination of effective parenting practices.

Additionally, the need for an infrastructure to support those training and implementing interventions through supervision and consultation as well as ongoing on-site coaching to support change in real-life settings is an important facet of intervention science. These support systems are often neglected or left unmentioned. Without proper training and ongoing support, evidence-based interventions are unlikely to be implemented with fidelity, minimizing the potential outcomes for children and families. In fact, the clinician supports should be considered as an integral part of the intervention. Implications for prevention and intervention science include the need for more transparency in the supports truly needed to adequately and effectively implement evidence-based interventions.

Lastly, intervention development must be thought of as an ongoing process rather than an endpoint given that new data gathered from ongoing research and clinical practice can inform improvements to the intervention. For instance, the IY Series implementation manuals (including handouts, books, and resources given to participants), vignettes, and even the suggested number of sessions have been refined over time based on these experiences. An important implication for prevention science is understanding that effective interventions continue to evolve and improve based on internal audits and feedback. As a parallel, consider that the safety features of cars continuously improve. Few people, when given the option, would opt to drive the old model without the safety additions of seat belts, and air bags. Gathering data on what works, eliciting ongoing feedback, and actively participating in the implementation of the intervention across a variety of contexts provides the needed information to improve interventions and meet the needs of broader diverse populations.

Conclusion

This chapter highlights the collaborative and systematic processes and principles that allow the IY parenting program to be adapted with high fidelity. Many of these processes and principles have been part of the program from the outset but others evolved iteratively with our research and repeated applications of the program over time and across settings. Continued refinements occur as the program continues to expand and as the science behind it improves. The most important lesson to date is that the principles and processes that support dissemination cannot be afterthoughts; rather they need to be essential, foundational aspects of the intervention if it is to be successfully transported. Only dynamic interventions with identifiable, non-reducible, and measureable elements will be broadly disseminated with fidelity to meet the needs of an increasingly diverse parent and family population.

Key Points

1. Without intervention, young children with disruptive behavior problems are at risk for later psychopathology including criminality and substance abuse.
2. The proportion of parents and their children actually receiving evidence-based programs (EBPs) is decreasing because of financial difficulties, lack of understanding how to deliver such programs with fidelity, and how to adapt programs to the cultural context of every family.
3. Convincing evidence exists that EBP program delivery fidelity (recommended program dosage and quality delivery) is predictive of significant positive outcomes across a number of different EBPs.
4. The Incredible Years (IY) Series utilizes a principle-driven, collaborative approach that guides implementation with high fidelity and adaptation. It has been the subject of over fifty randomized control group studies and shown

to improve parenting practices and children's social and emotional behavior in a diverse range of families.

5. Agencies or countries implementing IY programs need to provide a supportive infrastructure to deliver initial training to clinicians and fidelity implementation through clinician supervision, consultation, and coaching.

Discussion Questions

1. Why is it important to deliver evidence-based programs with fidelity?
2. How is fidelity of the Incredible Years program conceptualized?
3. For the Incredible Years Parent Program, is it possible to make adaptations in the program in regard to the culture of families or the child's developmental status?
4. What are the underlying theories that influence the Incredible Years programs?
5. What populations are the Incredible Years parenting programs suitable for?
6. What are the core parent training methods needed for delivering the Incredible Years programs to parents?
7. What is the rationale for becoming accredited as a clinician to deliver the Incredible Years programs?
8. What outcomes or benefits can you expect if the Incredible Years programs are delivered with fidelity?
9. What is the role of an Incredible Years group leader?
10. What kind of training and support is recommended for Incredible Years group leaders?

Additional Resources

Website

The Incredible Years® programs: http://incredibleyears.com/programs/

References

Ainsworth, M. (1974). Infant-mother attachment and social development: Socialization as a product of reciprocal responsiveness to signals, in M. Richards (Ed.), *The integration of the child into the social world.* Cambridge, UK: Cambridge University Press.

Bandura, A. (1977). *Social learning theory*. Englewood Cliffs, NJ: Prentice-Hall.

Bandura, A. (1982). Self-efficacy mechanisms in human agency. *American Psychologist, 84*, 191–215.

Baydar, N., Reid, M., & Webster-Stratton, C. (2003). The role of mental health factors and program engagement in the effectiveness of a preventive parenting program for Head Start mothers. *Child Development, 74*, 1433–1453.

Bowlby, J. (1980). *Attachment and loss: Loss, sadness, and depression.* New York: Basic Books.

Brown, A., & Palincsar, A. (1989). Guided cooperative learning and individual knowledge acquisition, in L. Resnick (Ed.), *Knowing, learning and intruction: Essays in honor of Robter Glaser* (pp. 393–451). Hillsdale, NJ: Lawrence Erlbaum.

Comer, J., Chow, C., Chan, P., Cooper-Vince, C., & Wilson, L. (2013). Psychosocial treament efficacy for disruptive behavior problems in very young children: A meta-analytic examination. *Journal of the American Academy of Child and Adolescent Psychiatry, 52*, 26–36.

Drugli, M., & Larsson, B. (2006). Children aged 4–8 years treated with parent training and child therapy because of conduct problems: Generalisation effects to day-care and school settings. *European Child and Adolescent Psychiatry, 15*, 392–399.

Drugli, M., Larsson, B., Fossum, S., & Morch, W. (2010). Five- to six-year outcome and its prediction for children with ODD/CD treated with parent training. *Journal of Child Psychology& Psychiatry, 51*, 559–566.

Eames, C., Daley, D., Hutchings, J., Whitaker, C., Jones, K., Hughes, J., & Bywater, T. (2009). Treatment fidelity as a predictor of behaviour change in parents attending group-based parent training. *Child: Care, Health and Development, 35*, 1–10.

Furlong, M., McGilloway, S., Bywater, T., Hutchings, J., Smith, S., & Donnelly, M. (2012). Behavioural and cognitive-behavioural group-based parenting programmes for early-onset conduct problems in children ages 3 to 12 years. *Cochrane Database of Systematic Reviews (2)*, Art. No.: CD008225.

Gardner, F., Burton, J., & Klimes, I. (2006). Randomized controlled trial of a parenting intervention in the voluntary sector for reducing conduct problems in children: Outcomes and mechanisms of change. *Journal of Child Psychology and Psychiatry, 47*, 1123–1132.

Gross, D., Fogg, L., Webster-Stratton, C., Garvey, C., & Grady, J. (2003). Parent training with families of toddlers in day care in low-income urban communities. *Journal of Consulting and Clinical Psychology, 71*, 261–278.

Henggeler, S., Schoenwald, S., Liao, J., Letourneau, E., & Edwards, D. (2002). Transporting efficacious treatments to field settings: The link between supervisory practices and therapist fidelity in MST programs. *Journal of Clinical Child & Adolescent Psychology, 31*, 155–167.

Hutchings, J., Gardner, F., Bywater, T., Daley, D., Whitaker, C., Jones, K., Eames, C., Edwards, R. T. (2007). Parenting intervention in Sure Start services for children at risk of developing conduct disorder: Pragmatic randomized controlled trial. *British Medical Journal, 334*, 678.

Larsson, B., Fossum, B., Clifford, G., Drugli, M., Handegard, B., & Morch, W. (2009). Treatment of oppositional defiant and conduct problems in young Norwegian children: Results of a randomized trial. *European Child Adolescent Psychiatry, 18*, 42–52.

Lavigne, J., LeBailly, S., Gouze, K., Cicchetti, C., Pochyly, J., Arend, R., Jessup, B., & Binns, H. (2008). Treating oppositional defiant disorder in primary care: A comparison of three models. *Journal of Pediatric Psychology, 33*, 449–461.

Lochman, J., Boxmeyer, C., Powell, N., Lou, L., Wells, K., & Windle, M. (2009). Dissemination of the Coping Power program: Importance of intensity of counselor training. *Journal of Consulting and Clinical Psychology, 77*, 397–409.

Lochman, J., Boxmeyer, C., Powell, N., Roth, D., & Windle, M. (2006). Masked intervention effects: Analytic methods for addressing low dosage of intervention. *New Directions for Evaluations, 110*, 19–32.

Menting, A., Orobio de Castro, B., & Matthys, W. (2013). Effectiveness of the Incredible Years parent training to modify disruptive and prosocial child behavior:A meta-analytic review. *Clinical Psychology Review*, *33*, 901–913.

Patterson, G., Reid, J., & Dishion, T. (1992). *Antisocial boys: A social interactional approach* (Vol. 4). Eugene, OR: Castalia.

Perrin, E., Sheldrick, R., McMenamy, J., Henson, B., & Carter, A. (2014). Improving parenting skills for families of young children in pediatric settings: A randomized clinical trial. *Journal of the American Medical Association Pediatrics*, *168*, 16–24.

Piaget, J., & Inhelder, B. (1962). *The psychology of the child*. New York: Basic Books.

Posthumus, J., Raaijmakers, M., Maassen, G., Engeland, H., & Matthys, W. (2012). Sustained effects of Incredible Years as a preventive intervention in preschool children with conduct problems. *Journal of Abnormal Child Psychology*, *40*, 487–500.

Raaijmakers, M., Posthumus, J., Maassen, G., Van Hout, B., Van Engeland, H., & Matthys, W. (2008). *The evaluation of a preventive intervention for 4-year-old children at risk for disruptive behavior disorders: Effects on parenting practices and child behavior* (Dissertation). University Medical Center Utrecht, the Netherlands.

Raver, C., Jones, S., Li-Grining, C., Metzger, M., Champion, K., Sardin-Adjei, L., & Young, T. (2008). Improving preschool classroom processes: Preliminary findings from a randomized trial implemented in Head Start settings. *Early Childhood Research Quarterly*, *23*, 10–26.

Reid, M., Webster-Stratton, C., & Beauchaine, T. (2001). Parent training in Head Start: A comparison of program response among African American, Asian American, Caucasian, and Hispanic mothers. *Prevention Science*, *2*, 209–227.

Reid, M., Webster-Stratton, C., & Hammond, M. (2007). Enhancing a classroom social competence and problem-solving curriculum by offering parent training to families of moderate-to-high-risk elementary school children. *Journal of Clinical Child and Adolescent Psychology*, *36*, 605–620.

Schoenwald, S., & Hoagwood, K. (2001). Effectiveness, transportability, and dissemination of interventions: What matters when? *Journal of Psychiatric Services*, *52*, 1190–1197.

Scott, S., Briskman, J., & O'Connor, T. (2014). Early prevention of antisocial personality: Long-term follow-up of two randomized controlled trials comparing indicated and selective approaches. *American Journal of Psychiatry*, *171*, 649–657.

Scott, S., Carby, A., & Rendu, A. (2008). *Impact of therapists' skill on effectiveness of parenting groups for child antisocial behavior*. London: King's College, Institute of Psychiatry, University College London.

Scott, S., Spender, Q., Doolan, M., Jacobs, B., & Aspland, H. (2001). Multicentre controlled trial of parenting groups for child antisocial behaviour in clinical practice. *British Medical Journal*, *323*, 1–5.

Scott, S., Sylva, K., Doolan, M., Price, J., Jacobs, B., Crook, C., & Landau, S. (2010). Randomised controlled trial of parent groups for child antisocial behaviour targeting multiple risk factors: the SPOKES project. *Journal of Child Psychology and Psychiatry*, *51*, 48–57.

Taylor, T., Schmidt, F., Pepler, D., & Hodgins, H. (1998). A comparison of eclectic treatment with Webster-Stratton's Parents and Children Series in a children's mental health center: A randomized controlled trial. *Behavior Therapy*, *29*, 221–240.

Tremblay, R., Nagin, D., & Seguin, J. (2004). Physical aggression during early childhood: trajectories and predictors. *Pediatrics*, *114*, 43–50.

Twentyman, C., & McFall, R. (1975). Behavioral training of social skills in shy males. *Journal of Consulting and Clinical Psychology, 43*, 384–395.

Webster-Stratton, C. (1981). Modification of mothers' behaviors and attitudes through videotape modeling group discussion program. *Behavior Therapy, 12*, 634–642.

Webster-Stratton, C. (1982). Teaching mothers through videotape modeling to change their children's behaviors. *Journal of Pediatric Psychology, 7*, 279–294.

Webster-Stratton, C. (1984). Randomized trial of two parent-training programs for families with conduct-disordered children. *Journal of Consulting and Clinical Psychology, 52*, 666–678.

Webster-Stratton, C. (1990a). Enhancing the effectiveness of self-administered videotape parent training for families with conduct-problem children. *Journal of Abnormal Child Psychology, 18*, 479–492.

Webster-Stratton, C. (1990b). Long-term follow-up of families with young conduct problem children: From preschool to grade school. *Journal of Clinical Child Psychology, 19*, 144–149.

Webster-Stratton, C. (1992). Individually administered videotape parent training: "Who benefits?" *Cognitive Therapy and Research, 16*, 31–35.

Webster-Stratton, C. (1994). Advancing videotape parent training: A comparison study. *Journal of Consulting and Clinical Psychology, 62*, 583–593.

Webster-Stratton, C. (1998). Preventing conduct problems in Head Start children: Strengthening parenting competencies. *Journal of Consulting and Clinical Psychology, 66*, 715–730.

Webster-Stratton, C. (2006). *The Incredible Years: A trouble-shooting guide for parents of children aged 2–8 years.* Seattle, WA: Incredible Years.

Webster-Stratton, C. (2011a). *Incredible Babies.* Seattle, WA: The Incredible Years.

Webster-Stratton, C. (2011b). *The Incredible Toddlers.* Seattle, WA: The Incredible Years.

Webster-Stratton, C. (2012). *Collaborating with parents to reduce children's behavior problems: A book for therapists using the Incredible Years programs.* Seattle, WA: Incredible Years.

Webster-Stratton, C., & Hammond, M. (1997). Treating children with early-onset conduct problems: A comparison of child and parent training interventions. *Journal of Consulting and Clinical Psychology, 65*, 93–109.

Webster-Stratton, C., & Herman, K. (2008). The impact of parent behavior-management training on child depressive symptoms. *Journal of Counseling Psychology, 55*, 473–484.

Webster-Stratton, C., Hollinsworth, T., & Kolpacoff, M. (1989). The long-term effectiveness and clinical significance of three cost-effective training programs for families with conduct-problem children. *Journal of Consulting and Clinical Psychology, 57*, 550–553.

Webster-Stratton, C., Kolpacoff, M., & Hollinsworth, T. (1988). Self-administered videotape therapy for families with conduct-problem children: Comparison with two cost-effective treatments and a control group. *Journal of Consulting and Clinical Psychology, 56*, 558–566.

Webster-Stratton, C., & Mihalic, S. (2001). *Blueprints for violence prevention, book eleven: The Incredible Years—Parent, Teacher, and Child Training Series.* Boulder, CO: Center for the Study and Prevention of Violence.

Webster-Stratton, C., & Reid, M. (2003). The Incredible Years parents, teachers and child training series: A multifaceted treatment approach for young children with conduct problems, in A. Kazdin & J. Weisz (Eds.) *Evidence-based psychotherapies for children and adolescents* (pp. 224–240). New York: Guilford.

Webster-Stratton, C., & Reid, M. (2010). The Incredible Years Parents, Teachers and Children Training Series: A multifaceted treatment approach for young children with conduct problems, in A. Kazdin & J. Weisz (Eds.) *Evidence-based psychotherapies for children and adolescents* (2nd ed.) (pp. 194–210). New York: Guilford.

Webster-Stratton, C., Reid, M., & Beauchaine, T. (2011). Combining parent and child training for young children with ADHD. *Journal of Clinical Child and Adolescent Psychology, 40*, 1–13.

Webster-Stratton, C., Reid, M., & Beauchaine, T. (2013). One-year follow-up of combined parent and child intervention for young children with ADHD. *Journal of Clinical Child and Adolescent Psychology, 42*, 251–261.

Webster-Stratton, C., Reid, M. J., & Hammond, M. (2001). Preventing conduct problems, promoting social competence: A parent and teacher training partnership in Head Start. *Journal of Clinical Child Psychology, 30(3)*, 283–302.

Webster-Stratton, C., Reid, M. J., & Hammond, M. (2004). Treating children with early-onset conduct problems: Intervention outcomes for parent, child, and teacher training. *Journal of Clinical Child and Adolescent Psychology, 33(1)*, 105–124.

Webster-Stratton, C., Reid, J., & Marsenich, L. (2014). Improving therapist fidelity during evidence-based practice implementation. *Psychiatric Services, 65(6), 789–795.*

Webster-Stratton, C., Rinaldi, J., & Reid, J. M. (2010). Long term outcomes of the Incredible Years Parenting Program: Predictors of adolescent adjustment. *Child and Adolescent Mental Health, 16(1)*, 38–46.

Wilson, S. J., & Lipsey, M. W. (2007). School-based interventions for aggressive and disruptive behavior: Update of meta-analysis. *American Journal of Preventive Medicine, (33)*, 130–143.

11

PARENTING WISELY

Using Innovative Media for Parent Education

Robert E. Pushak & Donald A. Gordon

Learning Goals

1. Learn about a highly accessible, cost-effective, research-based parent education program that has been shown to reduce child and adolescent behavior problems, teen and parent substance use, and problems at school
2. Learn how easy it is for families to access and use the program on their own.
3. Learn how for the same reasons this program is easy for service providers to use in multiple formats.
4. Learn how this program can achieve automatic high treatment integrity and therefore achieve effective outcomes without the need for intensive and expensive service provider training or quality assurance procedures.
5. Learn about research demonstrating the program can be effectively used with less-educated, low-income, ethnically diverse families, including families who had been resistant to, and did not benefit from, previous intervention efforts.

Introduction

Parenting Wisely (PW) is a video-based interactive computer training program for parents and families that reduces behavior problems, youth violence, youth substance use, school drop-out, and a host of other negative child outcomes (Gordon, 2003). The CD-ROM program, also in an online format, requires parents to have neither previous computer experience nor the ability to read (the computer reads all text aloud). If parents have never used a computer before, usually all they need is a short tutorial on how to use a computer mouse to be able to successfully use the program on their own. The visual, auditory, text, and interactive format of PW encourages maximum skill retention.

Theoretical Foundations and History

Program development started in the early 1990s based on two premises that are well established in the existing literature. The first premise is that parent self-administered video parent training based on social learning theory is an effective intervention for preventing and reducing child behavior problems (Webster-Stratton, 1990, 1992). The second premise is that interactive videodisk instruction is superior to conventional instruction such as lectures or reading (Niemiec & Walberg, 1987; Fletcher, 1990).

Parenting Wisely provides skill training in several areas including praise, prompting, contracting, clear expectations, planned ignoring, positive reinforcement, contingency management, mindful parenting, monitoring, and supervision. Communication skills such as active listening, I-messages, problem solving, and speaking respectfully are also covered. Parents also learn strategies that address risk factors that go beyond the immediate context of the family such as negative peer influences, substance abuse, and managing difficulties at school. This skill training occurs in the context of a family systems perspective (Gordon, 2003), which emphasizes the interdependence of family member interactions. The program has a cognitive emphasis (Alexander, Pugh, Parsons, & Sexton, 2000; Gordon, 2003) which depicts the thoughts of various family members as setting a context that shapes family interactions. In 2011, the program was revised to update the video content. Additional content included teaching parents about how the neurobiology of the brain affects their children's behavior. Additional content was added on mindfulness in relation to parenting. Mindfulness involves focusing on the present moment and avoiding thoughts about the past or the future. Mindfulness helps people to be more aware of their thoughts, feelings, and the sensations in their bodies. Mindfulness involves being open, curious, and accepting while avoiding being judgmental or critical towards oneself or others. Mindfulness has been shown to improve emotional self-control and decrease anxiety, anger, and depression. These latter emotions are often related to thoughts about the past or worries about the future. Research on mindfulness and parenting has been shown to enhance parent–child relationships (Duncan, Coatsworth, & Greenberg, 2009).

The adolescent program covers 10 problem scenarios chosen based on research identifying problems that frequently occur in many families, but are even more frequent in high-risk families (Segal, Chen, Gordon, Kacir, & Gylys, 2003). These include: getting children to do housework; helping children with school problems; curfew problems; step-parent–step-child conflict; monitoring school, homework, and friends; loud music and incomplete chores; speaking respectfully and sharing computer time; sibling conflict and aggression; getting children ready for school on time; and finding drugs in a teen's bedroom. Parents choose a problem scenario by clicking on a video of a family struggling with one of the above problems. Voice-overs from the actors communicate parents' and children's inner thoughts that contribute to family conflict. Next, parents are presented with three choices for responding to the problem and are prompted to choose the response they are most likely to use. The response options typically reflect authoritarian/harsh parenting, permissive parenting, or authoritative/nurturing parenting (Baumrind, 1967, 1978). After making a choice, another video depicts that solution followed by review questions and a critique that covers positive and negative consequences of that choice. Parents can make a second, and later, a third choice for responding to the problem scenario and watch videos depicting how these choices are likely to play out followed by another review quiz. This helps parents learn that child problem behavior can be significantly increased or reduced by how parents respond to that behavior. Text at the bottom of the screen helps parents to identify effective skills depicted by the actors. Sometimes the parents in the video of the effective solution still make a few mistakes, which communicates that use of new skills can improve family interactions even if the parent's performance is not perfect.

Parenting Wisely uses Behavior Modeling Training, which is one of the most effective methods for changing behavior (Burke & Day, 1986). With this approach, videotaped actors demonstrate common errors parents make, followed by use of skills to remediate these errors. The user's attention is directed to the model's behavior demonstrating skill use via guided questions that follow each video scene, by onscreen narrators, and by text at the bottom of the screen as the skills are depicted.

As parents use the program they can click on specific skills such as "Praise" or "Active Listening" which are highlighted in bold text. A voice along with written text defines and discusses the advantages of each skill. Clicking on a "Play Examples" button activates examples of the actors using that skill. The text includes footnotes which cover additional content on neuroscience in relation to parenting. Parents not interested in this more academic content can skip over it by not clicking on footnotes. A significant number of parents have provided feedback that they find this information on neuroscience helpful (Pushak & Pretty, 2008). After the most effective solution has been chosen and critiqued, parents complete an on-screen quiz which helps them to test themselves on how well they have learned the concepts and techniques taught in the program. Parents must view all three solutions and complete the review questions before the program allows them to proceed to the next problem scenario.

Parents can complete the computer portion of the program in about three to five hours. Parents receive a workbook (Gordon, 2011) which includes the written content of the program, including guided questions and answers, and reviews each skill followed by a list of advantages of the skills. Each skill is broken down into numbered "How to Use" steps followed by several examples of the skill. The workbook includes home practice skill assignments.

The program can be accessed on the Internet either in a family's home or on a computer made available at a community service agency or a public library, or via a mobile device such as a smartphone. The CD-ROM (or USB drive for the revised version), DVD, and the Internet-based versions of the program automatically track how much of the program has been completed and track the parent's progress on review questions. The online version of the program promotes ongoing skill practice and use via text prompts on the parent`s cellphone for six months and via email prompts with additional practice exercises, which can continue for a few years.

The program is versatile and can be used by parents individually, practitioners working with the parent, or in group parent training. Since the program was designed to be simple enough for parents to use on their own, it is also easy for practitioners to use. There is a need for practitioners to be cautious in using PW with parents because there is a possibility that some of the advantages of parents using the program on its own will be undermined. An evaluation by Cefai, Smith, and Pushak (2010), for example, showed parental self-efficacy increased when parents use the program on their own. When practitioners participate in the sessions, parents might attribute changes to the practitioner and not themselves. Two studies have shown that the practitioner's presence might compromise

TABLE 11.1 Comparison of Therapy and Interactive Computer-based Intervention

Therapist-guided education	*Self-administered interactive computer*
1. Focus on developing and maintaining therapist–client rapport	1. Exclusive focus on teaching good parenting
2. Client often feels judged by therapist	2. No perception of judgment by computer
3. Client defensiveness may impede progress	3. Minimal client defensiveness
4. Therapist may confront client on parenting mistakes	4. Client recognizes common parenting mistakes made by actors
5. Client rarely asks for repetition of unclear advice	5. Client can repeat any portion of the program at any time
6. Pace usually set by therapist	6. Client sets pace
7. Possible decreased self-efficacy if benefits of intervention are attributed to therapist	7. Increased self-efficacy because client attributes benefits to their own choices
8. Significant therapy time devoted to resistance	8. Virtually no program time devoted to resistance
9. Difficult to train or improve therapist skills in evidence-based practice	9. Easy to improve program structure and content as evidence base continues to develop
10. Maintaining program integrity expensive and often difficult	10. Program integrity is automatic
11. Ongoing costs of maintaining skilled practitioners are high	11. Ongoing costs are low

Source: Adapted from Gordon (2003). Reprinted with permission.

outcomes on measures of child behavior (Tattersall, Cooper, & Duffy, 2003; Cefai et al., 2010). Table 11.1 covers a number of advantages of a self-administered program compared with therapist-led parent education. Included with the program are manuals for using PW one-to-one with parents and there is a group parent training curriculum, both of which are described below. Use of these manuals should increase confidence that practitioner involvement will avoid the above concerns and achieve effective outcomes.

Needs Assessment and Target Audience

The group curriculum has a handout on protection and risk factors for child behavior problems. Service providers can use this handout as a guide for conducting a family need assessment if they wish. Information on functional behavioral assessment is included in the PW workbook and some additional information on this topic in the Foster Parent/Residential version of PW.

The target populations for PW are families with children between the ages of 0 to 18 who have behavior problems, including children who either are or at risk of becoming delinquent, developing substance abuse problems, dropping out of school, teen pregnancy, spouse relationship problems, employment problems, or premature death, all of which are shown to be associated to child behavior problems (Robins, 1996; Colman, Murray, Abbott, Maughan, Kuh, Croudace, & Jones, 2009). The text is written at a grade 6 reading level. Parenting Wisely is particularly appropriate for families who are unlikely to access, or who are likely to be resistant to, traditional parent training interventions. Single parent and stepfamilies' concerns are addressed in the program as these families are at higher risk for child behavior problems. Parents and teens can use the program together, especially the online format, where they can do it at home. The program can be used by all personnel who work with children, their parents, and their families. The program can be used on a continuum for either prevention or treatment (indicated or selected). The program has been used by schools, high school parent education courses, public health nurses, child protection agencies, substance abuse agencies, family therapy agencies, court and probation services, foster parent agencies, mental health agencies, hospitals, churches, jails, prisons, and the police.

Program Goals and Objectives

The initial goal in the development of PW was to create a cost-effective, highly accessible, and highly engaging research-based parent education intervention. Since child behavior problems are highly predictive of negative child outcome (Robins, 1996; Colman et al., 2009), a primary objective is to achieve significant and enduring reductions in child behavior problems. Other objectives include improved knowledge and use of effective parenting skills, enhanced parent–child relationships, improved family communication, enhanced mutual support between family members, reduced spousal and family violence, reduced parent and child substance abuse, and increased parental monitoring of school and peer relationships. The 2011 revision of PW increased the focus on the quality of the parent–child relationship so that parents learned more than simply controlling their children's behavior. The research support for achieving these objectives is discussed below.

Curriculum and Other Program Issues

No practitioner curriculum is needed for parents to self-administer the program. Further information that can guide parent/practitioner discussions can be found in the service provider's manual which comes with the program. Also included with the program is a six-session curriculum for practitioners using a combination of parent self-administered PW and six practitioner/parent sessions using a different version of the PW program. This approach maintains the advantages of self-administered PW listed in Table 11.1 and provides a second and different exposure to the program. The six-session manual provides service providers with guidance for conducting role plays to help parents practice skills. The importance of skill practice is supported by a meta-analysis from Kaminski, Valle, Filene, and Boyle (2008) which consistently found stronger effect sizes with parenting interventions that required practice of new parenting skills. Each of the six sessions includes home practice assignments found in the PW workbook. The manual includes strategies for increasing parent self-efficacy and reducing the parent's need for external professional supports. This curriculum is intended for families where the parents need additional structure and support to make changes to their relationships with their children. It was developed for higher-risk families where parents are unlikely or unwilling to attend group sessions. It can be substituted for family therapy, which requires more training and experience.

The program also includes a 100-page curriculum for group parent training. There are 10 sessions which are about 2 hours in length. The curriculum covers strategies for engaging parents in parent education and information on group management skills. Feedback from practitioners (Pushak & Niehe, 2005) indicated PW to be so successful at generating group discussion that there is a need for a curriculum to provide guidance on what content needs to be covered and emphasized for specific home practice assignments. Information for conducting role plays is provided and strategies for reducing parental resistance to each home practice assignment are covered. Strategies for increasing parental efficacy are also covered. The group program has fidelity measures for each session to maintain program integrity. An abbreviated example of a fidelity measure is presented in Figure 11.1.

It is possible to use self-administered PW followed by group use of PW using a different version of the program. This maintains the advantages of self-administered PW listed in Table 11.1 and adds additional benefits such as group discussion, social support from other parents, skill practice in role plays, greater accountability with home practice assignments, and repeated in-depth exposure

- ❑ Midweek support phone calls made.
- ❑ Home practice related to session on school collected and discussed.
- ❑ Role-plays on contacting the parents of child's friends completed.
- ❑ Discussion completed on how to use monitoring following problems related to peers.
- ❑ Handout provided on "Getting to Know Your Child's Friends."
- ❑ Home practice assigned on getting to know your child's friends

Estimated percentage of planned content covered: ________

Rate the following questions on this scale:

Not at all	Somewhat	Moderate	Fairly often	Very often
1.	2.	3.	4.	5.

Rate the overall amount of parental resistance:

Rate your success at dealing with parental resistance:

Were you able to reframe statements of hopelessness to communicate change is possible?

Were you able to keep discussion present focused and action oriented?

Were you able to reframe negative comments about family or peers with positive interpretations?

Were you able to give parents recognition for their input to discussions?

Were you able to reinforce parental self-efficacy?

Were you able to use role-plays of recommended skills in response to concerns or objections?

List any methods you used for responding to parent resistance:

FIGURE 11.1 Facilitator Self-Monitoring Measure Session 9 (abbreviated)

Source: Adapted from Pushak, (2011). Reprinted with permission.

to program content. If parents drop out of the group program prematurely they will at least have the benefits of the initial self-administered intervention.

One advantage of having practitioners using PW together with parents is that the service provider is repeatedly exposed to research-based content related to social learning theory, family systems theory, cognitive psychology, mindfulness, and neuroscience. In a survey of 21 practitioners in British Columbia who had used the PW program for over a year, all the service providers indicated that use of the PW program had increased the effectiveness of their work (Pushak & Niehe, 2005). The practitioners indicated that even when they were not using PW their previous exposure to the program helped them to be more competent in working with families.

Cultural Implications

Approximately 450,000 people have participated in PW. The program has been implemented in the USA, as well as in Australia, Canada, China, France, Ireland, New Zealand, Portugal, and the UK. English and Spanish versions of the program are available and the families depicted include African American, Hispanic-Latino, and Caucasian families. Research suggests there is a link between culturally similar videos and the likelihood for change (Orleans, Strecher, Schoenbach, Salmon, & Blackmon, 1989). A recent PW study (Cotter, Bacallao, Smokowski, & Robertson, 2013) showed moderate to strong effects for a sample that was mostly ethnic minority, with 53 percent Native American, 27 percent African American, and 8 percent Latino. The revision of PW in 2011 was preceded by focus groups of African American, Latino, and non-Hispanic Caucasians who viewed the earlier PW program and made recommendations for cultural modifications. In addition, academic experts from these ethnic groups made similar recommendations. Following the revision of the curriculum, including filming all scenarios, a study was conducted to test for differences among ethnic groups for efficacy. An evaluation by Feil, Gordon, Waldron, Jones, and Widdop (2011) was comprised of approximately equal numbers of African American, Latino, and non-Hispanic Caucasians. The PW program produced strong outcomes on deviant teen behavior, family relationships, and parenting self-efficacy regardless of ethnic group.

There is a UK urban teen version of the program and a young child version of PW for parents of children ages 0 to 9. The video vignettes for the young child version cover misbehaving at a grocery store; interrupting telephone conversations; problems getting along with friends; step-parent and step-child conflict; parenting with a grandparent who lives in the home who has different beliefs about parenting, school, and homework problems; sibling fighting; and how to get children to bed and ready for school on time. In addition, there is a foster/residential care version of PW that depicts foster parents and residential care staff responding to more extreme teen behaviors such as vandalism, theft, hygiene issues, bullying, peer aggression, and extreme defiance.

Evidence-based Research and Evaluation

The following review of research on PW will focus primarily on reduction of child behavior problems because problem behavior is one of the strongest predictors of negative child outcome (Robins, 1996; Colman et al., 2009).

Kacir and Gordon (1999) completed a randomized evaluation of PW with 72 mothers in a disadvantaged Appalachian community. Mothers using the program reported significantly lower rates of child problem behaviors and increased knowledge of adaptive parenting practices at one-month follow-up compared with wait-list control. At four-month follow-up these gains were maintained. The ES on the Eyberg Child Behaviour Inventory (ECBI) was 0.66 on the Problem Intensity scale, which measures the severity of child's behavior. In addition the program achieved an effect size of 0.51 on the ECBI Problem Number scale, which measures the number of behaviors the parent sees as problematic. Parents in the PW group showed a significant increase in knowledge of effective parenting skills and principles while the wait-list control showed no change.

An evaluation by Gordon, Kacir, & Pushak (1999) with court-referred, low-income parents of juvenile delinquents compared mandatory use of PW to a matched control group of youth who received probation services ($n = 80$). These families had previous involvement with either juvenile court or children services and been resistant to previous intervention efforts. Adolescents in the treatment group showed a 50 percent reduction in problem behavior on the ECBI and these gains were maintained at one, three, and six months. Effective parenting knowledge was significantly increased compared with control and these gains were maintained across all follow-up periods. Effect sizes ranged from 0.49 to 0.76. Eighty-two percent of youth in the treatment group who scored in the clinically significant range at pretest showed reliable change on the ECBI total problem scale (scoring in the normal range) at three-month follow-up compared with only 38 percent of the control group. The parents in the PW showed a significant increase in knowledge of effective parenting but there was no change in the control group.

Segal et al. (2003) evaluated use of PW with 42 parents at outpatient clinics or a residential treatment center for juvenile delinquents. There were significant decreases in the number and intensity of child problem behaviors on the ECBI, with a third to half of the children showing clinically significant change. Effect sizes ranged from 0.78 (ECBI) to 1.27 on the Parent Daily Report. Parents showed a significant improvement on a measure of knowledge of effective parenting skills. On a self-rating of their behavior, parents indicated they were using these skills.

Rolland-Staner, Gordon, Carlston, and Pushak (2008) evaluated school-based delivery of PW with 39 at-risk families. Using quasi-experimental design intervention, families showed a significant reduction for both spousal violence and violence towards children compared with the non-intervention control. These reductions in family violence were maintained at three- and six-month follow-up. Use of PW also decreased impulsive and hyperactive child behavior compared with the control condition. There was an improvement in parental communication and problem-solving skills and increased responsiveness from the children.

In an evaluation by Pushak and Pretty (2008) using a quasi-experimental design, 87 parents used PW in one of three ways: individually, in a 10-session group, or a combination of self-administered and group program. Parents of children ages 9 to 17 used the U.S. teen version of PW and parents of children 3 to 9 used the young child version of PW. Children in all groups showed significant improvement on the ECBI Intensity and Number scales at posttest and at one-year follow-up. The authors predicted that the young child version of PW would produce stronger outcomes than the teen version. There was, however no significant difference in the outcomes of the two programs. Effect sizes ranged from 0.51 to 1.52 on the ECBI scales, which are the strongest and most enduring outcomes achieved with PW to date.

An independent, randomized study of 116 parents in an Australian sample (Cefai et al., 2010) evaluated self-administered PW, a two-session group use of PW, and a wait-list control. Both treatment conditions significantly reduced child behavior problems and improved parental satisfaction, efficacy, and knowledge compared with the control group. These gains were maintained at three-month follow-up. Contrary to expectations, self-administered PW achieved significantly stronger reductions in child behavior problems and higher parental self-efficacy compared with group use of the program. Parent feedback indicated that the total of 4.5 hours for the group sessions was too rushed and not enough time was allowed for group discussion. Effect sizes for the two treatment conditions ranged from 0.45 to 1.04 on the ECBI Number and Intensity scales. This study using only two group sessions should not be used to discount the effectiveness of longer group sessions with specified session protocols.

In a pilot study of the new online version of PW mentioned above, Feil et al. (2011) recruited an ethnically diverse population of families from family service agencies, middle schools, and online advertisements. Youth that scored in the clinically significant range on the ECBI at pretest showed significant improvements on the Strengths and Difficulties Questionnaire. The effect size on this measure was 0.46. Parental self-efficacy showed modest improvement, with an effect size of 0.28 on the Parenting Sense of Competence Scale.

Two important studies were conducted at the Oregon Research Institute and at the University of North Carolina. Both studies used the revised PW program with the online format. The Oregon Research Institute study (Waldron, Hops, & Ozechowski, 2014) was done with parents of 280 delinquents referred for drug offenses. Three conditions compared PW Online plus a motivational interviewing (MET) condition for the youth, PW plus a drug education program (EDUC) for the youth, the motivational interviewing alone, or the drug education program alone. Parents randomly assigned to either of the PW conditions (MET+PW or EDUC+PW) reported significantly greater improvements at three months in adolescent pro-social behavior, emotional symptoms, conduct problems, and total behavior problems compared with parents assigned to non-PW conditions. Parents varied in how much of the PW program they completed. Higher amounts of PW completion by parents were associated with greater reductions in adolescent-reported levels of alcohol use, marijuana use, overall substance use, consequences for substance use, and drug avoidance self-efficacy skills. Likewise, greater amounts of PW completion by parents were associated with greater improvements in parent-reported levels of adolescent pro-social behavior. The authors of this independent evaluation conclude: "the fact that the PW intervention has a beneficial effect on the behavior of youth who were not direct recipients of the intervention is a particularly compelling endorsement of the potency of PW for youth in juvenile justice service contexts" (Waldron et al., 2014, p. 2). This is the first demonstration that parental use of PW decreases teen substance abuse. Previous studies showed reductions in risk factors for teen substance abuse.

A study of rural low-income, ethnic diverse minority families (n = 144) was conducted using quasi-experimental design (Cotter et al., 2013). Parents chose to participate in one of four formats of program delivery: parent-only intensive 1–2-day workshop; parent-only 5-week group; parent and adolescent 5-week group; and parent and adolescent online format. Findings show an association between PW participation and improvements in family problem solving, family roles, family involvement, parenting self-efficacy, parenting sense of competence, and decreased adolescent violent behavior. The parent adolescent 5-week group achieved the strongest reduction of adolescent behavior problems on the Child Behavior Checklist, with an effect size of 0.29, the strongest reduction of parent–child conflict on the Conflict Behavior Questionnaire with an ES of 0.47, and the strongest reduction on the Violence Behavior Checklist with a small ES of 0.2. On most measures the 1–2-day intensive PW workshops led by facilitators achieved the weakest outcomes.

Across the above studies, parents consistently reported high satisfaction with the PW program. Parents report they found the teaching format of the self-administered program easy to follow. Parents indicated the problem scenarios were realistic, relevant to their families, and the parenting skills were reasonable solutions to those problems. Further, parents felt confident they could apply these skills in their families. These parent perceptions are consistent with research on PW indicating quick gains in reduced child behavior problems and improved family functioning following use of the program. The parent completion rate for the above studies was between 70 to 95 percent. The consistency of these outcomes has led the developer of the program to provide a money-back guarantee for the program to improve child behavior and reduce family problems.

The implications of these studies are that an effective, very brief (3–5-hour) program can be effectively delivered remotely, online, without parents having to attend parenting classes. In the above evaluations many parents needed prodding to get them to log in or to complete the program, so Internet-delivered interventions require agency or court staff support. These parents are not usually proactive about seeking parent education and face daily chaotic challenges that make training a low priority. Even with this challenge, PW makes it considerably easier for high-risk families to participate and receive fairly immediate benefits for their families.

The research on PW has led to the program being designated as an effective program by Communities That Care (Fagan, Hanson, Hawkins, & Arthur, 2009), and an Exemplary Level 2 program by Strengthening American Families (Kumpfer, 1993 & 1999b). Parenting Wisely has been included in the National Registry of Evidence-based Programs and Practices (2008) based on the quality of research support and the ease of successful dissemination.

Professional Preparation and Training Issues

As mentioned above, one of the initial goals for the development of the program was to increase access to an evidence-based parent education program that did not require expensive practitioner training and also did not need ongoing, expensive quality assurance mechanisms. No practitioner training is required for parent self-administered PW. Practitioner training is recommended, but not required, if PW is being used for group parent training. Practitioner training for group use of PW is not as critical compared with other group parent education programs because all of the primary content is computer based. Therefore a high degree of program fidelity is automatic.

Conclusion

Parenting Wisely is a research-based parent education computer program that can be accessed anytime from any computer that has access to high-speed Internet. Parents can access the program over the Internet or using the CD-ROM on an agency's computer or laptop either on-site or at home. The program is easy to use, brief, and can be completed in about three to five hours. The program teaches parenting skills that have been shown to improve parent–child relationships, improve family communication, increase family unity, and promote healthy development in children ages 0 to 18. Reductions in behavior problems, teen depression, substance and alcohol abuse, and family violence have been found when parents use PW. Research shows the program reduces behavior problems that are linked to delinquency, teen pregnancy, school problems, and drop-out. The program has achieved significant outcomes with families resistant to or who have failed to benefit from previous intervention efforts. The program is based on social learning theory, family systems theory, cognitive psychology, mindfulness research, and neuroscience.

Users view 10 video enactments of common family problems. Parents choose from a list of solutions demonstrating different levels of effectiveness. Each solution is portrayed and then critiqued through interactive questions and answers. Each problem scenario ends with a quiz. After completing the computer program, parents receive a workbook which reviews program content and includes exercises that promote skill building practice. Because of the various formats for the program, repeated use is relatively easy to encourage. The cost per parent trained is very low compared with other evidence-based parenting programs. Sustainability of the PW program beyond grant support is more likely. Concerns about treatment fidelity being compromised when ongoing training or supervision by the developers is discontinued are minimal.

Key Points

1. Parenting Wisely is a research-based, highly cost-effective parent education program that is very accessible and easy for parents and service agencies to use.
2. The program has been shown to significantly reduce child and adolescent behavior problems, family violence, problems at school, and substance use and abuse.

Discussion Questions

1. How were the 10 problem scenarios used in the PW program selected?
2. What are some advantages of parents using a highly engaging, computer-based parent education program on their own without a clinician?
3. What kind of resistance are you likely to encounter as you attempt to engage parents in using a parent education program. What kind of strategies could you use to overcome resistance?
4. What criteria might you use to help choose a research-based parent education program for your community?
5. What would you need to do to successfully introduce a new parent education program in your community?

Additional Resources

Websites

If practitioners require additional support in implementing PW they can contact Family Works at http://familyworksinc.com/.

The Substance Abuse and Mental Health Services web site provides additional information on PW and an independent review of the research on PW: www.nrepp.samhsa.gov/ViewIntervention.aspx?id=35.

Abstracts and full articles on PW research can be found at www.familyworksinc.com/research.

References

Alexander, J. F., Pugh, C., Parsons, B., & Sexton, T. (2000). Book Three: Functional Family Therapy, in D. Elliott (Ed.) *Blueprints for violence prevention.* Golden, CO: Venture.

Baumrind, D. (1967). Child care practices anteceding three patterns of preschool behavior. *Genetic Psychology Monographs, 75(1)*, 43–88.

Baumrind, D. (1978). Parental disciplinary patterns and social competence in children. *Youth and Society, 9*, 238–276.

Burke, M., & Day, R. (1986). A cumulative study of the effectiveness of managerial training. *Journal of Applied Psychology, 71*, 232–245.

Cefai, J., Smith, D., & Pushak, R. (2010). The PW parent training program: An evaluation with an Australian sample. *Journal of Child & Family Behavior Therapy, 32*, 17–33.

Colman, I., Murray, J., Abbott, R., Maughan, B., Kuh, D., Croudace, T., & Jones, P. (2009). Outcomes of conduct problems in adolescence: 40 year follow-up of a national cohort. *British Medical Journal, 338*, a2981.

Cotter, K. L., Bacallao, M., Smokowski, P., & Robertson, C. (2013). Parenting interventions implementation science: How delivery format impacts the Parenting Wisely program. *Research on Social Work Practice, 23*, 639–650.

Duncan, L., Coatsworth, J., & Greenberg, M. (2009). A model of mindful parenting: Implications for parent–child relationships and prevention research. *Clinical Child and Family Psychology Review, 12*, 255–270.

Fagan, A., Hanson, K., Hawkins, J., Arthur, M. (2009). Translational research in action: Implementation of the Communities That Care prevention system in 12 communities. *Journal of Community Psychology, 37*, 809–829.

Feil, E., Gordon, D., Waldron, H., Jones, L., & Widdop, C. (2011) Development and pilot testing of an internet-based parenting education program for teens and pre-teens: Parenting Wisely. *The Family Psychologist, 27*, 22–26.

Fletcher, J. (1990). *Effectiveness and cost of interactive video disc instruction in defense training and education* (Report No. P-2372). Arlington, VA: Institute for Defense Analysis. ERIC number ED326194.

Gordon, D. (2003). Intervening with families of troubled youth: Functional Family Therapy and Parenting Wisely, in J. McGuire (Ed.) *Offender rehabilitation and treatment* (pp. 193–220). Sussex, UK: John Wiley.

Gordon, D. (2011). *Parenting wisely program workbook*. Athens, OH: Family Works.

Gordon, D., Kacir, C., & Pushak, R. (1999). Effectiveness of an interactive parent-training program for changing adolescent behavior for court-referred parents. Unpublished manuscript.

Kacir, C., & Gordon, D. (1999). Parenting adolescents wisely: The effectiveness of an interactive videodisk parent training program in Appalachia. *Child & Family Behavior Therapy, 21*, 1–22.

Kaminski, J., Valle, L., Filene, J., & Boyle, C. (2008). A meta-analytic review of components associated with parent training program effectiveness. *Journal of Abnormal Child Psychology, 36*, 567–89.

Kumpfer, K. (1993 & 1999b). *Strengthening America's families: Promising parenting and family strategies for delinquency prevention. A user's guide*. Prepared for the U.S. Department of Justice under Grant No. 87-JS-CX-K495 from the Office of Juvenile Justice and Delinquency Prevention, Office of Juvenile Programs, U.S. Department of Justice, Washington, DC. Also see www.strengtheningfamilies.org

Niemiec, R., & Walberg, H. J. (1987). Comparative effects of computer-assisted instruction: A synthesis of reviews. *Journal of Educational Computing Research, 3*, 19–37.

Orleans, C., Strecher, V., Schoenbach, V., Salmon, M., & Blackmon, C. (1989). Smoking cessation initiatives for Black Americans: recommendations for research and intervention. *Health Education Research, 4*, 13–25.

Pushak, R. (2011). *Parenting wisely: Teen, parent group curriculum, instructor's guide.* Athens, OH: Family Works.

Pushak, R., & Niehe, R., (2005). *Assessing community practitioners' use of an evidence based treatment program: Survey results on Parenting Wisely.* Unpublished manuscript.

Pushak, R. & Pretty, J. (2008). *Individual and group use of a CD-ROM for training parents of children with disruptive disorders.* Unpublished manuscript.

Robins, L. (1996). *Deviant children grown up: A sociological and psychiatric study of a sociopathic personality.* Baltimore, MD: William & Wilkins.

Rolland-Stanar, C., Gordon, D. A., Carlston, D., & Pushak, R. E. (2008). *Family violence prevention via school-based CD-ROM parent training.* Unpublished manuscript.

Segal, D., Chen, P. Y., Gordon, D., Kacir, C., & Gylys, J. (2003). Development and evaluation of a parenting intervention program: Integration of scientific and practical approaches. *International Journal of Human-Computer Interaction, 15*, 453–468.

Substance Abuse Mental Health Services Administration (2008). *National Registry of Evidence-based Programs and Practices.* See www.nrepp.samhsa.gov/ViewIntervention.aspx?id=35

Tattersall, A., Cooper, S., & Duffy, P. (2003). *Evaluation of the Junior Parenting Wisely Programme.* Unpublished manuscript.

Waldron, H., Hops, H., & Ozechowski, T. (2014). Report to National Institute on Drug Abuse on grant for treatment of adolescent substance abuse in juvenile courts. Bethesda, MD: National Institute on Drug Abuse.

Webster-Stratton, C. (1990). Enhancing the effectiveness of self-administered videotape parent training for families with conduct-problem children. *Journal of Abnormal Child Psychology, 18*, 479–492.

Webster-Stratton, C. (1992). Individually administered videotape parent training: "Who benefits?" *Cognitive Therapy and Research, 16*, 31–52.

12

SUPPORTING FATHER INVOLVEMENT PROJECT

A Value-added Co-parenting Program

Kyle D. Pruett, Marsha Kline Pruett, Carolyn Pape Cowan, & Philip A. Cowan

Learning Goals

After reading this chapter, the reader will increase their knowledge of the following:

1. SFI program history, different age and cultural versions, format or structure, and content addressed.
2. The theoretical foundations and core elements of SFI and other evidence-based family interventions.
3. Family-focused evidence-based prevention programs, steps to successful cultural adaptations, research outcomes of SFI for different populations. and comparative effectiveness reviews that found SFI to be the most effective substance abuse prevention program for youth.
4. The staffing and training required plus other resources to implement SFI successfully.
5. The need for new directions in prevention and treatment, including digitally delivered programming to reduce costs and increase dissemination capability rapidly.

Introduction

It is well established that parenting interventions offer substantial support for the development of competent and healthy children and families. Further, these interventions have the potential to strengthen the mental health of communities and their individual members (Panter-Brick & Leckman, 2013). But parenting education and support, until recently, has largely focused on maternal–child interactions, often failing to gather, report, or record paternal demographic data or variables of any kind (Phares, 2010), and completely failing to focus on the co-parenting relationship as the one that so heavily influences most of the relationships in the family. In a recent literature review of 15 parenting interventions in middle- and low-income countries purposed to formulate research priorities and make programmatic recommendations, fathers and father-related constructs were barely discussed (Engle, Fernald, Alderman, Behrman, et al. 2011). This remains theoretically and clinically problematic, given the many studies over the same time period that show the significance of fathers' positive involvement on the well-being of the child, the couple relationship, and the family (Pruett, 2000; Raeburn, 2014).

Even programs that are designed to encourage fathers to take an active role in their children's lives are rarely evaluated to determine whether they are effective or who is more likely to benefit from participating in them (Knox, Cowan, Cowan, & Bildner, 2011). The Supporting Father Involvement (SFI) Project is the first father involvement program that has been evaluated with a longitudinal randomized clinical trial research methodology. It was designed for and funded by the California Department of Social Service, Office of Child Abuse Prevention for low-income families from various cultural backgrounds to encourage fathers to become and stay positively involved in the rearing of their young children. While the program's title emphasizes paternal engagement as a goal and process in and of itself, it was equally clear to the research team that the ultimate goal of promoting paternal engagement was not father involvement in isolation, but rather, the promotion of paternal engagement with the goal of mutual co-parenting support within the couple relationship. The theoretical support for this approach rests on this fundamental finding from a number of studies of both middle- and low-income families: *The best predictor of whether a father will be positively involved with his children is the quality of his relationship with the children's mother.*

Theoretical Foundations and History

The SFI study is adopted and adapted from previous studies of married and divorced two-parent families (Belsky, 1984; Cowan & Cowan, 2000; Pruett, Insabella, & Gustafson, 2005) in which children's development and adaptation are predicted by risks and buffers in five interconnected family domains: (a) the mental health and well-being of individual family members, including depression and anxiety; (b) three-generational transmission of expectations and relationship behavior patterns; (c) parent–child relationship quality, notably parenting style and parenting stress; (d) parent-couple relationship quality, including communication and problem solving; and (e) the balance of life stresses and social supports in the family's relationships with peers, schools, work, and other social systems. In prior studies, each of these domains contributed unique variance to the prediction of children's cognitive, social, and emotional development and mental health status at different points in their development (Cowan, Cowan, & Heming,

2005). Risk and protective factors in these same domains are associated with fathers' positive involvement (Cookston, 1999; Parke, 2002) . These five domains, each one representing a central aspect of family life, are the areas of focus for the SFI curriculum. Our assumption was that if we could reduce symptoms of distress in the participants, affect the quality of their relationship as a couple and as co-parents, improve each of their relationships with the child and with their families of origin, and help them to use social supports more effectively to cope with life stress, we would have a positive preventive effect on child abuse and neglect and, more generally, on healthy family development.

While designing the intervention and its core curriculum, we needed to clarify how co-parenting as a process was different from traditional understandings of couples' systems dynamics. The triangle below shows the typical dyadic bidirectional dynamic influence that each pairing has on the others around the perimeter. We can easily see how a child with a difficult or easy temperament might influence mother and father, differently or similarly. We can also visualize how a sensitive couple relationship would support mother or father in parenting tasks, in comparison with a contentious relationship between the parents (Figure 12.1).

But the more salient co-parenting forces are at work inside the triangle. A mother who is supportive and appreciative of father–child time, versus one who is undermining and critically gatekeeping, has a very different influence on the father–child axis. A father who is substance-abusing or violent has a very different effect on the mother–child dyad than one who is nurturing of the couple domain and facilitates sensitive interactions between mother and child. A child with a flexible temperament can make both parents feel competent and secure, whereas a premie with colic can make one or both of them doubt their competence and feel unable to meet the child's needs.

To capture these nuances as we designed the curriculum, mindful of such familial dynamics, mothers and fathers need to be encouraged and supported separately and together, physically in couples groups, and conceptually through

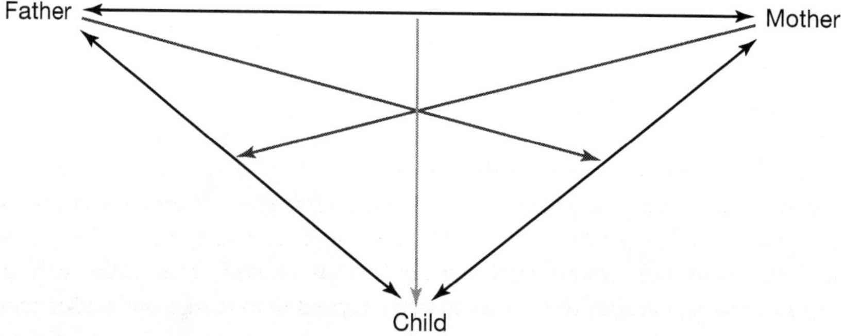

FIGURE 12.1 Co-parenting Dynamics

curricular content. We were all keenly aware that mothers and fathers nurture differently and that children draw on those differences in their relationships with each parent throughout their development (Pruett & Pruett, 2009).

An illuminating example is the different emphases of attachment behavior between mothers and fathers. Secure attachment behavior in mothering is classically interpreted as providing comfort when the child is distressed. Secure attachment in fathering differs in purpose and appears particularly in the context of monitored controlled excitement through sensitive and challenging support "when the child's exploratory system is aroused" (Grossman et al., 2002). Mothers' behavior is related in older children to their emotional competence, while fathers' behavior is more predictive of older children's school achievement, peer, and sibling relationships (Grossman et al., 2002). Such differences help explain parents' somewhat different observed behavior in novel or frustrating circumstances, and when comfortably integrated in the co-parenting context, can both be supportive of child's development. It is worth noting that such dimorphism is also observed in same-sex co-parenting couples.

The SFI project began in 2003 and was housed in local Family Resource Centers (FRCs) in five participating California counties, all of which volunteered to participate in the statewide invitation. Four of the centers served rural and urban families, with the latter two primarily rural and inclusive of many Hispanic migrant workers (San Luis Obispo, Santa Cruz, Tulare, and Yuba Counties) and one serving families in a low-income, predominantly African American urban setting (Contra Costa County). Parents were screened to affirm that they intended to co-parent their child, the child was younger than seven years old, and there was no serious substance abuse or any violence in the family (later cohorts of SFI did include families involved in the child welfare system, once safety of participating was confirmed for all family members). Parents who met these criteria and expressed interest in the program were invited to take part in one of the following programs on a randomly assigned basis, all with the same staff:

1. A one-time informational meeting for couples about positive paternal engagement (3-hour, low-dose control condition).
2. A semi-structured group primarily for fathers that met for 16 weeks (32 hours).
3. A semi-structured group primarily for couples that met for 16 weeks (32 hours).

Details of the programs are offered below. All three variations of the SFI program were delivered by clinically trained and experienced male–female pairs of group leaders, most of whom had master's level or higher degrees, or were students involved in licensing training. All families were also offered the support of a Case Manager/Family Worker to help with referrals to appropriate services as needed during their time in the project, as many of the families hovered at or near federal poverty-line income levels.

Needs Assessment and Target Audience

The first SFI trial study included 289 Mexican American (about two-thirds) and European American low-income families, their youngest child typically still in toddlerhood. Parents did not have to be married to each other or live together, but they did have to be involved in a co-parenting arrangement that allowed joint caregiving engagement, and participation in the family and the project.

Before families were randomized to one of the three conditions, the group leaders conducted an extensive 1.5-hour individual interview, some of which was conducted with parents together and some apart, typically the male group leader with the father and female group leader with the mother. Evidence or histories of active domestic violence, substance abuse, or untreated mental illness encountered during the course of these initial interviews were managed through referrals for service, and families were encouraged to return for participation after those more acute issues were resolved. Of 550 couples interviewed, 496 met eligibility and 405 completed the first interview. We planned to have another phase of study that would allow us to work with higher-risk families, but for Phase I we felt it imperative to document the efficacy and utility of the new intervention. The results revealed that the intervention had strong efficacy for parents and for their young children (Cowan, Cowan, Pruett, Pruett, & Wong, 2009).

A second study trial (Phase II) included 279 low-income families and added a small, primarily African American cohort of families. Non-parental co-parents (e.g., grandparents, a sibling of a parent) were included, as long as one member was a male, since father involvement was a major purpose of the program. Children of school age (upper age level was extended from 7 to 11) were also welcomed into Phase II. In this trial, mostly couples groups were conducted; the control group was not included since the previous trial strongly supported the efficacy of the ongoing intervention, especially given the fact that families' mental health and well-being declined in the control condition. None of the families had been referred for protective services the year before their participation in the study. Again, the study showed significant and positive results (Cowan, Cowan, Pruett, Pruett, & Gillette, 2014).

The final phase (Phase III) was a higher-risk family clinical trial in which half of the 230 participating couples had been referred by Child Welfare staff because they had been involved in cases of suspected or substantiated domestic violence and/or child abuse/neglect. This trial assigned couples to an immediate group treatment or a seven-month delay; this allowed everyone to be offered the group intervention, while still enabling a comparison of randomly assigned groups. Preliminary analyses suggested that there were significant advantages for even the high-risk couples in the immediate treatment condition.

Program Goals and Objectives

To reiterate briefly, the three trials' central purposes were to (a) increase fathers' positive involvement with their children; (b) strengthen the co-parenting relationship; and (c) promote positive parent–child relationships, in order to increase children's competence and prevent the rise of behavior problems. All of these outcomes represent key risk and protective factors in approaches to preventing child abuse and neglect.

The goal of the intervention was to deliver a structure with a series of supports from the co-leaders and group participants for achieving program goals, centered in a peer group experience, and organized by a curriculum delivered in a consistent, accessible manner to young children's families at varying levels of risk. We defined father involvement—a key program goal and outcome variable—as fathers who (a) provided direct care (feeding, dressing, soothing) to their child(ren); (b) provided indirect care (preparing meals, arranging doctor's appointment); (c) were actively and regularly thinking, feeling, and reflecting upon their child(ren) and their needs; (d) were present for play and exploration; and (e) were providing financial support. Men's needs were directly addressed in the program: jobs and job stability, being "responsible" as a father, and the legacy of his relationship with his own father.

The curriculum was typically presented two hours per week in groups of 5–7 couples or 6–8 fathers for 16 weeks, typically in the evening at the FRC, where a simple meal or pot luck was arranged just before the meeting started, and good-quality child care was provided while parents were engaged in the groups. Group leaders typically joined the families as they ate together as a group, helping to ease the transition from family's day time to fathers' or couples' group time. Child care workers—also considered active members of the teams at the FRCs, given their relationships with the parents and children—helped promote positive transitions at this time as well. Both parents were welcomed briefly in both conditions at the first session. Two of the sessions (weeks 5 and 13) involved fathers in supervised (videotaped for later coding and quality control) activities with their children. During these same sessions, mothers met separately with the other mothers and the female group leader.

Since most of the men had not been previously involved with the FRC, the often complex goal of recruiting and engaging the fathers in the project evolved over time from lessons learned and reflected the pooled knowledge of all five sites, each of which served a unique local population both culturally and socially (Pruett, Cowan, Cowan, & Pruett, 2009). The most productive recruitment methods avoided the usual barriers associated with maternal gatekeeping (both domestic and institutional) directly. Men were explicitly invited in person, and not simply via discussions with the mother about fathers being welcome. Male leaders in the community were recruited to be active recruiters themselves for SFI. Local public health initiatives about breastfeeding, depression screening, and personal health were approached as opportunities to engage men—often having been considered taboo topics before the FRC became more of a father-friendly setting and had yet to earn a reputation as such in the community.

SFI group process and curriculum differs from both traditional didactic parenting education approaches and open-ended group therapy approaches. In a psychoeducational approach, a specific curriculum is presented to the group, the leaders are presenters of what they consider to be important, and the goal is parents' acquisition of parenting skills. In group therapy, group members determine what is discussed, the leaders are guides or interpreters, and the goal is participants' insight and inner growth. SFI is also more than a hybrid of the two contrasting approaches. Its joint emphasis on group and individual process and curricular content is carefully titrated by skilled pairs of group leaders who use the group meetings as a way of role modeling good co-parenting collaboration styles. Spur-of-the-moment issues are integrated into the curricular topics as the leaders serve as guides more than interpreters of process or presenters of "correct" parenting practices. Its emphasis is less on skills training or insight *per se* and more on helping individuals and couples first articulate and then achieve their personal goals as both parents and partners.

Curriculum and Other Program Issues

From the beginning, SFI was not conceived as a classic parenting education effort. It was conceptualized as a preventive intervention with emphasis on understanding and utilizing familial processes as revealed over the course of the project's professionally supported discussion and reflection with peers. The curriculum relied on activities that were hands-on and able to be utilized verbally (discussions—dyadic, small group, or full group) or non-verbally (using metaphors and active, concrete examples) as group membership needs dictated.

Each session focused on one of the five domains (individual, couple, parent–child, three-generational, or stress/social support balance). Key points were articulated at the beginning of each session. An open-ended check-in opened each session, followed by a short didactic piece. Then an activity helped to deepen the concepts presented and guide participants to begin relating the concepts to themselves and their families. For example, to introduce father involvement, group members designed a want-ad for the father's role in the family, assuming he needed to be replaced for a period of time. These ads often evoked laughter and teasing among couples and participants, as serious content got woven into humorous acknowledgment of complex and sometimes contentious issues regarding fathers' roles. Communication style was taught by couples throwing bean bags to each other, facing each other, or with one parent's back turned, or through hard tosses designed to get the other's attention in a more combative, non-productive way. These styles were related to collaborative, avoidant, or aggressive styles, and the feelings and behaviors that resulted from such interchanges were explored. And written lists on an easel of traditions and habits from families of origin were attached by Velcro to categories representing "want to keep", "want to keep but change", or "want to get rid of"—eliciting discussion about how family of origin issues got brought into the family, potentially providing comfort, anxiety, and/or conflict. Finally, simple homework activities were assigned to encourage practice of new ideas and skills between group sessions.

Cultural Implications

The SFI curriculum, delivered in Spanish or English, has proven popular and effective with Americans of Mexican, African, and European descent. Many of the curricular tasks were centered on activities and/or art projects to de-emphasize heavy reliance on language competence, literacy, or communication skills. The SFI group intervention is also being implemented in other countries, and is reported to be useful with other ethnic and cultural groups with only minor adaptation. It has been found to be effective with low- and higher-income groups, more and less depressed parents, and parents living together married or unmarried.

What makes the program versatile is the balanced focus on process and pragmatics. Content is explicit but encouraged to be adapted as needed for each particular family or group. Rather than discussing examples of family problems provided by leaders, couples brought their ongoing disagreements into the group in ways that were relevant to their personalities and their culture. Guided discovery was substituted for prescriptions, so that values and judgments were left outside the Family Resource Center doors. Moreover, hiring of staff was done locally, and male–female pairs help ensure that all participants felt welcomed and represented.

Evidence-based Research and Evaluation

From the beginning, we worked closely with the FRC staffs to understand the importance of randomization and assessment, given that most of them were experienced, respected community care providers, not academic research colleagues. They also needed support to understand why we needed such a diversity of measures to document the change—if any—that these families might experience during this "preventive intervention". In the end we were able to administer and collect a wide variety of outcome measures, by interview, either in English or Spanish, documenting many important changes in the families, a sampling of which follows:

1. The Pie: Father Involvement. Psychological and behavioral paternal engagement (Cowan & Cowan, 1991). A parent divides a four-inch circle into sections reflective of how important (by salience, not by time) certain aspects of their lives were at the time (parent, partner/lover, worker/student,

leisure—e.g., gardener/sportsman, and me myself/alone); they then complete a second circle to represent their ideal sense of self. The size of the parent slices (real and ideal) were followed in this study. Parents could be compared to themselves and their partners, in terms of the central parts of their identities.

2. Who does what? (Cowan & Cowan, 1990). Daily child care for the youngest (feeding, pediatric visits, etc.) is rated according to "who does what": 1 = she does it all; 5 = done equally; 9 = he does it all. Correlations between parents' descriptions reveal similarity and differences in perception.
3. Parenting Stress Index (PSI; Lloyd & Abidin, 1985)—a questionnaire measure of each parent's level of distress in parenting their youngest (target) child.
4. Ideas about parenting (Heming, Cowan, & Cowan, 1991). Parents indicate agreement/disagreement with each other's parenting opinions and values.
5. Couple communication (Cowan & Cowan, 1991). Amount of conflict and strategies for resolving conflict.
6. Child Adaptive Behavior Inventory (CABI; Cowan, Cowan, & Heming, 1995). Positive and negative descriptors of children's cognitive and social competence, and behavioral problems, are given by each parent.

Outcomes

Using follow-up data collected at 9 and 18 months post intervention, we documented the following changes in SFI families:

1. Of 11 measures assessed, 10 revealed positive Baseline–Post 2 changes.
2. Fathers' involvement increased significantly, especially in child care tasks.
3. Both parents, especially fathers, showed reductions in anxiety symptoms.
4. Both parents', especially mothers', parenting stress declined.
5. Both parents maintained satisfaction with their relationship as a couple, while control group couples' satisfaction declined.
6. Mothers reported decline in violent problem-solving strategies used by the couple.
7. Mothers reported less harsh physical punishment of the children, and saw their children as less aggressive overall.

Additional findings showed that:

1. Fathers or mothers who participated in the *one-time informational meeting* did not show any positive changes over 18 months. They also showed negative changes over time in individual, couple, parent, and child outcome domains.
2. Couples group participants showed even more positive changes than those in the fathers-only groups over 18 months.

3. Organizational shifts were also documented in Family Resource Center father-friendliness. Based on systematic measurement, we found that in the first year of the study, the centers in which the SFI intervention was offered added policies and procedures addressed to fathers as well as mothers, and improved their reputation in the community for reaching out to fathers. Staff at the FRCs reported being better prepared to provide services specifically to fathers. These positive changes were maintained over the next five years, and improved even more in subsequent years. This finding emphasizes that positive change accompanied by a cultural shift takes time, and requires sustained programmatic effort and funding.

Child Welfare Trial

The final phase of the Supporting Father Involvement program began in July of 2009 in the original five California counties, and aimed to help families who had already come in contact with the Child Welfare System. Approximately 60 new families per site (230 total) participated. The families were referred to protective services for various reasons: 20 percent for domestic violence; 27 percent for child physical abuse; 5 percent for child sexual abuse; 8 percent for child emotional abuse; 32 percent for child neglect, and 6 percent for parental absence.

We should be clear that the child-abusing families and those involved in domestic violence in this study were assessed both by the Child Welfare Staff and SFI staff to ensure that they were not currently involved either in domestic violence or child abuse. That is, through careful assessment it was determined that (a) it was safe to see the parents together in pairs or groups, and (b) the children were safe to be with the parents. The results confirm that both the couples and fathers group interventions that we designed, but especially the couples groups, are effective with families from a range of ethnic backgrounds, income levels, and levels of risk.

The intervention effects in this phase of the project were tested by examining the differences at the 18-month posttest between families who had been enrolled in SFI groups immediately and those who had not been eligible for groups until seven months after their initial assessments (the delay control). Preliminary results are showing that:

1. As individuals, mothers and fathers *not* referred by CWS and enrolled in SFI immediately, significantly reduced their symptoms of anxiety and depression and their drug use over the 18 months of the study (greater reductions than those in the delay condition). The CWS-referred parents reduced their drinking over the same period of time, a welcome finding in that alcohol plays a significant role in domestic violence and child abuse.
2. Parents showed similar positive changes to those of parents in the earlier trials in terms of declines in parenting stress and psychological symptoms

> (depression and anxiety) and an increase in desire for closeness. They showed even greater positive change in reductions in violent problem-solving behavior, another salient outcome for families in protective services.

Important areas of improvement could be seen in their relationships as couples if they entered groups immediately, especially for CWS-referred parents. The couples were more likely to collaborate positively and their conflict as co-parents decreased. Finally, violent problem solving decreased over the course of the study both for CWS-referred and non-CWS-referred participants.

Significant findings were also documented in the quality of parent–child relationships. Father involvement increased to the first posttest for the non-CWS participants, while authoritarian, harsh parenting ideas decreased for both CWS and non-CWS-referred parents. There was a decrease in harsh parenting, as reported by both parents, for the CWS-referred participants who were enrolled in the groups immediately after their initial assessments (Figures 12.2 and 12.3).

When their parents participated in the intervention, there were significant benefits for children. In the first clinical trial (Phase I), when parents received only a single-session meeting (the low-dose control condition), the children's aggression, hyperactivity, social withdrawal, and anxiety/depression all increased over the course of the study. By contrast, children's problematic behaviors in the SFI ongoing group participant families remained stable. Similar findings were obtained in Phase II. For children whose parents were offered and took advantage of the immediate group condition, behavior problems either remained stable or improved, and both social competence and cognitive competence as rated by

Individual	Couple	Parent–child
• Anxiety decreased (non CWS) • Depressive symptoms decreased (non CWS) • Drug use decreased (non CWS) • Drinking reduced (CWS)	• Desire for close relationships increased (CWS) • Couple conflict decreased to PO1 (CWS) • Violent problem-solving decreased (non CWS to PO1, CWS) • Positive co-parenting increased (CWS)	• Father involvement increased to PO1 (non CWS) • Authoritarian parenting ideas decreased (non CWS, CWS) • Harsh parenting decreased (VWS)

FIGURE 12.2 Summary of Results for Individual, Couple, and Parent–Child Measures

Child older than 18 months at pre-test

Non CWS	CWS
No change in: • Aggression • Hyperactivity • Social withdrawal • Depression/anxiety Increase in: • Social competence • Cognitive competence	Decline in: • Aggression No change in: • Hyperactivity • Social withdrawal • Depression/anxiety Increase in: • Social competence • Cognitive competence

FIGURE 12.3 Summary of Results for Child Measures

their parents improved. The children of parents in the delay condition did *not* show these positive findings.

Two important additional findings occurred at the family level:

1. Family income increased by approximately $4,000 per year for those CWS-referred couples in the immediate treatment condition.
2. A nationally normed 77-item Child Abuse Potential questionnaire was filled out independently to assess each parent's own history of child abuse, depression/anger, feelings of rejection, perfection, loneliness, negative view of parenting, and couple/family conflict. Both non-CWS and CWS-referred families showed significant reductions in potential for child abuse.

Professional Preparation and Training Issues

We believe that at least one, preferably both, group leaders, need to have clinical training. Ideally, group leaders have skills in working with couples and groups, knowledge of child development, and cultural competency. While we recognize that this level of professionalism comes with a cost, we also believe it is why we have had continuously positive results for SFI, where other parenting programs have received somewhat less effective results. We also advocate to hold fast to the 32-hour curriculum. Analyses show that parents present for at least 80 percent of the time do indeed have more positive results than those who attend for less time. And finally, we give the curriculum away freely to other family professionals, but require staff at interested sites to be trained in order to seek fidelity to the model that allows the greatest opportunity for success.

The State of California has contracted with an existing training organization —Strategies—to disseminate the results of the Supporting Father Involvement program across California as a validated, evidence-based intervention. Their role is to:

1. Assess "father friendliness" in not-for-profit and county welfare agencies and increase their outreach to fathers.
2. Train staff to conduct Supporting Father Involvement groups in agencies that are poised to do so.

Dissemination projects are also occurring in other states and are ongoing in Alberta, Canada and in London, UK. Different populations and combinations of SFI with other evidence-based programs are under consideration, illustrating further the attractiveness and versatility of the intervention.

Conclusion

It should be understood that this is not truly a "final" report of the SFI results in the sense that the last of the data were collected only recently and the final analysis of the latest data and submission of papers for publication will continue over the next several years. For example, not all the Phase III data from the parents' reports have been analyzed. We also have observational measures at baseline and at the 18-month posttest—of couple discussions, and father–child and mother–child interactions that are in the process of being coded.

What we do know is that as a preventive intervention, SFI was equally effective (a) across the three ethnic groups evaluated; (b) for cohabitating and married couples, despite income levels; (c) as a curriculum that simultaneously and effectively can focus on both risk and protective factors across many aspects of family life and varying levels of risk within families; and that (d) it succeeds in making positive changes in father–child relationships whether it is focused primarily on fathers or couples.

The data overall yielded significant support for SFI as a couples–focused approach that has positive benefits on fathers' direct hands-on involvement in the care of their young children, as well as on the relationship between mothers and fathers, both parents' parenting styles and stress, and finally on their young children's behavior with them and with others. While interventions for couples and for fathers are often designed, funded, and carried out in separate administrative silos, we have shown that a unified approach, focusing on both couples and fathers, produces positive change in paternal involvement, couple relationship quality, and children's functioning. Our intervention approach encourages rethinking overall approaches to parental education less as skill building *per se*, and more as strengthening co-parenting processes in relationships that yield such protective results for children and families at risk.

Key Points

1. Family interventions that combine parenting skills, children's social skills, and family bonding components appear to be the most effective.
2. The SFI is a parent, youth, and family skill-building curriculum designed to prevent substance abuse and other behavior problems in children and youth, strengthen parenting skills, and build family strengths.
3. Research findings show that SFI has one of the largest impacts in preventing alcohol and substance abuse and also is cost-effective.
4. It is important to follow steps for cultural, age, and local adaptations to increase program effectiveness.
5. Careful staff selection and training help in delivering a successful implementation of EBPs.

Discussion Questions

1. Why is it important to address the co-parental relationships in parenting education?
2. What is the SFI project and how did it contribute to parenting education?
3. How is the SFI process and curriculum different from traditional parenting education approaches?

Additional Resources

Suggested Reading

Cowan, P. A., Cowan, C. P., Pruett, M. K., Pruett, K., & Wong, J. J. (2009). Promoting fathers' engagement with children: Preventive interventions for low-income families. *Journal of Marriage and Family*, *71*, 663–679.

Cowan, P., Cowan, C., Pruett, M. K., Pruett, K., & Gillette, P. (2014). Evaluating a couples group to enhance father involvement in low-income families using a bench comparison. *Family Relations*, *63*, 356–370.

Panter-Brick, C., Burgess, A., Eggerman, M., McAllister, F., Pruett, K., & Leckman, J. (2014). Practitioner review: Engaging fathers—recommendations for a game change in parenting interventions based on a systematic review of the global evidence. *Journal of Child Psychology and Psychiatry*, 55(11), 1187–1212.

Websites

fatherhoodinstitute.org
albertawellness.org/SFI
www.cebc4cw.org/program/supporting-father-involvement/detailed

References

Behavior Inventory (CABI). Unpublished manuscript. University of California, Berkeley.

Belsky, J. (1984). The determinants of parenting: A process model. *Child Development, 55,* 83–96.

Cookston, J. (1999). Parental supervision and family structure: Effects on adolescent problem behaviors. *Journal of Divorce & Remarriage, 32,* 107–122.

Cookston, J., Braver, S., Griffin, W. De Luse, S., & Jonathan, M. (2007). Effects of the *Dads for Life* intervention on interparental conflict and coparenting in the two years after divorce. *Family Process, 46,* 123–137.

Cowan, C., & Cowan, P. (1990a). *Couple Communication Questionnaire.* Berkeley, CA: Institute of Human Development, University of California, Berkeley.

Cowan, C., & Cowan, P. (1991). The pie, in J. Touliatos, B. Perlmutter, & M. Straus (Eds.). *Handbook of family measurement techniques* (pp. 278–279). Newbury Park, CA: Sage.

Cowan, C., Cowan, P., Pruett, M., & Pruett, K. (2005). Encouraging strong relationships between fathers and children. *Working Strategies, 8(4),* 1–11.

Cowan, C., Cowan, P., Pruett, M., & Pruett, K. (2007). An approach to preventing coparenting conflict and divorce in low-income families: Strengthening couple relationships and fostering fathers' involvement. *Family Process, 46,* 109–121.

Cowan, P., & Cowan, C. (1990b). Who does what? In J. Touliatos, B. Perlmutter, & M. Straus (Eds.) *Handbook of family measurement techniques* (pp. 447–448). Thousand Oaks, CA: Sage.

Cowan, P., & Cowan, C. (2010). How working with couples fosters children's development: From prevention science to public policy, in Schulz, M., Pruett, M., Kerig, P., & Parke, R. (Eds.). *Strengthening couple relationships for optimal child development: Lessons from research and intervention* (pp. 211–228). Washington, DC: American Psychological Association.

Cowan, P., Cowan, C., Cohen, N., Pruett, M., & Pruett, K. (2008). Supporting fathers' engagement with their kids, in J. D. Berrick & N. Gilbert (Eds.) *Raising children: Emerging needs, modern risks, and social responses* (pp. 44–80).

Cowan, P., Cowan, C., & Heming, G. (1995). *Manual for Child Adaptive Behavior Inventory (CABI).* Unpublished manuscript, University of California, Berkeley.

Cowan, P., Cowan, C., Pruett, M., & Pruett, K. (2009). Six barriers to father involvement and suggestions for overcoming them. *National Council of Family Relations Report,* p. 54.

Cowan, P., Cowan, C., Pruett, M., Pruett, K., & Gillette, P. (2012). Väterliches Engagement bei der Betreuung ihrer Kinder stärken: Ein familiensystemischer Ansatz./A family systems approach to supporting fathers' involvement in the care of their children. *Familiendynamik, 37(2),* 94–103.

Cowan, P., Cowan, C., Pruett, M., Pruett, K., & Wong, J. (2009). Promoting fathers' engagement with children: Preventive interventions for low-income families. *Journal of Marriage and the Family, 71,* 663–679.

Engel, P., Fernald, L., Alderman, H., Behrman, H., O'Gara, C., Yousafzai, A., Cabral de Mello, M., Hidrobo, M., Ulkuer, N. I., & Iltus, S. (2011). Strageties for reducing inequalities and improving developmental outcomes for young children in low-income and middle-income countries. *Lancet,* 378, 1339–1353.

Grossmann, K., Grossmann, K. E., Fremmer-Bombik, E., Kindler, H., Scheuerer-Englisch, H., & Zimmermann, P. (2002). The uniqueness of the child–father attachment relationship: Fathers' sensitive and challenging play as a pivotal variable in a 16-year longitudinal study. *Social Development, 11(3),* 307–331.

Heming, G., Cowan, P., & Cowan, C. (1991) Ideas about parenting, in J. Touliatos, B. Perlmutter, & M. Straus (Eds.) *Handbook of family measurement techniques* (pp. 362–363). Newbury Park, CA: Sage.

Knox, V., Cowan, P., Cowan, C., & Bildner, E. (2011). Policies that strengthen fatherhood and family relationships: What do we know and what do we need to know? *Annals of the American Academy of Political and Social Science, 635*, 216–239.

Loyd, B., & Abidin, R. (1985). Revision of the Parenting Stress Index. *Journal of Pediatric Psychology, 10*, 169–177.

Panter-Brick, C., & Leckman, J. (2013). Editorial commentary: Resilience in child development—interconnected pathways to wellbeing. *Journal of Child Psychology and Psychiatry, 54*, 333–336.

Parke, R. (2002). Fathers and families, in M. Bornstein (Ed.), *Handbook of Parenting: Vol. 3: Being and becoming a parent* (2nd ed., pp. 27–73). Mahwah, NJ: Lawrence Erlbaum.

Phares, V., Rojas, A., Thurston, I., & Hankinson, J. (2010). Including fathers in clinical interventions for children and adolescents, in M. Lamb (Ed.) *The role of the father in child development* (pp. 459–485). Hoboken, NJ: John Wiley.

Pruett, K, (2000). *Fatherneed: Why father care is as essential as mother care for your child.* New York: Free Press.

Pruett, K., & Pruett, M. (2009) *Patrnership parenting: How men and women parent differently—why it helps your kids and can strengthen your marriage.* New York: DaCapo Lifelong Books.

Pruett, M., Cowan, C., Cowan, P., & Diamond, J. (2012). Supporting father involvement in the context of separation and divorce., in K. Kuehnle & L. Drozd (Eds.) *Parenting plan evaluations: Applied research for the family court* (pp. 123–151). New York: Oxford University Press.

Pruett, M., Cowan, C., Cowan, P., & Pruett, K. (2009). Fathers as resources in families involved in the child welfare system. *Protecting Children, 24(2)*, 54–64.

Pruett, M., Cowan, C., Cowan, P., & Pruett, K. (2009). Lessons learned from the Supporting Father Involvement study: A cross-cultural preventive intervention for low-income families with young children. *Journal of Social Service Research, 35*, 163–179.

Raeburn, P. (2014). *Do fathers matter? What science is telling us about the parent we've overlooked.* New York: Farrar, Straus & Giroux.

13

PARENT MANAGEMENT TRAINING–OREGON MODEL

A Program to Treat Children's Behavior Problems

Margrét Sigmarsdóttir, Laura A. Rains, & Marion S. Forgatch

Learning Goals

Readers will gain knowledge about the Parent Management Training–Oregon model (**PMTO®**):

1. PMTO as a theoretical model and practice.
2. Specific criteria EBT programs need to fulfill.
3. The theoretical background of PMTO.
4. The core elements of positive parenting practices.
5. Important training methods that set up PMTO practitioners to learn and polish skills.
6. Why method fidelity is important and how it can be measured.
7. Existing evidence supporting PMTO and randomized controlled trial (RCTs) that have been conducted.
8. Important implementation strategies that need to be in place when a method is transferred from program developers to adopting sites.
9. Where and how PMTO has been implemented with high fidelity to the model.

Introduction

Parent Management Training–Oregon Model (PMTO), an evidence-based treatment (EBT) designed to prevent and reduce children's behavior problems, was developed by Gerald Patterson and his colleagues at the Oregon Social Learning Center (OSLC; e.g., Patterson, Reid, & Eddy, 2002; Forgatch

& Patterson 2010). PMTO meets EBT standards, including manual-based specification of program details, careful descriptions of client samples, demonstrated efficacy in several between-group-design experiments, and replications by independent investigators (Chambless & Hollon, 1998; Flay et al., 2005).

Needs Assessment and Target Audience

Children with behavior problems are at great risk of developing other adjustment disorders, including ADHD, depression, anxiety, academic difficulties, alcohol and drug abuse, delinquency, as well as limited social skills (Moffitt, Caspi, Rutter, & Silva, 2001; Karnik & Steiner, 2005; Kazdin, 2005). Patterson and colleagues

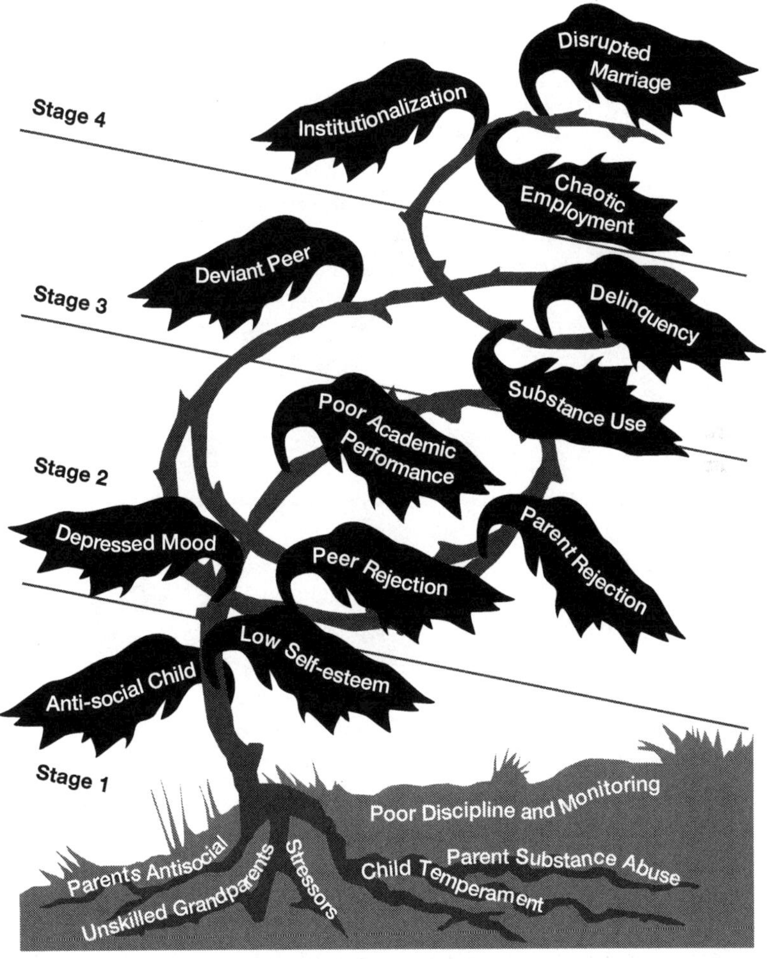

FIGURE 13.1 The Vile Weed: Stages in the Coercion Model

(Patterson, Reid, & Dishion, 1992) presented a stage model of deviancy in which family roots can influence a youngster's problems, which can develop throughout childhood and adolescence and carry into adulthood. Figure 13.1 illustrates the model and highlights the importance of intervening early in children's lives.

Interventions to strengthen effective parenting practices play a key role in the treatment of children's behavior problems in preschool and elementary school, with more reviews of outcome studies for parent training models than for other treatment approaches (Kazdin, 2005). A number of parent management training (PMT) interventions have been developed (e.g., Eyberg & Robinson, 1982; Webster-Stratton & Hammond, 1997; Sanders, 1999; Dishion et al., 2008) and, to some extent, PMTO is a prototype of other parent training EBTs (Brestan & Eyberg, 1998; Eyberg, Nelson, & Boggs, 2008). The PMTO program has been tested with samples of youngsters between the ages of 2 and 18 and has shown benefits to problems that include noncompliance, internalizing and externalizing behaviors, delinquency, substance abuse, and poor academic performance. It has shown to be effective for clinically referred cases and with at-risk samples to prevent problems and promote healthy development (Forgatch & Patterson, 2010). In clinical samples, families are assessed according to standard agency protocol to evaluate the level of functioning of both children and parents (only extreme cases of dysfunctions, like alcohol and drug abuse, are excluded). Prevention samples are selected in accordance with program goals and an example is recently separated mothers.

Program Goals and Objectives

PMTO is based on the social interaction learning model (SIL), which postulates that children learn behavior through their interactions with others as certain patterns of behavior are reinforced. Parents' child-rearing methods exert the primary influence on children's adjustment and have a direct effect on how children adapt to their environments. As children reach adolescence, peer influence becomes important as well (Dishion & Patterson, 2006). Parenting methods that are characterized by high rates of coercion (aversive behaviors, negative reciprocity, escalation, and negative reinforcement) increase the likelihood that children will develop behavior problems. Coercive patterns of behavior between parent and child can generalize from home to school as well as in relationships with others in the community (Ramsey, Patterson, & Walker, 1990). A key dimension of PMTO is to help parents replace **coercive interactions** (i.e., aversive behaviors, negative reciprocity, escalation, and negative reinforcement) with positive parenting methods consisting of five core components: *skill encouragement, setting limits, monitoring, problem solving*, and *positive involvement*. These components form the foundation of the intervention and are readily adapted to the unique characteristics of each family (Patterson & Forgatch, 2005). When used effectively, these parenting practices contribute to healthy child adjustment

(Forgatch, Patterson, DeGarmo, & Beldavs, 2009; Forgatch & Patterson, 2010). Stress-inducing factors such as financial difficulties, transitions in family life and family composition, trauma, children's challenging temperament, and parental physical or mental health problems can disrupt parenting skills. The SIL model postulates that such contextual adversities have an indirect impact on child adjustment through their disrupting influence on effective parenting (DeGarmo, Forgatch, & Martinez, 1999; Capaldi, DeGarmo, Patterson, & Forgatch, 2002). Figure 13.2 illustrates how contextual factors influence parenting practices, which then influence child/adolescent adjustment.

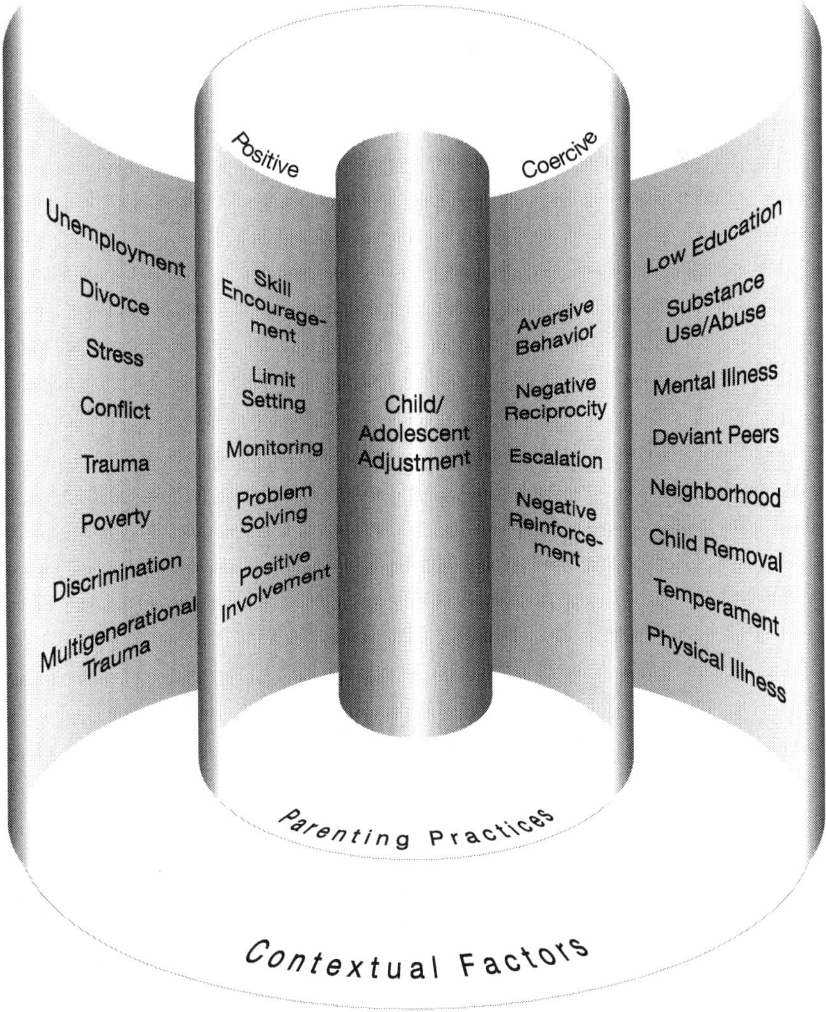

FIGURE 13.2 A Social Interactional Learning Model

Curriculum and Other Program Issues

PMTO has the flexibility of being offered to parents either in a group format or on an individual basis (Patterson et al., 2002; Forgatch & Patterson, 2010). Program components can be tailored to address specific family contexts and individual needs. Since parents are seen as the principal treatment agents for their children, they are the focus of the intervention. Therapists use active teaching approaches (e.g., role play, questioning process, and problem solving) to engage parents and introduce the five core PMTO components that are the putative mechanisms of child adjustment. Each component serves as a foundation for subsequent components. **Skill Encouragement** teaches parents to break behaviors into small steps and coach their children in pro-social behavior with practical, contingent processes such as token systems and incentive charts. **Limit Setting** helps parents reduce problem behavior with contingent, mild, noncorporal negative consequences such as time out, privilege removal, and brief work chores. **Supervision/ Monitoring** teaches parents to monitor children's whereabouts at home and in the community, the peers and adults in their lives, and adult supervision of the child's activities. The **Problem-solving** component includes strategies to resolve conflict and reach agreements on rules and consequences inside and outside the home. **Positive Involvement** promotes the many ways in which parents show children interest, love, and support. Parents practice weekly assignments at home between sessions and receive midweek calls to troubleshoot and support their practice. Parents also receive assistance in establishing positive working relationships with the schools, social services, and significant others.

The group format of the program ranges from 10 to 14 sessions, provided in weekly meetings of 1.5 to 2 hours with the parent groups conducted at agencies or at community sites. When families are treated individually, they receive treatment at agencies or in their homes in 60-minute sessions for 20–40 weeks (Patterson & Forgatch, 2005; Sigmarsdóttir, 2005; Forgatch et al., 2009; Forgatch & Patterson, 2010; Rains, Forgatch, & Knutson, 2010). Session structure varies; group sessions follow a set agenda, while individual sessions are more flexible. In all PMTO delivery, practitioners maintain a balance between following a structured agenda that introduces and rehearses core content and being responsive to family circumstances (Rains et al., 2010).

Professional Preparation and Training Issues

PMTO trains professionals who work in community agencies that are part of a wide-scale implementation. Professionals are recruited for PMTO training based on criteria across several dimensions, and a readiness checklist is used to help agencies select therapists. Preferred characteristics include education in a relevant discipline (e.g., psychology, social work, and counseling), clinical experience, an ability to adopt new intervention strategies, flexibility and creativity, belief in families, a strengths-based approach, and comfort with behavioral strategies.

Therapists are trained to certification in a comprehensive program for 12–18 months that uses best-practice adult-learning methods supplemented with detailed practitioner manuals and parent materials. Therapists attend workshop seminars, treat cases in community agencies, and receive coaching based on observations of video recorded therapy sessions. The number of workshop days averages 18 days in the first year, supplemented by live, written, and video feedback (Rains, Forgatch, Knutson, Sigmarsdóttir, & Duckert, 2013). Communities use a web-based, Health Insurance Portability and Accountability Act (HIPAA)-compliant database system that tracks progress and enhances communication. Agency support is essential.

The training program is prescriptive about practices and procedures; however, trainers emphasize that the parent-focused program is responsive to family context. PMTO uses a "show rather than tell" approach to family work and in training. Trainers model treatment strategies using what is called a **3D approach**, in which a practice is **D**emonstrated, **D**ebriefed, and **D**ifferentiated using role plays of ineffective and effective examples. Therapists learn to use problem-solving strategies to help parents address family issues and troubleshoot problems that commonly occur as they practice procedures with their children at home. Through the training process, therapists gain insight and practice in how to prevent and reduce parental resistance to the parenting techniques (Patterson & Forgatch, 1985; Patterson & Chamberlain, 1988, 1994) and instead begin to view the therapeutic interaction as a transactional process in which there is therapist responsibility and potential for influencing the outcome (Forgatch & Domenech Rodriguez, in press). During the training, therapists work with a minimum of three families until achieving a standard of proficiency that leads to invitation to begin treating two new "certification" families. Therapist candidates are certified when they attain a specified passing score on each of four sessions on core PMTO topics (Knutson, Forgatch, Rains, & Sigmarsdóttir, 2009).

The fidelity rating system used to certify therapists measures competent adherence to the PMTO model and method with an observation-based measuring tool: **Fidelity of Implementation Rating System** (FIMP; Knutson et al., 2009). FIMP assesses the interaction between therapist and parents during intervention sessions, with a focus on the therapist's competency and adherence to the model in five dimensions: Knowledge, Structure, Teaching, Process Skills, and Overall Development. Ratings are made using a nine-point Likert scale: 1–3 reflects *needs work*, 4–6 *acceptable work*, and 7–9 *good work*. To be certified, therapists must receive a mean FIMP score of 6.0 on each of the four certification sessions. After certification, therapists continue to receive regular coaching based on direct observation of therapy sessions. Studies assessing the predictive validity of FIMP show that high FIMP scores predict improvements in parenting practices (Forgatch, DeGarmo, & Beldavs, 2005; Ogden & Amlund Hagen, 2008; Forgatch & DeGarmo, 2011), as well as improvements in child outcome (Hukkelberg & Ogden, 2013).

Evidence-based Research and Evaluation

A review of key PMTO efficacy trials shows positive effects of the intervention for families assigned to PMTO compared with those in the control condition from both prevention and treatment populations (Forgatch & Patterson, 2010). Findings are based on RCTs, using **multi-method, multi-informant assessments, and intent-to-treat designs** (ITT). Outcomes that favor children in the experimental groups relative to the control groups include decreases in child deviant behavior assessed by direct observations and repeated telephone interviews; fewer delinquent behaviors assessed by parents and teachers; fewer recorded police arrests; less observed noncompliance and aggression; better school adjustment according to teacher ratings and standardized testing; and reduced self-reported depression and deviant peer association (Patterson, Chamberlain, & Reid, 1982; Bank, Marlowe, Reid, Patterson, & Weinrott, 1991; Chamberlain & Reid, 1998; Forgatch & DeGarmo, 1999; Forgatch et al., 2009; Forgatch & Patterson, 2010).

Parents also benefit from PMTO intervention. For example, the Oregon Divorce Study (ODS), a preventive intervention trial of 238 single mothers and their sons, obtained medium effect sizes for observed parenting practices, which mediated nine-year effects on youth adjustment (Forgatch et al., 2009). Other beneficial effects for parents include self-report of increased standard of living (e.g., income, occupation, education, financial stress, and rise out of poverty) and marital satisfaction, as well as decreased maternal depression and fewer reports of police arrests (DeGarmo, Patterson, & Forgatch, 2004; Forgatch & DeGarmo, 2007; Forgatch & Patterson, 2010; Patterson, Forgatch, & DeGarmo, 2010).

Studies outside of the U.S. have shown positive effects in practice in community treatment agencies (Ogden & Amlund Hagen, 2008; Sigmarsdóttir, Thorlacius, Guðmundsdóttir, & DeGarmo, in press), where the inclusion criteria were based on professionals clinical judgments of behavior problems (no formal screening or assessment). The first wide-scale RCT effectiveness trial, which was also the first PMTO study outside of the USA, was based on a nationwide implementation in Norway within two systems of care (i.e., child welfare and child mental health; Ogden & Amlund Hagen, 2008; Amlund Hagen, Ogden, & Bjørnebekk, 2011). In that study 112 children aged 4 to 12, referred for conduct problems, were randomly assigned to either a PMTO experimental group or a control group receiving services as usual (SAU). The results from the multiple-method and informant assessment yielded reductions in the children's externalizing problems and improvements in social competence in the PMTO group compared with the SAU group. Improvements in parental discipline predicted better child outcome, especially for the younger children (Ogden & Amlund Hagen, 2008; Amlund Hagen et al., 2011). In Iceland, pre/post results from an RCT conducted in community settings within a nationwide implementation revealed that the PMTO group condition showed greater reductions in child adjustment problems relative to the SAU controls. Participants in the study were families of 102 clinically referred children with behavior problems. Age and gender were not associated with change in outcomes, and the construct for child adjustment indicated that the PMTO intervention had a modest to medium effect (Sigmarsdóttir et al., in press). The Icelandic study showed no main effects on parenting but some interactional effects of maternal depression where PMTO prevented the expected damaging effects of depression (Sigmarsdóttir, DeGarmo, Forgatch, & Guðmundsdóttir, 2013).

Cultural Implications

PMTO, which was originally developed and evaluated in efficacy trials in the USA, has now been made available in community practice through several implementations. When attempting to bridge the gap between efficacy and effectiveness trials, a key question is whether the program can be provided as standard practice in community agencies with sustained adherence to the method (Fixsen, Naoom, Blasé, Friedmen, & Wallace, 2005; Carroll et al., 2007). PMTO implementations address this problem by working with large systems and gradually transferring the program into the hands of the community in a *full transfer* approach. Full transfer takes place in four stages over a period of at least three years, with extensive collaboration between the program purveyor and the adopting community (see Forgatch, Patterson, & Gewirtz, 2013). Many critical implementation steps need to be respected for successful outcome, including building infrastructure to support initiation and maintenance of the implementation (Fixsen et al., 2005; Chamberlain et al., 2008; Forgatch et al., 2013). For example in Iceland, where the program has been systematically implemented in several communities, a study has shown that the number of children referred for specialist services decreased following the implementation in comparison with control communities not receiving PMTO services (Sigmarsdóttir & Björnsdóttir, 2012).

The first PMTO implementation began in Norway in 1999. The Norwegian program was initiated following a careful survey by experts showing the need for programs that can effectively reduce youngsters' behavior problems (Ogden, Forgatch, Askeland, Patterson, & Bullock, 2005; Solholm, Askeland, Christiansen, & Duckert, 2005). Fifteen years later, the program continues to grow and extend its reach from treatment to prevention and immigrant populations. The first generation of PMTO therapists certified by the program developer in 2001 has grown from 30 to almost 300 countrywide, with the new practitioners trained and certified by the Norwegian team (Forgatch, Rains, & Sigmarsdóttir, 2014). Since then, three European countries have conducted nationwide implementations: Iceland, the Netherlands, and Denmark. In the USA, PMTO has been implemented in two statewide programs (i.e., Michigan in community mental health and Kansas in child welfare), and an adaptation for National Guard personnel returning from the wars in Afghanistan and Iraq (Gewirtz, Pinna,

Hanson, & Brockberg, 2014). Pilot projects have been carried out in the child welfare system in New York City and a prevention program in Mexico City. Finally, a pilot program is being conducted in Northern Uganda with war-displaced mothers. Each implementation, whether it is full-transfer or pilot, contributes unique learning points to the growth of implementation science.

An important question in relation to successful implementation—*Does method fidelity remain high from one generation of therapists to another?*—has been addressed in both the Norwegian and Icelandic programs (Forgatch & DeGarmo, 2011; Sigmarsdóttir & Guðmundsdóttir, 2013). In both countries, there was a small but significant drop in fidelity scores from generation 1 (G1), which was trained by the program purveyor to generation 2 (G2), trained by the adopting community. However, the G3 practitioners achieved scores equivalent to those attained by G1. In Iceland, the test was carried out to the fourth generation and showed that fidelity was sustained at the level of G1 and G3. These findings indicate that communities can sustain high levels of fidelity following transfer of the program with minimal involvement by the program developer. It is important to keep in mind that the implementation of PMTO adheres to the core components of PMTO while incorporating minor adaptations to adjust to cultural and contextual circumstances, which is in keeping with recommendations within the literature (Domenech Rodríguez, Baumann, & Schwartz, 2011). Further reading about the national and international implementation of PMTO can be found in papers by Forgatch and colleagues (Forgatch et al., 2013; Forgatch et al., in press).

Conclusion

The parent training program that became PMTO was originally designed in the mid-1960s. Since then, the program has developed as the result of integrating advances in methods and theory into the intervention it has become today (Forgatch et al., 2009; Patterson et al., 2010). PMTO has met EBT standards (Chambless & Hollon, 1998; Flay et al., 2005) with emphasis on treating cases—both clinical and at-risk samples (Forgatch et al., 2009; Forgatch & Patterson, 2010). In community agencies, cases are referred on the basis of clinical judgment of behavior problems. Therapists complete a structured training program to learn active teaching approaches, such as role play, questioning process, and problem solving, to help parents adopt positive parenting tools (Rains et al., 2013). Treatment integrity and the quality of treatment is measured with FIMP, a validated tool (Knutson et al., 2009) that allows program administrators to evaluate the extent to which model fidelity is sustained during community practice—a critical step in the complex process of implementing evidence-based practice (Fixsen et al., 2005; Chamberlain et al., 2008; Forgatch et al., 2013).

PMTO has successfully been implemented nationally and internationally (Forgatch et al., 2013). It is interesting to see how the parenting principles continue to play a key role in reducing children's behavior problems under different conditions. When community service programs choose treatment programs to treat children's adjustment problems, it is important to rely on data showing the program has shown good outcomes and can be maintained in the long run with sustained fidelity to the well documented model.

Key Points

1. PMTO is an evidence-based treatment (EBT) designed to prevent and reduce children's behavioral problems. PMTO is theory based—it carefully specifies client samples and provides manuals that describe practices and procedures and data demonstrating efficacy and effectiveness in several between-group-design experiments with replications by independent investigators.
2. PMTO is based on the social interaction learning model (SIL), which presumes that children learn behavior through reinforcing principles in their interactions with others. High rates of coercive parenting increase the likelihood that children will develop behavioral problems. PMTO therapists help parents replace coercive interactions with positive parenting practices that promote healthy child adjustment.
3. FIMP is an observational-based assessment tool used to measure therapists' competence and adherence to the PMTO method. Five dimensions are scored: knowledge, structure, teaching, process skills, and overall development. Tests of validity show that high FIMP scores assessed during intervention predict improvements in parenting practices assessed before and after intervention.
4. Evidence supporting PMTO is based on a number of RCTs conducted within and outside the USA Main outcomes show that PMTO contributes significantly to healthy child and parent adjustment.
5. PMTO developers implement using a method of full transfer to adopting sites. Full transfer requires adopting sites to develop infrastructure to sustain training, coaching, and rating of method fidelity. Studies have shown that high levels of fidelity sustain subsequent transfer of the program from PMTO purveyors to sites in Norway and Iceland.
6. PMTO has been implemented within diverse populations of ethnicities and cultures. Examples include: Norway, Iceland, the Netherlands, and Denmark within Europe; Mexico City in Central America; and Michigan, Kansas, Spanish-speaking families, and military families within the USA.

Discussion Questions

1. What evidence supports PMTO as an evidence-based treatment?
2. What is postulated in the SIL model?
3. What are the five core positive parenting practices that parents learn to replace coercive practices within families?

4. What is FIMP and how are FIMP scores correlated with PMTO outcomes?
5. Identify at least three RCTs that have been conducted on PMTO and where they have been conducted.
6. Why is it important to monitor FIMP scores from PMTO therapists on a regular basis when the program is practiced as part of regular services in communities?

Additional Resources

Additional Reading

Bjørknes, R., Kjøbli, J., Manger, T., & Jakobsen, R. (2012). Parent training among ethnic minorities: Parenting practices as mediators of change in child conduct problems. *Family Relations, 61*, 101–114.

Kjøbli, J. & Bjørnebekk, G. (2013). A randomized effectiveness trial of brief parent training: Six-month follow-up. *Research on Social Work Practice, 23*, 603–612.

Parra-Cardona, J., Domenech-Rodríguez, M., Forgatch, M., Sullivan, C., Bybee, D., Holtrop, K., Escobar-Chew, A., Tams, L., Dates, B., & Bernal, G. (2012). Culturally adapting an evidence-based parenting intervention for Latino immigrants: The need to integrate fidelity and cultural relevance. *Family Process, 51*, 56–72.

Patterson, G. (2005). The next generation of PMTO models. *Behavior Therapist, 28*, 25–32.

Patterson, G., Forgatch, M., & DeGarmo, D. (2010). Cascading effects following intervention. *Development & Psychopathology, 22*, 949–970.

Websites

www.cehd.umn.edu/fsos/projects/adapt; www.isii.net; www.oslc.org; www.pmto.no; www.pmto.is; www.pmto.nl; www.michiganpmto.com; www.socialstyrelsen.dk/born-og-unge/programmer-med-evidens/pmto

References

Amlund Hagen, K., Ogden, T., & Bjørnebekk, G. (2011). Treatment outcomes and mediators of parent management training: A one-year follow-up of children with conduct problems. *Journal of Clinical Child & Adolescent Psychology, 40*, 165–178.

Bank, L., Marlowe, J., Reid, J., Patterson, G., & Weinrott, M. (1991). A comparative evaluation of parent-training interventions for families of chronic delinquents. *Journal of Abnormal Child Psychology, 19*, 15–33.

Brestan, E., & Eyberg S. (1998). Effective psychosocial treatments of conduct-disorder children and adolescents: 29 years, 82 studies and 5,272 kids. *Journal of Clinical Child Psychology, 27*, 180–189.

Capaldi, D., DeGarmo, D., Patterson, G., & Forgatch, M. (2002). Contextual risk across the early life span and association with antisocial behavior, in J. Reid, G. Patterson & J. Snyder (Eds.) *Antisocial behavior in children and adolescents: A developmental analysis and model for intervention* (pp. 123–145). Washington, DC: American Psychological Association.

Carroll, C., Patterson, M., Wood, S., Booth, A., Rick, J., & Balain, S. (2007). A conceptual framework for implementation fidelity. *Implementation Science, 2*, 1–9.

Chamberlain, P., Brown, C. H., Saldana, L., Reid, J., Wang, W., Marsenich, L., Sosna, T., Padgett, C., & Bouwman, G. (2008). Engaging and recruiting counties in an experiment on implementing evidence-based practice in California. Administration and policy in mental health and mental health research, *35*, 250–260.

Chamberlain, P., & Reid, J. (1998). Comparison of two community alternatives to incarceration for chronic juvenile offenders. *Journal of Consulting and Clinical Psychology, 66*, 624–633.

Chambless, D., & Hollon, S. (1998). Defining empirically supported therapies. *Journal of Consulting and Clinical Psychology, 66*, 7–18.

DeGarmo, D., Forgatch, M., & Martinez, C., Jr. (1999). Parenting of divorced mothers as a link between social status and boys' academic outcomes: Unpacking the effects of SES. *Child Development, 70*, 1231–1245.

DeGarmo, D., Patterson, G., & Forgatch, M. (2004). How do outcomes in a specified parent training intervention maintain or wane over time? *Prevention Science, 5*, 73–89.

Dishion, T., & Patterson, G. (2006). The development and ecology of antisocial behavior in children and adolescents, in D. Cicchetti & D. Cohen (Eds.) *Developmental psychopathology. Vol. 3: Risk, disorder, and adaptation* (Revised ed., pp. 503–541). New York: Wiley.

Dishion, T., Shaw, D., Connell, A., Gardner, F., Weaver, C., & Wilson, M. (2008). The Family Check-Up with high-risk indigent families: Preventing problem behavior by increasing parents' positive behavior support in early childhood. *Child Development, 79*, 1395–1414.

Domenech Rodríguez, M., Baumann, A., & Schwartz, A. (2011). Cultural adaption of an evidence based intervention: From theory to practice in a Latino/a community context. *American Journal of Community Psychology, 47*, 170–186.

Eyberg, S., Nelson, M., & Boggs, S. (2008). Evidence-based psychosocial treatments for children and adolescents with disruptive behavior. *Journal of Clinical Child and Adolescent Psychology, 37*, 215–237.

Eyberg, S., & Robinson, E. (1982). Parent-child interaction training: Effects on family functioning. *Journal of Clinical Child Psychology, 11*, 130–137.

Fixsen, D., Naoom, S., Blase, K., Friedman, R., & Wallace, F. (2005). *Implementation research: A synthesis of the literature.* Tampa, FL: University of South Florida, Louis de la Parte Florida Mental Health Institute, National Implementation Research Network.

Flay, B., Biglan, A., Boruch, R., Gonzalez Castro, F., Gottfredson, D., Kellam, S., Mo_cicki, E., Schinke, S., Valentine, J., & Ji, P. (2005). Standards of evidence: Criteria for efficacy, effectiveness and dissemination. *Prevention Science, 6*, 151–175.

Forgatch, M., & DeGarmo, D. (1999). Parenting through change. An effective prevention program for single mothers. *Journal of Consulting and Clinical Psychology, 67*, 711–724.

Forgatch, M., & DeGarmo, D. (2007). Accelerating recovery from poverty: Prevention effects for recently separated mothers. *Journal of Early and Intensive Behavioral Intervention, 4*, 681–702.

Forgatch, M., & DeGarmo, D. (2011). Sustaining fidelity following the nationwide PMTO implementation in Norway. *Prevention Science, 12*, 235–246.

Forgatch, M., DeGarmo, D., & Beldavs, Z. (2005). An efficacious theory-based intervention for stepfamilies. *Behavior Therapy, 36*, 357–365.

Forgatch, M., & Domenech Rodríguez, M. (in press). Addressing coercion in intervention: Balancing content and process, in T. Dishion & J. Snyder (Eds.) *Oxford handbook of coercive relationship dynamics*. New York: Oxford University Press.

Forgatch, M., & Patterson, G. (2010). Parent Management Training—Oregon Model: An intervention for antisocial behavior in children and adolescents, in J. Weisz & A. Kazdin (Eds.) *Evidence-based psychotherapies for children and adolescents* (2nd ed., pp. 159–178). New York: Guilford.

Forgatch, M., Patterson, G., DeGarmo, D., & Beldavs, Z. (2009). Testing the Oregon delinquency model with nine-year follow-up of the Oregon Divorce Study. *Development and Psychopathology, 21(2)*, 637–660.

Forgatch, M., Patterson, G., & Gewirtz, A. (2013). Looking forward: The promise of widespread implementation of parent training programs. *Perspectives on Psychological Science, 8*, 682–694.

Forgatch, M., Rains, L., & Sigmarsdóttir, M. (2014). Early results from implementing PMTO: Full transfer on a grand scale, in M. Van Ryzin, K. Kumpfer, G. Fosco, & M. Greenberg (Eds.) *Family-centered prevention programs for children and adolescents: Theory, research, and large-scale dissemination*. New York: Taylor & Francis/Psychology Press.

Gewirtz, A., Pinna, K., Hanson, S., & Brockberg, D. (2014). Promoting parenting to support reintegrating military families: After deployment, adaptive parenting tools. *Psychological Services, 11*, 31–40.

Hukkelberg, S., & Ogden, T. (2013). Working alliance and treatment fidelity as predictors of externalizing problem behaviors in Parent Management Training. *Journal of Consulting and Clinical Psychology, 81*, 1010–1020.

Karnik, N., & Steiner, H. (2005). Disruptive behavior disorders, in W. M. Klykylo & J. L. Kay (Eds.) *Clinical child psychiatry* (2nd ed., pp. 191–202). Chichester: Wiley.

Kazdin, A. (2005). Child, parent, and family-based treatment of aggressive and antisocial child behavior, in E. Hibbs & P. Jensen (Eds.) *Psychological treatments for child and adolescent disorders: Empirically based strategies for clinical practice* (2nd ed., pp. 445–476). Washington, DC: American Psychological Association.

Knutson, N., Forgatch, M., Rains, L., & Sigmarsdóttir, M. (2009). *Fidelity of Implementation Rating System (FIMP): The manual for PMTO*. Eugene, OR: Implementation Sciences International.

Moffitt, T., Caspi, A., Rutter, M., Silva, P. (2001). *Sex differences in antisocial behavior: Conduct disorder, delinquency, and violence in the Dunedin longitudinal study*. Cambridge, UK: Cambridge University Press.

Ogden, T., & Amlund Hagen, K. (2008). Treatment effectiveness of Parent Management Training in Norway: A randomized controlled trial of children with conduct problems. *Journal of Consulting and Clinical Psychology, 76*, 607–621.

Ogden, T., Forgatch, M., Askeland, E., Patterson, G., & Bullock, B. (2005). Implementation of parent management training at the national level: The case of Norway. *Journal of Social Work Practice, 19*, 317–329.

Patterson, G., & Chamberlain, P. (1988). Treatment process: A problem at three levels, in L. Wynne (Ed.) *The state of the art in family therapy research: Controversies and recommendations* (pp. 189–223). New York: Family Process Press.

Patterson, G., & Chamberlain, P. (1994). A functional analysis of resistance during parent training therapy. *Journal of Clinical Psychology: Science and Practice, 1*, 53–70.

Patterson, G., Chamberlain, P., & Reid, J. (1982). A comparative evaluation of a parent-training program. *Behavior Therapy, 13*, 638–650.

Patterson, G., & Forgatch, M. (1985). Therapist behavior as a determinant for client noncompliance: A paradox for the behavior modifier. *Journal of Consulting and Clinical Psychology, 53*, 846–851.

Patterson, G., & Forgatch, M. (2005). *Parents and adolescents living together. Part 1: The basics.* Champaign, IL: Research Press.

Patterson, G., Forgatch, M., & DeGarmo, D. (2010). Cascading effects following intervention. *Development & Psychopathology, 22(Special Issue 04)*, 949–970.

Patterson, G., Reid, J., & Dishion, T. (1992). *A social interactional approach. IV. Antisocial boys.* Eugene, OR: Castalia.

Patterson, G., Reid, J., & Eddy, M. (2002). A brief history of the Oregon model, in J. B. Reid, G. Patterson & J. Snyder (Eds.) *Antisocial behavior in children and adolescents: A developmental analysis and model for intervention* (pp. 3–21). Washington, DC: American Psychological Association.

Rains, L., Forgatch, M., & Knutson, N. (2010). *A course in the basic PMTO model, vols. 1–5* [unpublished training manuals]. Eugene, OR: Implementation Sciences International.

Rains, L., Forgatch, M., Knutson, N., Sigmarsdóttir, M., & Duckert, M. (2013). *Manual for PMTO educators* [unpublished workshop training manual]. Eugene, OR: Implementation Sciences International.

Ramsey, E., Patterson, G., & Walker, H. (1990). Generalization of the antisocial trait from home to school settings. *Journal of Applied Developmental Psychology, 11*, 209–223.

Sanders, M. (1999). Triple P-Positive Parenting Program: Towards an empirically validated multilevel parenting and family support strategy for the prevention of behavior and emotional problems in children. *Clinical Child and Family Psychology Review, 2(2)*, 71–90.

Sigmarsdóttir, M. (2005). *Styðjandi foreldrafærni* [Positive parenting]. Hafnarfjörður: Skólaskrifstofa Hafnarfjarðar.

Sigmarsdóttir, M., & Björnsdóttir, A. (2012). Community implementation of PMTO™: Impacts on specialist services and schools. *Scandinavian Journal of Psychology, 53*, 506–511.

Sigmarsdóttir, M., DeGarmo, D., Forgatch, M., & Guðmundsdóttir, E. (2013). Treatment effectiveness of PMTO for children's behavior problems in Iceland: Assessing parenting practices in a randomized controlled trial. *Scandinavian Journal of Psychology, 54*, 468–476.

Sigmarsdóttir, M., & Guðmundsdóttir, E. (2013). Implementation of Parent Management Training—Oregon model (PMTO™) in Iceland: Building sustained fidelity. *Family Process, 52*, 216–227.

Sigmarsdóttir, M., Thorlacius, Ö., Guðmundsdóttir, E., & DeGarmo, D. (2014). Treatment effectiveness of PMTO for children's behavior problems in Iceland: Child outcome in a randomized controlled trial. *Family Process*, online first, November 19. doi: 10.1111/famp.12109

Solholm, R., Askeland, E., Christiansen, T. & Duckert, M. (2005). Parent Management Training—Oregon-modellen: Teori, behandlingsprogram og implementering i Norge [Parent Management Training—The Oregon Model: Theory, treatment program and implementation in Norway]. *Tidsskrift for Norsk Psykologforening, 42*, 587–597.

Webster-Stratton, C., & Hammond, M. (1997). Treating children with early onset conduct problems and improving school readiness: A comparison of child and parent training interventions. *Journal of Consulting and Clinical Psychology, 56*, 93–109.

14

NURTURING PARENTING PROGRAMS FOR THE PREVENTION OF CHILD MALTREATMENT

Stephen J. Bavolek

Learning Goals

After reading this chapter, readers will increase their understanding of the following:

1. The differences between positive and negative nurturing.
2. The role that empathy has in the formation and practice of positive nurturing.
3. The four personality traits developed during childhood and reinforced throughout life.
4. The five parenting constructs that define the practices of child abuse and neglect.

Introduction

The Nurturing Parenting Programs are family-centered programs designed for the prevention and treatment of child abuse and neglect. Both parents and their children participate in the sessions, which enhance the acquisition and application of new behaviors. Initially developed in 1979 from a three-year grant funded by the National Institute of Mental Health (NIMH), the lessons focus on helping parents and their children, prenatal to 18 years of age, replacing old and hurtful abusive and neglecting parenting practices and family patterns with positive nurturing ones. By applying the theory and practices of re-parenting, parents and their children learn new nurturing patterns that build and establish their knowledge and skills of empathy, empowerment, self-worth, cooperation, and parental guidance based on respect and dignity.

Today there are 25 different Nurturing Programs offered in communities worldwide to meet the unique learning needs of families. Programs are offered in three different models of delivery: home-based instruction (one-to-one); group-based instruction (12 to 15 parents); and a combination of group- and home-based instruction. The different models provide agencies the opportunity to select the model that best fits their agency's delivery of services as well as the needs of the families.

Programs also vary in dosage (i.e., the number of sessions offered to the families). The dosage reflects the degree of deficiency in positive nurturing, as well as other issues that often contribute to child maltreatment which include widespread family dysfunction, drug and alcohol addiction, intimate partner violence, and mental illness.

Based on thorough pre-program assessment followed by ongoing process assessment, core lessons provide education in the basic philosophy and practices of nurturing parenting. Supplemental lessons provide content and dosage that are tailored to meet the unique needs of families at three levels. The first level is designed for families with an assessed low risk for child maltreatment. Lesson dosage and content at this level ranges from five to ten sessions and is usually referred to as primary prevention or parent education. The second level of lesson dosage and content is designed for families who are assessed as being a moderate risk for child maltreatment. Lesson dosage at this level ranges from 12 to 20 sessions and is usually referred to as secondary prevention or intervention. The third level of lesson dosage and content is for families who are assessed as being a high risk for child maltreatment. Lesson dosage at this level ranges from 15 to 55 sessions and is usually referred to as tertiary prevention or treatment.

The lessons that make up the sessions of the Nurturing Programs are competency based. Lesson competencies are measured at the end of each session. If the lesson competencies have not been acquired by the parents at the end of the session, the following session(s) continues to work on helping parents acquire the skills and knowledge of the previous lesson. Previous lesson competencies must be learned before the following lesson's competencies are introduced. The lessons in the Nurturing Programs are taught in a sequenced order of difficulty. Recognizing that every skill has a necessary prerequisite skill, each lesson's competencies build upon the previous lesson. It is very likely that one lesson might take several sessions for some parents to acquire the lesson competencies.

Theoretical Foundations and History

The word **nurturing** comes from the Latin word *nutritura*, which means to promote, nurse, and nourish life. Nurturing is the single most critical process for creating and sustaining life. However, a closer examination of the processes of nurturing indicates all life as well as all behavior needs to be nurtured. The philosophy of the Nurturing Programs is based on the premise that two types of nurturing exist: positive and negative. In parenting, positive nurturing is nourishing the aspects of life we want in a child's personality. Negative nurturing is nourishing the aspects of life we don't want in a child's personality, but get anyway. Decades of behavioral research have shown the relationship between positive, healthy nurturing parenting practices in childhood and subsequent healthy lifestyles, and negative, destructive nurturing parenting practices in childhood and subsequent unhealthy lifestyles.

Positive nurturing is based on the characteristic of **empathy**. The word empathy comes from the Greek word *empatheia*, which means to project into or identify with another; and to enter fully through understanding another's feelings or motives. Empathy is the most important characteristics of a nurturing parent. Negative nurturing is called **abuse and neglect**. The word abuse comes from the Latin word *abusus*, which means to mistreat; cruel and harsh punishment. Neglect comes from the Latin word *neglegere*; *neg* means "not" and *legere* means "pick up". Neglectful parenting means not holding or touching children. Positive Nurturing and Negative Nurturing are two parenting patterns that exist on a continuum of frequency and intensity of zero to 10 (Figure 14.1).

The presence of positive nurturing parenting as a 10 is the complete absence (0) of negative nurturing. As positive nurturing parenting practices decrease, the frequency and intensity of abusive and neglectful parenting practices increase. A 10 in negative nurturing translates to the absence (0) of positive nurturing. The neurological networks and pathways that are created in childhood and influence our behavior are the result of the frequency and intensity of positive and negative nurturing. Events develop our personality characteristics. Personality characteristics lead to the development of personality traits. Over time, personality traits lead to full-blown personalities.

On the one hand, children who experience a high frequency and intensity of negative nurturing tend to develop abusive and neglecting personality characteristics very early in life. Over time, characteristics turn into more solid personality traits which, if the patterns continue, will turn into full-blown personalities. From a neurological perspective, the stress caused by constant experiences of abuse and

Positive Nurturing (Empathy)

Frequency	Always	Frequent	Sometimes	Infrequent	Never
Intensity	Very High	High	Average	Low	Not Present
	10	9 8 7	6 5 4	3 2 1	0

Negative Nurturing (Abuse and Neglect)

Frequency	Never	Infrequent	Sometimes	Frequent	Always
Intensity	Not Present	Low	Average	High	Very High
	0	1 2 3	4 5 6	7 8 9	10

FIGURE 14.1 Positive Nurturing (Empathy) and Negative Nurturing (Abuse and Neglect)

neglect creates diseased neurological networks and pathways by bathing neurons that are forming our neurological networks in high levels of stress hormones such as cortisol and adrenaline. When stress hormones are overactive, they can take over genetic regulation creating aberrant networks of connections between brain cells. The result is that depressive episodes occur instead of happy thoughts, and surges of rage occur instead of willingness to compromise. Abusive environments can cause genes important for survival to become overexposed, making a person more aggressive and violent.

Two dysfunctional personality traits are formed and reinforced through negative nurturing: the first dysfunctional trait is the **perpetrator**. This is the part of our personality that is abusive, hurts others physically, emotionally, spiritually, and sexually, and generally disregards the overall goodness of others. The second trait is the **victim**: the part of our personality that believes that hurt and pain given by others is justified and valid and for one's own good.

Children who experience a high frequency and intensity of positive nurturing in the form of empathy, self-worth, compassion, positive discipline, and empowerment create healthy neurological networks and pathways through the release of oxytocin and serotonin, our bonding and calming chemicals. The result is functional behavior which strengthens into positive character traits and personalities. Nurturing parenting practices reinforce a complex system of hormones and other chemical messengers in the brain that predisposes human beings to form and sustain strong attachments to other people. Two healthy personality traits are formed and reinforced through positive nurturing. The **nurturer** is the part of our personality that is capable of giving care, empathy, and compassion. The **nurtured** is the part of our personality that is capable of receiving care, seeking closeness and attachments, and accepts praise and positive touch.

The nurturing philosophy of parenting embraces the widely held and most sought-after belief of nonviolence in promoting in children the positive aspects of empathy for self and others; a strong sense of self-awareness; positive self-worth; empathic self-empowerment; and the ability to self-regulate emotions and behavior.

The Nurturing Parenting Philosophy of Change

The Nurturing Parenting philosophy of helping families change old unwanted patterns of interaction for healthier, more nurturing patterns is based on the theory of "emergence" and the practice of "re-parenting". In emergence theory, individuals already possess a degree of the sought-after desired traits. Abusive parents and abused children are capable of some level of nurturing. The goal of the facilitators is to enhance and build upon existing nurturing traits.

The practice of re-parenting entails interactive and experiential lessons that challenge existing thought and behavior patterns. Re-parenting instruction addresses the importance of self-awareness, understanding and acceptance, and

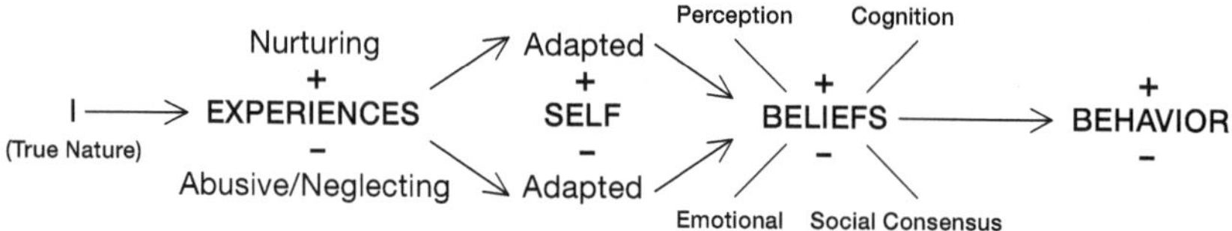

FIGURE 14.2 The Nurturing Parenting Philosophy of Change

persistence in replacing old dysfunctional existing thoughts and behaviors with newer, functional ones. The diagram presented (Figure 14.2) above describes how the environment plays a critical role in developing and shaping personality, and subsequently behavior.

The "I" represents our nature and the dispositional traits we receive from our parents' genes; the Self represents the adapted I which is the influence the environment has in forming our personality. In a summary Report of the Commission on Children at Risk entitled *Hardwired to Connect* (Commission on Children, 2003), the commission identified six key findings that show our nature is strongly influenced by our environment or nurture. Among their findings is that biological systems predispose human beings to form and sustain enduring, nurturing relationships. Experiences that we have growing up, however, can be positive nurturing, generating compassionate understanding, discipline, empathy, and empowerment, or they can be abusive and neglectful (negative nurturing), generating a violent, non-caring, painful childhood. The experiences that we have form the basis of our **adapted self**.

Simply, positive nurturing experiences form the basis of a positive adapted self. The abusive and neglecting experiences we have in childhood form the basis of our negative adapted self. The negative adapted self contains the traits of our personality that represent our victim and perpetrator that are capable of giving and receiving abuse and neglect. The positive adapted self, on the other hand, contains the traits of our personality that represent our nurturer and nurtured and are capable of giving and receiving compassion, caring, and love.

Needs Assessment and Target Audience

The Nurturing Parenting Programs have been validated with families at risk for abuse and neglect, families identified by local social services as abusive or neglectful, families in recovery for alcohol and other drug abuse, children at risk for delinquency, parents incarcerated for crimes against society, and adults seeking to become adoptive or foster parents. As such, a primary use of the Nurturing Parenting Programs is to treat child and adolescent maltreatment, prevent its recurrence, and build nurturing parenting skills in at-risk populations.

The goals, objectives, and educational lessons of the Nurturing Programs were developed from the previous research of Bavolek, Kline, and McLaughlin (1979) in identifying and assessing high-risk parenting behaviors. The first aspect of the research focused on identifying the critical behaviors of child maltreatment. The development of the Adult-Adolescent Parenting Inventory (AAPI-2) identified the following five basic constructs of child maltreatment which form the foundation of the Nurturing Programs:

Construct A

Inappropriate Parental Expectations. Beginning very early in the infant's life, abusive parents tend to inaccurately perceive the skills and abilities of their children. Inappropriate expectations of children are generally the result of three factors:

1. Parents simply don't know the needs and capabilities of children at various stages of growth and development.
2. Many parents who abuse their children generally lack a positive view of themselves and consequently of their children. Inadequate perceptions of self as an adult generally stem from early childhood experiences of failure, ridicule, and disappointment.
3. Abusive parents generally lack the empathy that is required to determine what an appropriate expectation is for children at different stages of development. The effects of inappropriate parental expectations upon children are debilitating. Many children perceive themselves as being worthless, as failures, and as unacceptable and disappointing to adults.

Construct B

Lack of an Empathic Awareness of Children's Needs. Empathic parents are sensitive to their children and create an environment that is conducive to promoting children's emotional, intellectual, physical, social, spiritual, and creative growth. Empathic parents understand their children from the inside, not from the outside as some interested observer. Parents lacking sufficient levels of empathy find children's needs and wants irritating and overwhelming. Everyday normal demands are perceived as unrealistic resulting in increased levels of stress. The needs of the child come into direct conflict with the needs of the parent, which are often similar in magnitude.

Lacking an empathic home life, children often fail to develop a solid moral code of conduct. Right and wrong, cooperation, and kindness are not important because they are not recognized as important values. The impact of one's negative actions on another is muted as the ability to care about the needs or feelings of another is not important. Children with low levels of empathy are often labeled as troublemakers, disobedient, and often engage in acts of cruelty to themselves, others, and animals.

Construct C

Strong Belief in the Use of Corporal Punishment. Physical punishment is generally the preferred means of discipline used by abusive parents. Rationale for the practice includes: teaching children right from wrong; as a cultural practice of discipline; as a practice sanctioned by the proverbs of the Old Testament; to punish children's misbehavior in a loving way; and just simply to punish misbehavior. Abusive parents often believe children should not be "given in to" nor allowed to "get away with anything". They must periodically be shown "who is boss" and to respect authority. Abusive parents not only consider physical punishment a proper disciplinary measure, but strongly defend their right to use physical force.

The effects of physical abuse are demonstrated in the observed inadequate behavior of children; their tendency to identify with the aggressive parent in an effort to gain some measure of self-protection and mastery; and the development of a set pattern of discharging aggression against the outside world in order to manage their own insecurities. Abused children, upon becoming parents, tend to punish their children more severely. As a result, abused children often become abusive parents.

Construct D

Parent–Child Role Reversal. A fourth common parenting behavior among abusive parents is their need to reverse parent–child roles. Children are expected to be sensitive to and responsible for much of the happiness of their parents. Parent–child role reversal is an interchanging of traditional role behaviors between a parent and child, so that the child adopts some of the behaviors traditionally associated with parents. In role reversal, parents act like helpless, needy children looking to their own children for parental care and comfort.

The effects of role reversal on abused children are destructive. Assuming the role of the responsible parent, children fail to negotiate the developmental tasks that must be mastered at each stage of life if they are to achieve normal development and a healthy adjustment. Failure to perform any of the developmental tasks not only hampers development in succeeding stages, but also further reinforces feelings of inadequacy. Children in a role reversal situation have little sense of self and see themselves as existing only to meet the needs of their parents.

Construct E

Oppressing Children's Power and Independence. Closely aligned with the value of physical punishment and the lack of an empathic awareness of children's needs is the belief that children's independence and power need to be oppressed. Parents fear that if children are permitted to use their power to explore their environment, or ask questions, or challenge parental authority, they will become "acting-out" and disrespectful. Hence, obedience and complete compliance to parental authority is demanded. When children's power and independence are oppressed, they are not allowed to challenge, to voice opinions, or to have choices, but rather are told to "do what they are told to do" without question.

This demand for compliance to parental authority has many negative consequences. Children often develop an emotional sense of powerlessness; feelings of inadequacy which often result in excessive dependence; power struggles with authority figures; and often fall easy prey to peer pressure.

Validation of the AAPI and Formation of the Nurturing Programs

The AAPI-2 is an inventory designed to assess the parenting and childrearing attitudes of adult and adolescent parent and pre-parent populations. Based on the known parenting and childrearing behaviors of abusive parents, responses to the inventory provide an index of risk for practicing behaviors known to be attributable to child abuse and neglect. The AAPI-2 is the revised and re-normed version of the original AAPI first developed in 1979.

Intended Populations

Both adult parent and pre-parent populations as well as adolescent parent and pre-parent populations. Adolescents as young as 13 years old can respond to the AAPI-2.

Normative Information

Abusive and non-abusive adults and abused and non-abused adolescents from around the country participated in the standardization of the AAPI-2. Normative data are provided by age (adult/adolescent) and sex (male/female). Individual responses can be compared to the responses of parents or adolescents to determine degree of risk for abuse.

Validation of the AAPI-2

1. Abusive parents express significantly ($p < 0.001$) more abusive beliefs than non-abusive parents.
2. Males, regardless of status (abusive or non-abusive) express significantly ($p < 0.001$) more abusive parenting beliefs than females.
3. Adolescents with histories of being abused express significantly ($p < 0.001$) more abusive parenting beliefs than non-abused adolescents.

4. Male adolescents express significantly ($p < 0.001$) more abusive parenting beliefs than female adolescents.
5. Each of the five parenting constructs of the AAPI-2, forming the five subscales of the inventory, shows significant diagnostic and discriminatory validity. That is, responses to the inventory discriminate between the parenting behaviors of known abusive parents and the behaviors of non-abusive parents. These findings hold true for abused adolescents and non-abused adolescents.
6. The development and validation of the AAPI-2 provided the basis for the development and validation of the Nurturing Parenting Programs.

Program Goals and Objectives

The Nurturing Parenting Programs are developed from a strong philosophical basis that supports the growth and development of parents and children as caring people who treat themselves, others, and the environment including animals with respect and dignity. This philosophical basis of caring forms the underlying structure that constitutes the morals and values that are mirrored in the attitudes, beliefs, strategies, and skills taught in the Nurturing Programs. To be effective in changing the way people behave, the morals defined by a program must represent the standards and practices of behaviors known to contribute to the overall health and functioning of a society.

The Nurturing Parenting Programs are founded on the following morals and values which form the basis of the Program's goals, objectives, and competencies:

Value One: Developing a Positive Self-Worth

Construct A: Appropriate Expectations

Having appropriate expectations of children's developmental stages is a first step in enhancing their self-worth. Positive self-worth is crucial in the ability to nurture one's self, nurture others, and nurture the environment, including animals. Parents and children who treat themselves with respect will in turn treat others with respect.

Value Two: Developing a Sense of Caring and Compassion

Construct B: Building Empathy in Children and Parents

Empathy is the ability to be aware of your own needs as well as the needs of others, and to take positive actions on the behalf of getting those needs met in healthy ways. Developing a sense of empathy is the cornerstone of the Nurturing Parenting Programs.

Value Three: Providing Children with Dignified Discipline

Construct C: Alternatives to Physical Punishment

Discipline comes from the Latin word *discipulus* which means to guide and teach. The purpose of discipline is to teach children to be respectful, cooperative, and contributing members to a family and society. Harsh and abusive language, hurting touch, and punishment are viewed as disrespectful and undignified practices promoting rebellious and acting-out behaviors. Parental practices of discipline must model the sought-after behavior of the child.

Value Four: Increasing Self-Awareness and Acceptance of Family Roles

Construct D: Appropriate Family Roles

Self-awareness and self-acceptance are importance values of nurturing parenting. Family role reversals and confusion are significant factors in robbing children of their proper responsibilities in being a child. Increasing self-awareness and self-acceptance team up with the other four constructs in building self-nurturing skills and proper family role responsibilities.

Value Five: Developing a Healthy Sense of Empowerment

Construct E: Developing Empowerment and Independence in Children and Adults

Children and adults need to feel empowered to make good choices and wise decisions through the use of their strong will and personal power. Developing a strong sense of personal power is a necessary characteristic in nurturing one's self and others.

Value Six: Humor, Laughter, and Fun

Construct F: All Five

Having fun in life, laughing, smiling, and enjoying being with the people who you love and who love you is a necessary part of positive nurturing. Brain research clearly shows that endorphins, which are the brain's feel-good chemicals, are released in times of joy and work in creating healthy cellular networks. Having fun as a family creates positive, healthy bonds between all family members which strengthen the positive neurological networks of the brain. The cycle of positive nurturing is reinforced.

Curriculum and Other Program Issues

Dosage and Levels of Prevention

Dosage (the number of lessons) is related to the severity of condition. Parents with more severe levels of dysfunction need more intense parenting instruction than parents with a desire to improve their already good parenting skills. To this end, the dosage is related to the levels of prevention (Table 14.1):

Primary Prevention or Education

Short term: 10 to 15 lessons; competency-based lessons; open-ended or closed group delivery; pre–post program assessment or individual session assessment.

Secondary Prevention or Intervention

Moderate term: 15 to 25 sessions; competency-based lessons; home visit or closed-group delivery; pre–post program assessment with longitudinal follow-up; family based.

Tertiary Prevention or Treatment

Long term: 25 to 60 sessions; competency-based lessons; home-, group-based, or combination home- and group-based delivery; pre–post program assessment with longitudinal follow-up; family-based program.

Session Content

The Nurturing Parenting Programs teach age-specific parenting skills. The program also addresses the need to nurture oneself. These two elements are considered equally important. Each program session is divided into parenting instruction and self-improvement instruction.

Parenting Instruction

Program topics related to parenting skills include:

1. Discipline—philosophy of discipline, alternatives to spanking, rewards and punishment, family rules, time out, loss of privilege, restitution, being grounded.
2. Nurturing—needs and self-esteem; developing empathy; ways to nurture others; praise; nurturing routines at meal time, bath time, bed time, dressing time; communicating with your child through touch.

TABLE 14.1 Nurturing Parenting Programs by Level of Prevention

	Group-based	*Home-based*	*No. of sessions*	*Session length (hours)*	*Child care or children's program curriculum*
Prevention Programs *(Primary Prevention)*					
Prenatal Families	X		9	2½	Child care
Community-based Education in Nurturing Parenting	X		12	1½	Parents only
Community-based Education in Nurturing Parenting—Military Families	X		7	1½	Parents only
Nurturing Skills for Families (80 lessons available)	X	X	Variable	Variable	Parents & children
ABCs for Parents and Their Children 5 to 7 years	X		7	2	(Pre-K and kindergarten)
Alcohol and Kids Don't Mix	X	X	5	1½	Parents only
Alcohol, Anger, and Abuse	X	X	5	2	Staff training/ parents only
Nurturing Skills for Latina, Arabic, and Haitian Families (80 lessons available)	X	X	Variable	Variable	Parents & children
"Nurturing God's Way" Parenting Program for Christian Families	X		21	2	Parents only
Parents and Their Children with Health Challenges	X		8	2	Parents & children
Intervention Programs *(Secondary Prevention)*					
Nurturing Skills for Families (80 lessons available)	X	X	Variable	Variable	Parents & children
Nurturing Skills for Teen Parents (60 lessons available)	X	X	Variable	Variable	Parents & children
Nurturing America's Military Families (78 lessons available)	X	X	78	Variable	Parents & children
Nurturing Skills for Latina, Arabic, and Haitian Families (80 lessons available)	X	X	Variable	Variable	Parents & children
Family Nurturing Camp Weekend Experience	X		N/A	N/A	Parents & children
Families in Substance Abuse Treatment and Recovery	X		18	1½	Parents & children
Hmong Parents and Their Adolescents	X		12	3	Parents & children

continued . . .

TABLE 14.1 Continued

	Group-based	*Home-based*	*No. of sessions*	*Session length (hours)*	*Child care or children's program curriculum*
Treatment Programs *(Tertiary Prevention)*					
Parents and Their Infants, Toddlers, and Preschoolers	X		27	2½	Parents & children
Parents and Their Infants, Toddlers, and Preschoolers		X	55	1½	Parents & children
Parents and Their School-Age Children 5 to 11	X		15	2½	Parents & children
Parents and Adolescents	X		12	3	Parents & children
Teen Parents and Their Families	X		26	2½	Parents & children
Teen Parents and Their Families		X	50	1½	Parents & children
Nurturing Fathers Program	X		13	2½	Fathers only
Crianza con Cariño (Latina Parents and Children Birth to 12 Years)		X	55	1½	Parents & children
Crianza con Carino (Latina Parents and Children Birth to 12 Years)	X		27	2½	Parents & children

3. Communication—redirecting, ignoring, communicating age-appropriate expectations, recognizing and understanding feelings, and taking ownership of one's feelings.
4. Attachment, attunement, and bonding.
5. Brain development; differences between male and female brains.
6. General health safety issues which include the dangers of second-hand smoke; dating and the responsibilities of parenting; stranger danger; and keeping children safe from predators.
7. Establishing morals, values, and rules.
8. Relationship between alcohol, anger, and abuse; possessive and violent relationships.

Self-nurturing Instruction

Program topics related to self-nurturing include:

1. Individual needs; self-esteem and self-concept.
2. Handling stress and anger; communicating needs and wants; personal power.
3. Personal space; pregnancy prevention; using alcohol and drugs.
4. Dating, love, and rejection; sex and sexually transmitted diseases; choices and consequences; and ways to care for oneself.

All concepts taught in the program are discussed in the context of the participant's personal history (e.g., what experience the person has with a concept such as time out, being hit, or feeling loved). Establishing a personal connection with the concept reinforces the likelihood that the individual will integrate it into his or her behavior, because understanding personal history plays an important role in changing old, unwanted, abusive parenting patterns.

Teaching Aids

The program uses the following teaching aids to engage parents and children on both cognitive and affective levels:

1. *Activities Manuals* (training manuals) for parents, children, and adolescents. These manuals are program specific and constitute the curriculum for each of the programs.
2. *Parent Handbooks* for parents and adolescents. These handbooks are written at a fifth-grade reading level.
3. *Implementation Manual* that describes the "how-to's" of implementing the programs, facilitating groups, gathering pre- and posttest data, recruiting families, and working with children.

4. *Instructional DVDs* in which actors demonstrate examples of abusive parenting with inappropriate behaviors such as hitting and yelling. Parents discuss the interactions dramatized in the video and alternatives to abusive behavior.
5. *Games* for parents and children that help build their nurturing skills and provide an opportunity for them to interact and have fun together. The games reinforce the concepts that are being presented.
6. *Instructional Aids* that include card games, pictures, and a questionnaire.

Cultural Implications

Adapted to meet the unique cultural and learning needs of families, currently there are 15 Nurturing Programs that honor the traditions, history, music, food, dress, and parental roles embedded in the philosophy of nurturing parenting. Programs with cultural adaptations include: parents in substance abuse recovery; parents with special learning needs; parents with special needs children; lesbian, gay, bisexual, transgender (LGBT) families, military families, and families of ethnic diversities including Hispanic, Arab, Hmong, Haitian, Chinese, Japanese, Liberian, Somalian, British, and Native American.

Evidence-based Research and Evaluation

Since the initial research study conducted in 1985, thirty additional validation studies support the Program's positive findings in treating and preventing the recurrence of child abuse and neglect. Implemented in state and community agencies in mental health, alcohol, and other drug addiction, domestic violence, and social services, the Nurturing Program classes are offered to families charged with child maltreatment. Research studies conducted during the past 31 years nationwide indicate the general research findings highlighted in selected studies:

1. Parents completing the sessions in their program continuously show significant positive pre–posttest gains ($p < 0.01$) in parenting beliefs in all five constructs of the Adult-Adolescent Parenting Inventory (Bavolek, McLaughlin, Comstock, 1983; Matteo-Kerney, & Benjamin, 2004; Bavolek, Keene, Weikert, 2005; Hodnett, Faulk, Dellinger, Maher, 2009).
2. Longitudinal follow-up research on families reported for child abuse and neglect who completed the Nurturing Parenting Programs consistently indicates low rates of recidivism. A 12-month follow-up of 100 families in the Midwest referred by CPS found a recidivism rate of only 7 percent of nearly 100 families completing the program. Forty-two percent of the families were no longer receiving services from the DSS for child abuse and neglect (Bavolek et al., 1983), A three-year study in Sacramento of 4,600 families with substantiated CPS reports and their 9,752 children who were receiving home-visitation sessions found a decline of 85 percent in CPS reports

one year after the program closed (LPC Consulting Associates, 2013). Maher, Marcynyszyn, Corwin, & Hodnett (2011), in their analysis of an extensive implementation of the Nurturing Programs throughout Louisiana, found that two years after participating, caregivers attending more sessions of the Nurturing Program were significantly less likely to have a substantiated maltreatment incident.

3. Findings reported by Bavolek et al. (1983) found retention rates for parents across all the studies averaged 84 percent. Low drop-out rates among families in child welfare attending a minimum of 12 group-based to a maximum of 55 sessions were reported in the Sacramento study. Client retention ranged from 46 to 85 percent across providers, with an overall retention rate of nearly 70 percent of program participants (n = 564) in the Louisiana study. This rate is significantly higher than research on other similar programs implemented in child welfare systems (Gershater-Molko, Lutzker, & Wesch, 2003).

A complete review of the entire peer-reviewed articles and agency-published research reports is available on our website: nurturingparenting.com.

Professional Preparation and Training Issues

Professionals in parent education, social work, psychology, education, public health, and the general helping fields (medicine, mental health, parent aide programs, and home visitor programs) and paraprofessionals in helping fields facilitate the parent, adolescent, and children's programs. Generally, two staff are required to facilitate the parents groups, and two or more staff are required to facilitate the children's and adolescents' groups. Professionals who have previously facilitated groups and taught parenting education and who subscribe to teaching nonviolent, nurturing parenting values and practices can successfully facilitate the Nurturing Parenting Programs.

Two professionals/paraprofessionals facilitate the parents' program; two staff (plus additional volunteers when necessary) facilitate the children's program.

1. Groups are held in sites ranging from classrooms to meeting rooms in various agencies.
2. Group-based programs generally run 2 to 3 hours per session with a 20-minute break.
3. Parents and children meet in separate groups that run concurrently.
4. 12 to 15 adults attend the group programs (single parents or intact couples); their children meet in their separate groups.

Many families attending the Nurturing Programs are either mandated by the courts, or required to attend as a stipulation of their treatment plan. Families who are not involved in abuse/neglect but wish to attend voluntarily sign up through news/flyer promotion.

Facilitator Qualifications and Training

Professionals and paraprofessionals with training in teaching low-risk parents and children-nurturing skills or professionals with a background in parent education, clinical social work, or clinical psychology are candidates to facilitate Nurturing Parenting Program classes. Empathy, positive self-worth, dependability, and sharing are desirable facilitator characteristics.

Instructor training workshops last from 3 to 5 days, depending on the group's level of sophistication. Costs also vary, depending on whether the workshops are sponsored by an agency seeking to implement the Nurturing Parenting Program or whether the training is provided by the community and participants register individually.

For more information regarding program facilitator training workshops, visit our website at nurturingparenting.com.

Conclusion

The focus of this chapter highlights the history, philosophy, implementation, and supporting evidence of the effectiveness of the Nurturing Parenting Programs in the prevention and treatment of child abuse and neglect. Child abuse and neglect is an age-old phenomenon dating back to the beginning of recorded history. For centuries children have been the victims of parental cruelty and death. Today we have the science, knowledge, and skills to help parents replace abusive and neglecting parenting practices with positive nurturing parenting practices. Child maltreatment can be treated and prevented. Over thirty years of research in measuring the effectiveness of the Nurturing Programs in treating and preventing the recurrence of child maltreatment has shown, with proper education and support, parents families can and want to change. Longitudinal follow-up studies show very impressive data on the low rate of parents who are charged with repeated maltreatment.

Preprocess–post-assessment, properly assigned lesson dosage to match the needs of the parents, and competent professionals committed to the philosophy and lessons of the Nurturing Programs have proven effectiveness in treating and preventing child maltreatment.

Key Points

1. Child abuse and neglect consists of five parenting practices that describe child maltreatment.
2. There exist both positive and negative parenting nurturing practices. There are four personality traits that develop in childhood resulting from the parenting practices we have as children.

3. Human nature is predisposed to form and sustain long-term positive nurturing relationships.
4. Dosage, or the number of lessons offered, is determined by the degree and frequency of the abuse and neglect.

Discussion Questions

1. What are the three levels of prevention and what is the significance of the lesson dosage?
2. What is empathy and what role does it play in the prevention of child abuse and neglect?
3. List and describe the four personality traits that develop from early childhood parenting experiences.
4. List and describe the five parenting constructs that constitute the practices of child abuse and neglect.

Additional Resources

Website

www.nurturingparenting.com/

References

Bavolek, S., Keene, R., & Weikert, P. (2005). *The Florida Report: Comprehensive examination of the effectiveness of the Nurturing Parenting Programs. Final report.* Asheville, NC. Family Development Resources.

Bavolek, S., Kline, D., & McLaughlin, J. (1979). Primary prevention of child abuse: Identification of high risk adolescents. *Child Abuse and Neglect: The International Journal, 3*, 1071–1080.

Bavolek, S., McLaughlin, J., & Comstock, C. (1983). *Nurturing Parenting Programs: A validated approach for reducing dysfunctional family interactions. NIMH Final Report.* Asheville, NC. Family Development Resources.

Commission on Children. (2003). *Hardwired to connect: The new scientific case for authoritative communities. Final Report.* New York: Institute for American Values.

Gershater-Molko, R., Lutzker, J., & Wesch, D. (2003). Project SafeCare: Improving health, safety, and parenting skills in families reported for and at risk for child maltreatment. *Journal of Family Violence, 18*, 377–368.

Hodnett, R., Faulk, K., Dellinger, A., & Maher, E. (2009). *Evaluation of the statewide implementation of a parent education program in Louisiana's Child Welfare Agency*. Louisiana Department of Social Services, Office of Community Services.

Langer, W. (1974). Europe's initial population explosion. *History of Childhood Quarterly, 2*, 129–134.

LPC Consulting Associates. Birth and Beyond Home Visitation Program. (2013). *Nurturing Parenting Program Child Protective Services, Outcomes Report, July 2010 through June 2013.* North Highlands, CA: Family Support Collaborative. Child Abuse Prevention Council.

Maher, E., Marcynyszyn, L., Corwin, T. & Hodnett, R. (2011). Dosage matters: The relationship between participation in the Nurturing Program for Infants, Toddlers and Preschoolers and subsequent child maltreatment. *Children and Youth Services Review, 33*, 1424–1426.

Matteo-Kerney, C., & Benjamin, S. (2004). *Rural Virginia Family Nurturing Project: Five year evaluation results.* Gloucester, VA: Middle Peninsula-Northern Neck Community Services Board.

15

TRIPLE P—POSITIVE PARENTING PROGRAM

Matthew R. Sanders and Karen M. T. Turner

Learning Goals

After reading this chapter readers will increase their understanding of the following:

1. The Triple P—Positive Parenting Program and its population-based approach to providing parenting support through a system of interventions of varying intensity.
2. The core positive parenting principles and skills.
3. The history, theoretical foundations, and evidence base of Triple P.
4. Rhe principle of minimal sufficiency in choosing program intensity and delivery formats that are matched to parents' needs and preferences.
5. A self-regulation framework for promoting parents' skills and independent problem solving.
6. A guided participation model for sharing assessment results and developing a shared case formulation and intervention plan.
7. Training and dissemination processes that underpin program fidelity as well as flexible program tailoring.
8. New areas of program development and research.

Introduction

The quality of parenting children receive has a major influence on their development, well-being, and life opportunities (Collins et al., 2000). It is increasingly recognized that if a society values the well-being of its children it must invest in effective prevention and early intervention programs that promote children's development (Biglan, Flay, Embry, & Sandler, 2012). Of all the potentially modifiable influences that can be targeted through intervention, none are more important than the quality of parenting children receive.

The Triple P—Positive Parenting Program is a tiered multi-level system of parenting support designed as a population-based strategy to enhance the knowledge, skills, and confidence of parents in the task of raising their children. It involves a unique blending of universal and targeted interventions on a continuum of increasing intensity and narrowing population reach. The five core principles of positive parenting that form the basis of the program are presented in Table 15.1.

Table 15.2 shows how these principles are operationalized into a range of specific parenting skills. Application of these principles and techniques of positive

TABLE 15.1 Principles of Positive Parenting

Principle	*Description*
A safe and engaging environment	Children of all ages need a safe, supervised and therefore protective environment that provides opportunities for them to explore, experiment, and play. This principle is essential to promote healthy development and to prevent accidents and injuries in the home.
A positive learning environment	This involves educating parents in their role as their child's first teacher, and specifically teaches parents to respond positively and constructively to child-initiated interactions (e.g., requests for help, information, advice, and attention) through incidental teaching and other techniques to assist children to learn how to solve problems for themselves.
Assertive and consistent discipline	Triple P teaches parents specific child management and behavior change strategies that are alternatives to coercive and ineffective discipline practices (such as shouting, threatening, or using physical punishment). The aim is to develop predictable and consistent responses and avoid factors that may maintain problem behavior (such as accidental rewards).
Realistic expectations	This involves exploring with parents their expectations, assumptions, and beliefs about the causes of children's behavior and choosing goals that are developmentally appropriate for the child and realistic for the parent. Parents who are at risk of abusing their children are more likely to have unrealistic expectations of children's capabilities.
Taking care of oneself as a parent	Parenting is affected by a range of factors that impact on a parent's self-esteem and sense of well-being. All levels of Triple P specifically address this issue by encouraging parents to view parenting as part of a larger context of personal self-care, resourcefulness, and well-being and by teaching parents practical parenting skills.

TABLE 15.2 Core Parenting Skills Introduced in Triple P

Basic Skills						*Enhanced Skills*	
Parent–Child Relationship Enhancement	*Encouraging Desirable Behavior*	*Teaching New Skills and Behaviors*	*Managing Misbehavior*	*Anticipating and Planning*	*Self-regulation*	*Mood and Coping Skills*	*Partner Support*
• Spending brief quality time • Talking with children • Showing affection	• Giving descriptive praise • Giving nonverbal attention • Providing engaging activities	• Setting a good example • Using incidental teaching • Using ask–say–do • Using behavior charts	• Establishing ground rules • Using directed discussion • Using planned ignoring • Giving clear, calm instructions • Using logical consequences • Using quiet time (non-exclusionary time out) • Using time out	• Planning and advanced preparation • Discussing ground rules for specific situations • Selecting engaging activities • Providing incentives • Providing consequences • Holding follow-up discussions	• Monitoring children's behavior • Monitoring own behavior • Setting developmentally appropriate goals • Setting practice tasks • Self-evaluation of strengths and weaknesses • Setting personal goals for change	• Catching unhelpful thoughts • Relaxation and stress management • Developing personal coping statements • Challenging unhelpful thoughts • Developing coping plans for high-risk situations	• Improving personal communication habits • Giving and receiving constructive feedback • Having casual conversations • Supporting each other when problem behavior occurs • Problem solving • Improving relationship happiness

parenting reduces behavioral and emotional problems; produces higher levels of readiness to enter the school system and other key developmental transitions by promoting children's social and emotional competence; reduces the risk of child maltreatment; and reduces the risk that children are on a developmental trajectory leading to poor outcomes such as school failure, substance abuse, juvenile offending, and risky behavior including sexually risky behavior.

Triple P incorporates five levels of intervention on a tiered continuum of increasing strength for parents of children from birth to age 16. Table 15.3 summarizes the multi-level Triple P approach which utilizes the principle of selecting the "minimally sufficient" effective intervention as a guiding principle to serving the needs of parents in order to maximize efficiency, contain costs, avoid over-servicing, and ensure that support becomes widely available to parents in the community. The suite of multi-level and multidisciplinary programs in the Triple P system is designed to create a 'family friendly' community context that better supports parents in the task of raising their children by offering a range of programs tailored to the differing needs of parents. This tiered continuum can also be described as adhering to the principle of proportionate universalism (Marmot, 2010).

Theoretical Foundations and History

The growth of Triple P, since the development of the foundation program in 1978, has involved a gradual transformation of an intensive clinical treatment model into a population-based system of parenting support. The origins of Triple P lie in social learning theory and the behavioral and cognitive therapy principles and techniques of behavior, cognitive, and affective change articulated in the 1960s and 1970s. Triple P was developed as a multi-level system of parenting interventions designed to improve the quality of parenting advice available to all parents (Sanders 1999; Sanders, Turner, & Markie-Dadds, 2002). From its beginnings as a home-based intervention for parents of disruptive preschool-aged children (Sanders & Glynn, 1981), the program has evolved over a 35-year period into the current population-based public health model of parent support. This has involved the collective efforts of a number of colleagues and postgraduate students at the University of Queensland's Parenting and Family Support Centre in the School of Psychology.

Needs Assessment and Target Audience

Within a public health perspective, the multi-level Triple P system can be adopted as a population-based approach, to achieve broad exposure to quality parenting information, reduce stigma associated with seeking support, allow for universal and targeted prevention and early intervention efforts, and facilitate the access of high-risk families to intensive support. Public health principles are also

TABLE 15.3 The Triple P Multi-level System

Level of Intervention	*Target Population*	*Intervention Methods*	*Facilitators*
Level 1 Communications strategy • Universal Triple P	All parents interested in information about parenting and promoting their child's development.	Coordinated communications strategy raising awareness of parent issues and encouraging participation in parenting programs. May involve electronic and print media (e.g., brochures, posters, websites, television, talk-back radio, newspaper and magazine editorials).	Typically coordinated by communications, health, or welfare staff.
Level 2 Health promotion strategy/ brief selective intervention • Selected Triple P • Selected Teen Triple P	Parents interested in parenting education or with specific concerns about their child's development or behavior.	Health promotion information or specific advice for a discrete developmental issue or minor child-behavior problem. May involve a group seminar format or brief (up to 20 minutes) telephone or face-to-face clinician contact.	Practitioners who provide parent support during routine well-child healthcare (e.g., health, education, allied health- and child care staff).
Level 3 Narrow focus parent training • Primary Care Triple P • Triple P Discussion Groups • Triple P Online Brief • Primary Care Teen Triple P • Teen Triple P Discussion Groups	Parents with specific concerns as above who require consultations or active-skills training.	Brief program (about 80 minutes over four sessions, or 2-hour discussion groups) combining advice, rehearsal, and self-evaluation to teach parents to manage a discrete child problem behavior. May involve telephone contact.	Same as for Level 2.

continued . . .

TABLE 15.3 Continued

Level of Intervention	*Target Population*	*Intervention Methods*	*Facilitators*
• Primary Care Stepping Stones Triple P	Parents of children with disabilities, with concerns as above.	A parallel program with a focus on disabilities.	Same as above.
Level 4 Broad focus parent training • Standard Triple P • Group Triple P • Self-directed Triple P • Triple P Online Standard • Standard Teen Triple P • Group Teen Triple P • Self-directed Teen Triple P	Parents wanting intensive training in positive parenting skills. Typically parents of children with behavior problems such as aggressive or oppositional behavior.	Broad focus program (about 10 hours over 8–10 sessions) focusing on parent–child interaction and the application of parenting skills to a broad range of target behaviors. Includes generalization-enhancement strategies. May be self-directed, online, involve telephone or face-to-face clinician contact, group sessions.	Intensive parenting intervention workers (e.g., mental health and welfare staff, and other allied health and education professionals who regularly consult with parents about child behavior).
• Standard Stepping Stones Triple P • Group Stepping Stones Triple P • Self-directed Stepping Stones Triple P	Parents of children with disabilities who have or are at risk of developing behavioral or emotional disorders.	A parallel series of tailored programs with a focus on disabilities.	Same as above.

Level 5 Intensive family intervention • Enhanced Triple P	Parents of children with behavior problems and concurrent family dysfunction such as parental depression or stress, or conflict between partners.	Intensive individually tailored program with modules (60–90-minute sessions) including practice sessions to enhance parenting skills, mood management and stress coping skills, and partner support skills.	Intensive family intervention workers (e.g., mental health and welfare staff).
• Pathways Triple P	Parents at risk of child maltreatment. Targets anger management problems and other factors associated with abuse.	Intensive individually tailored or group program with modules (60–120-minute sessions depending on delivery model) including attribution retraining and anger management.	Same as above.
• Group Lifestyle Triple P	Parents of overweight or obese children. Targets healthy eating and increasing activity levels as well as general child behavior.	Intensive 14-session group program (including telephone consultations) focusing on nutrition, healthy lifestyle, and general parenting strategies. Includes generalization enhancement strategies.	As above plus dieticians/nutritionists with experience in delivering parenting interventions.
• Family Transitions Triple P	Parents going through separation or divorce.	Intensive 12-session group program (including telephone consultations) focusing on coping skills, conflict management, general parenting strategies, and developing a healthy co-parenting relationship.	Intensive family intervention workers (e.g., counselors, mental health and welfare staff).

adopted by the system including the selection of "minimally sufficient" interventions, a concept that refers to the selection of interventions aimed at achieving a meaningful clinical outcome in the most cost-effective and time-efficient manner (Sanders, 2008). Other public health principles include ensuring flexible and responsive program delivery, developing culturally acceptable interventions that are consumer informed, and supporting dissemination through a sustainable implementation model (Sanders & Kirby, 2012).

Although positive parenting methods are relevant to all parents, parents of children who are demanding, disobedient, defiant, aggressive, or generally disruptive are particularly likely to benefit from more intensive levels of Triple P. Many of the principles and techniques have been successfully applied in intervention programs for children clinically diagnosed with severe behavior problems (particularly children with oppositional defiant disorder, conduct disorder, or attention-deficit/hyperactivity disorder). The early evaluation of Triple P attesting to the efficacy of the standard program was delivered within a treatment context of children with aggressive and disruptive behavior problems, and families with adversity factors such as low socioeconomic status, low parental education levels, low parent income, and single parent status. If Triple P is used in children with severe disruptive behavior disorders or attention-deficit/hyperactivity disorder, comprehensive clinical assessment is needed to determine whether other school or pharmacological interventions may be required in addition.

Program Goals and Objectives

The primary aim of Triple P is to prevent severe behavioral, emotional, and developmental problems in children, and child maltreatment, by enhancing the knowledge, skills, and confidence of parents, and promoting parents' self-sufficiency in managing future difficulties. Competent parenting is defined as warm, responsive, consistent caregiving that provides nurturing and secure attachments, as well as boundaries and contingent limits for children in a low-conflict family environment. Triple P teaches parents strategies to encourage their child's social and language skills, emotional self-regulation, independence, and problem-solving ability. Different Triple P variants may focus on preventive information (Level 1), one or two specific behavior problems or developmental issues that are a current concern (Level 2–3), intensive parenting skills training (Level 4), or broader family issues (Level 5).

The key objectives of the programs are to increase parents' knowledge, competence, and confidence in raising children by:

1. Increasing their skills in managing common behavioral and emotional problems and developmental issues.
2. Helping them be more positive and proactive in their daily interactions with children.

3. Reducing family conflict and coercive and punitive methods of discipline.
4. Improving their communication about parenting issues.
5. Reducing levels of stress, anxiety, depression, and relationship conflict over parenting issues.

Attainment of positive parenting skills promotes family harmony, reduces parent–child conflict, fosters successful peer relationships, and prepares children for successful experiences at school and in later life. These outcomes can be achieved by creating a safe learning environment for parents where they can self-disclose, receive practical information about parenting skills that they can incorporate into everyday interactions with their children, and receive constructive feedback on their implementation of strategies.

Curriculum and Other Program Issues

Teaching Procedures

Triple P aims to help parents make informed decisions by sharing knowledge and skills derived from contemporary research into effective childrearing practices. Programs employ an active skills training process within a self-regulation framework to help parents acquire new knowledge and skills. The sessions provide opportunities for parents to learn through observation, discussion, practice, and feedback. DVD segments and/or live modeling are used to demonstrate parenting skills. These skills are then practiced within sessions. Parents receive constructive feedback about their implementation of skills in an emotionally supportive context. Between sessions, parents complete homework tasks to consolidate their learning.

Self-regulation Framework

The educative approach used in Triple P to promote parental competence views the development of a parent's capacity for self-regulation as a central skill. This involves teaching parents skills to modify their own ways of thinking and behaving that enable them to become independent problem solvers (Karoly, 1993). From a therapeutic perspective, self-regulation is a process whereby parents are taught skills such as selecting developmentally appropriate goals for their child or personal goals as a parent, monitoring a child's or their own behavior, choosing an appropriate solution for a particular problem, implementing the solution, self-monitoring their implementation; identifying strengths and limitations in their performance; and setting future goals for action. This self-regulatory framework is operationalized to include five components.

The first component is self-sufficiency. As a parenting program is time limited, parents need to develop the knowledge, skills and resourcefulness to maintain the gains achieved through the program and to become independent in tackling future challenges. The aim is for them to parent effectively, trust their own judgment, seek support if they need it, and to view their parenting approach and decisions as their own responsibility and choice.

Second, self-efficacy refers to a parent's belief that they can effectively deal with a parenting situation or child management problem. Parents seeking help from parenting programs typically have low self-efficacy in relation to global expectations (e.g., *I'm a bad parent*), managing specific child behavior problems (e.g. *I can't cope with temper tantrums*), or parenting demands or tasks (e.g., *I can't manage them when we're out in public*). As parents try out new skills, experience success, and reach goals, their self-efficacy increases. This is in turn related to resilience and persistence in the face of future setbacks.

The third component involves self-management. As each parent is responsible for the way they choose to raise their children, parents select those aspects of their own and their child's behavior they wish to work on, set goals, choose specific parenting and child management techniques they wish to implement, and self-evaluate their success with their chosen goals.

Fourth, personal agency is an important part of self-regulation. Parents develop attributions about why problems happen and why change occurs. In developing a sense of personal agency, the aim is to help parents attribute positive changes to their own or their child's efforts rather than external factors like chance, maturation, or other uncontrollable events (e.g., the child's genetic makeup, the actions of other parents or carers). This is achieved by prompting parents to identify what they are doing differently through the course of the program that has contributed to the positive change in their own or their child's behavior. This can empower parents, motivate them to continue their efforts, reduce dependence on the practitioner, and minimize relapse when contact is terminated.

A final aspect of self-regulation is problem solving. This refers to parents' ability to apply the skills they learn to issues beyond the presenting concern. Rather than focusing on the development of discrete parenting skills in isolation, the aim is to help parents become active problem solvers. This means being able to clearly define a problem, identify and evaluate potential solutions, develop a tailored parenting plan, try it out, review how the plan went in practice, and refine as necessary. The success of a parenting intervention is not simply parents' ability to resolve current issues, but their capacity to address a diverse range of family challenges over time with relative autonomy. For more information on enhancing parents' self-efficacy see Sanders and Mazzucchelli (2013).

Guided Participation Approach to Self-regulation

Practitioners are trained to develop a personalized functional assessment and case formulation for each family. Presenting problems must be viewed within a developmental and sociocultural context. The practitioner's task is to arrive at an understanding of the nature of the behavioral or emotional problem the child is experiencing, and to determine whether there is a significant deviation from normal development. A working knowledge of normal development, familiarity with different types of child psychopathology, and experience in working with children and families are important in making such judgments. The extent to which a child's behavior deviates from normal development is based on interview, self-report measures, behavioral monitoring, and where possible, direct observation.

A personalized functional assessment is developed for parents and children. It considers excesses, deficits, and assets of parents and child to inform targets for change, and also explores antecedents and consequences that may maintain problem behavior. It may also include competing behaviors analysis to develop strategies for change (to alleviate triggers, teach new skills and behaviors, reward goal behaviors, and remove rewards for problem behaviors).

The case formulation includes the practitioner's conclusions concerning the nature, extent, severity, etiology, maintaining factors, and prognosis of the child's problem. It involves integrating various assessment sources to formulate conclusions supported by data that can guide the tailoring of the intervention. In working with families, the formulation particularly focuses on the role of family interactions in maintaining problem behavior. In most cases, the role of family factors is best understood by carefully describing the child's behavior problems in their situational context. To be useful in planning an intervention, a case formulation needs to identify potentially modifiable risk factors (e.g., coercive, inconsistent, or lax parenting) and protective factors (e.g., close relationships, partner support) which could influence the course of the child's future development. Such a formulation will usually indicate the extent to which other family factors (e.g., parental conflict) are implicated in maintaining a problem. There are two levels of case formulation. The first is based on the practitioner's judgments and conclusions. The second is the shared understanding derived collaboratively with the parent through a process of discussing the assessment data collected on the family. The parent's own formulations lay the foundations for parents being receptive to intervention suggestions.

A guided participation model (Sanders & Lawton, 1993) is recommended for sharing assessment results, developing a shared perspective of the family's difficulties, and negotiating an intervention plan. It involves inviting parents to identify, from trigger material depicting social learning causes of problem behavior, which of the causes they consider relevant to their family. When a parent identifies a possible cause, they are prompted to explain why they consider it important and to provide an example. This process encourages parents to take responsibility for understanding their child's actions, and how their own actions may be contributing to a problem. Therefore, practitioners are encouraged to use the guided participation model to develop a shared understanding of the nature and possible causes of the presenting problems, and to offer suggestions rather than prescriptions when alternative parenting strategies are introduced.

Practitioners must be prepared to confront and work through process issues such as disengagement, resistance, defensiveness, dependency, hostility, conflict between partners, and attempts to blame others (e.g., partner, relatives) as problems arise. They must also be prepared to facilitate parents' application to session tasks such as role plays and between-session homework. For more information on effective parent consultation see Sanders and Burke (2013). These processes apply to face-to-face programs.

Self-directed Learning

Triple P has variants that are partly or entirely self-directed. These include books, self-help workbooks, video material, and interactive online programs. In each case, our goal has been to present content and active skills training that are equivalent to the face-to-face programs, and elicit the same key learning processes and take home messages. For example, Triple P Online Standard (Turner & Sanders, 2013) is an interactive, self-directed positive parenting program delivered via the Internet. The intervention provides instruction in the use of the 17 core positive parenting skills in eight sequenced modules. As with face-to-face programs, this online program has an emphasis on promoting parental self-regulation through dynamic and demonstration-driven video content, teaching parents self-management skills (goal setting, self-evaluation) and prompting parents' ongoing participation, without the need for personal contact with a practitioner. It incorporates elements designed to engage participants and improve knowledge acquisition, positive self-efficacy and behavior activation. These elements include: (a) video-based modeling of parenting skills, and diverse parent "vox pops" describing their experiences; (b) personalized content including goal setting, review, and feedback; (c) interactive exercises to prompt parental problem solving, decision making, and self-regulation; (d) downloadable worksheets and podcasts to review session content; (e) automated text messaging and email prompts to increase the likelihood of program completion; and (f) a downloadable workbook that records program content, parents' goals, and responses to exercises. Cultural sensitivity is addressed through the use of multicultural video models and the self-regulatory framework that enables parents to select goals informed by their own values and traditions.

Cultural Implications

Mainstream parenting programs have historically had difficulty in recruiting and maintaining the involvement of culturally and linguistically diverse parents, suggesting the need for more culturally appropriate parenting programs tailored to their needs. For parenting programs to be successful across cultures, they must be sensitive to the broader cultural context in which parenting takes place. Kumpfer, Alvarado, Smith and Bellamy (2002) argue that cultural adaptation of existing programs requires sensitivity and responsiveness to language barriers, cultural factors that influence receptivity to programs, and practical concerns in the local setting. While culturally specific versions of a program may not significantly improve positive behavioral change outcomes, they may result in better recruitment and retention of families (Kumpfer et al., 2002).

Positive parenting principles and strategies can cross cultures. What may vary according to culture are the goals and target behaviors, practical implementation of strategies, and ways of sharing information. Triple P resources have to date had 21 language translations and been disseminated in 25 countries to date, with surprisingly little need for adaptation. Programs have been deployed in many different cultural contexts including ethnically diverse populations in Australasia (e.g., Australia, New Zealand), the UK (e.g., England, Scotland), North America (e.g., Canada, the USA), Western Europe (e.g., Ireland, Sweden, Germany, Belgium, the Netherlands, Switzerland), Middle East (e.g., Iran, Turkey), South America (e.g., Chile), Asia (e.g., Japan, Hong Kong, Singapore), and with Indigenous parents in Australia, Canada, New Zealand, and the USA.

The one major cultural adaptation of Triple P has been for Australian Indigenous families when the mainstream program was sought by Indigenous workers, but potential barriers for families were identified. Community consultation with elders, professionals, and parents resulted in the development of culturally adapted resources and minor program delivery variation (Turner, Richards, & Sanders, 2007). As Triple P is designed to be tailored to target identified risk factors for each family, it can accommodate culturally sensitive implementation.

Culturally diverse parents have reported that the positive parenting principles and strategies introduced in Triple P are highly acceptable and highly useful. Further, they were very likely to use or currently used the strategies, and the program materials were rated as very culturally appropriate (Morawska et al., 2011). Flexible delivery tailored to client needs while maintaining program fidelity is a key feature of any Triple P intervention (Mazzucchelli & Sanders, 2010).

Evidence-based Research and Evaluation

Proper empirical appraisal of Triple P is complex as there are multiple levels of intensity, delivery modalities, target populations, age groups, and intervention methods employed. As there are many individual variable components in the system that need to be evaluated, as well as the synergistic effects of the multilevel system, it is not surprising that Triple P has attracted considerable empirical scrutiny. At the time of writing this includes over 400 authors, from 121 institutions around the world. It is arguably the most extensively evaluated parenting intervention yet developed. Its evidence base comprises a range of quantitative and qualitative methodologies including controlled single-subject experiments, uncontrolled case studies, small-scale randomized clinical trials, larger-scale randomized trials, service-based evaluations, controlled population-level evaluations, quasi-experimental service-based evaluations, and meta-analyses. It also includes a mixture of developer-led and independent evaluations.

The most comprehensive meta-analysis reported on outcome findings from 101 empirical studies that include published and unpublished studies, developer-led and independent studies, RCTs and uncontrolled studies (Sanders, Kirby, Tellegen, & Day, 2014). The main findings supported the conclusion of seven prior meta-analyses that Triple P works. As expected, largest effect sizes were associated with targeted rather than universal programs, however significant intervention effects were found for each level of the intervention, on a range of outcome measures. The largest significant effect sizes across levels were for improvements in children's social, emotional, and behavioral problems and parenting practices, showing the proximal targets of intervention changed. There were also significant effect sizes for parental satisfaction, parental adjustment, and parental relationships.

Professional Preparation and Training Issues

Triple P International is a dissemination organization licensed by the University of Queensland to disseminate Triple P professional training and resources globally. The professional skills training model developed in the Parenting and Family Support Centre was deployed from 1996, and has undergone continual refinement since that time. The standardized system of professional training has several key features. It adopts an active skills training approach that involves didactic input, video and live demonstrations, small group exercises to practice core consultation skills, problem-solving exercises, course readings, and competency-based assessment and accreditation.

Training courses are developed for each level and variant of the program once sufficient evidence is compiled showing the program is effective. This is usually on the basis of at least one published randomized trial. A recent empirical evaluation of the effects of the Triple P professional training system on practitioner self-efficacy from a sample of 5,109 practitioners from 15 countries (Sethi, Sanders, & Ralph, 2014) showed that the training program was robust, producing consistent increases in practitioners' self-efficacy in relation to the content of the program, and the consultation process used to implement it with parents.

Although the development of multinational professional training programs targeting an existing workforce is a major advance over the "train and hope" model used in much continuing professional education, a broader systems-contextual perspective is needed to embed evidence-based programs. Sanders and Murphy-Brennan (2010) argue that a range of organizational factors are important in taking an intervention to scale including organizational leadership, preparation of staff to undertake training, establishing implementation targets, supporting staff who have been through training, and ensuring adequate infrastructure support and supervision. Some follow-up studies of trained practitioners have highlighted the potential for program drift, non-implementation, and failure to achieve implementation targets practitioners (Shapiro et al., 2014). Although high-quality training experiences are important and have been well documented, they are rarely sufficient to ensure programs are implemented with fidelity. Drawing upon the National Implementation Research Network (NIRN) Active Implementation Frameworks (Fixsen, Naoom, Blasé, Friedman, & Wallace, 2005), and the RE-AIM Framework (Glasgow, Vogt, & Boles, 1999), Triple P International has developed an implementation framework to guide and support organizations and communities to successfully implement Triple P. This framework is summarized in Figure 15.1.

Sanders and Kirby (2014) outline a research and development model that informs the ongoing translational research process that is employed to promote Triple P. Another recent development has been the establishment of an international research network, TPRN (www.tprn.org) to promote knowledge exchange between researchers involved in research on Triple P. This network provides technical information and support to research groups to secure funding and conduct quality research. The goals of the network are: (a) to advance the

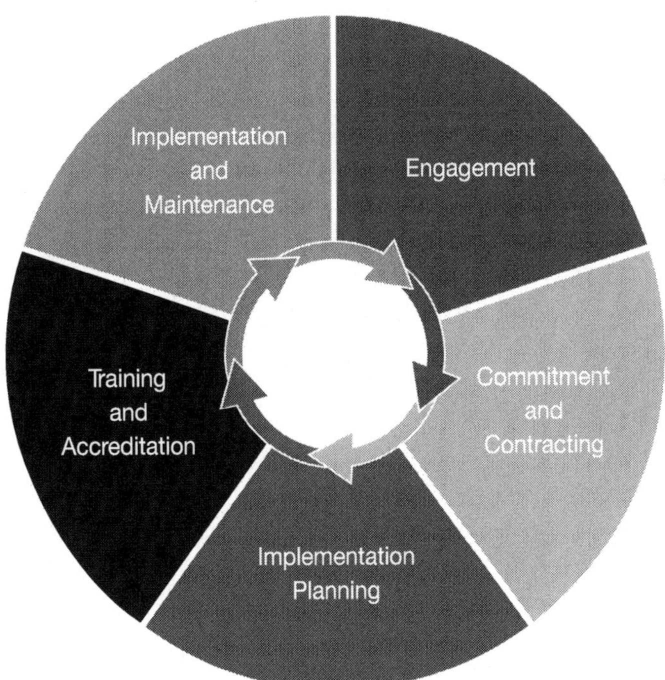

FIGURE 15.1 Triple P Implementation Framework Diagram (simplified)

Reprinted with permission from Triple P International Pty, Ltd.

knowledge on parenting and evidence-based systems of intervention in the prevention and treatment of child social-emotional and behavior problems; (b) to conduct rigorous science to develop best practices to improve the functioning of children, parents, and families from an individual level to a population level; (c) to assist in population-level reductions in the prevalence of child social, emotional, and behavior problems; (d) to increase the quality and quantity of research output and collaborative grants for network members; and (e) and to facilitate communication about research, policy, and practice with researchers, policy makers, and practitioners.

A notable feature of TPRN is to host an annual Triple P research conference (Helping Families Change Conference, HFCC) that brings together researchers, policy makers, and practitioners from around the world to discuss latest developments and innovations and to encourage critical appraisal of the Triple P system (www.helpingfamilieschange.org). Now in its 17th year, the HFCC has been a fundamental translational research activity to foster better knowledge exchange between various stakeholders.

Conclusion

From fledgling beginnings in the late 1970s, the Triple P system of parenting support sought to transform a prevailing clinical model for the individual or group treatment of parents of disruptive children into a public health population-based strategy for all families. Triple P has built a solid empirical foundation following decades of prior behavioral research by pioneers of the parent training movement, and influenced by the growing scientific literature on the importance of parenting programs that documents the efficacy of the intervention system to assist a culturally diverse range of parents and children. However, there is much to be done. Although considerable progress has been made in improving access to evidence-based programs, Triple P is less accessible for families living in poverty, minority groups, refugee families, parents with mental illness or substance abuse problems, incarcerated parents, and foster parents. There is a pressing need to develop and rigorously test parenting programs in resource-poor settings and countries where levels of child maltreatment and family violence remain high and where most evidence-based programs remain inaccessible (Mejia, Calam, & Sanders, 2014). The development of the Triple P system has involved the dedicated efforts of a large number of people that have shared a unified vision of improving the lives of children through quality, evidence-based systems of parenting support to meet the needs of all parents, and will continue to do so.

Key Points

1. Behavioral family interventions have evolved over recent decades and, as an example, the Triple P—Positive Parenting Program has developed to

encompass a multi-level, multidisciplinary, population-based system ranging from universal to targeted interventions to meet families' needs and preferences for parenting support.

2. The key objectives are to increase parents' knowledge, competence, and confidence in raising children by: building on their skills in managing common behavioral and emotional problems and developmental issues; helping them be positive and proactive in their daily interactions with children; reducing family conflict and coercive and punitive methods of discipline; and improving their communication about parenting issues.
3. The core principles of Triple P include: creating a safe and engaging environment; having a responsive, positive learning environment; using assertive and consistent discipline; having realistic expectations of children and oneself; and taking care of oneself as a parent.
4. These principles translate into specific skills in the areas of: parent–child relationship enhancement; encouraging desirable behavior; teaching new skills and behaviors; managing misbehavior; anticipating and planning ahead; self-regulation; mood management and coping skills; and partner support and communication skills.
5. Triple P interventions use a self-regulation framework to help parents develop skills to become self-reliant, confident, self-directed, empowered, independent problem solvers.
6. A guided participation approach is used to share a personalized functional assessment formulation, and negotiate an intervention plan with each family.
7. Tailoring of program goals and delivery to individual needs is a key feature of any Triple P intervention. This approach also underpins culturally sensitive ways of working with families.
8. To be effective, large-scale dissemination of evidence-based interventions must blend flexibility to community and family capacity with fidelity to core program content and therapeutic processes.
9. Program development and dissemination processes are never static. Rather, they should be continually evolving in response to research outcomes and consumer feedback.
10. Innovation in program development can increase access to quality parenting support for previously under-serviced, hard-to-reach families, minority groups, and resource-poor communities and countries.

Discussion Questions

1. Does a manualized program which has been proven effective in research trials necessarily limit professional judgment and program tailoring in real-world practice?

2. How can practitioners balance program fidelity and flexible delivery to provide evidence-based practice that is tailored to individual needs?
3. What needs to be considered in developing an individual case formulation and intervention plan?
4. What is the difference between a universal and targeted intervention approach? How might they conflict with or complement each other?

Additional Resources

Websites

More information about Triple P research and evidence base can be found at www.pfsc.uq.edu.au.

For details about training and parent resources, see www.triplep.net.

References

Biglan, A., Flay, B. R., Embry, D. D., & Sandler, I. N. (2012). The critical role of nurturing environments for promoting human wellbeing. *American Psychologist, 67*, 257–271.

Collins, W., Maccoby, E., Steinberg, L., Hetherington, E., & Bornstein, M. (2000). Contemporary research on parenting: The case for nature and nurture. *American Psychologist, 55*, 218–232.

Fixsen, D. L., Naoom, S. F., Blasé, K. A., Friedman, R. M., & Wallace, F. (2005). *Implementation research: A synthesis of the literature*. Tampa, FL: University of South Florida, Louis de la Parte Florida Mental Health Institute, National Implementation Research Network. (FMHI Publication No. 231).

Glasgow, R. E., Vogt, T. M., & Boles, S. M. (1999). Evaluating the public health impact of health promotion interventions: The RE-AIM framework. *American Journal of Public Health, 89*, 1922–1927.

Karoly, P. (1993). Mechanisms of self-regulation: A systems view. *Annual Review of Psychology, 44*, 23–52.

Kumpfer, K. L., Alvarado, R., Smith, P., & Bellamy, N. (2002). Cultural sensitivity in universal family based prevention interventions. *Prevention Science, 3(3)*, 241–244.

Marmot, M. (2010). *Fair society, healthy lives: The Marmot Review; Strategic review of health inequalities in England post-2010*. London: The Marmot Review.

Mazzucchelli, T. G. & Sanders, M. R. (2010). Facilitating practitioner flexibility within an empirically supported intervention: Lessons from a system of parenting support. *Clinical Psychology: Science and Practice, 17(3)*, 238–252.

Mejia, A., Calam, R., & Sandes, M. R. (2014). Examining delivery preferences and cultural relevance of an evidence-based parenting program in a low-resource setting of Central America: Approaching parents as consumers. *Journal of Child and Family Studies*, published online February 2014.

Morawska, A., Sanders, M., Goadby, E., Headley, C., Hodge, L., McAuliffe, C., et al. (2011). Is the Triple P-Positive Parenting Program acceptable to parents from culturally diverse backgrounds? *Journal of Child and Family Studies, 20*, 614–622.

Sanders, M. R. (1999). The Triple P-Positive Parenting Program: Towards an empirically validated multi-level parenting and family support strategy for the prevention of behavior and emotional problems in children. *Clinical Child and Family Psychology Review, 2*, 71–90.

Sanders, M. (2008). Triple P-Positive Parenting Program as a public health approach to strengthening parenting. *Journal of Family Psychology, 22*, 506–517.

Sanders, M. R. (2011). Adopting a public health approach to the delivery of evidence-based parenting interventions. *Association for Child and Adolescent Mental Health Occasional Papers: Increasing Access to CAMHS, 30*, 11–19.

Sanders, M. R. (2012). Development, evaluation, and multinational dissemination of the Triple P-Positive Parenting Program. *Annual Review of Clinical Psychology, 8*, 1–35.

Sanders, M. R., & Burke, K. (2013). The "hidden" technology of effective parent consultation: A guided participation model for promoting change in families. *Journal of Child and Family Studies*, published online September 2013.

Sanders, M. R., & Glynn, E. L. (1981). Training parents in behavioral self-management: an analysis of generalization and maintenance effects. *Journal of Applied Behaviour Analysis, 14*, 223–237.

Sanders, M. R., & Kirby, J. N. (2012). Consumer engagement and the development, evaluation and dissemination of evidence-based parenting programs. *Behavior Therapy, 43*, 236–250.

Sanders, M. R. & Kirby, J. N. (2014). Surviving or thriving: Quality assurance mechanisms to promote innovation in the development of evidence-based parenting interventions. *Prevention Science*, published online March 2014.

Sanders, M. R., Kirby, J. N., Tellegen, C. L., & Day, J. J. (2014). Towards a public health approach to parenting support: A systematic review and meta-analysis of the Triple P-Positive Parenting Program. *Clinical Psychology Review, 34(4)*, 337–357.

Sanders, M. R., & Lawton, J. M. (1993). Discussing assessment findings with families: A guided participation model of information transfer. *Child and Family Behavior Therapy, 15*, 5–35.

Sanders, M. R., & Mazzucchelli, T. G. (2013). The promotion of self-regulation through parenting interventions. *Clinical Child and Family Psychology Review, 16(1)*, 1–17.

Sanders, M. R., & Murphy-Brennan, M. (2010). Creating conditions for success beyond the professional training environment. *Clinical Psychology: Science & Practice, 17*, 31–35.

Sanders, M. R., Turner, K. M., & Markie-Dadds, C. (2002). The development and dissemination of the Triple P-Positive Parenting Program: A multilevel, evidence-based system of parenting and family support. *Prevention Science, 3*, 173–189.

Sethi, S., Sanders, M. R., & Ralph, A. (2014). The international dissemination of evidene-based parenting interventions: Impact on practitioner content and process self-efficacy. *International Journal of Mental Health Promotion, 16(2)*, 126–137.

Shapiro, C. J., Prinz, R. J., & Sanders, M. R. (2014). Sustaining use of an evidence-based parenting intervention: Practitioner perspectives. *Journal of Child and Family Studies, 24(6)*. doi: 10.1007/s10826–014–9965–9.

Turner, K. M., Richards, M., & Sanders, M. R. (2007). Randomised clinical trial of a group parent education programme for Australian indigenous families. *Journal of Paediatrics and Child Health, 43(6)*, 429–437.

Turner, K. M. & Sanders, M. R. (2013). *Triple P Online* [8 module interactive internet program]. Brisbane, QLD, Australia: Triple P International Pty.

16

FAMILIES AND SCHOOLS TOGETHER (FAST)

Lynn McDonald

Learning Goals

1. To recognize that "improving parenting" is a complex goal, which may benefit from complex, multi-systemic interventions that apply theories from sociology and psychology, which recognize the impacts of stress and social isolation on families, build protective factors for all children against risks at home, in school, and in communities, and adults' experiential learning in groups, repetition, and positive emotion.
2. To promote the successful engagement of parents, especially socially marginalized parents, into proven parent interventions and the retention of those parents in the programs requires strategies related to (a) awareness of power and sharing power; (b) respect for the elders (parents) and different types of knowledge; (c) relationship building, social inclusion, and cultural representation; and (d) program flexibility and promotion of local adaptation for a cultural fit in the co-production of sustainable strategies with parents taking a lead with professionals to "improve parenting".
3. About the successful replication of the "proven" parenting programs, across urban and rural settings, across race and ethnic groups, and across countries in thousands of settings, offer lessons: planning, training of teams and of local trainers; repeated on-site visits by certified program trainers to monitor program integrity and quality of implementation; pre–post evaluations using standardized instruments; and requiring parent and practitioner feedback to lead to constant improvement of the program.

Introduction

Families and Schools Together (FAST) is a multi-systemic intervention in which multi-family groups held after school bring together all young children (ages 4–7), whole families, schools, and communities to build relationships over time to increase child well-being (see www.familiesandschools.org). FAST applies theories from sociology and psychology to systematically increase positive outcomes for all children by building social capital in local primary schools located in disadvantaged communities, by empowering parents to feel effective and to form a collective voice of interdependent parents; and by coaching parents of children as they enter school to practice leading family activities and positive parenting to build family cohesion, the parent–child bond, and every child's learning readiness. FAST has an established track record of increasing family engagement with low-income, diverse families (Caspe & Lopez, 2006), and is recognized by the United Nations (UNODC, 2010) as an evidence-based, universal, family skills model for drug prevention.

Theoretical Foundations and History

Since 1988, FAST has changed from targeting a few "at-risk" children at a school with a combination of clinical and community development strategies (McDonald, Billingham, Conrad, Morgan, & Payton, 1997) to a universal, community-based, public health parenting model to reduce inequalities in health, education, and social care. This shift is based on consumer feedback from FAST parent graduates who said "all parents should be able to do this", from practitioners in the field and with new theories and research. Eight weekly group sessions are followed by two years of monthly multi-family booster sessions led by FAST parent graduates to maintain gains in social capital, parent–child bonds, and community norms about positive parenting. Primary schools aim to engage 40 kindergarten families at a time to come at least once; high retention rates of 80 percent are based on whether a family comes once and whether families attend six or more times. FAST has now been adapted, implemented with supervision, and evaluated in 20 countries with families of many races, income levels, ethnicities, languages, religions, and in both rural and urban settings.

Trained teams are encouraged to locally adapt about 60 percent of the processes, while also implementing the core components of FAST (40 percent). Certified trainers supervise teams in three on-site observations of the eight weekly sessions, to monitor the core components and to celebrate local adaptations. In addition, pre–post quantitative evaluations are required for each implementation, partially because of the large numbers of local adaptations. New school districts or Ministries of Education are supported to create cultural adaptation teams, translate materials, and pilot FAST in their social contexts. With a five-day Training of Trainers (T of T) and supervision of their own training efforts at a new school, authorities can invest in developing capacity of local certified FAST trainers, which in turn increases sustainability of the two-year, community-building family skills program.

One "core component" of FAST is that each team is culturally representative of the families participating in the groups. Race, ethnic and language "matching" increases feelings of social inclusion for parents on the team as well as for parents participating in the groups. This is a power shift towards "shared governance" to show respect for the knowledge of the "lived experience" of local parents and contribute to predictably high retention rates (McDonald et al., 2012). FAST teams are also required to be a partnership of local parents, teachers, and community professionals or leaders. The collaborative team co-produces planned local adaptations to fit their unique social-cultural contexts (Lee, Altschul, & Mowbray, 2008), with 60 percent of FAST processes being flexible and open to local cultural adaptation.

Teams of 20 partners host 4 multi-family groups in 4 classrooms at a school, serving 10 whole families each. Team members are trained to respect parents and to coach parents to lead family routines each week. The experiential learning and practice approach helps participating parents to build mastery of positive parenting over eight weekly repetitions. The 2.5 hours of family, dyadic, and small group interactions repeated each week reduce family conflict and lead to strengthened relationships. The strengthened relationships are protective factors against risk for the young child; caring relationships buffer and reduce "toxic stresses" of child neglect, abuse, and of parental dysfunction (Gerhardt, 2004). Adult outcomes show increases in feelings of self-efficacy by 80 percent who graduate, as well as unanticipated results (e.g., a return to further education (44 percent), starting employment (35 percent), making a new friend whom they still see four years later (86 percent) (McDonald & Sayger, 1998)), and statistically significant increases in parent graduates becoming volunteers and community leaders (Layzer et al., 2001). Other community outcomes include building social capital defined as parents befriending other parents of their children's friends at school (Gamoran et al., 2012). After FAST compared with a year later, children continue to increase their levels of well-being and their academic achievements (Kratochwill et al., 2004).

Universal FAST parenting groups are offered within a particular social and historical context: the United Nations Convention on the Rights of the Child (1989) (www.unicef.org.uk/Documents/Publication-pdfs/UNCRC_summary.pdf) asserts the right of each child in the world to grow up safe, happy, and healthy with 43 specific provisions. UNICEF monitors, assesses, and published reports in 2007 and 2013 on "child well-being" levels in 29 rich industrialized nations. The studies on child well-being included in-depth interviews of children, government data on child abuse and neglect, rates of infant death, delinquency, and surveys evaluating 40 distinct factors (www.unicef-irc.org/Report-Card-11/). Relationships with parents and peers were assessed with the statements: "it is easy to talk to my mother", "it is easy to talk to my father", and "my classmates are kind and helpful". Wide variability showed up between the 29 countries and aggregate scores were used to rank countries. There is perhaps an increased awareness by governments of the universal need for all parents to participate in parenting programs, versus only parents of children with conduct disorders.

Policy makers are starting to recognize that there are significant healthcare costs resulting from not offering universal parenting classes based on research on adverse childhood events (ACE). In the ACE research, health assessments of middle-aged, middle-class women in California were correlated with survey responses to an ACE list completed retrospectively. Rates of adult health and morbidity, emergency room visits, and frequency of outpatient and pharmacy use were correlated with ACE (under age seven). Exposure to ACE as young children included child abuse (physical, sexual, or psychological), domestic violence, parental addiction, depression, or incarceration. Results showed that over 50 percent reported at least one ACE, and 25 percent reported two. Experiencing four or more ACE showed dramatic increases in rates of adult suicide, depression, alcoholism, adult pulmonary disease, cancer, compromised health, and lung and liver disease (Felitti, Anda, Nordenberg, Williamson, Spitz, Edwards, Koss, & Marks, 1998). The original ACE study has now been widely replicated by state and federal governments (Bellis, Hughes, Leckenby, Hardcastle, Perkins, & Lowey, 2014). Policy makers are calling for social-family-parenting interventions to reduce ACE in childhood, based on these research findings.

Children raised in poverty have double the increased risk for ACE by parents with the additional stresses of struggling to provide housing, food, and healthcare for their young child. The parents need support and young children will benefit from protective factors against these stresses, of stronger attachment and the parent–child bond, and the parental–child having repeated positive interactive sequences. In the UK (Lindsay et al., 2014), a recent evaluation report describes the evaluation of government pilot-offered vouchers for free parenting classes for all parents with children 0–5. Three local authorities were selected for the pilot and all parents given a choice of about 10 parenting programs. There was a choice provided of 14 parenting programs; four were taken up by 67 percent of the participants (including FAST).

> The specific research connecting social capital to health outcomes via a social support mechanism is vast. In this sense, social capital has been empirically linked to, among other things, improved child development and adolescent well-being, increased mental health, lower violent crime rates and youth delinquency, reduced mortality, lower susceptibility to binge drinking, to depression, and to loneliness, sustained participation in anti-smoking programmes, and higher perceptions of well-being and self-rated health. Where urban neighbourhoods and rural communities (and particular subpopulations) are demonstrably low in social capital, residents report higher levels of stress and isolation, children's welfare decreases, and there is a reduced capacity to respond to environmental health risks and to receive effective public health service interventions.
>
> (Szreter & Woolcock, 2004)

Wilkinson and Pickett (2010) examined whether income disparities in individual countries contribute to lower overall "child well-being" levels as published by UNICEF. He analyzed indicators of extreme disparities and correlated them with the UNICEF child well-being rankings. The results showed dramatic correlations. Wilkinson suggested that governments create policies which provide financial support for families, income transfers, universal healthcare, public housing benefits, good schools, child protection services, and community infrastructures for all children to lift the national levels of child well-being.

FAST applies both sociological and psychological theories into a simple program for raising "child well-being" levels for all children. Reaching out to all children, including targeted children, especially in low-income communities, can help reduce disparities of race and income inequalities. Values expressed in the FAST program are those of social justice: social inclusion, co-production with parents (i.e., service users), respecting parents as leaders of their own family, cultural representation of the families being served, and program flexibility to stimulate the local practitioners and parents to fit the FAST to their local sociocultural priorities. The values, research, and theory foundations of FAST are each discussed at the two-day FAST trainings by the local teams, prior to the supervised implementations and evaluations.

Ten sociology and psychology theories underpin the multi-family group processes with families, dyads, and small groups: (a) community-organizing strategies of outreach, engagement, and empowerment of adults in small, open-discussion groups of parents to develop a collective voice (Freire, 1995); (b) group work theory is applied in FAST through the multi-family group, the parent group, and the support of the collaborative team as a group (MacFarlane, 2002; Ephross & Vassil, 2005); (c) systemic theories of structural family therapy in low-income communities (Minuchin et al., 1967; Minuchin, 1974) support building parental hierarchy and authority, increasing family cohesion, and reducing family conflict; functional family therapy (Alexander & Robbins, 2011) promotes learning skills of turn-taking in families, positive inquiry to reduce conflict, and structured expressed warmth; (d) experiential learning strategies for adult learning are expressed in the coaching of parents as they lead positive family games and routines, repeated each week to increase parenting skills to mastery; (e) social learning theory is expressed through role modeling with opportunities for parents to observe others doing positive parenting, promoting attendance behaviors using social and tangible reinforcements; repetition with coaching of parenting behaviors towards mastery, successive approximation towards the target behavior; and multiple embedded compliance requests delivered by the parents (Patterson et al., 1992); (f) the theory of reciprocal adult pair relationships supports marital therapy strategies (Gottman, 2014); the theory of daily social support of talking with a friend for improving parenting of stressed, depressed, and low-income mothers (Belle & Doucet, 2003). The isolated "insular" mother compromise follow-up outcomes of recently learned parenting skills; the mutuality of friendships are essential to sustained effective parenting (Wahler, 1980); (g) theory of play for young children in parent-delivered play therapy and "attachment repair" strategies between parent and young child, in which parents are coached to be more responsive to their child in "special play" for 15 minutes, rather than bossing and teaching (Kogan & Gordon, 1975; Webster-Stratton et al., 2004); (h) family stress theory (Hill, 1958; Boss, 2002) suggests that social networks and hope can function as protective factors for families and reduce the pile-up effects on family functioning of multiple stressors. Building protective factors to reduce the impact of risk factors for children under stress at home, in school, or in the community (Farrington & Ttofi, 2012) can reduce bad trajectories of children (e.g., delinquency). In FAST, family stress reduction strategies include building positive energy through singing as a group and playing as a family; the theory of sustained positive emotion (Fredrickson, 2003) suggests that promoting family fun by coaching parents to lead positive family interaction games increases the curiosity to learn and wish to socialize more with others; (i) the social capital and social inclusion theory (Wilkinson, 1997; Wilkinson & Pickett, 2010; Shoji et al., 2014) suggests that communities with "bonds, bridging and linking relationships" (Szreter & Woolcock, 2004) correlate many kinds of outcomes, including child well-being and health, and education. Coleman (1994) theorized on social capital in his research on schools; "intergenerational closure" is when parents form trusting reciprocal small networks among 4–5 parents of children who are friends with their child and attend the same school (Coleman, 1994; Gamoran et al., 2012); and (j) empowerment theory, to support the parent as having essential knowledge of "lived experience" needed for the FAST team to be effective, coaching participating parents to be the family leaders, inviting parent graduates to lead the monthly booster sessions, and inviting a FAST parent graduate panel to provide feedback for team certification.

Needs Assessment and Target Audience

There is no needs assessment of individual young children in FAST. An assumption is made that there is a universal need for all young children to experience positive parenting, including children in poverty and/or with conduct problems. This right is in the United Nations Charter for Children's Rights. Another assumption of FAST is that all parents love their child and want the best for them. FAST provides the support structures to all parents as their child enters school and offers them an opportunity to meet other parents of their children's friends, help their child's motivation to learn, practice positive parenting activities within a socially inclusive and respectful group setting, and receive personal coaching on family skills offered by a trained, culturally representative local team of parents and professionals.

Working in partnership with primary schools makes it possible to reach all young children and their parents. Parents of at-risk children do not feel stigmatized or excluded, because all children are invited to FAST (about 40 percent of FAST children exhibit mental health symptoms). Trained teams make "face-to-face" contact and provide additional parent outreach and repeated home visits, as needed.

Eligibility is universal for all kindergartners, with a special focus on primary schools located in disadvantaged communities. After assessing community-level indicators of risk, a head teacher would be approached serving in a community with elevated poverty levels, high mobility, or local government indicators of high rates of delinquency, domestic violence, addiction, school drop-out, low reading scores, or child abuse and neglect. By working with all parents in primary schools in disadvantaged communities, one increases changes in both the immediate and long-term sustainable systems (Wilkinson, 1997; Wilkinson & Pickett, 2010). Public health theory suggests that one can reduce inequalities in health by offering a universal parenting program with wide reach and high retention rates, which both empowers a collective voice as well as connecting isolated parents. A community approach has a chance to shift norms across the local community towards positive parenting. Building shared expectations of groups of parents about positive parenting who have social capital of reciprocal exchange, mutual support among parents, and more parent involvement at school, should lower stress levels at home and boost children's learning. These multi-systemic impacts can reduce disparities in education and child abuse and neglect, while improving "child well-being".

The goal for FAST is to reach more than half of all children starting school. To achieve this "reach", two groups a year are offered at a school with open enrollment over the eight weeks, with 20–40 families attending weekly group sessions each time. On average, retention rates for coming once to FAST are 80 percent who complete the weekly sessions (McDonald et al., 2012). These are high rates for parents in low-income settings. In a recent UN family skills initiative in several Central Asian developing countries (Tajikistan, Kyrgyzstan, & Kazakhstan), 20–30 families participated in FAST in six schools per country and completed eight sessions with almost 100 percent retention rates (McDonald & Doostgharin, 2013). In three favelas of Brazil, funded by the UN, the FAST average retention rate was 81 percent with 20–40 families per community center completing the weekly groups. Across the UK, on average 23 families have graduated from FAST in 400 schools, each located in high-poverty areas (McDonald & Puniskis, 2013) with a 78 percent retention rate. In the south-western USA, the average number of families of first graders who graduated per school was 22 (of 26 urban schools with high proportions of low-income Hispanic families, primarily Mexican immigrant families (Shoji et al., 2014). In inner city Philadelphia at 30 failing schools in 2013–2014, on average 18 kinder-gartners and their whole families came once and 86 percent returned, in communities which were predominantly low-income African American (unpublished i3 report, 2014). The high numbers of parents engaged enables a shift and change in the school climate to support positive parenting norms.

Program Goals and Objectives

Goals

To increase child well-being and education achievement for all children and to reduce education and health disparities (for bullying and aggression in school, child mental health problems, juvenile delinquency, violence, and drug and alcohol addiction).

Objectives

To increase parental self-efficacy; improve the parent–child bond (with the kindergartner); enhance family functioning; reduce family conflict and stress of child and parents; increase the social network with other parents; increase parent engagement with school and the community; and make appropriate referrals for parental depression, anxiety, addiction, and domestic violence.

Curriculum and Other Program Issues

There are three stages of this two-year parenting program: outreach, weekly multi-family groups, and monthly parent, graduate-led, multi-family group sessions. There are no handouts for parents and no written curriculum for parents, as the learning is entirely based on practicing interactive positive family experiences while being coached for success by trained team members. The team members, however, have FAST manuals, quality of implementation checklists, and program integrity checklists made available to them through the nonprofit FAST, based in Madison, WI (www.familiesandschools.org).

Outreach Process

The school head teacher sends a letter inviting all kindergarten (or first grade) children to try FAST once. Teachers and team members meet parents at the school and tell them about FAST. Posters are on the wall and fliers sent home to also provide information. Some families get repeated home visits by parents on the FAST team in non-traditional hours to assure the participation of socially excluded families. Successful outreach to all families is enhanced by flexibility about time and place to meet with parents, persistence and caring, discussion of social inclusion and the importance of listening respectfully, and providing free transport, infant care, weekly family meals, and a lottery gift for every participating family.

Weekly Program

1. Eight weekly programs are held after school for groups of 10 families in a classroom; a primary school hosts four groups at a time (for 40 families) in order to be able to reach all children of the entering class.
2. Weekly sessions are 2.5 hours with repeated routines; if you come once, you learn it; by repeating it each week, both the child and parent master the pattern of family activity, transition, activity, etc.
3. Family table activity (60 minutes): parent(s) are supported by trained team members to be the head of the family table: parent(s) lead a family meal, lead family introductions, sing songs as a group; parent(s) lead a family craft activity, lead a family drawing and communication game, and lead a feelings identification game; then, transition time.
4. Peer activity (60 minutes): the generations go into separate areas/rooms for mothers, fathers, grandparents, teenagers, young children, and babies; children play (no TV) and adults talk (no lectures); then transition time.
5. Parent–kindergarten child activity (15 minutes): one-to-one free play activity in which the team member coaches the parent to respond rather than lead and to focus on the play of the child.
6. Closing traditions (15 minutes): all families and team gather into a large circle at the end of the session; the group recognizes birthdays and invites personal announcements and claps; then silence and finally, movements move around the circle which sound like RAIN.
7. Weekly groups are followed by a graduation ceremony for participating families celebrating success. The head teacher congratulates the parents and gives a certificate of recognition for the family, thus, simulating a high school graduation ceremony to lift expectations for school completion.

Monthly Program

1. Two years of monthly sessions planned and led by parent graduates to maintain gains over time.
2. In grade 1, FAST parent graduates can volunteer to be on FAST teams to lead, host, and coach the entering kindergarten families.
3. In grade 2, open family nights are held at school for all second children with whole families (whether or not they went to FAST in kindergarten); these are co-produced by teachers and FAST graduate parent leaders: math night, science night, reading night, etc.

The curriculum is based entirely on experiential learning through structured interactive processes, with team members coaching parents and supporting the parents to take a lead on positive parenting; parents present imbedded compliance requests and lead enactments of positive parenting while leading family activities. With repetition each week, reciprocal trust relationships on multiple levels are strengthened between parents and children, parent to parent, and parent to team members. Parents experience increased self-efficacy and learn that with social support, they can be more effective as a parent. They experience parenting within a socially inclusive community each week and month over two years. Gradually they experience a "social safety net" of long-term relationships which function as protective factors in stressful times; social capital systematically builds up within the school community. Social capital is correlated with improved academic success, reduced crime, drugs, increased health, and longevity.

Cultural Implications

FAST groups have engaged hundreds of thousands of families, including in favelas and primary schools in Brazil, in schools in Malaysia, Philippines, in Germany, Austria, and Holland; and in Russia, Uzbekistan, Kazakhstan, Kyrgyzstan, Turkmenistan, Tajikistan (McDonald & Doostgharin, 2013), and Iran. FAST has been implemented widely in England, Wales, Scotland, Northern Ireland, Canada, Australia, and in 49 states in the USA. Explicit strategies enable the cross-cultural successes and high retention rates across widely differing cultures and rural and urban settings (McDonald et al., 2012).

Teams are trained and supervised while implementing the groups by an assigned certified trainer, who over time forms a relationship of trust and advises the team and meets with the team multiple times on-site. FAST manuals are translated into the local language, including both the majority and minority languages. FAST teams are encouraged to make local cultural adaptations at each site by requiring that teams are culturally representative of the families being served. Recognizing many types of knowledge and bringing everyone to the table for solving social problems is a key strategy for increasing family engagement.

A core component of FAST is that the culture/language/religion/race of the participating families must be represented on the implementation teams. In addition, an assumption made in each country is that there will probably be inequalities and disparities in education and health related to racism and social exclusion. Discussions are held about the powerful versus powerless in each setting, related either to a dominant versus minority religion, language, ethnicity, race, or immigrant status, social class, etc.

With every team required to be culturally representative of the local families, the power on the team shifts. The minority representatives inform the majority representatives on the team and advise the team and the FAST trainer. Local teams co-produce the cultural adaptations, and unique variations emerge. Local teams adapt 60 percent of the curriculum and follow the core components (40 percent). The required on-site observations by a certified FAST trainer give feedback on whether the adaptations are "drift". Then the required pre–post evaluations enable monitoring of the impact of locally developed adaptations on the expected child well-being outcomes. This is how the flexibility of FAST has increased over time.

Native Americans in the USA reported to the U.S. government that what they appreciate about FAST is (a) the respect towards the elders, (b) the holistic, multi-systemic, relationship-based approach, and (c) the program flexibility which enables introduction of local native tribal ceremonial practices. Retention rates on average are very high in these diverse rural and urban communities for FAST groups: 80 percent who come once usually complete six of eight sessions. Within a year, each country or city has usually invested in training and supervision of their own local certified FAST trainers to sustain the pilots, and then to expand and train other local community schools in "scale-ups".

Evidence-based Research and Evaluation

Several rigorous experimental research studies on program impact of FAST in low-income communities have been conducted in collaboration with academic researchers, community partners of nonprofit family counselling agencies, and local schools. The studies were funded by U.S. government departments (e.g. Health, Education, Child Welfare and Justice (Layzer et al., 2001; Kratochwill et al., 2004, 2009; McDonald et al., 2006)). Randomized controlled trials (RCTs) are required in order for a parenting program to become listed as an "evidence-based practice". Based on five RCTs on FAST since 2001, FAST is now rated at the highest levels of evidence on government lists (i.e., USA, UK, Australia, and Canada), as well as the European Union (EU) and the United Nations (UNODC).

The National Institute of Child and Human Development (NICHD: 2008–2013)-funded RCT was led by sociology academics interested in testing FAST as a strategy for systematically building social capital in 52 primary schools serving communities with predominantly low-income, Hispanic populations. Another RCT (2013–2018), funded by an Investing in Innovation (i3) U.S. Department of Education award, is aimed at using FAST to reduce education disparities by changing school climate through engagement and reducing social obstacles to learning which exist outside the classroom. This RCT is ongoing in Philadelphia, PA (www.PhillyFASTi3.com) with the school district and a nonprofit family counselling agency, in 60 urban failing schools with predominantly low-income African American populations. Each of the FAST RCTs was in a low-income setting, led by a distinct research team, in which the founder consulted to insure the program integrity of the group implementations.

Routine evaluations of FAST replications are done to insure that the expected outcomes are achieved, especially given the high level of local adaptation of the multi-family groups. The evaluation design uses a pre and post mixed methods evaluation design, with two independent reporters (parent and teacher), standardized instruments with established validity and reliability, and one-tailed, paired *t*-test analyses. In addition, comments are solicited from parents and teachers with open-ended questions. The evaluations are required at each new school, community, or country as part of the Quality Assurance Structure (QAS) developed and tested for widespread dissemination and "scale-ups" of FAST. Use of the FAST QAS produces expected child, family, school, and community outcomes and high retention rates. The QAS includes training, on-site supervision, monitoring program integrity with a checklist, and process and outcome evaluations. To assess whether specific objectives are actually achieved in new settings, a questionnaire was developed, tested, and revised over the years. The FAST questionnaire is used widely across many countries and includes well-recognized instruments with established validity and reliability (and standardized norms), as well as several developed and tested by the founder with colleagues.

Domain: Measures Used for Routine FAST Evaluation of Each School

- Parent empowerment: Parental Efficacy (Sherer et al., 1982).
- Parent–child bond: Parent Relationship Scale (McDonald, 2008).
- Child well-being: Strengths and Difficulties Questionnaire (SDQ, Goodman et al., 1998).
- School competence: Social Skills Research Scale (SSRS, Gresham & Elliot, 1990).
- Family conflict/cohesion: Moos Family Environment Scale (FES, Moos & Moos, 1981).
- Parent involvement in school: Parent Involvement in Education (Epstein & Salinas, 1993).
- Social capital and support: Community Involvement Scale (McDonald & Moberg, 2003).
- Consumer satisfaction: Parent/Teacher Satisfaction Scale (McDonald & Billingham, 1992).

Pre–post data are anonymized and submitted to the nonprofit FAST evaluation center, analyzed for statistical significance, and the results are sent in a 50-page outcome evaluation report to the local site. Quantitative outcomes for each site are written out as well as presented in bars and graphs. To put local outcomes into perspective, the local results are placed alongside the norms of the SDQ and FESs instrument, and also alongside national or state norms of aggregated FAST outcomes. The outcome evaluation report is reviewed and discussed in person by the FAST trainer with the funders, trained team, and consumer parents. The heuristic goal is to explicitly tie local outcomes to local practice, with reflective time to advise and make plans on strategies to improve outcomes with better performance.

The process evaluation is led by the certified FAST trainer, who makes three on-site visits per FAST group to observe the local adaptations and to coach the quality of implementation. After the weekly program is completed, the FAST trainer meets with the team again to evaluate the pilot. The trainer has team members complete a program integrity checklist (PIC scored per site), leads the team discussion of the outcome evaluation report, and leads the questioning of a FAST parent graduate panel about their experiences. For a site to become certified to implement FAST independently and over time, the entire QAS must be in place.

Professional Preparation and Training

The best team member for FAST is probably a FAST parent graduate, who is culturally representative of the families, has "lived experience", shows warmth and respect towards low-income participating parents, and shows a commitment to follow the core components while also culturally adapting the processes. Local FAST parent graduates on the team are required after the first pilot and offer a unique strength related to sustainability; they insure that the parent voice is respected during team planning. Each team includes practitioners from education, health, and social care. Teachers are excellent team members, enthusiastic about FAST, and protect the program integrity. Other functions of the team include referring parents to appropriate intensive services for depression, addiction, or domestic violence.

For sustainability, funders' investing in having local certified trainers is very important. One can become a certified FAST trainer within 12 months. A certified FAST trainer trains a team to deliver group services. The criteria for trainers include being a professional who has been on a FAST team, attended the Training of Trainers (T of T) five-day seminar, and has been supervised to train a team by a certified FAST supervisor. The FAST training and supervision model for the team is also used for the trainer interns, and comes from family therapy training. One is observed and supervised while delivering services. Trainers host local team workshops for 20 team members per school for two days. On Day 1, the manuals are introduced and a trainer DVD is provided (see image from the DVD; Figure 16.1). The certified team trainer introduces FAST and explains each of the family activities with role plays on coaching the parent to lead the activity. On Day 2, the values and research are taught and discussed by the team, followed by team planning for implementation. The certified trainer then supervises the team implementation by coming to the site for observation of three of the eight weekly sessions. This face-to-face support to each hub-team is given as they implement the group processes for the first time with up to 10 families per classroom. In the FAST International Training model, a team also has a chance to observe another team implement a session. The trainer provides feedback using the quality of implementation checklist (QUIK) the next morning. The final day of team training is reflective and evaluative, and takes place a month after the graduation event for the families. The trainer reviews what was learned and asks team members

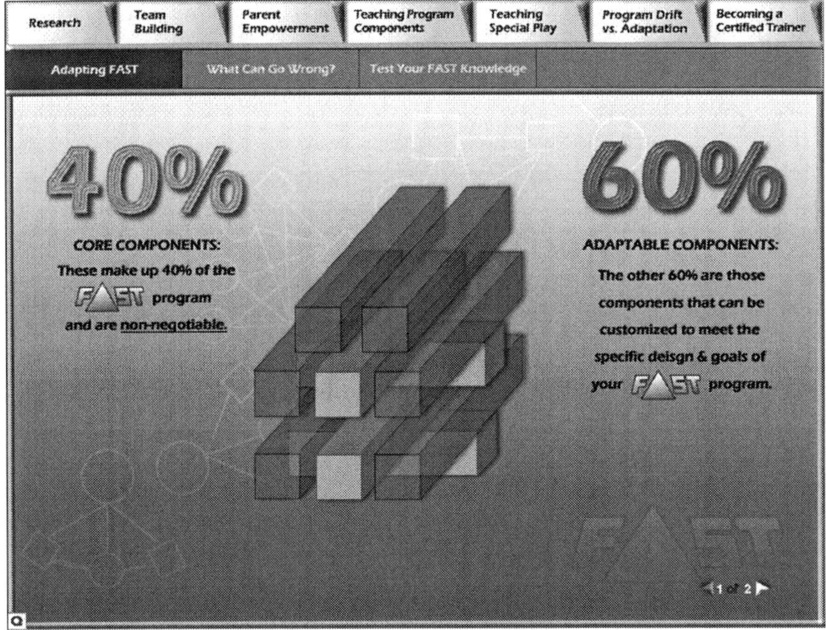

FIGURE 16.1 Components of FAST

to self-evaluate using the program integrity checklist (PIC). The team members are appreciated for their own good efforts, which led to the results on the site outcome evaluation report. The team sees the data of pre to post changes across domains of child, family, school, and community. In addition, a FAST parent graduate panel is convened for their evaluation report. Then the team members become certified.

All team members who complete the FAST training can receive university credits if they complete a 3,000-word paper (Middlesex University, UK; Department of Health and Education). Middlesex University now offers an accredited one-year postgraduate degree in Supervision of Evidence-based Parenting Programs. This course offers classroom instruction as well as supervised field placements and visits and supervision for becoming a FAST supervisor. Supervisors train FAST trainers.

Building local capacity of certified trainers in counties and countries is important for "scale-ups". FASTUK has "scaled up" 400 sites in partnership with Save the Children UK and Middlesex University 2010 (www.familiesandschoolstogether.com.). New international FAST replications are led through the Tavistock Institute for Human Relations (TIHR) in London.

The nonprofit home organization for FAST is based in Madison, WI; it directs the quality assurance packages for manuals, training, supervision, and evaluation for FAST for all pilots, and produces materials and supports for the widespread dissemination of this evidence-based parenting program in small and large initiatives. Contractual agreements are made for national "scale-ups" (www.familiesandschools.org).

Conclusion

FAST is recognized for its track record in engaging low-income, socially marginalized families into multi-family groups to increase child well-being outcomes. FAST requires cultural representation and local parents on every team, and because it is flexible it can be locally co-produced. The issues of social justice and social exclusion are managed for disenfranchised, ethnic minority parents in such a way that they feel respected, with anti-oppressive practices. The high retention rates by families from disadvantaged communities are on average 80 percent of those who come once, to complete six or more of the eight weekly sessions and continue to help lead the monthly booster sessions for two years. With several large RCTs completed, and based on both sociological and psychological theories, FAST is "evidence based". Whole families of all kindergartners entering school are invited to build reciprocal relationships within the family and across local families and with schools and communities. FAST multi-family groups build social capital for families at a community level, and provide social support for stressed parents who are struggling to do their best. Parents strengthen their bonds with their young child, as they practice being positive and responsive in free play with their child. With repetition each week and booster sessions, the enactments seem to become habits, which increase child well-being.

Key Points

Families and Schools Together (FAST)

1. Multi-family groups for whole families of all kindergartners as they enter primary school, especially in low-income communities, serving 40 at once.
2. Aims to increase child well-being and motivation for learning at school by increasing family bonds, parent to parent supports, and ties between family, school, and community.
3. Trained teams coach repetition of positive, parent-led family activities for mastery in eight weekly sessions, with 22 monthly booster sessions led by FAST parent graduates to maintain relationship gains.
4. Partnership teams of culturally representative parents and professionals increase parent engagement/retention rates (80 percent) to reduce disparities.
5. Builds protective factors (layers of relationships) against child stress.
6. Builds social capital among parents and with schools and community.
7. Teams respect and empower parent group to form a collective voice.

8. Co-produced by supervised teams in which there is 60 percent program flexibility to enable local ownership and a fit with cultural priorities.
9. Based on 10 sociological and psychological theories.
10. Experiential learning only; values of social inclusion and social justice.
11. Evidence-based, manualized family skills model replicated in 20 countries.
12. Quality assurance structure includes three on-site supervision visits, pre–post evaluation, program integrity checklist, and feedback panel of parents.

Discussion Questions

1. Which social ecological domains are involved in FAST?
2. How is the main outcome of child well-being assessed in FAST?
3. How would you characterize the parent role in FAST?
4. In what ways does this family skills strategy seek to reduce disparities in health, education, and social care?
5. Can you identify the protective factors built in FAST to reduce the impact of a child's experiences of stress and adverse childhood events?
6. What quality control efforts are used to replicate FAST in 20 countries?

Additional Resources

Websites

Some links which describe and evaluate the FAST evidence base are given below:

www.countyhealthrankings.org/policies/families-and-schools-together-fast
www.crimesolutions.gov/ProgramDetails.aspx?ID=185
www.nrepp.samhsa.gov/ViewIntervention.aspx?id=30
www.wsipp.wa.gov/ReportFile/1469
www.unodc.org/docs/youthnet/Compilation/10–50018_Ebook.pdf
www.education.gov.uk/commissioning-toolkit/Programme/Detail/37
investinginchildren.eu/interventions/families-and-schools-together-fast

Links to FAST in several countries
FAST UK:

www.tavinstitute.org/news/stunning-new-partnership-with-families-and-schools-together-fast/
www.mdx.ac.uk/our-research/centres/drugs-and-alcohol-research-centre/families-and-schools-together
(Northern Ireland) www.familysupportni.gov.uk/listing/families-and-schools-together-belfast/

Canada:
cbpp-pcpe.phac-aspc.gc.ca/interventions/families-schools-fst/

Links to several videos of FAST
Liverpool, UK:

www.tes.co.uk/teaching-resource/Teachers-TV-Strengthening-the-Family-6044186/

Australia Northern Territories FAST by Aborigine leaders:
www.youtube.com/watch?v=XuazxqUnFFw
Australia Northern Territory FASTWORKS:
www.youtube.com/watch?v=NRxX5x1yftk
www.youtube.com/watch?v=nU37bd3kft4&feature=youtu.be
www.facebook.com/FASTfamiliesandschoolstogether
Philadelphia, PA, U.S. inner city failing schools:
www.phillyfasti3.com/fast-fastworks.html
www.youtube.com/watch?v=ZgLVpW8vwpM FAST Song

References

Achenbach T. (1991). *Manual for the Child Behavior Checklist/4–18 and 1991 profile.* Burlington, VT: University of Vermont, Department of Psychiatry.

Ahmed, S. (2005). What is the evidence of early intervention, preventative services for black and minority ethnic group children and families? *Practice: Social Work in Action, 17*, 89–102.

Alexander, J., & Robbins, M. (2011). Functional family therapy, in R. Murrihy, A. Kidman, & T. Ollendick (Eds.) *Clinical handbook of assessing and treating conduct problems in youth* (pp. 245–273). New York: Springer.

Alinsky, S. (1971). *Rules for radicals: A pragmatic primer for realistic radicals.* New York: Random House.

Aymer, C., & Otilkipi, T. (2003). Social work with African refugee children and their families. *Child & Family Social Work, 8*, 213–222.

Bandura, A. (1977). *Social learning theory.* New York: General Learning Press.

Barlow, J., & Calam, R., (2011). A public health approach to safeguarding in the 21st century. *Child Abuse Review, 20*, 238–255.

Barlow, J., & Stewart-Brown, S. (2003). Why a universal populational-level approach to the prevention of child abuse is essential. *Child Abuse Review, 12*, 279–281.

Belle, D., & Doucet, J. (2003). Poverty, inequality, and discrimination as sources of depression among U.S. women. *Psychology of Women Quarterly, 27*, 101–113.

Bellis, M., Hughes, K., Leckenby, N., Hardcastle, K., Perkins, C., & Lowey. L. (2014). Measuring mortality and the burden of adult disease associated with adverse childhood experiences in England: A national survey. *Journal of Public Health* advance access, August, 1–10. doi: 10.1093/pubmed/fdu065. See jpubhealth.oxfordjournals.org/content/early/2014/08/30/pubmed.fdu065.full.pdf

Bernard, C., & Gupta, A. (2008). Black African children and the child protection system. *British Journal of Social Work, 38*, 476–492.

Boss, P. (2002). *Family stress management* (2nd ed.). Thousand Oaks, CA: Sage.

Boyd-Franklin, N. (2003). *Black families in therapy: Understanding the African American experience* (2nd ed.) New York: Guilford.

Boyd-Franklin N., & Bry, B. (2000). *Reaching out in family therapy: Home-based, school, and community interventions.* New York: Guilford.

Bowlby, J. (1988). *A secure base: Parent–child attachment and healthy human development.* New York: Basic Books.

Brondolo, E., Gallo, D. C., Meyers, H. F. (2009). Race, racism, and health: disparities, mechanisms, and interventions. *Journal of Behavioural Medicine, 32*, 1–8.

Bronfenbrenner, U. (1979). *The ecology of human development: Experiments by nature and design.* Cambridge, MA: Harvard University Press.

Caspe, M., & Lopez, M. (2006). *Lessons from family-strengthening interventions: Learning from evidence based practice.* Cambridge, MA: Harvard Family Research Project.

Chand, A. (2008). Every child matters? A critical review of child welfare reforms in the context of minority ethnic children and families. *Child Abuse Review, 17*, 6–22.

Coleman, J. (1994). *The foundations of social theory.* Cambridge, MA: Harvard University Press.

Comer, J., & Gates, H., Jr. (2005). *Leave no child behind: Preparing today's youth for tomorrow's world.* New Haven, CT: Yale University Press.

Courtney, M., & Skyles, A. (2003). Racial disproportionality in the child welfare system. *Children and Youth Services Review, 25*, 355–358.

Ephross, P., & Vassil, T. (2005). *Groups that work: Structure and process.* New York: Columbia University Press.

Epstein, J., & Salinas, K. (1993). *School and family partnerships: Surveys and summaries.* Baltimore, MD: Johns Hopkins University, Center on Families, Communities, Schools and Children's Learning.

Farrington, D., & Ttofi, M. (2012). Protective and promotive factors in the development of offending, in T. Bliesener, A. Beelmann, & M. Stemmler (Eds.) *Antisocial behavior and crime: Contributions of developmental and evaluation research to prevention and intervention* (pp. 71–88). Gottingen and Cambridge, MA: Hogrefe.

Felitti, V., Anda, R., Nordenberg, D., Williamson, D., Spitz, A., Edwards, V., Koss, M., & Marks, J. (1998). Relationship of childhood abuse and household dysfunction to many of the leading causes of death in adults. The Adverse Childhood Experiences (ACE) Study. *American Journal of Preventive Medicine, 14*, 245–258. Available at www.ajpmonline.org/article/S0749-3797(98)00017-8/pdf

Flanagan, S., & Hancock, B. (2010). Reaching the hard to reach: Lessons learned. *BMC Health Services Research, 10*, 92.

Fraenkel, P. (2006). Engaging families as experts: Collaborative family program development. *Family Process, 42*, 237–257.

Fredrickson, B. (2001). The role of positive emotions in positive psychology: The broaden-and-build theory of positive emotions. *American Psychologist, 56*, 218–226.

Fredrickson, B. (2003) The value of positive emotions. *American Scientist, 91*, 330–335.

Freire, P. (1995). *Pedagogy of hope: Reliving pedagogy of the oppressed.* New York: Continuum.

Gamoran, A., Lopez-Turley, R., Turner, A., & Fish, R. (2012, May). *Social capital and inequality in child development: First year findings from an experimental study.* Presentation at International Sociological Association, Beijing, China.

Gerhardt, S. (2004). *Why love matters: How affection shapes a baby's brain.* Hove, UK: Brunner Routlege.

Goodman, R. (1997). The Strengths and Difficulties Questionnaire: A research note. *Journal of Child Psychology and Psychiatry, 38,* 52–58.

Goodman, R., Meltzer, H. & Bailey, V. (1998). The Strengths and Difficulties Questionnaire: A pilot study on the validity of the self-report version. *European Child and Adolescent Psychiatry, 7,* 125–130.

Gorman-Smith, D., Henry, D., & Tolan, P. (2004). Exposure to community violence and violence perpetration: The protective effects of family functioning. *Journal of Clinical Child and Adolescent Psychology, 33*, 439–449.

Gottman, J. (2014). *What predicts divorce: The relationship between marital process and marital outcome.* New York: Psychology Press.

Gresham, F., & Elliott, S. (1990). *Social skills rating system.* Circle Pines, MN: American Guidance Service.

Gross, D., Julian, W., & Fogg, L. (2001). What motivates participation and drop out rates among low-income urban families of color in a prevention intervention. *Family Relations, 50*, 246–254.

Hansen, S. Giles, & M. Fearnow-Kenney (Eds.). *Improving prevention effectiveness* (pp. 235–250). Greensboro, NC: Tanglewood Research.

Hill, R. (1958). Social stresses on the family: Generic features of families under stress. *Social Casework, 39*, 139–150.

Kazdin, A. (2001). Treatment of conduct disorders, in J. Hill & B. Maughan (Eds.) *Conduct disorders in childhood and adolescence* (pp. 408–448). Cambridge, UK: Cambridge University Press.

Kogan, K., & Gordon, B. (1975). A mother-instruction program. *Child Psychiatry and Human Development, 5*, 189–200.

Kratochwill, T., McDonald, L., Levin, J., Scalia, P., & Coover, P. (2009). Families and Schools Together: A randomized trial of school based family support for children's mental health. *Journal of School Psychology, 47*, 245–265.

Kratochwill, T., McDonald, L., Levin, J., Youngbear-Tibbetts, H., & Demaray, M. (2004). Families and Schools Together: An experimental analysis of a parent-mediated, multi-family group intervention for American Indian children. *Journal of School Psychology, 42*, 359–383.

Layzer, J., Goodson, B., Bernstein, L., & Price, C. (2001). *National Evaluation of Family Support Programs. Vol B. Research studies. Final report.* Prepared by Abt Associates. Washington, DC.: U.S. Department of Health and Human Services, Administration of Children, Youth and Families.

Lee, S., Altschul, I., & Mowbray, C. (2008). Using planned adaptation to implement evidence based programs with new populations. *American Journal of Community Psychology, 41*, 290–303.

Lindsay, G., Cullen, M. A., Cullen, S., Totsika, V, Bakopoulou, I., Goodlad, S., Brind, R., Pickering, E., Bryson, C., Purdon, S., Conlon, G., & Mantovani, I. (2014). *CANparent trial evaluation: Final research report.* London: UK Department for Education (DFE).

Lowe, F. (2006) Containing persecutory anxiety: Child and adolescent health services and black and ethnic minority communities. *Journal of Social Work Practice, 20*, 5–25.

McDonald, L., & Billingham, S. (1992). *FAST orientation manual and elementary school FAST program workbook.* Madison, WI: FAST International.

McDonald, L., Billingham, S., Conrad., T., Morgan., A., & Payton, E. (1997). Families and Schools Together (FAST): Integrating community development with clinical strategy. *Families in Society, 78*, 140–155.

McDonald, L., Coover, G., Sandler, J., Thao, T., & Shalhoub, H. (2012). Cultural adaptation of an evidence based parenting programme with elders from South East Asia in the US: Co-producing Families and Schools Together: FAST. *Journal of Children's Services, 7, 113*–128.

McDonald, L., & Doostgharin, T. (2013). UNODC Global Family Skills Initiative: Outcome evaluation in Central Asia of Families and Schools Together (FAST) multi-family groups. *Social Work & Social Sciences Review, 16*, 51–75.

McDonald, L., Fitzroy, S., Fuchs, I., Fooken, I., & Klasen, H. (2012). Strategies for high retention rates of low-income families in FAST (Families and Schools Together): An evidence-based parenting programme in the USA, UK, Holland and Germany. *European Journal of Developmental Psychology, 9*, 75–88.

McDonald, L., & Moberg, D. (2002). *Social relationships questionnaire.* Madison, WI: FAST National Training and Evaluation Center.

McDonald, L., & Moberg, D. (2002). Families and schools together. FAST strategies for increasing involvement of all parents in schools and preventing drug abuse. In W. Hansen, S. Giles, & M. Fearnow-Kenney (Eds.), *Improving prevention effectiveness* (pp. 235–250). Greensboro, NC: Tanglewood Research.

McDonald, L., Moberg, D., Brown, R., Rodriguez-Espiricueta, I., Flores, N., & Burke, M. (2006) After-school multi-family groups: A randomised controlled trial involving low-income, urban, Latino children. *Children and Schools*, *28*, 25–34.

McDonald, L. & Puniskis, M. (2013). *FASTUK Aggregate Evaluation Report.* London: FASTUK Middlesex University.

McDonald, L., & Sayger, T. (1998). Impact of a family and school based prevention program on protective factors for high risk youth: Issues in evaluation. *Drugs and Society*, *12*, 61–85.

MacFarlane (2002). *Multi-family groups in the treatment of severe psychiatric disorders.* New York: Guilford.

Marmot, M. (2010). *Strategic Review of Health Inequalities in England post-2010 (the Marmot Review).* London: Institute of Health Equity, University College. Available at www.ucl.ac.uk/gheg/marmotreview.

Miller, L., Southan-Gerow, M., & Allin, R., Jr. (2008). Who stays in treatment? Child and family predictors of youth client retention in a public mental health agency. *Child Youth Care Forum*, *37*, 153–170.

Minuchin, S. (1974). *Families and family therapy.* Cambridge, MA: Harvard University Press.

Minuchin, S., Montalvo, B., Guerney, B., Rosman, B., & Schumer F. (1967). *Families of the slums.* New York: Basic Books.

Moos, R., & Moos, B. (1981). *Family Environment Scale manual.* Palo Alto, CA: Consulting Psychologists Press.

Muir, J. A., Schwartz, S. J., & Szapocznik, J. (2004). A program of research with Hispanic and African American families: three decades of intervention development and testing influenced by the changing cultural context of Miami. *Journal of Marriage and Family Therapy*, *30*, 285–303.

Murry, V., & Brody, G. (2007). Partnering with community stakeholders: engaging rural African American families in basic research and the Strong African American Families preventive intervention program. *Journal of Marital and Family Therapy*, *3*, 271–285.

Okitikpi, T., & Aymer, C. (2003). Social work with African refugee children and families. *Child and Family Social Work*, *8*, 213–222.

Patterson, G., Reid, J., & Dishion, T. (1992). *Antisocial boys: A social interactional approach.* (Vol. 4). Eugene, OR: Castalia.

Putnam, R. (1999). *Bowling alone: The disappearance of civic America.* Cambridge, MA: Harvard University Press.

Rutter, M. (2002). Resilience concepts and findings: Implications for family therapy. *Journal of Family Therapy*, *29*, 119–144.

Rutter, M. (2006). Stress, coping, and development: Some issues and some questions. *Journal of Child Psychology and Psychiatry*, *22*, 323–356.

Sandler, J. (2007). Community based practices: integrating dissemination theory with critical theory of power and justice. *American Journal of Community Psychology*, *4*, 272–289.

Scott, S., Knapp, M., Henderson, J., & Maughan, B. (2001). Financial cost of social exclusion: follow up study of antisocial children into adulthood. *British Medical Journal*, *323*, 191–194.

Sherer, M., Maddux, J., Mercandante, B., Prentice-Dunn, S., Jacobs, B., & Rogers, R. (1982). The Self-Efficacy scale: Construction and validation. *Psychological Reports*, *51*, 663–671.

Shoji, M., Haskins, A., Rangel, D., & Sorensen, K. (2014). The emergence of social capital in low-income Latino elementary schools. *Early Childhood Research Quarterly, 29*, 600–613.

Stuart, O. (2009). User participation in health care services. *Inequalities in Health and Social Care, 2*, 50–59.

Szreter, S., & Woolcock, A. (2004). Health by association? Social capital, social theory, and the political economy of public health. *International Journal of Epidemilogy, 33(4)*, 650–667.

Terrion, J. (2006). Building social capital in vulnerable families. *Youth & Society, 38*, 155–176.

Terrion, J., & Horgrebe, A. (2007). A Canadian experience with an intervention progamme for vulnerable families: Lessons for German social work and policy. *European Journal of Social Work, 10*, 401–416.

Truswell, D., & Bryant-Jefferies, R. (2010). Responding to the Delivering Race Equality (DRE) agenda in mental health services: National recommendations informed by local experiences. *Inequalities in Health and Social Care, 3*, 30–46.

UNODC (2010). Drug prevention: Compilation of recommended evidence based family skills. www.unodc.org/docs/youthnet/Compilation/10–50018_Ebook.pdf

Van der Linden, J., Drukker, M., Gunther, N., Feron, F., & Van Os, J. (2003). Children's mental health service use, neighbourhood socioeconomic deprivation, and social capital. *Social Psychiatry and Psychiatric Epidemiology, 38*, 507–514.

Wahler, R. (1980). The insular mother: Her problems in parent child treatment. *Journal of Applied Behavior Analysis, 13*, 207–219.

Webster-Stratton, C., Reid, M., & Hammond, M. (2004). Treating children with early-onset conduct problems: intervention outcomes for parent, child, and teacher training. *Journal of Clinical Child and Adolescent Psychology, 33*, 105–124.

Werner, E., & Smith, R. (1982). *Vulnerable but invincible: A longitudinal study of resilient children and youth*. New York: McGraw-Hill.

Wilkinson, R. (1997). *Unhealthy societies: The affliction of inequality*. London: Routledge.

Wilkinson, R., & Pickett, K. (2010). *The spirit level: Why equality is better for everyone*. London: Penguin Books.

Williams, C., & Soydon, H. (2005). When and how does ethnicity matter? A cross-national study of social workers response to ethnicity in child protection cases. *British Journal of Social Work, 35*, 901–920.

17

THE PARENTS MATTER! AND FAMILIES MATTER! PROGRAMS

Kim S. Miller

Learning Goals

After reading this chapter, the reader will be able to:

1. Describe the Families Matter! Program, its theoretical basis, history and evidence base.
2. Identify factors that make it possible for FMP to operate successfully at scale while maintaining high levels of quality, fidelity, contextual relevance, and community acceptance.
3. Describe the program goals and objectives and the curriculum for low-literacy learners that supports these.

Introduction

Many parents and caregivers need support both to effectively protect and guide their children as they navigate adolescence, and also to define and communicate their values and expectations about sexual behavior. The Families Matter! Program (FMP) is an evidence-based intervention for parents and caregivers of 9–12-year-olds in sub-Saharan Africa that promotes positive parenting practices and effective parent–child communication about sex-related issues and sexual risk reduction (Miller et al., 2013). FMP was adapted for use in Kenya from a U.S. evidence-based intervention in 2003–2004. The U.S. Centers for Disease Control and Prevention (CDC) now provide technical support for its implementation in eight African countries, where it has been delivered to over 400,000 families.

Program Overview

The goal of FMP is the reduction of sexual risk behaviors among adolescents, including delayed onset of sexual debut. FMP pursues this goal by giving parents the tools they need to protect and guide their children by enhancing their parenting and communication skills. FMP is a community-based, group-level intervention that is delivered over six consecutive sessions lasting approximately three hours apiece. Each session builds upon the foundation laid in the previous session.

The intervention curriculum focuses on raising awareness about the sexual risks teens face today and encouraging general parenting practices that increase the likelihood that children will not engage in risky sexual behaviors. Parenting skills and practices, including parental monitoring, positive reinforcement, and the building of a strong parent–child relationship, are addressed. The program also strives to help parents overcome common parent–child communication barriers and improve parents' ability to effectively communicate with their children about sexuality and sexual risk reduction. Recent enhancements to the program address the difficult issues of child sexual abuse (CSA) and gender-based violence (GBV) through culturally acceptable content, highlighting the key role parents can play in protecting their children from CSA and GBV.

Theoretical Foundations and History and Evidence-based Research and Evaluation

The conceptual framework that guides FMP is based on a collection of social and behavioral theories widely employed in explaining the role of parenting in child socialization and in explaining and predicting adolescent sexual risk behavior. FMP is primarily grounded in four theories which have received extensive empirical support: social learning theory (Bandura, 1975), especially as it relates to parenting (see Kotchick, Shaffer, Dorsey, & Forehand, 2004); problem behavior theory (Jessor & Jessor, 1977); the theory of reasoned action (Fishbein & Ajzen, 1975); and social cognitive theory (Bandura, 1986). These theories have been tested in hundreds of research studies and often form the basis of programs which target adolescent sexual risk behavior directly. FMP extends previous research by applying these theories to a program involving the parents of young adolescents, rather than adolescents themselves. FMP is predicated on the hypothesis that reductions in adolescent sexual risk behavior will result from changes in parenting behaviors and family environment that have been found to relate to several constructs which are important determinants of adolescent behavior.

Social learning theory emphasizes the role of external reinforcement, expectations, self-efficacy, and behavioral outcomes in the learning, performance, and maintenance of behavior (Bandura, 1975). With its focus on positive reinforcement, modeling, and practice, social learning theory forms the foundation of most behavioral interventions designed to reduce or prevent child behavior problems across several domains (Kotchick et al., 2004). FMP uses the principles of social learning theory (e.g., reinforcement, modeling) and the format of parent training interventions (e.g., didactic presentation, practice) to deliver the intervention to parents with the goal of preventing a problem behavior (i.e., sexual risk behavior) before it happens. Specifically, parents are encouraged to provide supportive environments, positively reinforce competence-promoting (and thus risk-reducing) behavior, and structure or monitor children's environments so that exposure to problem or "risk" models is limited. It should be noted that the parent-training approach is not new in public health; drug, alcohol, and tobacco prevention programs have employed this methodology successfully for many years (Elmquist, 1995; Bauman et. al, 2002). Efforts in the parent training field have focused on using this model to prevent high-risk behaviors successfully (Conduct Problems Prevention Research Group, 2002). FMP adds to this body of research by applying the parent training model to the prevention of adolescent sexual risk behavior and its consequences.

Additionally, the premise of FMP is based, in part, on problem behavior theory (Jessor & Jessor, 1977; Jessor, Donovan, & Costa, 1991). According to problem behavior theory, adolescent sexual risk behavior is part of a constellation of risky or problematic behaviors, all of which are the product of an interaction between the environment and the adolescent's psychological risk or resource factors, such as motivation, expectations, and self-esteem. According to this model, reducing HIV risk behavior must include efforts to enhance general competencies, such as school achievement and positive interpersonal relationships, as well as mobilize the family as a social context which promotes sexual health and safety. Thus FMP seeks to bolster pre-adolescent and adolescent perceived competence by providing parents with the skills to appropriately reinforce positive behavior and structure the social environment so as to reduce opportunities for engaging in problem behaviors, such as substance use, that may promote sexual risk-taking.

According to the theory of reasoned action (Fishbein & Ajzen, 1975), behavior is a function of behavioral intentions, although many factors may interfere with the intention-to-behavior relationship. Behavioral intentions are, in turn, a function of two types of cognition: attitudes toward the behavior and perceived social norms. Intervention efforts based on the theory of reasoned action seek to impact upon an adolescent's intentions and behavior by attempting to change and/or add to the beliefs which comprise the adolescent's attitudes and norms. The FMP intervention attempts to modify adolescent attitudes and norms by providing parents with the tools they need to communicate their own attitudes and expectations regarding sexual behavior, in the hope that their children will incorporate those expectations into their own attitudes and intentions. Additionally, FMP seeks to promote more positive attitudes and expectations among parents toward discussing sexuality with their children by providing useful communication strategies and increasing their confidence in their ability to engage their children in effective dialogues about sexual issues.

In contrast to the focus on attitudes, values, and beliefs prominent in the theory of reasoned action, the most important construct in Bandura's (1986) social cognitive approach is an individual's perceived self-efficacy with regard to performing a behavior. Self-efficacy reflects one's actual ability to perform a specific behavior as well as one's confidence in one's ability to perform that behavior. Interventions based on the social cognitive approach often aim to increase adolescents' self-efficacy for refusal of sexual intercourse and for condom or contraceptive negotiation and use. This is typically accomplished by increasing adolescents' skills and confidence in their abilities around refusal and condom or contraceptive use. FMP applies the social cognitive model to both adolescent and parent behavior: for adolescents, FMP seeks to increase self-efficacy by promoting open and well-informed dialogue between parents and children about sexual risk reduction strategies; for parents, FMP directly targets their self-efficacy for communicating with their children about sexual topics.

FMP was adapted from the U.S. evidence-based intervention, the *Parents Matter! Program* (PMP) (Miller et al., 2011). PMP was developed based on research conducted on the parenting practices and parent–child communication patterns of African American families in the USA, which highlighted the critical role of parents in prevention of adolescent sexual risk. A randomized controlled trial of PMP found that parents participating in the enhanced intervention, relative to the control, demonstrated higher levels of parent–preadolescent sexual communication and comfort with and responsiveness to sex-related questions (Forehand et al., 2007). Using a systematic adaptation process, PMP was adapted for use in Kenya in 2003–2004 and renamed the *Families Matter! Program* (Poulsen et al., 2010).

From 2004–2006, an outcome evaluation of FMP was conducted using a pre–post intervention design. Evaluation data were collected from 375 parents and their children at baseline and one year post-intervention. The intervention's effect was measured on six composite scores reported separately by parents and their children, comprising parenting (monitoring, positive reinforcement, relationship) and parent–child communication (sexuality education, sexual risk, communication responsiveness) variables. Evaluation results showed the adapted evidence-based parenting program retained its effectiveness, successfully increasing parenting skills and parent–child communication about sexuality and sexual risk reduction (Vandenhoudt et al., 2010). Based on the positive results in Kenya, countries across sub-Saharan Africa have requested the Families Matter! Program. Since 2008, FMP has been conducted in eight countries: Kenya, Tanzania, Cote d'Ivoire, South Africa, Zambia, Botswana, Mozambique and Namibia. Over 400,000 families in rural, semi-urban, and urban communities have participated in the intervention, which has been translated into 16 languages. FMP is well received in partner countries, by officials at the Ministries of Health, by implementing organizations, and by the participants themselves. Partners collect continuous process monitoring data which show high levels of participation and retention—on average over 90 percent of participants complete all FMP intervention sessions.

Needs Assessment and Target Audience

The first step of the FMP implementation process is to conduct formative work including a community needs assessment (CNA) to ensure there is a need and desire for FMP in the chosen communities. A CNA or similar activity is particularly needed during this initial stage in resource-constrained settings (Poulsen et al., 2010), as involving local stakeholders and building community support for the intervention is an important step towards creating sustained interest and ownership of an intervention in communities facing multiple health concerns (González Castro, Barrera, & Martinez, 2004). Furthermore, findings from a CNA allow the implementing organization to identify risk behaviors, structural and environmental risks, and community norms and practices that may be important to integrate into the program during the adaptation process (Resnicow, Soler, Braithwaite, Ahluwalia, & Butler, 2000; Poulsen et al., 2010).

Program Goals and Objectives

The goal of FMP is the reduction of sexual risk behaviors among adolescents, including delayed onset of sexual debut. FMP pursues this goal by giving parents and other caregivers the knowledge, skills, comfort, and confidence to discuss sex-related issues with their children. FMP is unique in that it does not dictate what parents should say to their children, but instead guides them in defining the values and messages they want to convey. Session-by-session goals are outlined in Box 17.1.

Box 17.1 FMP Session-by-Session Goals

1: Introduction to FMP and Steps to Understanding Your Child

Session 1 Goals

To provide parents and caregivers with an understanding of the purpose and goals of the *Families Matter! Program.*

To increase parents' and caregivers' awareness of the situations their children face that may put them at risk and the important role they play in keeping their children safe and healthy.

To introduce parents and caregivers to the physical, emotional, and social changes their pre-adolescents are going through and the need to provide guidance and support to children during this important period.

2. Good Parenting Skills

Session 2 Goals

To help parents and caregivers understand that their children need and value their guidance and support during this difficult period of adolescence.

To provide parents and caregivers with information and strategies to protect and guide their children through this important period.

To help parents and caregivers practice general parenting skills that support their children and protect them from risky situations.

3. Parents' Role in Educating their Children about Sexuality

Session 3 Goals

To make parents and caregivers more aware of the need for them to be sex educators for their children.

To increase parents' and caregivers' understanding of the physical and reproductive changes their children will be going through during puberty and adolescence.

To help parents and caregivers to define their values about sex and to learn ways to communicate their values to their children.

To provide parents and caregivers with tools and strategies for communicating with their children about sex.

4. Information to Increase Comfort and Skills in Discussing Sex and Sexuality

Session 4 Goals

To provide parents and caregivers with information on family planning, sexually transmitted infections (STIs), HIV, and AIDS and other sexual health issues.

To provide parents and caregivers with direct linkages to community health resources.

To increase parents' and caregivers' comfort and skills in discussing difficult sex-related issues with their children, including HIV stigma and disclosure.

5. Discussing Sexuality and Pressures Faced by Children

Session 5 Goals

To continue improving parents' and caregivers' comfort in discussing sex and sexuality with their child.

To give parents and caregivers an opportunity to work on their communication skills with their child.

To introduce parents and caregivers to pressures their children face from peers, partners, and adults, such as pressure to have sex, that could keep their children from reaching their life goals.

6. Understanding Child Sexual Abuse

Session 6 Goals

To raise parents' and caregivers' awareness about child sexual abuse.

To increase parents' and caregivers' understanding of their role in preventing child sexual abuse.

To increase parents' and caregivers' awareness of their role in protecting and supporting their children when responding to child sexual abuse.

Curriculum and Other Program Issues

The intervention increases parental awareness and parenting skills through a series of six weekly three-hour sessions. The sessions focus on increasing parental awareness about the issues children face, improving parents' ability to communicate with their children about sex, and encouraging parenting practices that increase the likelihood that children will not engage in sexual risk behaviors. Parents are also asked to bring their child to a designated session in order to practice the communication skills learned during the intervention. The goal is that, upon completion of the program, parents have enhanced parenting skills to navigate their child's adolescence and will feel more competent and comfortable in addressing issues related to sex and sexuality with their children. FMP is delivered in a small group setting using two trained and certified facilitators per group (one male and one female) who share equal responsibility for delivering the curriculum.

FMP utilizes a mixture of structured learning experiences, discussion, audiotapes, role plays, and group exercises. In addition, a combination of verbal and visual instruction techniques is incorporated in the curriculum to meet auditory and visual learning preferences. A number of different strategies and learning methods are used during the six sessions. These include: group interaction activities such as proverb/poster discussions, large group discussions, brainstorming, role plays, songs and ice-breakers; audio presentations and follow-up discussion; mini-lectures; participant handouts; and homework assignments.

Recently, a number of updates have been made to the FMP curriculum in order to keep it as current, beneficial, and culturally attuned as possible. These enhancements include content specific to CSA and GBV, the addition of a sixth session which specifically addresses these issues, and the strengthening of direct linkages between FMP and the priority U.S. Government goals for HIV set during 2011 World AIDS Day events (Clinton, 2011).

Child Sexual Abuse and Other Forms of Gender-based Violence

CSA is globally pervasive, difficult to discuss, and associated with increased sexual risk-taking among youth. FMP has been identified as a valuable platform for addressing CSA because the program is widely accepted within communities and teaches parenting skills that closely map onto protective factors identified in previous studies on CSA. Integrating CSA into FMP provides an opportunity to increase parents' awareness of CSA and the role they can play in helping prevent it, and thereby to address sexual abuse as a risk factor for sexual risk-taking.

A new sixth session on understanding CSA has recently been added to the curriculum. In addition, content covering both CSA and GBV has been infused throughout the program. GBV focuses on unequal power relations between genders and on physical and sexual violence, usually against women, which increases vulnerability to HIV and other STIs. The enhanced FMP curriculum promotes reflection, dialogue, and action across the broad spectrum of GBV issues, from gender norms and the role they play in HIV-related risk to CSA. These difficult topics are addressed in culturally sensitive ways, seeking to promote lasting change and avoid confrontation that can be counterproductive.

FMP introduces parents to the risks for sexual violence that their children face, both as potential victims and potential perpetrators. The program's interactive curriculum incorporates skills-building role play exercises and audio resources which reflect the voices, perspectives, and everyday experiences of young Africans. Development of these resources and activities drew on stories written by young people across Africa for the Scenarios from Africa/Global Dialogues scriptwriting competitions (www.globaldialogues.org). Parents learn to recognize and respond to situations where their children are—or may be—being abused or where they may be at greater risk of abuse. Parents are encouraged to open a dialogue with their children about sex-related issues and personal safety; to use parenting skills, like monitoring and supervision, to protect their children; and to help their children recognize and, through role play, prepare for situations that may put them at risk. Recognizing that parents may not be able to stop an adult from forcing their child to have sex, the CSA-focused session addresses actions parents can take at the family and community level in the event that their child or a child in their community is sexually abused.

Cultural Implications

FMP is culturally and linguistically adapted for implementation in countries that request the program. The program is currently available in English, Spanish, French, Portuguese, Kiswahili, Setswana, Lozi, Tonga, isiXhosa, isiZulu, Afrikaans, Xitsonga, isiSwati, Sesotho, and Oshiwambo.

Professional Preparation and Training Issues

To strengthen capacity among implementing partners, we offer the following elements: (a) central technical assistance unit available for site visits, phone, or email communication/consultation; (b) tools to conduct a community needs assessment verifying that the program is wanted and needed by the community; (c) guided program adaptation workshops to ensure that FMP is adapted in a scientific and culturally appropriate way; (d) all curriculum materials needed for program delivery and implementation; (e) technical support materials for recruiting, training, certifying, and hiring qualified facilitators; (f) guidance documents to conduct pilot testing and monitoring activities; (g) process and outcome evaluation tools that directly assess the objectives of the evidence-based intervention; (h) a central reporting system to monitor program implementation and fidelity; (i) annual site visits to monitor quality assurance of program delivery; and (j) a feedback communication loop of lessons learned from country implementation efforts.

To prepare facilitators to deliver FMP with fidelity, we employ these key elements: (a) candidate recruitment through clearly delineated qualification requirements, interview, and selection procedures; (b) a theoretically based training portfolio with extensive knowledge- and skills-building components and practice, demonstration, and feedback sessions; (c) certification—training attendance does not sufficiently indicate command of skills and intervention concepts required to successfully facilitate FMP. Thus, only participants who meet key criteria (e.g., thorough understanding of FMP and importance of maintaining curriculum fidelity, demonstration of necessary facilitation skills) are certified and hired as facilitators; (d) mentorship—post-training practice, facilitator debriefs, and support and mentorship from program managers; (e) supervision—review of retention rates and challenges (via monitoring forms), at least one unannounced program manager site visit per wave, and annual site visits by CDC staff. This model has promoted low facilitator turnover, high recruitment and retention of FMP participants (indicative of quality program facilitation, as no participant incentives are offered), and high-fidelity delivery of FMP content (which is monitored through site visits). These characteristics set FMP apart from other HIV prevention evidence-based interventions and have sustained FMP's growth and success for the past 10 years, expanding from one country to eight and reaching nearly 500,000 families in sub-Saharan Africa.

Conclusion

FMP reaches parents with skills and resources they need to protect and guide their children as they navigate through the challenges of adolescence in contexts of high prevalence of HIV, unintended pregnancy, and gender-based violence. Community needs assessment, facilitator training and certification, and capacity strengthening of implementing partners allow it to operate successfully at scale while maintaining high levels of quality, fidelity, and community acceptance. Ongoing program enhancements and monitoring and evaluation help ensure it remains responsive to evolving needs and optimally effective.

Key Points

1. The Families Matter! Program (FMP) is an evidence-based intervention for parents and caregivers of 9–12-year-olds in sub-Saharan Africa that promotes positive parenting practices and effective parent–child communication about sex-related issues and sexual risk reduction.
2. Community needs assessment, facilitator training and certification, and capacity strengthening of implementing partners allow FMP to operate successfully at scale while maintaining high levels of quality, fidelity, contextual relevance, and community acceptance.
3. Ongoing program enhancements and monitoring and evaluation help ensure FMP remains responsive to evolving needs and optimally effective. Recent enhancements to the program address the difficult issues of child sexual abuse (CSA) and gender-based violence (GBV).

Discussion Questions

1. What is the Families Matter! Program?
2. Why is it important to promote parent–child communication about sexuality in sub-Saharan Africa today?
3. Why are parents particularly well placed to educate their children about sex and sexuality?
4. What are the main barriers to effective parent–child communication about sexuality? What tools do parents need in order to be able to communicate effectively with their children about sexuality?
5. According to the theoretical framework, what factors help adolescents avoid risky sexual behavior? What parenting practices help foster those factors?
6. Why do you think it is important for parents to define their values and expectations about sexual behavior?
7. Why is it important to address gender norms in a program about sexuality?
8. Why is it necessary to culturally adapt the program to different settings?
9. Why is a community needs assessment conducted prior to program implementation?
10. What pedagogical approaches does FMP use and why are these important?
11. What steps help ensure that FMP operates successfully at scale while maintaining high levels of quality, fidelity, and acceptance?
12. What program enhancements have recently been incorporated into FMP and why?
13. Why is it important to monitor and evaluate FMP on an ongoing basis?
14. If you were the parent of a 9–12-year-old child, what would you want your child to know about sexuality? What would you like to have known when you were that age?

Additional Resources

Suggested Reading

Miller, K., Lasswell, S., Riley, D., & Poulsen, M. (2013). Families matter! Presexual risk prevention intervention. *American Journal of Public Health, 103(11)*, e16–e20.

Miller, K., Lin, C., Poulsen, M., Fasula, A., Wyckoff, S., Forehand, R., Long, N., & Armistead, L. (2011). Enhancing HIV communication between parents and children: Efficacy of the Parents Matter! Program. *AIDS Education and Prevention, 23*, 550–563.

Poulsen, M., Vandenhoudt, H., Wyckoff, S., Obong'o, C., Ochura, J., Njika, G., Otwoma, N., & Miller, K. (2010). Cultural adaptation of a U.S. evidence-based parenting intervention for rural Western Kenya: From Parents Matter! to Families Matter! *AIDS Education and Prevention, 22*, 273–285.

Vandenhoudt, H., Miller, K., Ochura, J., Wyckoff, S., Obong'o, C., Otwoma, N., Poulsen, M., Menten, J., Marum, E., & Buvé, A. (2010). Evaluation of a U.S. evidence-based parenting intervention in rural Western Kenya: From Parents Matter! to Families Matter! *AIDS Education & Prevention, 22*, 328–343.

Websites

www.cdc.gov/globalaids/publications/fmp-2-pager-final-jan-2014.pdf
www.cdcnpin.org/parentsmatter/
http://hopeeducation.org/what-we-do/families-matter/
www.tmarc.or.tz/l/projects/families-matter/

References

Bandura, A. (1975). *Social learning theory*. Englewood Cliffs, N.J.: Prentice-Hall.

Bandura, A. (1986). *Social foundations of thought and action: A social cognitive theory*. Englewood Cliffs, NJ: Prentice-Hall.

Bauman, K., Ennett, S., Foshee, V., Pemberton, M., King, T., & Koch, G. (2002). Influence of a family program on adolescent smoking and drinking prevalence. *Prevention Science, 3*, 35–42.

Clinton, H. (2011). Remarks on "Creating an AIDS-Free Generation". Retrieved January 9, 2014, from www.state.gov/secretary/rm/2011/11/176810.htm

Conduct Problems Prevention Research Group. (2002). The implementation of the Fast Track Program: An example of a large-scale prevention science efficacy trial. *Journal of Abnormal Child Psychology, 30*, 1–17.

Elmquist, D. (1995). A systematic review of parent-oriented programs to prevent children's use of alcohol and other drugs. *Journal of Drug Education, 23*, 251–279.

Epstein, J., & Salinas, K. (1993). *School and family partnerships: Surveys and summaries.* Baltimore, MD: Johns Hopkins University, Center on Families, Communities, Schools and Children's Learning.

Fishbein, M., & Ajzen, I. (1975). *Belief, attitude, intention and behavior: An introduction to theory and research*. Reading, MA: Addison-Wesley.

González Castro, F., Barrera, M., Jr., & Martinez, C., Jr. (2004). The cultural adaptation of prevention interventions: Resolving tensions between fidelity and fit. *Prevention Science, 5*, 41–45.

Goodman, R. (1997). The Strengths and Difficulties Questionnaire: A research note. *Journal of Child Psychology and Psychiatry, 38*, 52–58.

Goodman, R., Meltzer, H. & Bailey, V. (1998). The Strengths and Difficulties Questionnaire: a pilot study on the validity of the self-report version. *European Child and Adolescent Psychiatry*, 7, 125–130.

Gresham, F., & Elliott, S. (1990). *Social Skills Rating System*. Circle Pines, MN: American Guidance Service.

Jessor, R., Donovan, J., & Costa, F. (1991). *Beyond adolescence: Problem behavior and young adult development*. New York: Cambridge University Press.

Jessor, R., & Jessor, S. (1977). *Problem behavior and psychosocial development: A longitudinal study of youth*. New York: Academic Press.

Kotchick, B., Shaffer, A., Dorsey, S., & Forehand, R. (2004). Parenting antisocial children and adolescents, in M. Hoghughi & N. Long (Eds.), *SAGE handbook of parenting*. Newbury Park, CA: Sage.

McDonald, L., & Billingham, S. (1992). *FAST orientation manual and elementary school FAST program workbook*. Madison, WI: FAST International.

McDonald, L., & Moberg, D. (2002). *Social relationships questionnaire*. Madison, WI: FAST National Training and Evaluation Center.

McDonald, L., & Moberg, D. (2002). Families and schools together. FAST strategies for increasing involvement of all parents in schools and preventing drug abuse. In W. Hansen, S. Giles, & M. Fearnow-Kenney (Eds.), *Improving prevention effectiveness* (pp. 235–250). Greensboro, NC: Tanglewood Research.

Miller, K., Lasswell, S., Riley, D., & Poulsen, M. (2013) Families Matter! Presexual risk prevention intervention. *American Journal of Public Health, 103(11)*, e16–e20.

Miller, K., Lin, C., Poulsen, M., Fasula, A., Wyckoff, S., Forehand, R., Long, N., & Armistead, L. (2011). Enhancing HIV communication between parents and children: Efficacy of the Parents Matter! Program. *AIDS Education and Prevention, 23*, 550–563.

Moos, R., & Moos, B. (1981). *Family Environment Scale manual*. Palo Alto, CA: Consulting Psychologists Press.

Poulsen, M. N., Vandenhoudt, H., Wyckoff, S., Obong'o, C., Ochura, J., Njika, G., Otwoma, N. J., & Miller, K. S. (2010). Cultural adaptation of a U.S. evidence-based parenting intervention for rural Western Kenya: From Parents Matter! to Families Matter! *AIDS Education and Prevention, 22*, 273–85.

Resnicow, K., Soler, R., Braithwaite, R., Ahluwalia, J., & Butler, J. (2000). Cultural sensitivity in substance use prevention. *Journal of Community Psychology, 28*, 271–290.

Sherer, M., Maddux, J., Mercandante, B., Prentice-Dunn, S., Jacobs, B., & Rogers, R. (1982). The Self-Efficacy scale: Construction and validation. *Psychological Reports, 51*, 663–671.

Vandenhoudt, H., Miller, K., Ochura, J., Wyckoff, S., Obong'o, C., Otwoma, N., Poulsen, M., Menten, J., Marum, E., & Buvé, A. (2010). Evaluation of a U.S. evidence-based parenting intervention in rural Western Kenya: from Parents Matter! to Families Matter! *AIDS Education & Prevention, 22*, 328–343.

18

STRENGTHENING FAMILIES PROGRAM

Karol L. Kumpfer, Cátia Magalhães, & Jeanie Ahearn Greene

Learning Goals

After reading this chapter, the reader will increase their knowledge of the following:

1. The SFP program history, different age and cultural versions, format or structure and content addressed.
2. The theoretical foundations and core elements of SFP and other evidence-based family interventions.
3. The family-focused evidence-based prevention programs, steps to successful cultural adaptations, research outcomes of SFP for different populations, and comparative effectiveness reviews that found SFP to be the most effective substance abuse prevention program for youth.
4. The staffing and training required plus other resources to implement SFP successfully.
5. The need for new directions in prevention and treatment, including digitally delivered programming to reduce costs and increase dissemination capability rapidly.

Introduction

The Strengthening Families Program (SFP) is a highly structured, evidence-based family skills training preventive intervention. SFP is effective because both parents and children participate in two-hour weekly family group sessions for 10–14 weeks. In the first hour, children and parents attend separate classes each led by one female and one male culturally competent group leader. Children learn social and emotion-regulation skills, peer resistance skills, problem solving, and effective communication, while parents learn parenting skills (e.g., attention and rewards, clear communication, family organization and weekly meetings, effective discipline, substance use education, problem solving, and limit setting (Kumpfer & Hansen, 2014). Both learn the importance of family play and togetherness time, effective family communications, family meetings to enhance or reduce stress and conflict, which they practice together in the second hour. Offering transportation, dinners, babysitting, incentives for attendance and participation, and a graduation party removes barriers and promotes recruitment and retention.

Theoretical Foundations and History

SFP was developed in 1982 by Dr. Karol Kumpfer, psychologist and professor at the University of Utah, as a 14-session selective prevention intervention for high-risk elementary school children of parents with substance use disorders (SUDs) on a National Institute on Drug Abuse (NIDA) research grant. The objective was to prevent drug abuse in children by improving parenting and nurturing skills in drug-abusing parents. The program significantly improved parenting, reduced family and children's risk factors, and increased protective factors and resilience for drug abuse (DeMarsh & Kumpfer, 1985; Kumpfer & DeMarsh, 1986). SFP has been shown effective in a wide variety of community settings (e.g., schools, mental health and addictions treatment, family and youth services, churches, public housing, refugee and homeless shelters, adult and youth corrections, and hospitals) and for many nationalities and ethnic groups (Kumpfer, Alvarado, Tait, & Turner, 2002; Kumpfer & Hansen, 2014).

Culturally specific versions of SFP were developed and evaluated in the 1990s on five separate phase-in studies for rural and urban African Americans, Pacific Islanders, Hispanics, and American Indians. They recorded positive results and improved recruitment and retention when culturally adapted and implemented with fidelity (Kumpfer, Alvarado, Smith & Bellamy, 2005). These newer versions addressed the needs not just of children of substance abusers, but also children of abusive, antisocial or mentally ill, and single parents often living in poverty.

A shorter seven-session junior high school-age version for universal prevention in schools, called SFP 10–14, was developed by Drs. Kumpfer and Molgaard on an NIDA grant to Iowa State University (Kumpfer, Molgaard, & Spoth, 1996). In two longitudinal studies lasting up to 10 years, SFP 10–14 was found more effective in reducing substance use initiation and use than *Preparing for the Drug-free Years* (now called *Guiding Good Choices*) and Botvin's *Life Skills Program* (Spoth, Redmond, Shin, & Azevedo, 2004). The SFP 10–14 version was adapted for African American youth in schools and called *Strong African American Families* (SAAF) by Dr. Gene Brody and associates in Georgia with an emphasis on HIV prevention. In a 10-year follow-up epigenetic study of gene–environment interaction, SAAF reduced by 50 percent diagnosed genetic diseases (e.g., substance abuse, depression, anxiety, and HIV) related to short alleles of the 5-HTTLPR serotonin gene or DRD4 7-repeat dopamine gene (Brody et al., 2012, 2013).

SAAF also reduced telomere length shortening and cytokines or inflammation levels (Brody, 2014).

In the mid-2000s, SFP 6–11 was revised to be culturally sensitive rather than specific. Versions for children ages 3–5 and 12–16 were developed. SFP 12–16 has been especially successful in Canada, the Netherlands, Spain, and Ireland (Kumpfer, Xie, & O'Driscoll, 2012). Agencies have successfully added a second children's group and divided the family practice period to deliver more than one age variant at a time, for example with both SFP 3–5 and SFP 6–11 separate children's groups.

A 10- to 14-session DVD SFP 7–17 Years video version was developed by Dr. Kumpfer and Jaynie Brown. It was found effective for home or clinic use or as an adjunct to family groups in schools (Kumpfer & Brown, 2012), family services agencies, homeless shelters, refugee communities, and juvenile courts, and in limited trials has had slightly larger effect sizes compared with the regular 14-session SFP group versions. This DVD has sound-tracks in both English and Spanish. Several countries (e.g., China, France, and Austria) are considering creating cheaper language subtitles and using the MP3 format for delivery on smartphone apps, the web, or YouTube for no-cost delivery.

Translated and culturally adapted versions of the original 7- and 14-session, group-based SFP have been implemented in over 35 countries by local researchers (Kumpfer, Pinyuchon, de Melo, & Whiteside, 2008; Kumpfer, Magalhães & Xie, 2012; Kumpfer, Fenollar, & Jubani, 2013). Cultural adaptations by culturally sensitive group leaders are essential to fidelity in *every* SFP implementation. At the very least, content should be altered to suit local culture (i.e., incorporating local songs, music, foods, games, and stories). Cultural adaptations of SFP increase community engagement, recruitment, and retention by an average of about 40 percent.

The program conceptualizes adolescent drug use risk as a "family disease" based on genetic, epigenetic, biological, and environmental family risk factors. The theoretical rationale of SFP integrates intervention theories of **family systems theory** (Bowen, 1991) with **social learning/efficacy theory** (Bandura, 2001). These behavior change theories are targeted to the most critical risk/resilience factors found in Kumpfer and her colleagues' Structural Equations Model (SEM)-tested **Social Ecology Model**, which found that the pathway of family attachment, supervision, and communication of positive values and expectations was most protective of negative outcomes (Kumpfer, Alvarado, & Whiteside, 2003) particularly for girls (Kumpfer, 2014). SFP is also based on the Kumpfer (1999) **Resilience Framework** stressing dreams, goals, and purpose in life in promoting positive outcomes. The SFP teaches parents to use positive reinforcement (attention, praise) for increasing wanted behaviors and ignoring unwanted behaviors that are highly effective clinical methods developed by Dr. Patterson and associates in Oregon.

Needs Assessment and Target Audience

The one-year stratified cluster needs assessment conducted prior to developing the original SFP 6–11 identified significant differences in a convenience sample of drug abusers in treatment with children aged 6 to 11 years compared with large samples of both normal and demographically matched non-drug-abusing families (Kumpfer & DeMarsh, 1986). By comparison, drug-abusing parents were higher in family conflict, spent half as much time with their children, used inconsistent and abusive discipline, offered little praise for good behavior, and had unrealistic developmental expectations. They did not praise new skills because their children "should" have had those skills two years earlier. They did little to promote parent–child attachment and provided little guidance, supervision, or monitoring. Oddly, parents were highly enmeshed with each other, but not with their children—later explained as co-dependency.

SFP has been tested successfully in many types of families and settings (mentioned earlier) to prevent a wide range of undesirable adolescent outcomes including alcohol and drug use, depression/anxiety, violence and aggression, delinquency, early sexuality and HIV risk, and school and job failure. To reduce obesity and diabetes, SFP was successfully tested with Pacific Islanders using an SFP physical activity module prior to SFP sessions and nutrition education during meals. In large state dissemination trials, SFP reduced substance abuse in New Jersey, Virginia, DC, and Canada, and child maltreatment in Maine, North Carolina, Oklahoma, Iowa, and Kansas (Brook, McDonald, & Yan, 2012).

Program Goals and Objectives

SFP's goals are to reduce child maltreatment, substance abuse, delinquency, and school failure by training parents to improve their positive parenting, parental efficacy, and parental–child involvement. The family skills training sessions increase family bonding, strengths and resilience, family organization, and effective family communication and reduce family conflict. The children's skills training sessions improve concentration, social skills, conflict resolution, peer resistance skills, and reduce depression and overt and covert aggression. These objectives improve significantly by posttest and are causally related to the four long-term outcome goals as found in the Social Ecology Model (Kumpfer, Alvarado, & Whiteside, 2003).

Curriculum and Other Program Issues

SFP includes three one-hour classes: (a) a behavioral parent training (PT) class that teaches discipline, supervision, limit setting, and family management skills; (b) children's skills training class (CT) that teaches social and life skills (i.e., peer resistance, problem solving, communication, stress management, and anger control); and (c) a family skills training class that teaches family activities, communication, cohesion, planning and organization, and managing family conflict by providing practice opportunities for positive play, communication and family meetings, problem solving, and effective discipline to encourage non-punitive interaction. These classes are taught in consecutive weekly sessions, beginning with a meal followed by simultaneous parents' and children's classes, and ending with the joint family class, in 14 weeks for higher-risk families and 7 weeks for lower-risk general/universal population families. The new DVD SFP 7–17 version includes 20- to 30-minute sessions taught in 10 to 14 weeks depending on family risk level, and including downloadable handouts and home practice assignments.

The key to SFP's success is that both parents and children attend and participate together in the family sessions, as found in the first component RCT study (Kumpfer & DeMarsh, 1985) and when family sessions are removed except for graduations (Skärstrand, Larsson, & Andreasson, 2008). The whole family then knows and reminds each other what they are to work on together in their home practice sessions. Another key element used in most of the effective parenting programs is teaching non-directive play, called *Child's Game* or *Our Time*, for teens to increase parent–child attachment and bonding.

Core Essential Components of Family Interventions

A cost–benefit analysis conducted by Miller and Hendrie (2008) revealed that the most effective prevention programs were family programs that teach skills, rather than those that just educate participants on the dangers of substance abuse. Family skills training, including interactive training such as role playing, group discussion, and homework assignments, is more effective than reading and lecturing (Kumpfer & Alvarado, 2003). A Centers for Disease Control and Prevention (CDC) meta-analysis found that prevention programs including role plays, homework assignment, and family practice time were more successful in preventing child maltreatment (Kaminski, Valle, Filene, & Boyle, 2008). The following four content components were found to significantly predict larger effect size: Practicing with Own Child with Family Coach, Positive Interactions with Child, Emotional Communication, and Consistent Responding. The first two of these skills are beneficial because they improve the parent–child relationships, which subsequently improves behavior. In youth and children, social skills and emotion regulation skills best prevent delinquency (Kumpfer, Alvarado, & Whiteside, 2003). These skills create self-reinforcing pro-social behaviors that allow the child/adolescent to bond with positive adults, authority figures, and peers. Focusing on strengths and resilience, involving fathers, adapting the program to the family's needs and cultural or local realities, having the appropriate intervention dose, and providing incentives and transportation improve retention and also increase program success (Kumpfer & Alvarado, 2003).

Trainers

Careful staff selection is critical for a successful implementation of evidence-based programs (EBPs) (Turner & Sanders, 2006; Kumpfer et al., 2008). Quality training increases practitioners' willingness to implement EBPs and improves fidelity. Therapist characteristics (e.g., warmth, genuineness, and empathy) are linked with higher levels of engagement and positive treatment outcomes (Truax & Carkhuff, 1967). Prevention facilitator characteristics have rarely been studied; however, SFP researchers (Kumpfer, Park, Magalhães, Amer, & Orte, in preparation) found that effective facilitators are both warm and welcoming and committed to client change results. They are on time, well prepared, and communicate high expectations for behavior change and home practice completion including family meetings, chore charts, and Child's Game. SFP facilitators who accept cognitive behavioral skills training principles have experience in running groups, understand the importance of fidelity to the SFP model, and believe in the effectiveness of SFP and convey this enthusiasm to the families, which is more effective in recruiting and retaining families and getting better results. "True believers" in SFP make the best facilitators. For best results, facilitators should be ethnically and linguistically matched to the target population and culturally competent (Webster-Stratton, 2007; Kumpfer et al., 2008; Kumpfer, Magalhães, & Xie, 2012). Clinical supervisors should meet with SFP group leaders immediately after sessions to debrief and to review weekly the program and family's progress.

Evidence-based Research and Evaluation

Effectiveness studies of SFP

SFP has a long history of substantial research demonstrating its effectiveness with numerous ages of children and ethnic populations. While originally developed and tested from 1982 to 1986 on an NIDA four-group randomized component condition control trial (RCT) with 288 families as a *selective* prevention program for 6- to 12-year-old children of substance abusers, the *universal* prevention school- and community-based version has been found in 12 RCTs to be effective in reducing multiple risk factors and preventing adolescent substance use and other adolescent problem behaviors (Spoth et al., 2000, 2004; Kumpfer, Alvarado, Tait, & Turner, 2002; Gottfredson et al., 2006; Brody, 2012, 2013).

The initial NIDA-funded experimental study used a component analysis design to compare outcomes for four conditions: parent training alone, parent training plus child skills training, parent and child training plus family skills, and a no-treatment control condition. The outcome assessments included highly reliable and valid standardized measures assessing parenting skills (discipline, positive communication, parenting efficacy and confidence, parental involvement) and parents' stress, depression, and drug use; family environment (cohesion, conflict, organization, communication); and child behavior outcomes (drug use, internalizing and externalizing behaviors, social skills, and grades). Each program component resulted in significant changes in the targeted risk factors (and there were limited crossover effects), but overall, the program containing all three modules worked best in reducing the most risk factors and reducing substance use (DeMarsh & Kumpfer, 1985; Kumpfer & DeMarsh, 1986).

An independent quasi-experimental pre- and posttest study (Harrison, Boyle, & Farley, 1999) also showed positive program effects with a large sample size of 421 parents and 703 high-risk youth. At immediate posttest, youth reported fewer behavior problems and families indicated more cohesion and less conflict compared with a comparison program. A five-year follow-up study using family interview data with experimentally treated families showed that parents reinforced the continued use of skills learned during training, reported improved family relations, and a high percentage (33 percent) of the families still held weekly family meetings and 58 percent monthly family meetings to communicate better and plan fun family activities.

Considerable effectiveness research in many states and counties finds SFP to be very robust even when implemented on a large scale. A statewide dissemination study with 1,600 high-risk families in New Jersey of the four age versions of SFP (3–5, 6–11, 10–14, and 12–16 years) in 75 different community agencies found SFP 6–11 produced the greatest effect sizes (Kumpfer, Greene, Allen, & Miceli, 2010). The effect sizes were larger compared with prior SFP clinical RCT outcomes, possibly because of employing seasoned prevention specialists versus graduate students often used in RCTs. Also, excellent training workshops and online and phone supervision by the program developers possibly enhanced the effect sizes.

An RCT of SFP 6–11 in two Utah school districts compared with an 88-session teacher-delivered youth skills training program (I Can Problem Solve) found that those schools randomly assigned to access both programs had the best outcomes, with almost additive effect sizes of each of the individual programs. SFP 6–11 outcomes did improve over the five-year follow-up, while the results for the youth-only program decreased over time (Kumpfer, Alvarado, Tait, & Turner, 2002).

In the mid-1990s the original developer, Drs. Karol Kumpfer and Virginia Molgaard, developed a shorter seven-session SFP for universal families recruited through schools in Iowa. This program, called Iowa SFP (ISFP) and now SFP 10–14 Years, was tested in a five-year NIDA RCT in 20 counties and found to be very effective in reducing substance abuse. Ten-year follow-ups of ISFP found large reductions in mental health problems (depression, social anxiety, phobias, and personality disorders), delinquency, and substance abuse with no methamphetamine use compared with 3.2 percent users in the no-treatment schools (Spoth, Clair, Shin, & Redmond, 2006).

A UN Office of Drugs and Crime review found many youth-only EBP prevention programs are effective for boys but not for girls. Most family-based EBP interventions, however, did have positive results for both boys and girls (Kumpfer, 2014; Kumpfer & Magalhães, in press). A recent gender subgroup analysis of SFP (Kumpfer, 2014; Magalhães & Kumpfer, in press) of a large SFP normative database of over 4,000 families from agencies worldwide found the traditional 14-session SFP equally effective for girls and boys. For some risk factors, SFP was even more effective for girls than boys, despite lower base rates of risk factors, possibly because girls are more influenced by family relationship.

Culturally Adapted Versions

One critical core element in SFP is that *every* implementation is culturally and locally adapted by the implementing agency and facilitators, called group leaders. SFP has been culturally adapted for many different ethnic and cultural groups worldwide (Kumpfer, Alvarado, Smith, & Bellamy, 2002), and the program has been widely disseminated internationally (Kumpfer, Pinyuchon, de Melo, & Whiteside, 2008).

U.S. Ethnic Adaptations

Five 5-year phase-in studies, or one for each major U.S. ethnic population (e.g., urban and rural African Americans, Hispanics, Pacific Islanders, Asian and Native Americans), started with using the generic SFP version for two years while developing and implementing the cultural and local adaptations in the last two years. The culturally adapted SFP versions resulted in 40 percent better average recruitment and retention of families (Kumpfer, Alvarado, Smith, & Bellamy, 2002), but outcomes were not significantly different. The program developers expect local and cultural adaptations as a core component of fidelity to the model. Research examining cultural adaptations reinforces the need to maintain program fidelity while instituting "surface structure" adaptation to achieve cultural competence and improve recruitment and retention. At the very least, program format and delivery should be altered to suit local cultures (i.e., incorporating local songs, music, foods, games, and stories). The SFP developers stress that group leaders should closely adhere to the core content.

Steps to Cultural Adaptation

The cultural adaptation teams are encouraged to follow the steps to implementation and cultural adaptation found to produce the most effective outcomes, described in the recent UNODC publication (UNODC, 2009) and in journal publications (Kumpfer, Pinyucheon, de Melo, & Whiteside, 2008; Kumpfer, Magalhães, & Xie, 2012). These include: (a) conduct a local family needs assessment; (b) review

EBP family programs and select the best program for age, ethnicity, and risk level of families (e.g., universal, selective, or indicated prevention); (c) create a cultural adaptation team including family members and the original program developer; (d) translate into the local language; (e) implement at first "as is" with minimal cultural adaptation; (f) make gradual cultural changes based on what works (culturally appropriate language, stories, songs); (g) make continuous cultural adaptations with repeated implementations; (h) conduct annual pre- and posttest evaluations to determine whether the local cultural adaptations are making the program better or worse; (i) make adjustments by adding or dropping new cultural adaptations; and (j) disseminate to similar cultural groups if the outcome evaluations show it is as effective as the SFP norms.

A survey by Burkhart at ECDDMA (Burkhart, 2013) of implementers of SFP and other EBP substance abuse prevention programs in Europe found unanimous belief that SFP can be culturally adapted with excellent outcomes if implemented with fidelity and steps to cultural adaptations are followed. The involvement of consultants from the local population is essential for this success.

International SFP Cultural Adaptations

Multiple age and cultural adaptations of SFP have found it to be robust in producing positive outcomes when culturally adapted for new populations (Kumpfer, Pinyuchon, de Melo, & Whiteside, 2008). SFP is probably the most widely translated and culturally adapted family therapeutic intervention in the world. Dissemination by the UN Office of Drugs and Crime (UNODC) to developing countries in three regions of the world (Balkans, Central America, and Southeast Asia), the Pan American World Health Organization (PAWHO) in Latin American countries, the International Rescue Committee (IRC) for refugees, and many international governments has helped bring SFP to more than 35 countries. An RCT study funded by the Thai government found that if both mothers and fathers attend rather than only mothers, the outcomes were better (Pinyuchon, 2010).

Replications of SFP in RCTs and quasi-experimental studies in different countries (USA, Canada, Ireland, UK, Netherlands, Spain, Thailand, and Italy) with different cultural groups by independent evaluators have found SFP to be an effective program in reducing multiple risk factors for later alcohol and drug abuse, mental health problems, and delinquency by increasing family strengths and children's social competencies and improving parent's parenting skills (Kumpfer, Alvarado, Smith, & Bellamy, 2002). For a summary of outcomes from foreign studies see Kumpfer, Pinyuchon, de Melo, and Whiteside's work (2008).

Among these countries, 13 are in Europe, including 4 that have one to two years of pre–post test outcome results conducted independently by researchers at the University of the Balearic Islands in Spain (Orte, March, Ballester, &Touza, 2007), in the Netherlands at the Trimbos Institute, in Sweden at the Karolinski

Institute, and at Oxford Brook University in the UK (Allen, Coombes, & Foxcroft, 2007). These studies were all non-experimental or quasi-experimental designs, but their positive results suggest that SFP can be culturally adapted and replicated in other countries with positive results. Each of these studies with different cultural groups by independent evaluators have found SFP to be an effective program in reducing multiple risk factors for later alcohol and drug abuse, mental health problems, and delinquency by increasing family strengths and children's social competencies and improving parent's parenting skills (Kumpfer et al., 2002a; Kumpfer & Johnson, 2007; Orte et al., 2007). The Spanish results in particular have been excellent, with effect sizes slightly higher than the SFP norms.

Excellent results have also been found in other countries (Portugal, Ireland, Northern Ireland, Italy, France, Slovenia, and Austria) with semi-independent replications. These have all been quasi-experimental pre-and posttest designs and the agencies used the recommended SFP testing instruments allowing comparison to the country's SFP or international norms. In addition, Portugal and the Azores have implemented SFP 6–11 with excellent outcomes. Norway is implementing SFP 10–14 and 6–11 as has the UK. The first Asian country to conduct research on SFP was Thailand. The Thai government supported the cultural adaptation and dissemination of SFP 6–11. An RCT found having fathers also attend produced better results (Pinyuchon, 2010).

A multi-country, quasi-experimental evaluation of an Irish cultural adaptation for indicated prevention of youth probation in Ireland (Kumpfer, Xie, & O'Driscoll, 2012) produced Cohen's *d*-effect sizes 20 percent larger than the U.S. SFP norms, possibly because the families were so needy and alcohol use rates were higher at pretest. All 21 measured teen, parent, and family outcomes were significantly improved in the 288 families. A unique collaborative coalition recruitment and staffing model including probation services, local drugs task forces, schools, and Garda (i.e., police) produced sustainability and enhanced recruitment.

When not culturally adapted and implemented in high-crime and disorganized communities by primarily contracted staff, one NIDA RCT with 715 primarily high-risk African Americans in the Washington, DC region, still found good results but reduced effect sizes and recruitment and retention compared with other SFP RCTs (Gottfredson et al., 2006). Program modifications in format and length reduce fidelity. An unfortunate Swedish modification of the recommended seven-session SFP 10–14 Years format resulted in non-significant outcomes (Skärstrand, Larsson, & Andreasson, 2008). To save money after making expensive new videos, they eliminated all but two of the weekly family sessions and some of the parenting classes at night. Omitting meals, incentives for homework completion, and babysitting reduced parent attendance to only 33 percent of the families. School teachers offered a longer SFP with more drug education information to their full classroom of students, thus increasing the possibility of a "negative contagion effect" described earlier by Dishion in his *Adolescent*

Transitions Program when implementers are not skillful in maintaining control over the youth. This natural experiment demonstrated that a critical core component of SFP's success is bringing the family together to improve the family communications and relations by eating together, learning the same family skills, and playing games and role plays together to practice their interaction.

Comparative Effectiveness Reviews

Two meta-analyses of school-based alcohol prevention by the Cochrane Systematic Review at Oxford (Foxcroft, Ireland, Lister-Sharp, Lowe, & Breen, 2003; Foxcroft & Tsertsvadze, 2012) and one meta-analysis of non-school-based substance abuse prevention (Gates, McCambridge, Smith, & Foxcroft, 2006) concluded that SFP 10–14 Years is twice as effective in preventing alcohol and drug misuse as any program with at least two years of follow-up data. These positive SFP outcomes are based on eight independent replications in NIAAA/NIDA/NIMH/CSAP-funded RCT with up to 10 years of follow-ups (Kumpfer, Alvarado, Tait, & Turner, 2002; Spoth, Redmond, Shin, & Azevedo, 2004).

Cost–Benefit of SFP

Cost–benefit studies (Spoth, Guyll, & Day, 2002; Miller & Hendrie, 2008) noted a positive cost–benefit ratio of $9.60–11.00, which underestimated the total benefit to the family as they were based only on direct financial benefits to school districts in reducing truancy. Video-based in-home delivery of SFP holds considerable potential for improving cost–benefit ratios. However, by using a more efficient delivery system to effectively engage more families, the high cost of SFP at $1,000 per family can be considerably reduced to $4 per family for the DVD and handbook and about $100 if adding family coaching.

Miller and Hendrie (2008) also reported that no other substance abuse prevention program prevented as many adolescents from using substances as SFP. Their tables show that 18 percent of all youth participating in SFP will reduce or never initiate alcohol use compared with no-treatment youth and 15 percent for marijuana, 11 percent for other drugs, and even 7 percent for tobacco. The next most effective prevention program, *Adolescent Transitions Program* was also a family program that prevented 14 percent of youth from using alcohol and 12 percent from using tobacco. These percentages of youth prevented from using alcohol and drugs were higher than all other family-focused or youth-only prevention programs. For example, *Life Skills Training* (LST) prevented 1 percent of youth from using alcohol and 3 percent from using marijuana. The *All Stars* program was the most cost-beneficial youth-only program at $32 saved per dollar spent. Staff costs for delivering the program, however, were excluded from this calculation of cost and benefit. *All Stars* prevented 11 percent of youth from using alcohol and 6 percent from using tobacco or marijuana. Spoth and associates (2005) reported that at 22 years of age in a 10-year follow-up, lifetime diagnosed mental health problems (depression, anxiety, social phobias, and personality disorders) were reduced by 230–300 percent.

Professional Preparation and Training Issues

SFP group leaders are typically staff of community agencies and trained on-site in two-day training workshops by two certified SFP trainers. The contents of the training workshops cover the need for parenting programs and effective parenting or basically why Parenting is Prevention; the implementation needs, content, and staffing, resource needs; and SFP research results. In the afternoon, the participants are taught how to train families to implement special play called Child's Game or Our Time for adolescents, clear communications, effective discipline, and family meetings. The second day is spent with pairs of trainees delivering a preprepared lesson to a group of other participants role playing typical parents and youth. These role plays highlight group process issues that are then processed in brief discussions. These practice lessons are interspersed with discussions of recruitment and retention issues and solutions, cultural and local adaptations, group process, and other implementation issues. In addition to group leader intro and advanced trainings, site visits, quality and fidelity assessments, and outcome evaluations are offered by Ahearn Greene and Associates, sole authorized providers for North America. International evaluations and trainings are offered by Dr. Karol Kumpfer, the program developer at Alta Institute in Salt Lake City, Utah.

Conclusion

This chapter has reviewed the need for family interventions to improve developmental outcomes for high-risk children. It also reviewed the 30-year history of studies on SFP including mandated cultural adaptations and SFP results in many countries. The developers' major goal is to improve the happiness and quality of life of families worldwide. As described in this chapter, SFP is a tool for strengthening families to achieve this goal. Future worldwide dissemination of SFP and other family skills training programs could contribute greatly to improving outcomes for children and youth.

Key Points

1. Family interventions that combine parenting skills, children's social skills, and family bonding components appear to be the most effective.
2. The SFP is a parent, youth, and family skill-building curriculum designed to prevent substance abuse and other behavior problems in children and youth, strengthen parenting skills, and build family strengths.

3. Research findings show that SFP has one of the largest impacts in preventing alcohol and substance abuse and also is cost-effective.
4. It is important to follow steps to cultural, age, and local adaptations to increase program effectiveness.
5. Careful staff selection and training help with delivering a successful implementation of EBPs.

Discussion Questions

1. What is the SFP intervention and how does it engage parents?
2. What is the key element to the effectiveness of SFP?
3. Why is it important to culturally and locally adapt SFP implementation?
4. How is SFP indicative of evidence-based practices?

Additional Resources

USA and Canada SFP trainings, manuals on CDs, and evaluations are ordered from Ahearn Greene and Associates (AGA) in Washington, DC on forms downloadable on the SFP website at www.strengtheningfamiliesprogram.org. Other international trainings and evaluations are contracted from Dr. Kumpfer of the Alta Institute. The CDs include a master set of all manuals, parent and youth handbooks, and implementation manual with permanent license to copy course materials as needed for own agency use. The video SFP 7–17 DVDs are also ordered from the SFP website for $5 each. A DVD group curriculum is also available with a separate DVD to show video clips in the parent and child sessions.

Helpful Websites

Center for Substance Abuse Prevention (CSAP): www.prevention.samhsa.gov
National Institute on Drug Abuse: www.nida.nih.gov
OJJDP and CSAP's matrix and descriptions of EBP parenting interventions: www.strengtheningfamilies.org
Strengthening Families Program: www.strengtheningfamiliesprogram.org
UNODC Compilation of Evidence-based Family Skills Training Programs www.unodc.org/documents/prevention/family-compilation.pdf

References

Allen, D., Coombes, L., & Foxcroft, D. (2007). Cultural accommodation of the Strengthening Families Programme 10–14: UK Phase I study. *Health Education Research*, *22*, 547–560.

Bandura, A. (2001). Social cognitive theory: An agentic perspective. *Annual Review of Psychology*, *52*, 1–26.

Bowen, M. (1991). Alcoholism as viewed through family systems theory and family psychotherapy. *Family Dynamics Addiction Quarterly, 1*, 94–102.

Brody, G., Chen, Y., Kogan, S., Yu, T., Molgaard, V., DiClemente, R., & Wingood, G. (2012). Family-centered program to prevent substance use, conduct problems, and depressive symptoms in Black adolescents. *Pediatrics, 129*, 108–115.

Brody, G., Yu, T., Chen, E., Miller, G., Kogan, S., & Beach, S. (2013). Is resilience only skin deep? Rural African Americans' socioeconomic status-related risk and competence in preadolescence and psychological adjustment and allostatic load at age 19. *Psychological Science, 24*, 1285–1293.

Broning, S., Kumpfer, K., Kruse, K., Sack, P., Schaunig-Busch, I., Ruths, S., Moesgen, D., Pflug, E., Klein, M., & Thomasius, R. (2012). Selective prevention programs for children from substance-affected families: A comprehensive systematic review. *Journal of Substance Abuse Treatment, Prevention, and Policy*, 7, 23. Available online at http://link.springer.com/article/10.1186%2F1747–597X-7–23#page-1

Brook, J., McDonald, T., & Yan, Y. (2012). An analysis of the impact of the Strengthening Families Program on family reunification in child welfare. *Children and Youth Services Review, 34*, 691–695.

Burkhart, G. (2013). North American drug prevention programmes: Are they feasible in European cultures and contexts? European Monitoring Center for Drugs and Drug Addiction, ISBN/ISSN:1725–1767. Electronic Document.

DeMarsh, J., & Kumpfer. K. (1985). Family-oriented interventions for the prevention of chemical dependency in children and adolescence, *Journal of Children in Contemporary Society: Advances in Theory and Applied Research, 18(122)*, 117–151.

Foxcroft, D., Ireland, D., Lister-Sharp, D., Lowe, G., & Breen, R. (2003). Longer-term primary prevention for alcohol misuse in young people: A systematic review. *Addiction, 98*, 397–411.

Foxcroft, D., & Tsertsvadze, A. (2012). Universal alcohol misuse prevention programmes for children and adolescents: Cochrane systematic reviews. *Perspectives in Public Health, 132*, 128–134.

Gates, S., McCambridge, J., Smith, L. A., & Foxcroft, D. (2006). Interventions for prevention of drug use by young people delivered in non-school settings. *Cochrane Database of Systematic Reviews (1)*, CD005030.

Gottfredson, D., Kumpfer, K., Polizzi-Fox, D., Wilson, D., Puryear, V., Beatty, P., & Vilmenay, M. (2006). The Strengthening Washington D. C. Families Project: A randomized effectiveness trial of family-based prevention. *Prevention Science*, 7, 57–74.

Harrison, S., Boyle, S., & Farley, O. (1999). Evaluating the outcomes of a family-based intervention for troubled children: A pretest-posttest study. *Research on Social Work Practice, 9*, 640–655.

Kaminski, J., Valle, L., Filene, J., & Boyle, C. (2008). A meta-analytic review of components associated with parent training program effectiveness, *Journal of Abnormal Psychology, 36*, 567–589.

Kumpfer, K. (1991). How to get hard-to-reach parents involved in parenting programs, in Pines, D., Crute, D., & Rogers, E. (Eds.) *Parenting as prevention* (pp. 87–95). Rockville, MD: OSAP.

Kumpfer, K. (1999). Factors and processes contributing to resilience: The resilience framework, in M. Glantz & J. Johnson (Eds.) *Resilience and development: Positive life adapations.* New York: Kluwer Academic/Plenum.

Kumpfer, K. (2014). Family-based interventions for the prevention of substance abuse and other impulse control disorders in girls. Invited Spotlight Article, *ISRN Addiction*, Hindawi.

Kumpfer, K., & Alvarado, R. (2003). Family-strengthening approaches for the prevention of youth problem behaviors. *American Psychologist, 58*, 6–7.

Kumpfer, K., Alvarado, R., Smith, P., & Bellamy, N. (2002). Cultural sensitivity in universal family-based prevention interventions. *Prevention Science, 3(3)*, 241–244.

Kumpfer, K., Alvarado, R., Tait, C., & Turner, C. (2002). Effectiveness of school-based family and children's skills training of substance abuse prevention among 6–8 year old rural children, *Psychology of Addictive Behaviors, 16(4 Suppl.)*, S65–71.

Kumpfer, K. Alvarado, R., & Whiteside, H. (2003). Family-based interventions for substance abuse prevention. *Substance Use and Misuse, 38(11–13)*, 1759–1789.

Kumpfer, K., & Brown, J. (2012). New way to reach parents: A SFP DVD. Western States Substance Abuse Annual ATOD conference, Boise, ID. Sept. 22, 2012.

Kumpfer, K., & DeMarsh, J. (1986). Family environmental and genetic influences on children's future chemical dependency, in S. Ezekoye, K. Kumpfer, & W. Bukoski (Eds.) *Childhood and chemical abuse: Prevention and intervention*. New York: Haworth.

Kumpfer, K., Fenollar, J., & Jubani, C. (2013). An effective family skills-based intervention for the prevention of health problems in children of alcohol and drug-abusing parents, in *Pedagojia Social, Revisita Interuniversitarie, 21*, 85–108.

Kumpfer, K., Greene, J., Allen, K., & Miceli, F. (2010). Effectiveness outcomes of four age versions of the Strengthening Families Program in statewide field sites. *Group Dynamics: Theory, Research, and Practice, 14(3)*, 211–229.

Kumpfer K., & Hansen, W. (2014). Family based prevention programs, in L. Scheier & W. Hansen (Eds.) *Parenting and teen drug use* (pp. 166–192). New York: Oxford University Press.

Kumpfer, K., & Johnson, J. (2011). Enhancing positive outcomes for children of substance-abusing parents, in B. A. Johnson (Ed.) *Addiction medicine: Science and practice* (pp. 1307–1329). New York, NY: Springer Verlag.

Kumpfer, K., Magalhães, C., & Xie, J. (2012). Cultural adaptations of evidence-based family interventions to strengthen families and improve children's outcomes. *European Journal of Developmental Psychology, 9*, 104–116.

Kumpfer, K., Molgaard, V., & Spoth, R. (1996). The Strengthening Families Program for the prevention of delinquency and drug use, in R. Peters & R. McMahon (Eds.) *Preventing childhood disorders, substance abuse, and delinquency* (pp. 241–267). Thousand Oaks, CA: Sage,

Kumpfer, K., Park, M., Magalhães, C., Amer, J. & Orte, C. (in preparation). The impact of client satisfaction and quality of the facilitator on family intervention outcomes. *Journal of Health Education Research*.

Kumpfer, K., Pinyuchon, M., de Melo, A., & Whiteside, H. (2008). Cultural adaptation process for international dissemination of the Strengthening Families Program (SFP). *Evaluation and Health Professions, 33(2)*, 226–239.

Kumpfer, K., Xie, J., & O'Driscoll, R. (2012). Effectiveness of a culturally adapted Strengthening Families Program 12–16 Years for high risk Irish families. *Child and Youth Care Forum, 41*, 173–195.

Magalhães, C., & Kumpfer, K. (in press). Effectiveness of the Strengthening Families Program 6–11 Years among US Portuguese immigrant families and families in Portugal compared to SFP norms. *Journal of Child Services*.

Miller, T., & Hendrie, D. (2008). *Substance abuse prevention: Dollars and cents: A cost-benefit analysis;* Center for Substance Abuse Prevention (CSAP), SAMHSA. DHHS Pub. No. 07-4298, Rockville, MD.

Orte, C., March, M., Ballester, L., & Touza, C. (2007). Results of a family competence program adapted for Spanish drug abusing parents (2005–2006). Presentation at annual conference of the Society for Prevention Research, Washington, DC.

Pinyuchon, M. (2010). The effectiveness of father involvement in the Strengthening Thai Families Program. Paper at NIDA International Forum, Scottsdale, AZ, June 12, 2010.

Skärstrand, E., Larsson, J., & Andreasson, S. (2008). Cultural adaptation of the Strengthening Families Programme to a Swedish setting. *Health Education, 108*, 287–300.

Spoth, R., Clair, S., Shin, C., & Redmond, C. (2006). Long-term effects of universal preventive interventions on methamphetamine use among adolescents. *Archives of Pediatrics & Adolescent Medicine, 160*, 876–882.

Spoth, R., Guyll, M., & Day, S. (2002). Universal family-focused interventions in alcohol-use disorder prevention: Cost-effectiveness and cost-benefit analyses of two interventions. *Journal of Studies on Alcohol, 63*, 219–228.

Spoth, R., Redmond, C., Shin, C., & Azevedo, K. (2004). Brief family intervention effects on adolescent substance initiation: School-level growth curve analysis 6 years following baseline. *Journal of Consulting and Clinical Psychology, 72*, 535–542.

Spoth, R. L, Trudeau, L. S., Guyll, M., & Shin, C. (2012). Benefits of universal intervention effects on a youth protective shield 10 years after baseline. *Journal of Adolescent Health, 50(4)*, 414–417.

Spoth, R., Trudeau, L, Guyll, M., Shin, C., & Redmond, C. (2009). Universal intervention effects on substance use among young adults mediated by delayed adolescent substance initiation. *Consulting and Clinical Psychology, 77(4)*, 620–32.

Truax, C., & Carkhuff, R. (1967). *Towards effective counseling and psychotherapy*. Chicago, IL: Aldine.

United Nations Office on Drugs and Crime (UNODC, 2009). *Guide to implementing family skills training programs for drug abuse prevention*. Geneva: UN Publications.

United Nations Office on Drugs and Crime (UNODC, 2010). *Compilation of evidence-based family skills programmes*. United Nations Office of Drugs and Crime (UNODC), Vienna, Austria. Both UNODC monographs available online at www.unodc.org/unodc/en/drug-prevention-and-treatment/publications.html

Van Ryzin, M., Kumpfer, K., Falco, G. & Greenberg, M. (Eds.) (2015). *Family-centered prevention programs for children and adolescents: Theory, research, and large-scale dissemination*. New York: Academic Press.

19

NOBODY'S PERFECT PROGRAM

Deborah J. Kennett & Gail Chislett

Learning Goals

After reading this chapter, the reader will increase their understanding of the following:

1. The goals and objectives of the Nobody's Perfect Program.
2. The core values and key concepts of the program.
3. The curriculum and delivery of Nobody's Perfect.
4. The body of evidence supporting the program.

Introduction

The **Nobody's Perfect Parenting Program** helps parents of children up to five years of age, who have difficulty accessing resources or support in the community, to increase their parenting knowledge and skills, and promote the healthy development of their children. In short, it informs parents about the "whens", "whats", and "whys" of childhood (Public Health Agency of Canada—PHAC website: www.phac-aspc.gc.ca/hp-ps/dca-dea/parent/nobody-personne/index-eng.php). This chapter describes Nobody's Perfect's development and theoretical framework, objectives and values, target audience, and implementation, as well as the empirical evidence supporting its efficacy across Canada and in other parts of the world.

Theoretical Foundations and History

In the early 1980s, the Atlantic Office of the Health Promotion Directorate of Health and Welfare Canada (as it was then known) embarked on a joint health promotion venture with the Departments of Health of New Brunswick; Newfoundland and Labrador; Nova Scotia; and Prince Edward Island, and formed the Atlantic Regional Health Promotion Committee. Recognizing the importance of providing an effective community-based parenting program for parents with limited resources and young children (Strachan, 1988; VanderPlaat, 1989), this working committee invested five years in consultation, program development, and field-testing. The outcome was the *Nobody's Perfect Parenting Program* (i.e., Nobody's Perfect), which was implemented and evaluated between October 1986 and June 1987 (VanderPlaat, 1989), and was introduced nationally in 1987. Today, Nobody's Perfect is owned by the **Public Health Agency of Canada (PHAC)**, and coordinated nationally through the Division of Children, Seniors and Healthy Development. Nobody's Perfect has a well-established network across the country that is built upon partnerships with the provinces and territories, as well as with non-governmental organizations.

Nobody's Perfect can be considered an empowerment-oriented social intervention (VanderPlaat, 1998). The adult education approach provides the program's emancipatory underpinnings (encouraging the collective development of understanding based on experience, a sense of collective identity, mutual support, and the exploration of common need), and promotes individual empowerment, self-reflection, self-confidence, and coping skills. Thus, its core social education (examining one's own attitudes and behaviors, learning and developing skills), is combined with the transformative learning occurring at the individual level (Inglis, 1997; VanderPlaat, 1998).

Kropotkin's mutual aid theory appears to have influenced program development, with "mutual support" featured in objectives, facilitator guides (e.g., Strachan, 1988; Wood Catano, 2000), and findings of the original evaluation (VanderPlaat, 1989). As well, the program resonates with many theories informing parent education (Mann, 2008), such as andragogy, constructivism, humanistic person-centered learning and adult human development.

For a program developed in the early 1980s, Nobody's Perfect was a pioneer. Nobody's Perfect predates and is consistent with the *Ottawa Charter for Health Promotion* (World Health Organization et al., 1986; Health Canada, 1994). Furthermore, the theoretical health framework on which Nobody's Perfect is grounded bears a remarkable resemblance to current social determinants of health theory (Mikkonen & Raphael, 2010). In fact, the program's basic tenets (Atlantic Regional Health Promotion Committee, 1989), which may be based more on experience than theory, include: "Health problems must be viewed both in terms of individual and social factors: To be born poor is to face a greater likelihood of ill health; and . . . Income, cultural and social milieu, and the community in which we live largely determine the extent to which we are and can be concerned about or devote resources to child health" (p. 9). In addition, Nobody's Perfect seems to have been solidly based on the socio-ecological theory of Bronfenbrenner (1979) before it became widely established (Skrypnek & Charchun, 2009).

The adult education model; respect for parents' diversity, values and experience; social justice and power-sharing values; promotion of mutual support;

flexible, participant-centered approach; and the focus on positive parenting are likely responsible for Nobody's Perfect`s enduring popularity with parents, and to have influenced the development of many subsequent parenting programs.

Program Goals and Objectives

The goal of the NPP, as outlined by the Atlantic Health Promotion Directorate (VanderPlaat, 1989; Skrypnek & Charchun, 2009), is to improve participants' capabilities to maintain and promote the health of their young children, and remains the same today. The program objectives have been restated to some degree (Rootman et al., 1998; Wood Catano, 2000; Leskiw et al., 2002; Government of Canada, n.d.), with no apparent change in meaning. They are to: promote positive parenting; increase parents' understanding of children's health, safety, and behavior; help parents build on the skills they have and learn new ones; improve parents' self-esteem and coping skills; increase self-help and mutual support; bring parents in contact with community services and resources; and prevent family violence.

A core ideology of Nobody's Perfect is that the program is "participant-centred" (Wood Catano, 2000). The parent is at the heart of the program: acknowledged, accepted, valued, supported, listened to, and respected. The parent is also part of a mutual support network within the group, offering acceptance, peer support, encouragement, and friendly social interaction. Respect is a cornerstone of the program, including non-judgment and acceptance of diversity and differences in values and beliefs.

The program is **learner-centered** and **participant-driven**, not expert-driven. As such, Nobody's Perfect uses an adult education delivery model (Strachan, 1988; Atlantic Regional Health Promotion Committee, 1989; VanderPlaat, 1989; Wood Catano, 2000; Rodgers, 2006; Russell, 2006; Svensson, Barclay, & Cooke, 2008; Government of Canada, n.d.). Participants are self-directed and actively involved in their own learning, choosing topics relevant to them and setting personal goals. They reflect on, share, and build on their own knowledge and life-experience. Delivery involves cooperative learning (e.g., group discussions, small group work, problem-solving activities); uses practical materials; and provides opportunities for practice. Facilitators, not educators, conduct sessions. Participation in the program is voluntary. Such an approach is empowering to parents.

Another key concept is the use of "**experiential learning**" (Wood Catano, 2000). Nobody's Perfect "uses the experience of parents as a recognized and valued part of the knowledge base" (VanderPlaat, 1989, p. i). Nobody's Perfect does not tell parents what or how to do something. Instead, the program offers topic-related experiences which parents examine (noting all aspects of the experience to gain information and insight), consider what relates to them personally, and apply what is relevant to their own situation.

Needs Assessment and Target Audience

Nobody's Perfect is an education and support program for parents (male and female) of children from birth through to five years of age. The program is designed to meet the needs of parents who may be young; single; socially, geographically, or culturally isolated; or who may have a low income or a limited formal education (VanderPlaat, 1989; Wood Catano, 2000; Government of Canada, n.d.). As such, parents attending Nobody's Perfect may experience barriers to accessing community or web-based parenting programs (i.e., the inability to afford fees, transportation, child care, or Internet), or have a low literacy level or lack a support network to fall back on. Additionally, they may fear being negatively judged and think most programs are not relevant to them, for cultural reasons or simply because they are young.

Curriculum and Other Program Issues

Nobody's Perfect has no set program of study, however learning resources are provided to parents free of charge. The program is built around five books: Mind, Body, Safety, Behaviour, and Parents. The books are illustrated and easy to read. They are available in English and French, and have been translated into Spanish, Portuguese, Chinese, Vietnamese, Punjabi, Inuktitut, and Japanese. Revised parent books are expected to be available in 2015. "The books are intended to provide information to parents and to help cope with stresses and inevitable situations which arise in the course of parenting" (VanderPlaat, 1989, p. ii), and include topics such as health, safety, nutrition, child development, child behavior management (using non-physical forms of discipline), feelings, stress management, and healthy relationships. Moreover, parents decide what they want to learn at Nobody's Perfect based on their needs, by consensus. Using the Facilitator's Guide (Wood Catano, 2000), facilitators design and conduct sessions.

Professional Preparation and Training Issues

Provincial and Territorial Coordinators provide training and resources, in addition to coordinating the network of trainers and facilitators in their jurisdiction. Nobody's Perfect facilitator training takes place over four full days. The training provides the knowledge and skills necessary for parent recruitment and successful program delivery. A training manual (Wood Catano, 2000) is used (the fourth edition is expected to be released soon). Facilitators learn about the goals, principles, resources, and delivery of Nobody's Perfect, including the target audience, adult education methods, participant-centered delivery, experiential learning, and session planning. Community workers, family support workers, early childhood educators, and public health nurses are regularly trained. Because Nobody's Perfect does not follow an expert model, parents who have completed the program may train to become facilitators. Ongoing support and refresher courses are available for facilitators and trainers.

Cultural Implications

The simplicity and adaptability of Nobody's Perfect, as well as its participant-centered, empowering approach have contributed to the program being successfully implemented in a wide range of settings and circumstances. In Canada, the program may be found throughout the provinces and territories in urban and rural settings, homes, neighbourhoods, family resource centers, organizations, and First Nations communities. As well, there is growing international interest in Nobody's Perfect (e.g., in the Caribbean, South America, and Asia).

Implementing the Program

Nobody's Perfect is usually offered as a series of six to eight two-hour sessions held once a week; however, this can be modified to meet the needs of parents or the sponsoring organization(s). For example, the series can be expanded to 10–12 weeks, have three-hour sessions (Kennett & Chislett, 2012), or even be provided as full-day sessions over several weekends (Wood Catano, 2000). The program is offered free of charge, provided by a sponsoring organization, sometimes in partnership with other agencies, services, or facilities and volunteers. To make the program accessible, parenting books, transportation assistance, child care, and snacks are provided. The group meets in a community location. At completion, parents receive a certificate based on consistent attendance. One or two trained facilitators lead the group, using an interactive, fun, and empathetic approach. Cooperative learning strategies, reflection, role playing, and skill-building activities promote learning and build group cohesiveness. A participant-crafted "group agreement" guides group functioning. One-on-one *Nobody's Perfect* series are helpful for parents who are not ready or unable to attend a group.

Evidence-based Research and Evaluation

Evaluations of Nobody's Perfect have been ongoing across the Canadian provinces since the program's inception, to determine whether Nobody's Perfect achieves its aim. One of the first evaluations was completed by Rootman et al. (1998) in Ontario from six different geographical regions. The study interviewed parents recently completing the Nobody's Perfect program and parents (control group) who were about to complete the program, as well as Nobody's Perfect facilitators. For both parent groups, many were having challenges with their child at the time of the interview, with most Nobody's Perfect participants using the provided books and information received at their meetings, as well as the support of friends and other social resources. Nobody's Perfect parents in comparison with the control group also discussed being more aware of nutritional foods, spending more time with their children, showing less anger, being more patient, and spanking less. Although both groups knew that children need love and attention, Nobody's Perfect appeared to provide participants ideas for activities with their children, explanations as to why their children act the way they do, and ways for talking with their children and handling their behaviors. Facilitators thought Nobody's Perfect worked well for those parents able to admit that they had learning to do, open to change and new ideas, willing to share, comfortable in a group, and not in crisis.

Leskiw and associates' (2002) report on Nobody's Perfect Manitoba is another widely cited early study. Research methods included pre–post surveys, focus groups, and telephone and in-person interviews with Nobody's Perfect participants. Their findings revealed that participation in Nobody's Perfect changed ways in how parenting responsibilities are viewed, provided learning about being a parent, built parenting skills, and helped parents to become stronger and more confident as parents. The authors note that this progression occurred in small steps, at different times, and at different rates depending on the experiences and ability of the parent.

Considering more recent investigations, in Chislett and Kennett's (2007) study, participants from Peterborough, Ontario, completed demographic information, along with self-report measures assessing the types of interactions with their children, parent resourcefulness, knowledge and use of resources, parent competency, satisfaction, and self-efficacy, prior to the program, and again after the program, and at a two-month follow-up testing. Parents earning certificates demonstrated and maintained an increase in parenting resourcefulness, warm/positive parent–child interactions, sense of parenting competency and satisfaction, and use of community resources. The more sessions parents attended, the better their parenting resourcefulness and warm/positive parent–child interaction at program completion and at follow-up, and the less their angry and punitive parenting at follow-up. Moreover, parents who had attended other parenting programs before this one had higher parenting resourcefulness scores at entry, and attended more Nobody's Perfect sessions. They left the program with increased levels of parenting resourcefulness, better parent–child interactions, and more effective child management skills.

Given that Chislett and Kennett (2007) found that only 55 percent of the participants earned certificates, Kennett, Chislett, and Olver (2012) additionally wanted to determine whether parents not earning certificates possessed a low repertoire of general learned resourcefulness. Over the course of a lifetime, people develop to varying degrees the learned resourcefulness skills to self-regulate emotions and thoughts, and to facilitate change in behaviors. These skills include the use of positive self-instructions, problem-solving strategies, and the delay of immediate gratification in order to achieve emotional and psychological stability when various crises or disruptions become part of their lives (Rosenbaum,

1990, 2000). Higher learned resourcefulness, as measured by Rosenbaum's (1980) Self-Control Schedule (SCS), has been shown in past studies to predict higher attendance rates (Kennett, 1994; Kennett & Ackerman, 1995; Kennett, Stedwill, Berrill, & Young, 1996), and more positive behavioral outcomes in educational and other programs promoting personal control and achievement (Kennett & Campbell, 2004; Kennett, O'Hagan, & Cezer, 2008). Thus, along with the pre, post, and follow-up parenting measures, Kennett et al. (2012) included Rosenbaum's SCS.

Replicating their earlier study, Kennett et al. (2012) observed significant improvements over time for parenting satisfaction, knowledge and use of community resources, and parenting resourcefulness. Although participants in both samples attained comparable scores on the parenting inventories, and shared similar demographic features, a significantly higher percentage of the participants earned a certificate in the Kennett et al. study (83 percent versus 55 percent in the Chislett and Kennett study)—a finding they suggested could be attributed to a greater previous exposure to parenting programs (70 versus 58 percent). Nonetheless, for pretest scores and when parents not earning certificates were included, parents completing a higher percentage of Nobody's Perfect sessions were observed to have more education, higher parenting efficacy competency, and greater beliefs in their ability to overcome the stressors of being a parent. Thus, future studies need to determine to what extent education level and heightened parental confidence serve to promote better attendance.

With the inclusion of general resourcefulness, two additional hypotheses were proposed by Kennett et al. (2012). Namely, that parents having higher pretest learned resourcefulness scores would be more likely to earn a certificate and attend a higher percentage of sessions, and given Nobody's Perfect's experiential learning focus, increases in general learned resourcefulness would be seen over the course of the study. Although improvements in general resourcefulness were observed for those earning a certificate, pretest resourcefulness scores failed to predict program completion. The latter finding they explain may be due to the fact that, for many parents, participating in Nobody's Perfect was not entirely voluntary, as was the case in the past cited studies (e.g., Kennett, 1994), but, instead, they were advised by child welfare to attend.

Additionally, the Kennett et al. (2012) study, using Hake's (1998) gain factor, found that relative gain in one parenting variable was associated with relative gains in others. For example, parents showing greater relative gains in general resourcefulness had greater relative gains in parenting resourcefulness and parenting efficacy, and greater relative gains in knowledge about community resources associated with a greater relative gain in parenting effectiveness. More importantly, these observed relative gains were unrelated to most of the demographic features of the sample, suggesting that Nobody's Perfect helped even the most socially and economically disadvantaged parents.

Although the important gains observed in parenting resourcefulness better equip parents to deal with problematic child-rearing situations that will undoubtedly arise, and improvements in warm/positive parent–child interactions provide a protective factor against abuse in a child's life, Chislett and Kennett (2007) and Kennett et al. (2012) suggest several recommendations to improve Nobody's Perfect's outcomes. Namely, to have coverage of core topics to better improve parenting self-efficacy, and longer sessions to provide parents opportunities to practice situation-specific and effective child management strategies. Moreover, parents who attend parenting programs repeatedly are reasonably good at problem solving, know about community resources, and have good parent–child interactions. Longer sessions would allow them to share their experiences and knowledge with other parents.

Kennett and Chislett's (2012) study incorporated these recommendations, but this time with parents who were all clients of the child welfare system. Their enhanced Nobody's Perfect was composed of 12 three-hour weekly sessions, and participants were assigned homework to practice the skills learned and to showcase the strategies they used at subsequent meetings. To open communication channels and foster trust, each session ended with a focus group discussion on how they liked the session, whether it was helpful, and how it could be improved. Facilitators responded to concerns and followed suggestions as much as possible. All groups discussed positive communications, healthy relationships, and community resources, and chose at least eight other topics. More importantly, in this mixed-method design, in addition to the three series of inventories used in the Kennett et al. (2012) study, participants completed an exit focus group interview asking them what they liked and gained from the program. Facilitators also completed two questionnaires during each series, to monitor delivery and practitioner feedback at mid-program, and to determine their views of the "enhanced" series after the series ended.

Fifty-three percent of parents completed the program and earned a certificate, with non-completers more likely having less education. Nonetheless, 80 percent of participants attended at least 5, three-hour sessions, in spite of living in circumstances with multiple risks. For program completers, even though the clientele of the Kennett and Chislett (2012) study had at pretest substantially lower parenting resourcefulness and practices scores than clients of the regular Nobody's Perfect series, significant improvements were observed in knowledge and use of community resources, positive parenting interactions, and parenting resourcefulness, with gains in parenting competence and efficacy approaching significance. Some of the positive improvements over time were not observed until follow-up, rather than immediately at the end of the program, as expected. Moreover, taking into account parents' skill and belief level at the start of the program and examining the relative gains they made over the 12 weeks of the program using Hake's (1998) gain factor, even though relative gains in one parenting attribute were moderately to strongly associated with relative gains in other parenting attributes, there was a tendency for non-custodial parents, in comparison with custodial parents, to have greater relative gains in positive parenting practices and general resourcefulness, thus increasing their chances of being reinstated with their children.

According to Kennett and Chislett (2012), it was the exit focus group transcripts providing the richest data. There was nothing parents disliked about the content of the program, with some wishing the series was longer or wanting to take the program again. Parents not having custody of their children reported it was difficult for them to do homework and practice newly learned skills. But, more importantly, further analysis of the focus group structure also revealed that medium-sized groups having a blend of males and females, custodial and non-custodial parents, skill levels and life experiences, fared much better than extremely large groups of more than 15 people or small groups composed of predominantly severely challenged, non-custodial parents. Thus, when the group was mixed, even the most multi-stressed parent reaped great benefits from the program.

From the facilitators' perspective, there was overwhelming and unanimous support for the enhanced over the original version of the program. All facilitators indicated that the increased number of sessions and the longer session duration allowed for more repetition of the material, a sense of trust to develop, client involvement/input, more time to talk about "routine", and bonding among parents. Facilitators concurred that parents completing the homework came back to the group with a more positive outlook and ideas. One facilitator who had better success with homework compliance distributed prizes for its completion.

Kennett and Chislett (2012) attribute the popularity of this enhanced program chiefly to the weekly focus group sessions. Asking parents what they liked about the session, how it was helpful, and how it could be improved likely instilled a sense of care, trust, and personal agency, especially for those parents having a low written literacy level, and when their responses were reviewed and suggestions were followed in subsequent weeks. Second, the three-hour sessions were never rushed, and allowed parents to have more productive and interactive sessions. Third, more food was provided than in regular Nobody's Perfect programs, which was likely appreciated by exceptionally low-income parents. Attesting to the enhanced Nobody's Perfect's value, many clients were at a loss to see the program end.

Utilizing similar survey measures, as well as social support and parenting stress scales, Skrypnek and Charchun (2009) compared a non-equivalent wait list control group (consisting of parents waiting for a Nobody's Perfect program planned for the future) to Nobody's Perfect participants completing pre and post testing; and Nobody's Perfect participants completing pre, post, and follow-up testing, to determine what parental changes could be attributed to the program. Nobody's Perfect participants were drawn from programs housed across the provinces of British Columbia, Saskatchewan, Manitoba, and Newfoundland. A multiple number of key changes in parenting behaviors could be attributed to participation in Nobody's Perfect, as these changes were not observed for the control group. For example, effects of Nobody's Perfect that were maintained over time included the increased use of positive discipline strategies, decreased use of punitive strategies, and increased use in parent stress coping skills and problem solving, which continued to develop at follow-up. In contrast, the increase in frequency of positive parent–child interactions was observed to be a temporary effect and diminished over time. Effects that appeared to need time to develop were the use of active approaches to discipline and use of behavior modification strategies. All groups, including the control group, however, showed similar increases in parenting confidence, and knowledge about the community resources.

Skrypnek and Charchun (2009) found that Nobody's Perfect participants completing the program and taking part in focus groups, expressed positive cognitive (e.g., Nobody's Perfect increased their self-respect), behavioral (e.g., Nobody's Perfect taught them how to give their child choices), and emotional (e.g., Nobody's Perfect helped them to relate to their child on an emotional level) changes. Importantly, some remarked that they learned they were not alone in terms of their issues as a parent, and described the social support they received from each other. As noted in the Kennett and Chislett (2012) study, parents liked their facilitators, enjoyed activities, appreciated the provision of child care and food, and wanted the program to be longer. A poignant comment made by one parent was "children keep changing, and we have to keep up". Many of these parents, too, had participated in other parenting programs before Nobody's Perfect. In comparison they described Nobody's Perfect as more comprehensive, in-depth, and interactive, allowing for more opportunity to discuss the information being provided.

Facilitators also completed a series of questionnaires prior to the program, after each session, and after the final Nobody's Perfect session. They thought the group setting and interactive support from other parents was instrumental to the changes that occurred. Aside from the need for more adequate funding (a fundamental comment made in all the aforementioned studies interviewing facilitators), facilitators recommended they receive more intensive training, refresher courses, methods of networking with other facilitators, and more provincial and national coordination.

Nobody's Perfect has recently gone virtual with its delivery in Manitoba, using the **Families First Home Visitors (FFHV)** program (Paterson-Payne, 2013). In Paterson-Payne's study, parents were visited at their homes, where they did activities together, using the Nobody's Perfect books. But here, parents' questions and concerns were additionally documented in a book and were later shared with other families participating in this study for their input. In short, the book became a living forum for parents, whereby parents engaged in broader discussions with each other. Of the 10 parents participating in FFHV, 9 completed both the pre and post surveys modelled after Skrypnek and Charchun's (2009) evaluation. The most dramatic changes seen from this program included parents taking more time for themselves, using the social media to learn more about parenting and child development, decreasing their use of physical punishment and yelling at their children, and using more problem-solving strategies based on a child's developmental stage. All of the parents enjoyed the process of being involved with other parents, even though not being with them face-to-face, with most remarking on how they "felt normal" and not alone in their struggles.

Given the program's success at helping young and often marginalized parents in Canada, it has been adapted and incorporated in other countries (McLennan, Leon, Haffey, & Barker, 2009; Goto, Yabe, Sasaki, & Yasumura, 2010). Goto et al. (2010) describe that, in Japan, fathers are not as involved in the child's care as those in other countries. Mothers in Japan are also required to report their pregnancy and childbirth to a municipal office, and are invited to attend health checkups. Checkups not only assess the child's physical health, but also the mother's parenting, mood, self-efficacy, and depression. In Goto et al.'s study, mothers at risk for depression and low self-efficacy, or who responded negatively to parenting questions involving confidence, were invited to participate in Nobody's Perfect, which consisted of 5 two-hour group sessions scheduled approximately three weeks apart. Mothers participating in Nobody's Perfect (high-risk Nobody's Perfect participants) were compared to both non-risk non-participants and high-risk non-participants for changes in parenting confidence, mood, and self-efficacy between the 3–4-months and 9–10-months child health checkups. Mothers of the groups were similar in age, employment status, medical history, and their child had similar characteristics. The only group difference was that Nobody's Perfect mothers were more likely to be first-time mothers. Supporting the effectiveness of the program, mothers of the Nobody's Perfect group showed more positive changes in mood and self-efficacy (particularly social support efficacy) than the other two groups, with mothers attending all Nobody's Perfect sessions showing the most significant change in these measures. The majority of Nobody's Perfect participants highly agreed or agreed that following the program they had become better parents, found the lessons from class useful in parenting, and got out more often than before. Less endorsed were improvements with family relationships.

With a different focus, McLennan et al.'s (2009) paper describes how the Nobody's Perfect Parenting Program was exported to the Dominican Republic (DR). Although the efficacy of this adapted program still needs to be determined, much care was taken selecting the original elements of the program (e.g., encouraging active participation, emphasizing facilitation over didactic teaching, using experiential learning), as well as incorporating new topics that are relevant locally in their community (e.g., diarrhea prevention and treatment strategies). It was also decided to have a set content for their first offering of the eight-week Nobody's Perfect. More importantly, the DR team valued its collaboration with the Canadian team and believed that a substantial amount of additional time would have been required getting this program into place had this relationship between exporters and importers not existed.

Conclusion

Each year, Nobody's Perfect reaches 12,000 to 20,000 parents across Canada (PHAC brochure), and is becoming popular worldwide. Nobody's Perfect exhibits many of the attributes of effective parenting programs as outlined in the literature, having parent development or self-help as a primary goal (Layzer, Goodson, Bernstein, & Price, 2001). Nobody's Perfect, however, allows the flexibility to address wider problems that families experience (Moran, Ghate, & van der Merwe, 2004); and offers child care and transportation assistance to help overcome barriers to attendance (Forehand & Kotchick, 2002; Law, Plunkett, Taylor, & Gunning, 2009).

More importantly, empirical evidence validates the objectives of the Nobody's Perfect program, because studies show that parents completing the program are being more confident, resourceful, knowledgeable about parenting, and using healthier positive parenting practices in disciplining and managing their children. Studies also affirm that Nobody's Perfect participants are relieved to learn that their parenting struggles are not unique, express the desire to attend Nobody's Perfect more than once, reap more benefits with multiple exposures, and desire more series with longer sessions. Nobody's Perfect groups also work best when group members are mixed in terms of gender, age, education, and parenting capability. Facilitators identify the need for more funding, upgrades in training, refresher courses, peer support, and more provincial support and coordination.

In conclusion, Nobody's Perfect is a valuable program, and pivotal in the eyes of the participants. The growing international interest in Nobody's Perfect attests its success, as does its efficacy in meeting the needs of the most marginalized populations both in and outside of Canada.

Key Points

The Nobody's Perfect Parenting Program is:

1. for parents with few resources and children up to five.
2. learner-centered and uses a supportive adult education model.
3. participant-centered, experienced-based, and respectful.
4. voluntary, accessible, and free of charge.
5. evidence-based.

Discussion Questions

1. Why was the Nobody's Perfect Parenting Program developed and implemented across Canada?
2. What barriers and challenges could the target audience face when accessing resources and parenting programs?

3. How did theory and core values guide the design of the program?
4. What features of program delivery support the achievement of program objectives?
5. What evidence would you cite in support of the provision of Nobody's Perfect?

Additional Resources

Websites

One of the best supplementary resources for facilitators and parents is the Nobody's Perfect website, www.nobodysperfect.ca, developed and hosted by the province of Manitoba. This website has become a National Knowledge Sharing Forum for all Nobody's Perfect coordinators, trainers, and facilitators.

Equally helpful are the excellent downloadable Nobody's Perfect Fact Sheets for parents (Mind, Body, Safety, Behaviour, and Parents) developed by The BC Council for Families. These are found at http://bccf.ca/professionals/programs/nobodys-perfect and www.nobodysperfect.ca

Other commonly used supplemental resources are the developmental charts provided with each set of parent books: Fathers book and Feelings book.

References

Atlantic Regional Health Promotion Committee. (1989). *Nobody's Perfect administrative manual.* Ottawa, ON: Public Health Agency of Canada.

Bronfenbrenner, U. (1979). Contexts of child rearing: problems and prospects. *American Psychologist, 34,* 844–850.

Chislett, G., & Kennett, D. (2007). The effects of the Nobody's Perfect program on parenting resourcefulness and competency. *Journal of Child and Family Studies, 16,* 473–482.

Forehand, R., & Kotchick, B. (2002). Behavioral parent training: Current challenges and potential solutions. *Journal of Child and Family Studies, 11,* 377–384.

Goto, A., Yabe, J., Sasaki, H., & Yasumura, S. (2010). Short-term operational evaluation of a group-parenting program for Japanese mothers with poor psychological status: Adopting a Canadian program into the Asian public service setting. *Health Care for Women International, 31,* 636–651.

Government of Canada (n.d.). Canadian Best Practises Portal: Nobody's Perfect. Retrieved from cbpp-pcpe.phac-aspc.gc.ca/~cbpp/public/wp-content/themes/wet-boew306/print-interventions.php?pID=2630&lang=en

Hake, R. (1998). Interactive-engagement versus traditional methods: A six-thousand student survey of mechanics test data for introductory physics courses. *American Journal of Physics, 66,* 64–74.

Health Canada (1994). *Nobody's Perfect's Health Canada National Strategic Plan.* Working document. Ottawa, ON: Health Canada.

Inglis, T. (1997). Empowerment and emancipation. *Adult Education Quarterly, 48,* 3–17.

Kennett, D. (1994). Academic self-management counseling: Preliminary evidence for the importance of learned resourcefulness on program success. *Studies in Higher Education, 19*, 295–307.

Kennett, D., & Ackerman, M. (1995). Importance of learned resourcefulness to weight loss and early success during maintenance: Preliminary evidence. *Patient Education and Counseling, 25*, 197–203.

Kennett, D., & Campbell, K. (2004). Women with life controlling issues: The importance of learned resourcefulness scores (pp. 14–15), in *Showcase 2004: Trent University's Institute for Health Studies*. Trent, ON: James Publishing.

Kennett, D., & Chislett, G. (2012). The benefits of an enhanced Nobody's Perfect Parenting Program for child welfare clients including non-custodial parents. *Children and Youth Services Review, 34*, 2081–2087.

Kennett, D., Chislett, G., & Olver, A. (2012). A reappraisal of the Nobody's Perfect program. *Journal of Child and Family Studies, 21*, 228–236.

Kennett, D., O'Hagan, F., & Cezer, D. (2008). Learned resourcefulness and the long-term benefits of a chronic pain program. *Journal of Mixed Methods Research, 2*, 317–339.

Kennett, D., Stedwill, A., Berrill, D., & Young, A. (1996). Co-operative learning in a university setting: Evidence for the importance of learned resourcefulness. *Studies in Higher Education, 21*, 177–187.

Law, J., Plunkett, C., Taylor, J., & Gunning, M. (2009). Developing policy in the provision of parenting programmes: Integrating a review of reviews with the perspectives of both parents and professionals. *Child: Care, Health and Development, 35*, 302–312.

Layzer, J., Goodson, B., Bernstein, L, & Price, C. (2001). *National evaluation of family support programs. Volume A: The meta-analysis. Final report.* Cambridge, MA: Abt Associates. Retrieved from www.abtassociates.com/reports/NEFSP-VolA.pdf.

Leskiw & Associates. (2002). *Nobody's Perfect Manitoba outcome evaluation. Highlights of the final report.* Prepared for the Manitoba Nobody's Perfect Advisory Committee. Winnipeg, Manitoba. Retrieved from www.youville.ca/_uploads/PageContent/documents/Highlights%20of%20the%20Final%20Report%202002.pdf

Mann, B. (2008). *What works for whom? Promising practices in parenting education.* Canadian Association of Family Resource Programs (FRP Canada). Retrieved from www.frp.ca/index.cfm?fuseaction=page.viewpage&pageid=932

McLennan, J., Leon, T., Haffey, S., & Barker, L. (2009). Exporting a Canadian parenting education program to the Dominican Republic. *Public Health Nursing, 26*, 183–191.

Mikkonen, J., & Raphael, D. (2010). *Social determinants of health: The Canadian facts.* Toronto, ON: York University School of Health Policy and Management. Retrieved from www.thecanadianfacts.org/

Moran, P., Ghate, D., & van der Merwe, A. (2004). *What works in parenting support? A review of the international evidence.* UK: Policy Research Bureau, Department for Education and Skills. Research Report 574, Retrieved from www.education.gov.uk/research/data/uploadfiles/rr574.pdf

Paterson-Payne, C. (2013). *Nobody's Perfect Home Visitors adaptation of a 1:1 and 'virtual' group delivery project. Parent outcome evaluation report. October 2012 to May 2013.* Retrieved from www.youville.ca/_uploads/PageContent/documents/report%20and%20module%20june27.pdf

Public Health Agency of Canada: *Nobody's Perfect* (website). Retrieved from www.phac-aspc.gc.ca/hp-ps/dca-dea/parent/nobody-personne/index-eng.php

Public Health Agency of Canada: *Nobody's Perfect* (brochure). Retrieved from www.nobodysperfect.ca/_uploads/PageContent/documents/New%20brochure%20-%20FINAL%20E.pdf

Rodgers, J. (2006). Guidance on delivering effective group education. *British Journal of Community Nursing, 11*, 476–482.

Rootman, I., Goodstadt, M., Weir, N., Moazami, S., Barr, V., & Walsh G. (1998). *An evaluation of the Nobody's Perfect Parenting Program in Ontario.* Funded by the Health Policy Branch and the Public Health Branch of the Ministry of Health. Retrieved from www.bccf.ca/sites/default/files/Rootman%20et.%20al.%20Nobody'sPerfect.ON_.EVAL-FinalWRUP.pdf

Rosenbaum, M. (1980). A schedule for assessing self-control behaviors: Preliminary findings. *Behavior Therapy, 11*, 109–121.

Rosenbaum, M. (Ed.). (1990). *Learned resourcefulness: On coping skills, self-control, and adaptive behavior.* New York: Springer Publishing.

Rosenbaum, M. (2000). The self-regulation of experience: Openness and construction, in P. Dewe, A. Leiter, & T. Cox (Eds.), *Coping and health in organizations* (pp. 51–67). London: Taylor & Francis.

Russell, S. (2006). An overview of adult-learning processes. *Urologic Nursing, 26*, 349–352, 370.

Skrypnek, B., & Charchun, J. (2009). *An evaluation of the Nobody's Perfect Parenting Program.* Ottawa, ON: Canadian Association of Family Resource Programs (FRP Canada). Retrieved from www.parentsmatter.ca/document/docWindow.cfm?fuseaction= document.viewDocument&documentid=420&documentFormatId=1110

Strachan, D. (1988). *Nobody's Perfect leader's guide.* (2nd ed.). Ottawa, ON: Health and Welfare Canada.

Svensson, J., Barclay, L., & Cooke, M. (2008). Effective antenatal education: Strategies recommended by expectant and new parents. *Journal of Perinatal Education, 17*, 33–42.

VanderPlaat, M. (1989). *Nobody's Perfect: Process and impact evaluation report.* Ottawa, ON: Health and Welfare Canada. Prepared for the Atlantic Regional Health Promotion Committee.

VanderPlaat, M. (1998). Empowerment, emancipation and health promotion policy. *Canadian Journal of Sociology, 23*, 71–90.

Wood Catano, J. (2000). *Working with Nobody's Perfect: A facilitators' guide* (3rd ed.). Ottawa, ON: Minister of Public Works and Government Services.

World Health Organization, Health and Welfare Canada, & Canadian Public Health Association. (1986). *Ottawa Charter for Health Promotion.* Ottawa, ON. Retrieved from www.phac-aspc.gc.ca/ph-sp/docs/charter-chartre/pdf/charter.pdf

PART IV

Future Directions and Conclusion

20

FUTURE TRENDS IN PARENTING EDUCATION

Nicholas Long

Learning Goals

1. To better understand anticipated trends regarding evidence-based parenting programs.
2. To better understand issues and anticipated trends in training those who provide parenting education services.
3. To understand how genetics and biological factors may influence parenting education in the future.

Introduction

Parenting education has long been validated and deemed important, but what does the future hold for the field? What current trends will continue? What new trends might we see in the future? Making such predictions is challenging because the future direction will reflect not only current professional, societal, scientific, political, and fiscal perspectives but also ways in which these perspectives will evolve and change over time. The predictions regarding anticipated trends in parenting education that are expressed in this chapter reflect opinions predicated on these various perspectives.

At the end of the twentieth century it was postulated that we were entering the third generation of parenting education, predicted to be marked by several trends that included a greater focus on outcomes, an increased emphasis on accountability, an increase in the use of targeted programs, a greater focus on training parenting educators, an increased use of parenting interventions in the provision of child mental health services, and an increased use of technology in delivering parenting education (Long, 1997). All of these predicted trends have materialized, some more than others. This chapter focuses on discussing current perspectives on some of these trends as well as discussing other anticipated trends.

Before delving into the specific trends in parenting education, it should be noted that the field has developed from many disciplines and perspectives and, as a result, is rife with the use of various terminologies. Terms such as parenting education, parent education, parent training, parenting programs, parenting interventions, and parenting services are often used interchangeably. Terms used for those who provide parenting education services are also varied and include parent educator, parenting educator, parent trainer, practitioner, provider, family life educator, and home visitor. For the purposes of this chapter the terms "parenting education", "parenting program", and "provider" will be used most often for the purpose of consistency.

The Era of Evidence-based Parenting Education

In 1997 it was predicted that "There will be an increasing need to establish more clearly the effectiveness and cost-effectiveness of parent education programs in order to be more successful in obtaining financial support for the expansion of parent education programs" (Long, 1997, p. 503). There is no doubt that this prediction has come true. However, as the evidence-based movement progresses, it is likely not only to strengthen but also to expand and adapt to changing needs. In this section we will explore some of the trends and anticipated future directions related to evidence-based programs and practice.

Benefit–Cost

Benefit–cost will likely become the major determining factor in the widespread funding for parenting education programs. As government budgets tighten, policy makers will increasingly use business models to help determine how to best invest public funds. This will involve a focus on "return on investment" (ROI). Policy makers will be increasingly persuaded by evidence that their "investment" in a program (costs of implementing the program) will eventually yield a cost savings (e.g., in reduced mental health costs, reduced healthcare costs, reduced costs related to delinquency) that is greater than their investment. Those programs that are able to demonstrate cost savings will be best positioned to receive government funding. Perhaps the best example of how this type of research has impacted public policy and funding regards evidence-based home visiting programs in the USA As part of healthcare reform in the USA, $1.5 billion over a 5-year period was allocated (under the Patient Protection and Affordable Care Act of 2010) for home visiting through the Department of Health and Human Services' Maternal Infant and Early Childhood Home Visiting (MIECHV) program. This funding was a direct result of research, primarily conducted with the Nurse Family Partnership program that found significant cost savings in health-care as well as other areas as a result of the home visiting program.

As a function of the increasing focus on benefit–cost analyses in this area, the Institute of Medicine and the National Research Council (2014) recently assembled researchers to discuss the lack of uniformity in the methods and assumptions used in these studies. The goal is to create standards for conducting benefit–cost analyses in areas of prevention related to child, youth, and families. This initiative provides further support that these types of analyses will become increasingly important for the advancement of parenting education.

Anticipated Trends

1. There will be an increased utilization of business models to determine the value of parenting education from a benefit–cost perspective.
2. ROI will be increasingly used to inform public policy and funding decisions related to parenting education services.

Evidence-based Designation

Numerous clearinghouses have been created over the past decade to review the evidence supporting the effectiveness of various programs, including parenting education programs. Both public and private funders are increasingly funding parenting education programs only if the program has been rated by one of these clearinghouses at a level for the program to be considered "evidence-based". Examples of such clearinghouses in the USA include the California Evidence-based Clearinghouse for Child Welfare as well as several others developed by different agencies within the U.S. Government. The U.S. Department of Health and Human Services Substance Abuse and Mental Health Services Administration (SAMHSA) has developed the National Registry of Evidence-based Programs and Practices (NREPP). The U.S. Office of Juvenile Justice and Delinquency Prevention has developed the Model Programs Guide. The U.S. Department of Health and Human Services has also created the Home Visiting Evidence of Effectiveness (HomVEE) program to assess the level of evidence for various home visiting models that target expectant parents and parents of young children. Of particular significance is that the HomVEE designation of "evidence-based" is being used to determine which programs are eligible for the $1.5 billion of MIECHV funding to expand home visiting services in the USA. There is not a specific clearinghouse in the USA that focuses exclusively on assessing the level of evidence for the broad continuum of parenting programs. However, in the UK the "Commissioning Toolkit" offered through the Department of Education is a searchable database of parenting interventions that have been reviewed by researchers from the National Academy of Parenting Research against best practice standards. Since that database includes a very broad list of parenting programs available in the UK. it is not surprising that relatively few of the parenting education programs listed meet the criteria for being evidence-based (Asmussen, 2011).

While an evidence-based designation will continue to be used for specific funding purposes (e.g., grants and initiatives), a growth in legislation/laws that specify government entities must utilize evidence-based programs when they offer or support parenting education services is likely to follow. For example, in the USA there has been an initiative in the home visiting area to develop a policy framework (Pew Center on the States, 2011). The purpose of this framework is to help guide policy makers and funders in how to obtain the best outcomes for families and the best returns on taxpayer investments. This framework focuses on the importance of clearly defining the purpose of the program and expected outcomes. It also promotes the investment of public funds in proven programs. Other aspects of this framework focus on the need to have a plan to monitor and evaluate these programs on an ongoing basis. This framework has recently been used by several states to pass bills that mandate that when state government funds are used to support home visiting programs, the vast majority of funding must be used for evidence-based programs (i.e., as designated by HomVEE).

Anticipated Trends

1. It will become increasingly difficult to obtain significant funding to deliver parenting education programs unless the program has been classified as evidence-based by a government agency or clearinghouse.
2. Public policies and legislation will increasingly use wording to mandate the use of evidence-based programs/practice.
3. Evidence-based home visiting services will continue to receive strong federal support in the USA (provided the programs continue to demonstrate effectiveness through the MIECHV program).

Implementation and Dissemination

Researchers will increasingly try to identify the most effective strategies for implementing evidence-based programs at scale. That is, how are programs that have been found to be efficacious in research studies expanded to reach a much larger population and be effective? In regard to parenting education programs, there have been relatively few that have been successfully taken to significant scale (e.g., Triple P, Incredible Years, Nurse Family Partnership) (Institute of Medicine and National Research Council, 2014a).

One of the concerns that many providers have about implementing evidence-based programs regards the issue of fidelity; that is, the need for strict adherence to the program's protocol. A frequent concern is that such rigidity does not allow the provider to adapt to meet diverse parent needs. There has been recent attention given the issue of adherence and flexibility. It has been argued that having some flexibility leads to practitioners having greater satisfaction with the intervention, improves their critical thinking about how the intervention is delivered, and in turns leads to greater adherence and fidelity (Mazzucchelli & Sanders, 2010). This has led to a call for researchers and program developers to address issues regarding "flexibility within fidelity" as part of their effectiveness trials and implementation/dissemination research in terms of improving practitioner adoption and adherence (Forehand, Dorsey, Jones, Long, & McMahon, 2010). This is likely critical as the widespread success of these programs may be dependent, to a large degree, on how they can be tailored to meet the various social contexts of targeted families (Law, Plunkett, Taylor, & Gunning, 2009).

Anticipated Trends

1. There will be increased attention paid to the science of effective implementation and dissemination of parenting education programs.
2. There will be greater attention given to strategies that promote both fidelity as well as flexibility within parenting education programs.

Core Components of Evidence-based Programs

As the number of evidence-based parenting programs grows, it is predicted that there will be an increased focus on examining the shared core components of effective programs. This will help identify what components of programs might be most important to include as new programs are developed. This type of data might also be helpful to parenting education program developers in helping them optimize their interventions by removing program components that may not be contributing significantly to the effectiveness of their program. For example, the Centers for Disease Control and Prevention (CDC, 2009) has published a guide for practitioners based on meta-analyses (Kaminski, Valle, Filene, & Boyle, 2008) of 77 "parent training" studies that focused on parents of children from birth to seven years of age. Specifically, "parent training" is the term often used for parenting programs developed within the fields of psychology and mental health to improve parent–child interactions, improve child behavioral and emotional problems, and prevent or reduce mental health problems. A meta-analysis, such as the one used by the CDC, allows researchers to quantitatively examine a large number of studies together in order to draw objective/aggregated conclusions about the findings across the various studies. The CDC study examined which program components were most, as well as least, strongly related to improving parenting skills and to decreasing children's disruptive behavior. Accordingly, a significant increase in studies such as this that analyze the most robust core elements and processes of evidence-based parenting programs that target specific groups (e.g., parents of children with behavior problems) and/or specific modes of intervention (e.g., home visiting) is likely to occur.

Anticipated Trends

1. There will be increasing efforts to identify the shared core components of effective programs that target specific groups and/or outcomes.
2. There will be a focus on examining core components of specific service delivery systems (e.g., home visiting programs) to identify those components that are most, and least, associated with effectiveness.

Examining Effectiveness as well as Moderating and Mediating Factors

While efficacy studies continue to be important in evaluating new parenting programs, there will be an increasing focus on effectiveness trials. Efficacy is demonstrated when an intervention is found to be successful under restricted and well-controlled conditions (e.g., within a randomized trial at a university setting). Effectiveness is then demonstrated when the intervention is found to be successful in real-world settings. The growing interest in effectiveness trials reflects the need for programs to increasingly demonstrate meaningful real-world outcomes.

What factors moderate or mediate an intervention's effectiveness? Moderators typically specify for whom and under what conditions an intervention works. Mediators refer to the possible mechanisms through which the intervention works (e.g., changes in parental discipline approaches, changes in injury prevention practices). There will be an increased focus on gaining a better understanding of the factors that moderate and mediate the effectiveness of evidence-based interventions. One area that is likely to receive greater attention in this regard is parental depression. The impact of parental depression on parenting and children is now well recognized (National Research Council and Institute of Medicine, 2009) and there will be growing interest in how parental depression may play a moderating and/or mediating role in the effectiveness of parenting programs. This is an especially important area for parenting education given the prevalence of depression in the families who receive these services. For example, across several home visiting studies, the percentage of mothers who exceeded clinical cutoff scores on measures of depression ranged from 28.5 to 61 percent (see Ammerman, Putman, Bosse, Teeters, & Van Ginkel, 2010).

Anticipated Trends

1. While there will be continued attention paid to efficacy trials, there will be increased attention paid to effectiveness trials in determining which parenting programs are considered evidence-based.

2. There will be an increased focus on research that examines what factors moderate and mediate the effectiveness of parenting education services.
3. There will be greater attention paid to the impact of maternal depression on the effectiveness of parenting education programs. There will also be an increased focus on developing parenting education programs for depressed parents.

Directly Comparing Evidence-based Programs

There has been a paucity of studies that have directly compared parenting education programs in randomized controlled trials. As such, there is a need for comparative efficacy/effectiveness trials to directly compare outcomes for different evidence-based programs. For example, a recent randomized control trial examined the efficacy of a parenting program that was specifically designed for parents of children with attention deficit hyperactivity disorder (ADHD) to the efficacy of a parenting program that focused more generically on improving young children's behavior (Abikoff et al., in press). Both approaches were evidence-based interventions, and the question was whether the more specialized parenting program was more efficacious than the generic program. Interestingly, the specialized parenting program was not found to be better than the generic program and, in fact, on several outcome measures the generic program was found to be superior. These types of studies will help determine the relative efficacy/effectiveness of programs that target specific groups and provide guidance in terms of selecting programs to use.

Anticipated Trends

1. There will be an increase in comparative efficacy and effectiveness trials.
2. The results of comparative effectiveness trials that examine parenting programs utilized in mental health services to address specific disorders will be used to inform practice guidelines for those disorders.

Modifying Existing Evidence-based Parenting Programs

It is predicted that there will be a continuing trend to modify existing evidence-based programs, to reduce costs and to have a broader reach (while maintaining effectiveness). This will probably involve numerous strategies including taking current programs that are costly to provide (e.g., those that involve working with families individually) and examining less costly service delivery approaches (e.g., fewer number of sessions, parenting class/group approaches, self-guided approaches) that still include key components of the original intervention (e.g., Morawska & Sanders, 2006; Forehand et al., 2010, 2011; Kling et al., 2010; Malmberg & Field, 2013).

Evidence-based parenting programs will be increasingly modified for use in health and mental healthcare settings. Parenting programs have a long history as evidence-based intervention in mental health programs to address disruptive behavior problems. However, it is anticipated that parenting interventions will be utilized more frequently to address other mental health problems such as child anxiety (Forehand, Jones, & Parent, 2012). There will also be an increased focus on modifying parenting education programs for implementation in the primary healthcare setting (e.g., pediatricians' offices).

Anticipated Trends

1. There will be an increased focus on modifying existing evidence-based programs to reduce costs as well as broaden their reach.
2. Parenting programs will be used with increasing frequency to address mental health problems beyond conduct/disruptive behavior problems.
3. There will be an increased use of parenting education in primary healthcare settings.

Use of Technology in Parenting Education

Emerging technologies may drastically change the landscape of parenting education over the coming decades. However, it is important to realize that technology has a long history of use within the field (Long, 2004). For example, videotapes were introduced in early evidence-based programs in the 1980s (e.g., Webster-Stratton, 1994) followed in the 1990s by the use of evidence-based self-administered programs that involved the use of interactive technology (Gordon, 2000). More recently, online parenting interventions are being used with increased frequency in order for programs to have a broader reach (Sanders, Baker, & Turner, 2012; McGrath et al., 2013). Newer technologies such as podcasts (Morawska, Tometzki, & Sanders, 2014) and smartphones (Jones et al., 2014) have also been utilized effectively. In addition to the use of technology in delivering parenting education services to parents it will be used with increased frequency to facilitate the dissemination and scaling of evidence-based programs. This will include the training and supervision of providers of parenting education services. Technology is advancing so quickly it is hard to predict what future technologies will be available to deliver parenting education. However it is clear that technology will be used with increased frequency within the field of parenting education.

Anticipated Trends

1. Technology will be increasingly utilized in delivering parenting education services.

2. Technology will also be increasingly utilized for provider training as well as in dissemination efforts.

Parenting Education Providers: Training and Workforce Development

Having a well-trained and competent workforce is critical to long-term success in any field. Unfortunately, it is extremely difficult to clearly define the qualifications of a typical parenting education provider. These providers represent diverse backgrounds, varying levels of education, and various disciplines. As a result, various job titles are used including parenting educator, parent educator, family life educator, home visitor, parent trainer, parenting program provider, parenting practitioner, parenting facilitator, therapist, and parenting coach. Providers who have professional-level training in a specific discipline typically identify first with their primary discipline (e.g., social work, education, psychology, or nursing) rather than as a parenting education provider. Thus providers, as well as parenting programs, are often embedded in different disciplines. The situation is even more complex as there are also paraprofessionals and peer providers who provide parenting education services who are not college educated.

As the field of parenting education advances and parenting programs become more widely implemented, there will be increased pressure to better define who should be providing services. A workforce needs to be adequately prepared to successfully take on the challenges of evidence-based practice. In that regard, there is evidence that providers with at least a bachelor's degree are not only more willing to use evidence-based interventions but also more likely to implement them effectively (Korfmacher, O'Brien, Hiatt, & Olds, 1999; Asmussen et al., 2010; Olds, Robinson, Pettitt, Luckey, Holmberg, Ng, Isacks, Sheff, & Henderson, 2004; Sanders et al., 2009).

While several individual parenting education programs provide certification in their particular program, there are many that believe a broader credentialing process is needed. Several states and groups in the USA have developed core competencies for parenting educators (Cooke, 2006). The National Parenting Education Network in the USA is currently working toward developing a set of national core competencies and guidelines. It remains to be seen whether such national competencies/standards will gain widespread acceptance in the USA; however, in the UK the National Occupational Standards for "Work with Parents" have been created. These standards define the competencies required to carry out the functions in this area rather than specific job roles. An issue related to core competencies is that they are often used to develop a certification, credentialing, or licensure process. While there have been attempts to realize this in the USA (Bryan, DeBord, & Schrader, 2006; Cooke, 2006), it is extremely challenging given that parenting education involves peer educators, paraprofessionals, and professionals from numerous disciplines delivering various types of services (Jones et al., 2013). Since parenting education services are not regulated, there is limited motivation at present for individuals to become certified. However, this could change if certification were required for employment purposes or if the provision of parenting education services became regulated (which would be extremely difficult). For such reasons, past efforts for general certification as parenting educators have had only limited success. This is an issue that will receive ongoing attention as evidence-based programs are more broadly disseminated and there is a greater demand not just for providers to effectively implement programs but also for those who are also able to engage in evidence-based practice as they work with parents more broadly (Asmussen, 2011).

Training issues that will gain more attention as the parenting education field moves forward include the roles of ongoing supervision and professional development in improving the effectiveness of services. Traditional approaches for training providers (e.g., attending a single training workshop and providing a provider manual) have typically not been found to be very effective in terms of competence and adherence in the use of evidence-based interventions in other related fields such as mental health (Long, 2008). What happens after the initial training (e.g., ongoing training and supervision) is now being viewed as critical for effective implementation of evidence-based programs (Beidas & Kendall, 2010). Issues that need to be addressed more empirically include determining the most effective modes of training/supervision, the most effective approaches to training/supervision, and the frequency and intensity of training/supervision that yield the best outcomes. There will also be an increased focus on ongoing professional development (e.g., determining specific needs, developing effective strategies) as a mechanism to improve the competencies of parenting educators.

Anticipated Trends

1. There will be an increase in studies that examine how provider knowledge, training, and skills impact the effectiveness of different parenting education services.
2. There will be an increased focus on identifying core competencies as well as ethical guidelines for parenting educators.
3. There will be a growing interest in certifying those who provide parenting education services (beyond program-specific certification).
4. There will be a greater focus on how to most effectively train and supervise providers of parenting education services.

Influence of Genetics and Biological Factors on Parenting Education

The sequencing of the human genome through the Human Genome Project, completed in 2003, has led to the identification of specific genes and genetic variants that are associated with a wide variety of medical disorders. As a result, the field of medicine is entering the era of "personalized medicine" where healthcare will be customized for individuals based on knowledge of their specific genetic genome. Medical decisions and treatments will increasingly be "personalized" for individuals based on genetic information to optimize effectiveness. Will parenting education services ever be tailored for specific parents based on genetic information? Let's look at some of the research that suggests this might in fact occur in the future.

The sequencing of the human genome is making it possible to identify gene variants that are associated with differences in human behavior. For example, a recent large-scale study found that during adverse macroeconomic conditions (economic adversity at the community level) mothers who have a specific genotype of the DRD2 gene (approximately half of mothers) were significantly more likely to engage in harsh parenting practices (e.g., screaming, threatening, and excessive punishment) than mothers who do not (Lee et al., 2013). The DRD2 gene impacts the neurotransmitter dopamine which is involved in regulating emotional and behavioral responses to environmental threats and rewards. Other lines of research have found that children with certain genotypes (related to dopamine-related genes) are more sensitive to both negative and positive environments (Bakermans-Kranenburg & Van IJzendoorn, 2011). Further evidence suggests that the variant of genes related to serotonin or dopamine influences how sensitive children are to rewards and punishments (Pedersen, 2013). Collectively, these studies suggest that a parent's genotype puts them at risk for negative parenting and that children's genotype might make them more or less sensitive to specific parenting interventions. Will this type of genetic information be used in the future to suggest who might benefit most from parenting education and/or which programs might be most effective for specific families?

In a recent study, the majority of new parents reported they would be interested in obtaining whole-genome sequencing of their newborns (Goldberg, Dodson, Davis, & Tarini, 2014). This would provide information to parents on their child's risk for various diseases as well as mental health disorders. As this type of information becomes more accessible to parents it will raise many ethical, social, and practical issues for the field of parenting education. How will parents interact differently with their children if they know their children are at risk for certain diseases and/or mental health disorders? How will parenting change when genetic information is readily available? Will parenting programs be specifically developed for parents and children with certain genotypes?

In the past the prevailing thought was that genes influence behavior, but it is becoming increasingly clear that behaviors also influence genes. The field of epigenetics is examining how experiences impact the DNA molecule to influence gene activity. This type of research will help us understand how the social and physical environment experienced in childhood modulates the expression of one's genotype (Shonkoff, Garner, & AAP Committee members 2012). Of particular interest will be helping to explain the mechanism by which "toxic stress" (e.g., abuse, neglect, exposure to domestic violence, living with someone with mental health or substance abuse problems) experienced during childhood is related to significant health problems in adulthood including obesity, cardiovascular reactivity, systematic inflammation, mental health problems, as well as various other issues including shorter lifespans (Brown et al., 2009; Shonkoff, Boyce, & McEwen, 2009). Additionally, it appears as if the impact of environmental influences on gene expression can be inherited. That is, the influence of toxic stress experienced during an individual's childhood may be passed on to their children through a process known as epigenetic inheritance (Hackett, Sengupta, Zylicz, Murakami, Lee, Down, & Surani, 2013).

Researchers are also exploring the role of hormones on parenting. Recent animal research has found that specific hormones (e.g., estrogen, progesterone, oxytocin, prolactin) interact with dopamine to impact neural systems to motivate parents to nurture and bond with their offspring. The influence of vasopressin and testosterone on paternal care is also being explored. Although this research has been with animals, there is growing evidence that human and animal parenting share many subcortical neural and neurochemical mechanisms (Rilling & Young, 2014). Will this eventually lead to the possible use of pharmaceutical agents to increase parental sensitivity, motivation, and drive (e.g., in regard to nurturing and bonding)? How will society react to the ethical dilemmas that this will introduce?

A recent research study, related to ameliorating genetic risk and reducing inflammation, has potentially profound implications for the field of parenting education. Excessive inflammation, a chronic overactivation of parts of the immune system, has been found to be related to a number of health problems later in life (e.g., heart disease, diabetes) as well as to depression and psychosis (Khandaker, Pearson, Zammit, Lewis, & Jones, 2014). The study found that an intervention delivered when children were 11 years old, and which focused on strengthening families through improving parenting, parent–child communication, and helping children develop strategies for dealing with a variety of issues and stressors, actually resulted in reducing inflammation. What is more remarkable is that it was a randomized controlled study involving low-socioeconomic status (SES) families and that the extent of inflammation was assessed 8 years after the intervention, when the children were 19 years old (Miller, Brody, Yu, & Chen, 2014). Inflammation was lowest among youth who received, as a result of the intervention, more nurturing-involved parenting and less harsh/inconsistent parenting. They also found that the intervention was most effective in reducing inflammation with the most disadvantaged families. This same longitudinal study (Brody, Chen, Beach, Philibert, & Kogan, 2009) was also the first to demonstrate that a preventative intervention can ameliorate a genetic risk for increasing involvement in health-compromising risk behaviors in early adolescence. Young adolescents who had a specific genetic vulnerability factor and were assigned to the control group displayed greater increases in risk behaviors than those adolescents, with the same genetic risk, who received the family-strengthening intervention. This study provides evidence that parenting interventions, when combined with other strengthening family components, can impact biological markers and ameliorate a genetic risk for behaviors that are related to long-term health issues. If additional studies are able to replicate such findings with other parenting programs it will significantly increase support for, and credibility of, the field of parenting education.

Anticipated Trends

1. There will be growing evidence that the relationship between parenting and child outcomes are moderated by gene-related polymorphisms.
2. There will be growing evidence that parenting interventions have differential effectiveness based on child and/or parental genotypes.
3. Biological indices (e.g., inflammation) will be used with increased frequency as outcome measures in studies examining the effectiveness of parenting education interventions.
4. There will be an increase in the number of studies that specifically examine whether parenting programs ameliorate genetic risk related to specific outcomes.
5. Parenting programs that can demonstrate amelioration of genetic risk for key outcomes and/or significant changes on specific biological markers will be well positioned to receive significant support for widespread dissemination.
6. Parenting education will increasingly be impacted by genetic and biological studies including decisions on what parenting education services are most appropriate for which families. "What works for whom and why?" will be taken to a new level.

Conclusion

As the field of parenting education moves forward, the current focus on evidence-based programs and practice will continue to strengthen and expand. Trends in this regard will include an increasing focus on the cost-effectiveness of parenting education services, on effective implementation and dissemination, as well as the use of technology both in providing parenting education services as well as in training and dissemination. There will also be a greater focus on workforce development and the training of parenting education providers. Finally, there will be an increasing influence of genetics and biological factors on the field of parenting education.

Key Points

1. Funding for parenting education services will increasingly be focused on parenting programs that have been independently designated as "evidence-based".
2. Government funding agencies will increasingly use benefit–cost data to determine the value of parenting education in making funding decisions.
3. There will be increased attention paid to the science of effective implementation and dissemination of evidence-based parenting education programs.
4. There will be increased investigation of the shared core components of effective programs that target specific groups and/or outcomes.
5. Factors that moderate and/or mediate the effectiveness of parenting education services will receive increased attention.
6. There will be more efficacy and effectiveness trials that directly compare different parenting programs.
7. There will be increased pressure to modify existing evidence-based programs to reduce costs as well as broaden their reach.
8. Technology will be increasingly used in delivering parenting education programs as well as in training those that provide these services.
9. There will be a greater focus on how provider knowledge, training, and skills impact the effectiveness of different parenting education services.
10. There will be more attention on how to most effectively train and supervise providers of parenting education services.
11. Core competencies as well as ethical guidelines for parenting educators will receive increased attention.
12. There will be a growing interest in certifying those who provide parenting education services (beyond program-specific certification and discipline-related certification/licensure).
13. Evidence will accumulate indicating that parenting programs have differential effectiveness based on specific child and/or parent genotypes.
14. Biological measures (e.g., inflammation) will be used more frequently in studies assessing the effectiveness of parenting education programs.
15. Research studies will increasingly examine whether parenting programs ameliorate genetic risk related to specific outcomes.

Discussion Questions

1. What concerns will arise as government agencies increasingly use benefit–cost analyses to make funding decisions regarding the support of parenting education programs?

2. How might currently emerging technologies be used to impact the delivery of parenting education services?
3. What level of education and training do you think should be required for an individual to be designated as a "parenting educator"?
4. What moral and ethical issues will arise if a drug becomes available that is shown to increase parental sensitivity more so than traditional parenting education interventions?

Additional Resources

Websites

Evidence-based clearinghouses:

California Evidence-based Clearinghouse for Child Welfare: www.cebc4cw.org

National Registry of Evidence-based Programs and Practices (NREPP)-United States: www.nrepp.samhsa.gov

HomVEE (Home Visiting Evidence of Effectiveness)–United States: http://homvee.acf.hhs.gov

Commissioning Toolkit of Parenting Programmes-United Kingdom: www.parentinguk.org/your-work/programmes/commissioning-toolkit

References

Abikoff, H., Thompson, M., Laver-Bradbury, C., Long, N., Forehand, R., Miller-Brotman, L., Klein, R., Reiss, P., Huo, L., & Sonuga-Barke, E. (in press). Parent training for preschool ADHD: A randomized controlled trial of specialized and generic programs. *Journal of Child Psychology and Psychiatry.*

Ammerman, R., Putman, F., Altaye, M., Stevens, J., Teeters, A., & Van Ginkel, J. (2013). A clinical trial of in-home CBT for depressed mothers in home visitation. *Behavior Therapy, 44*, 359–372.

Ammerman, R., Putman, F., Bosse, N., Teeters, A., & Van Ginkel, J. (2010). Maternal depression in home visitation: A systematic review. *Aggression and Violent Behavior, 15*, 191–200.

Asmussen, K. (2011). *The evidence-based parenting practitioner's handbook.* New York: Routledge.

Bakermans-Kranenburg, M., & Van IJzendoorn, M. (2011). Differential susceptibility to rearing environment depending on dopamine-related genes: New evidence and a meta-analysis. *Development and Psychopathology, 23*, 39–52.

Beidas, R., & Kendall, P. (2010). Training therapists in evidence-based practice: A critical review of studies from a systems-contextual perspective, *Clinical Psychology: Science and Practice, 17*, 1–30.

Brody, G., Chen, Y., Beach, S., Philibert, R., & Kogan, S. (2009). Participation in a family-centered prevention program decreases genetic risk for adolescents' risky behaviors. *Pediatrics, 124*, 911–917.

Bryan, G., DeBord, K., Schrader, K. (2006). Building a professional development system: A case study of North Carolina's parenting education experiences. *Child Welfare, 85*, 803–818.

Centers for Disease Control and Prevention. (2009). *Parent training programs: Insight for practitioners*. Atlanta, GA: Centers for Disease Control.

Cooke, B. (2006). Competencies of a parent educator: What does a parent educator need to know and do? *Child Welfare, 85*, 785–802.

Forehand, R., Armistead, L., Long, N., Wyckoff, S., Kotchick, B., Whitaker, D., Shaffer, A., Greenberg, A., Murry, V., Jackson, L., Kelly, A., McNair, L., Dittus, P., & Miller, K. (2007). Efficacy of a family-based, youth sexual risk prevention program for parents of African-American pre-adolescents. *Archives of Pediatric and Adolescent Medicine, 161*, 1123–1129.

Forehand, R., Dorsey, S., Jones, D., Long, N., & McMahon, R. J. (2010). Adherence and flexibility: They can (and do) co-exist! *Clinical Psychology: Science and Practice, 17*, 258–264.

Forehand, R., Jones, D., & Parent, J. (2012). Behavioral parenting interventions for child disruptive behaviors and anxiety: What's different and what's the same. *Clinical Psychology Review, 33*, 133–145.

Forehand, R., Merchant, M., Long, N., & Garai, E. (2010). An examination of *Parenting the strong-willed child* as bibliotherapy for parents. *Behavior Modification, 34*, 57–76.

Forehand, R., Merchant, M., Parent, J., Long, N., Linnea, K, & Baer, J. (2011). An examination of a group curriculum for parents of young children with disruptive behavior. *Behavior Modification, 35*, 235–251.

Goldberg, A., Dodson, D., Davis, M., & Tarini, B. (2014). Parents' interest in whole-genome sequencing of newborns. *Genetics in Medicine, 16*, 78–84.

Gordon, D. (2000). Parent training via CD-ROM: Using technology to disseminate effective prevention practices. *Journal of Primary Prevention, 21*, 227–251.

Hackett, J., Sengupta, R., Zylicz, J., Murakami, K., Lee, C., Down, T., & Surani, M. (2013). Germline DNA demethylation dynamics and imprint erasure through 5-Hydroxymethylcyctosine. *Science, 339*, 448–452.

Institute of Medicine and National Research Council. (2014a). *Considerations in applying benefit-cost analysis to preventive interventions for children, youth, and families: Workshop summary*. Washington, DC: The National Academies Press.

Institute of Medicine and National Research Council. (2014b). *Strategies for scaling effective family-focused preventive interventions to promote children's cognitive, affective, and behavioral health: Workshop summary*. Washington, DC: The National Academies Press.

Jones, D., Forehand, R., Cuellar, J., Parent, J., Honeycutt, A., Khavjou, O., Gonzalaz, M., Anton, M., & Newey, G. (2014). Technology-enhanced program for child disruptive behavior disorders: Development and pilot randomized control trial. *Journal of Clinical Child and Adolescent Psychology, 43*, 88–101.

Jones, S., Stranik, M., Hart, M., McClintic, S., & Wolf, J. (2013). *A closer look at diverse roles of practitioners in parenting education: Peer educators, paraprofessionals, and professionals*. NPEN White Paper. National Parenting Education Network. Accessed May 20, 2014 at http://npen.org/resources-for-parenting-educators/papers-articles.

Kaminski, J., Valle, L., Filene, J., Boyle, C. (2008). A meta-analytic review of components associated with parent training program effectiveness. *Journal of Abnormal Child Psychology, 26*, 567–89.

Khandaker, G., Pearson, R., Zammit, S., Lewis, G., & Jones, P. (2014). Association of serum interleukin 6 and c-reactive protein in childhood with depression and psychosis in young adult life: A population-based longitudinal study. *JAMA Psychiatry*, published online August 13, 2014. Doi:10.1001/jamapsychiatry.2014.1332.

Kling, A., Forster, M., Sundell, K., & Melin, L. (2010). A randomized controlled effectiveness trial of parent management training with varying degrees of therapist support. *Behavior Therapy, 41*, 530–542.

Korfmacher, J., O'Brien, R., Hiatt, S. & Olds, D. (1999) Differences in program implementation between nurses and paraprofessionals providing home visits during pregnancy and infancy: A randomized trial. *American Journal of Public Health, 89*, 1847–1851.

Law, J., Plunkett, C., Taylor, J., & Gunning, M. (2009). Developing policy in the provision of parenting programmes: Integrating a review of reviews with the perspectives of both parents and professionals. *Child: Care, Health and Development, 35*, 302–312.

Lee, D., Brooks-Gunn, J., McLanahan, S., Notterman, D., & Garfinkel, I. (2013). The great recession, genetic sensitivity, and maternal harsh parenting. *Proceedings of the National Academy of Sciences 2013*. PNAS Early Edition accessed August 6, 2013 at www.pnas.org/cgi/doi/10.1073/pnas.1312398110

Long, N. (1997). Parent education/training in the USA: Current status and future trends. *Clinical Child Psychology and Psychiatry, 2*, 501–515.

Long, N. (2004). E-parenting, in M. Hoghughi & N. Long (Eds.) *Handbook of parenting: Theory and research for practice* (pp. 369–379). London: Sage.

Long, N. (2008). Closing the gap between research and practice: The importance of practitioner training. *Clinical Child Psychology and Psychiatry, 13*, 187–190.

McGrath, P., Lingley-Pottie, P., Ristkari, T., Cunningham, C., Huttunen, J., Filbert, K., Minna Aromaa, M., Corkum, P., Hinkka-Yli-Salomäki, S., Kinnunen, M., Lampi, K., Penttinen, A., Sinokki, A., Unruh, A., Vuorio, J., & Watters, C. (2013). Remote population-based intervention for disruptive behavior at age four: Study protocol for a randomized trial of Internet-assisted parent training (Strongest Families Finland-Canada). *BMC Public Health, 13*, 985.

Malmberg, J., & Field, C. (2013). Preventative behavioral parent training: A preliminary investigation of strategies for preventing at-risk children from developing later conduct problems. *Child and Family Behavior Therapy, 35*, 212–227.

Mazzucchelli, T., & Sanders, M. (2010). Facilitating practitioner flexibility within an empirically supported intervention: Lessons from a system of parenting support. *Clinical Psychology: Science and Practice, 17*, 238–252.

Miller, G., Brody, G., Yu, T., & Chen, E. (2014). A family-oriented psychosocial intervention reduces inflammation in low-SES African American youth. *Proceedings of the National Academy of Sciences 2014*. PNAS Early Edition accessed July 21, 2014 at www.pnas.org/cgi/doi/10.1073/pnas.1406578111

Morawska, A., & Sanders, M. R. (2006). Self-administered behavioural family intervention for parents of toddlers: Effectiveness and dissemination. *Behaviour Research and Therapy, 44*, 1839–1848.

Morawska, A., Tometzki, H., & Sanders, M. R. (2014). An evaluation of the efficacy of a Triple P-Positive Parenting Program podcast series. *Journal of Developmental and Behavioral Pediatrics, 35*, 128–137.

National Research Council and Institute of Medicine. (2009). *Depression in parents, parenting, and children: Opportunities to improve identification, treatment, and prevention*. Committee on Depression, Parenting Practices, and the Healthy Development of Children. Board on Children, Youth, and Families. Division of Behavioral and Social Sciences and Education. Washington, DC: The National Academies Press.

Olds, D., Robinson, J., Pettitt, L., Luckey, D., Holmberg, J., Ng, R., Isacks, K., Sheff, K., & Henderson, C. (2004). Effects of home visits by paraprofessionals and by nurses: Age 4 follow-up results of a randomized trial. *Pediatrics, 114*, 1560–1568.

Pedersen, T. (2013). Brain chemical genes influence sensitivity to reward, punishment. *Psych Central*. Retrieved March 17, 2014, from http://psychcentral.com/news/2013/11/24/brain-chemical-genes-influence-sensitivity-to-reward-punishment/62417.html

Pew Center on the States. (2011). *Policy framework to strengthen home visiting programs*. Philadelphia, PA: The Pew Charitable Trusts.

Reeves, R., & Howard, K. (2013). *The parenting gap*. Washington, DC: The Brookings Institution.

Rilling, J., & Young, L. (2014). The biology of mammalian parenting and its effect on offspring social development. *Science, 345*, 771–776.

Sanders, M., Baker, S., Turner, K. (2012). A randomized controlled trial evaluating the efficacy of Triple P Online with parents of children with early-onset conduct problems. *Behaviour Research and Therapy, 50*, 675–684.

Sanders, M., Prinz, R., & Shapiro, C. (2009). Predicting utilization of evidence-based parenting interventions with organizational, service-provider and client variables. *Administration and Policy in Mental Health, 36*, 133–143.

Shonkoff, J., Boyce, W., & McEwen, B. (2009). Neuroscience, molecular biology, and the childhood roots of health disparities. *Journal of the American Medical Association, 301(21)*, 2252–2259.

Shonkoff, J., Garner, A., & AAP Committee members. (2012). The lifelong effects of early childhood adversity and toxic stress. American Academy of Pediatrics Technical Report. *Pediatrics, 129*, e232–246.

Webster-Stratton, C. (1994). Advancing videotape parent-training: A comparison study. *Journal of Consulting and Clinical Psychology, 62*, 583–593.

21

THE FUTURE OF EVIDENCE-BASED PARENTING EDUCATION AROUND THE WORLD

James J. Ponzetti, Jr.

Learning Goals

1. Understand the fundamentals of parenting education (e.g., best practices, theory).
2. Describe conceptual and theoretical frameworks for Parenting Education (PEd).
3. Differentiate inventory based from skills-based programs.
4. Comprehend the utility of evidence-based parenting education (PEd) with various distinct groups and the unique needs of each.

Introduction

Evidence-based Parenting Education: A Global Perspective offers a comprehensive overview of the foundations of evidence-based parenting education as well as a review of many of the most significant programs available globally. Early chapters recommended steps for designing evidence-based parenting education. These steps include developing a vision, assessing the needs of the target audience, identifying theoretical bases for content, determining goals and specific learning outcomes, and planning the assessment of effectiveness. The importance of choosing an implementation framework and evaluating implementation strategies is discussed. Finally, program fidelity, one of the most complex but important implementation outcomes, is briefly described.

Evaluation requires careful consideration of purpose and scope. In planning the evaluation, evaluators need to consider the characteristics of the participants, appropriate evaluation design, measurement, data collection, and efficient design of databases. Understanding issues of implementation fidelity, bias, and confounding are critical to interpretation of the evaluation. Conceptual and methodological issues related to the evaluation of parenting programs are ordered according to three questions that are posed in evaluation research: Does a program work? For whom and under which conditions does a program lead to positive outcomes? And how does a program work?

The Cooperative Extension Service has supported families in raising their quality of life. The National Extension Parenting Education Model (NEPEM) makes a major contribution to the field of parenting education. Conceptualized in 1994, the NEPEM model provides a definition of parenting along with 29 critical parenting practices divided into six skill categories. Expanding on NEPEM, a second framework called the National Extension Parenting Educators' Framework (NEPEF) was created. NEPEF addresses the processes and skills needed for parenting educators' professional development and educational certification.

A contemporary overview of the progress of evidence-based parenting education efforts in Europe includes examples of policies, parental support initiatives, and evidence-based parenting programs that may impact the well-being of the child and the family. The implementation of the Council of Europe recommendation on positive parenting through evidence-based parenting programs (EBPs) is essential for the future of parenting programs in Europe.

The incidence and prevalence of child maltreatment, delinquency, and substance abuse in Asia offer a foundation for parenting education unique to the Asian culture and parenting style. Because there has been less research on EBPs in Asia and the Pacific Region, the review EBP parenting programs covers the most popular EBPs (e.g., *Triple P, Incredible Years, Strengthening Families, and Family Matters*). The use of digital technology to disseminate EBP parenting programs in Asia and the Pacific Region and strengthen families as Eastern and Western cultures overlap is critical to promoting child development.

Parenting has always been a challenging task. The types of resources available to parents have increased over the years, particularly a notable increase in online resources. Parents are more likely to have access to and use the Internet than non-parents. Professionals need to learn how parents use the resources that are available to them, including the Internet. In addition, practitioners need to create responsible and useful online parenting materials and teach parents how to be informed consumers of these resources.

The Incredible Years (IY) parent training programs utilize a principle-driven, collaborative approach that guides implementation with high fidelity and adaptation. It has been the subject of over fifty randomized control group studies and shown to improve parenting practices and children's social and emotional behavior in a diverse range of families. A core feature of IY is that it utilizes video-based modeling that shows participants actual parents using effective behavior management skills.

Parenting Wisely is a cost-effective, research-based parent education program that has been shown to reduce child and adolescent behavior problems, family conflict, problems at school, and teen and parent substance use. Parents can access the program online and use it on their own, or service providers can use the program for individual or group parent training.

While father engagement has recently become more common as a feature of parenting education, very few such programs are systematically and prospectively evaluated as to efficacy, especially for low-income and minority families. Supporting Father Involvement (SFI), one of the only randomized clinical trials of the effects of positive father engagement in at-risk families, evaluated Mexican and European American families in the first phase of a 16-week study. SFI has since expanded as a significant parenting intervention worldwide.

Parent training programs are the best-documented interventions for treating children's behavior problems. The Parent Management Training–Oregon Model (PMTO) has a long history of theory-based research and treatment development. The theoretical model, social interaction learning (SIL), emphasizes that children learn behavior through their interactions with others. Parents regulate children's social environments; thus therapists work directly with parents as the agents of change. Findings are based on randomized controlled trials (RCTs) with positive outcomes for both children and parents. Mediated models support the theory that parenting practices are mechanisms of change for children's outcomes. PMTO is effective for clinically referred cases and with at-risk samples to prevent problems and promote healthy development.

The Nurturing Parenting programs are family-centered, evidence-based programs designed for the prevention and treatment of child abuse and neglect. Both parents and their children participate in sessions. Lesson dosage varies by level of prevention: primary (education), secondary (intervention), and tertiary (treatment). There are 25 different Nurturing Programs offered in communities worldwide designed to meet the varying educational capabilities of parents and their children, as well as their culturally based parenting patterns and family practices. All lessons in the Nurturing Programs are competency based.

The Triple P—Positive Parenting Program provides a multi-level, multi-disciplinary parenting support system designed to enhance parents' knowledge, skills, and confidence. Core positive parenting principles and skills, the history and theoretical foundations of Triple P, and its growing evidence base are presented; the principle of minimal sufficiency, with program intensity and delivery format tailored according to families' needs; the focus on the development of a parent's capacity for self-regulation as a central skill; and a guided participation model of sharing case formulation and intervention planning are exemplary of the Triple P educational approach.

Families and Schools Together (FAST) is recognized for engaging low-income, socially marginalized families into multi-family groups to increase child well-being outcomes and reduce inequalities. FAST requires cultural representation and local parents on every team, and, because of its flexible structure, the teams can locally adapt it. Accordingly, FAST has high retention rates and is evidence-based with several large RCTs completed.

The Families Matter! Program (FMP) is an evidence-based intervention for parents of 9–12-year-olds that promotes positive parenting practices and effective parent–child communication about sexuality. FMP seeks to reduce sexual risk behaviors among adolescents by giving parents the tools they need to protect and guide their children by enhancing their parenting and communication skills. The intervention is grounded in four theories, which have received extensive empirical support: social learning theory, especially as it relates to parenting; problem behavior theory; reasoned action theory; and social cognitive theory. FMP was adapted from the U.S. evidence-based Parents Matter! Program (PMP).

The Strengthening Families Program (SFP) is a research-based prevention program for high-risk children of substance abusers. Its effectiveness is attributed to the engagement of the whole family for 7–14 weeks, so that the family system is changed long term through direct practice together and home practice assignments. SFP has been found to be twice as effective as any program in preventing substance abuse when implemented in schools. Cultural adaptation is a core element in program fidelity. Hence, SFP has been proven effective in over thirty-five countries with dissemination to many undeveloped countries.

The Nobody's Perfect Parenting Program was developed in Canada to help parents of young children who have difficulty accessing resources in the community, to increase their parenting knowledge and skills, and promote the healthy development of their children. The program is learner-centered and participant-driven. As such, Nobody's Perfect uses an adult education delivery model. It is offered as a series of six to eight two-hour weekly sessions; however, this can be modified if necessary. The growing international interest in Nobody's Perfect attests its success, as does its efficacy in meeting the needs of the most marginalized populations both in and outside of Canada.

Anticipated trends in the field of parenting education are presented. The three primary areas of focus are: (a) expansion of the evidence-based movement; (b) greater focus on provider training; and (c) increasing influence of genetic and biological research on parenting education. In regard to the evidence-based movement, specific areas covered include the increasing influence of cost–benefit studies in making funding decisions, a greater focus on effective implementation and dissemination of evidence-based programs, and the investigation of shared core program components. In regard to training, specific areas discussed include the increasing need to articulate the knowledge and skill set for those providing parenting education, ascertaining the most effective training/supervision strategies to build a competent workforce, and exploring the need for specific credentialing in parenting education.

SUBJECT INDEX

AUTHOR INDEX